CAPITALIST PATRIARCHY
AND THE CASE FOR
SOCIALIST FEMINISM

CAPITALIST PATRIARCHY AND THE CASE FOR SOCIALIST FEMINISM

edited by Zillah R. Eisenstein

Monthly Review Press
New York

Library of Congress Cataloging in Publication Data
  Main entry under title:
  Capitalist patriarchy and the case for socialist feminism.
  Includes bibliographical references.
    1. Feminism—United States—Addresses, essays, lectures. 2.
  Women and socialism—Addresses, essays, lectures. I. Eisenstein,
  Zillah R.
  HQ1426.C244   301.41'2   77-76162
  ISBN 0-85345-419-1

Monthly Review Press
155 West 23rd Street
New York, N.Y. 10011

Manufactured in the United States of America

10 9 8 7 6

I ain't gonna die.
I'm goin' home like a shootin' star.
—Sojourner Truth

For my sister Sarah Eisenstein,
who died before any of us
were ready to part with her.

CONTENTS

Capitalist Patriarchy and Female Work

Patriarchy in Revolutionary Society

Socialist Feminism in America

ACKNOWLEDGMENTS

There are many people to thank for helping me in the preparation of my articles and this book. Sarah Eisenstein, Ellen Wade, Jackie Fralley, Miriam Brody Kramnick, Isaac Kramnick, Rayna Reiter, and Mary Ryan have all been helpful and generous in criticizing and commenting on my articles and in making organizational suggestions for the book. Most sincere thanks to my excellent editor, Susan Lowes. Carol Stevenson typed many of the earliest drafts of my articles and Judy Humble has typed endless drafts and carried on much of the correspondence necessary for this volume.

My students at Ithaca College, especially those who have participated in the socialist feminist tutorial 1975, 1976, 1977 and graduate students at Cornell with whom I work, have been invaluable in allowing me to share and test my ideas with them. I would also like to thank the politics department of Ithaca College which has funded a Socialist Feminist Speakers series for the last three years. Several of the articles here were first delivered as papers in that series.

Final thanks to Beau Grosscup who has been intimately linked with the book in reading and assessing it. And to my parents Morris L. Eisenstein and Fannie Price Eisenstein who taught me how to use a body of ideas, while never losing the right to criticize it. Lastly, I thank the women's movement itself, particularly the socialist feminists who are working so hard and who have shared their work in this book.

INTRODUCTION

Socialist feminism, both as theory and in practice, is very much in the process of developing. This volume gives a statement of where socialist feminism has developed to and at the same time focuses upon what it must move toward. These articles lay a foundation, from which further socialist feminist study and activity can build. Earlier beginning points were found either within the traditions of Marxist analysis or feminist theory. This volume makes public a political and intellectual commitment to understanding the problem of woman's oppression in terms of a real synthesis between the two. This does not mean merely adding one theory to the other but rather redefining each through the conflict that derives from and between both traditions. The synthesis must formulate the problem of woman as both mother and worker, reproducer and producer. Male supremacy and capitalism are defined as the core relations determining the oppression of women today. This volume is devoted to understanding the dynamic of power involved, which derives from both the class relations of production and the sexual hierarchical relations of society.

It is sometimes helpful to say what a book is not intended to do. This volume is not a presentation of the historical development of socialist feminism, nor is it a complete collection of socialist feminist writings to date. It is rather a collection of representative work being done by a much larger community of women than can be collected here. The articles should be read in relation to each other. Some articles stress patriarchy more than capitalism. Others focus more on socialism than

1

feminism. This reflects the imbalanced existing scholarship most of our authors must use as a beginning point. Separately, the articles are limited by time, space, knowledge, etc.; the outlines of a socialist feminist analysis of woman's oppression emerges from the collection of articles seen together as a whole.

At the same time that we are mapping out where we have come from, a statement of where we need to direct our energy emerges. The recognition of these needs, and a setting of priorities, is part of the development of our theory. This is what it means to say that theory and practice are in process.

Developing Socialist Feminist Questions as Theory

All of the articles in this volume have been chosen for their commitment to socialism and to feminism. Each tries to develop a fuller understanding of the relationship between patriarchy and capitalism. The three articles in this first section outline some theoretical priorities, particularly for the underdeveloped dimensions of feminism within a socialist feminist perspective. To the extent that socialist theory and practice has a more developed history than that of socialist feminism, it is particularly important to be aware of where we are in constructing the feminist dimensions of socialist feminism. Women throughout the movement have committed themselves to this task, and these first articles are only a small part of that effort. They are an outgrowth of much collective activity and of previous work by other feminists in socialist, feminist, radical feminist, lesbian, and socialist feminist theory.

My articles attempt to formulate socialist feminist questions by using the Marxist method, transformed by feminist commitments. Nancy Hartsock focuses on the transformation of politics through the feminist commitment in the personal realm. Although this argument has been reduced to defining the political solely in terms of the personal, rather than emphasizing the *relations* defining the connections between the two, the emphasis on the importance of everyday life is integral to a meaningful socialist feminist analysis. Hartsock is also concerned with constructing theory from reality rather than plastering one onto the other, with creating a dialectic between theory and practice rather than deriving one from the other. How can theory guide and direct action while growing out of the needs of everyday life, when everyday life embodies both real and false needs? The basic conflict that feminists must deal with is that in having everyday life define theory, theory cannot be defined in its totality by everyday life. Theory must grow out of reality, but it must be able to pose another vision of reality as well.

Much work has preceded the development of socialist feminism and was necessary for its inception. Shulamith Firestone's *The Dialectic of Sex* (1970) presented crucial but incomplete ideas to the women's movement about patriarchal power. Her book laid the basis for critical analyses and new developments, which were elaborated by Juliet Mitchell in *Woman's Estate* (1971), an important criticism of both radical feminism and socialist theory on the woman question. We have here the beginnings of a self-aware socialist feminism. This self-awareness takes clearer form in Sheila Rowbotham's *Women, Resistance, and Revolution* (1972), as well as in her *Woman's Consciousness, Man's World* (1973). At the same time, there were important developments in radical feminist analysis as presented by Ti Grace Atkinson in *Amazon Odyssey* (1974) and by Redstockings in *Feminist Revolution* (1975). The different priorities but similar commitments evident in all these works take a new turn in Juliet Mitchell's *Psychoanalysis and Feminism* (1974), Sherry Ortner's critique of this—"Oedipal Father, Mother's Brother & the Penis . . ." in *Feminist Studies* (1975), and Gayle Rubin's "The Traffic in Women: Notes on the Political Economy of Sex," in *Toward an Anthropology of Women* (1975), all of which show a commitment to understanding the universality of patriarchy through Freud and psychoanalysis. Whether there can be a meaningful synthesis of Marx and Freud depends on whether it is possible to understand how the unconscious is reproduced and maintained by the relations of the society. This part of the ongoing discussion of socialist feminism reflects the new understanding of how the system of male supremacy is reproduced through the sexual ordering of the society, both consciously and unconsciously. In this sense, and in the sense that socialist feminism proposes a synthesis between Marxist theory and radical feminism, both of which are still being defined, socialist feminist theory is still in the process of being formulated.

Related Reading

Burris, Barbara, et al., "Fourth World Manifesto," *Notes from the Third Year*.

Kollias, Karen, "Class Realities: Create a New Power Base," *Quest* 1, no. 3 (Winter 1975).

Lichtman, George, "Marx and Freud," *Socialist Revolution* 6, no. 43 (October-December 1976): 3–57.

Magas, Branka, "Sex Politics: Class Politics," *New Left Review* 66 (March-April 1971): 69–96.

Reed, Evelyn, *Woman's Evolution, from Matriarchal Clan to Patriarchal Family* (New York: Pathfinder Press, 1975).

Sontag, Susan, "The Third World of Women," *Partisan Review* (1973): 180–206.

Willis, Ellen, "Economic Reality and the Limits of Feminism," *Ms.* (June 1973): 90–111.

"Women in Struggle," *NACLA Newsletter* 6, no. 10 (December 1972).

"Women's Labor," *NACLA Newsletter* 9, no. 6 (September 1975).

Zaretsky, Eli, "Male Supremacy and the Unconscious," *Socialist Revolution* 4, no. 21–22 (January 1975).

DEVELOPING A THEORY OF CAPITALIST PATRIARCHY AND SOCIALIST FEMINISM

Zillah Eisenstein

Introduction

Radical feminists and male leftists, in confusing socialist women and socialist feminists, fail to recognize the political distinction between being a woman and being a feminist. But the difference between socialist women and socialist feminists needs to be articulated if the ties between radical feminism and socialist feminists are to be understood. Although there are socialist women who are committed to understanding and changing the system of capitalism, socialist feminists are committed to understanding the system of power deriving from capitalist patriarchy. I choose this phrase, capitalist patriarchy, to emphasize the mutually reinforcing dialectical relationship between capitalist class structure and hierarchical sexual structuring. Understanding this interdependence of capitalism and patriarchy is essential to the socialist feminist political analysis. Although patriarchy (as male supremacy) existed before capitalism, and continues in postcapitalist societies, it is their present relationship that must be understood if the structure of oppression is to be changed. In this sense socialist feminism moves beyond singular Marxist analysis and isolated radical feminist theory.

This is a slightly revised version of an article that appeared in The Insurgent Sociologist 7, no. 3 (Spring 1977). The article was first delivered as a paper in the spring of 1975 at Cornell University's women studies weekly seminar.

Power is dealt with in a dichotomous way by socialist women and radical feminists: it is seen as deriving from either one's economic class position or one's sex. The critique of power rooted in the male/female distinction focuses most often on patriarchy. The critique of power rooted in the bourgeoisie/proletariat distinction focuses on capitalism. One *either* sees the social relations of production *or* the social relations of reproduction,[1] domestic *or* wage labor, the private *or* public realms, the family *or* the economy, ideology *or* material conditions, the sexual division of labor *or* capitalist class relations as oppressive. Even though most women are implicated on both sides of these dichotomies, *woman* is dealt with as though she were not. Such a conceptual picture of woman hampers the understanding of the complexity of her oppression. Dichotomy wins out over reality. I will attempt here to replace this dichotomous thinking with a dialectical approach.[2]

The synthesis of radical feminism and Marxist analysis is a necessary first step in formulating a cohesive socialist feminist political theory, one that does not merely add together these two theories of power but sees them as interrelated through the sexual division of labor. To define capitalist patriarchy as the source of the problem is at the same time to suggest that socialist feminism is the answer. My discussion uses Marxist class analysis as the thesis, radical feminist patriarchal analysis as the antithesis, and from the two evolves the synthesis of socialist feminism.

Thesis: Woman as Class

1. *Marx: Revolutionary Ontology and Women's Liberation*

The importance of Marxist analysis to the study of women's oppression is twofold. First, it provides a class analysis necessary for the study of power. Second, it provides a method of analysis which is historical and dialectical. Although the dialectic (as method) is most often used by Marxists to study class and class conflict, it can also be used to analyze the patriarchal relations governing women's existence and hence women's revolutionary potential. One can do this because Marxist analysis provides the tools for understanding all power relations; there is nothing about the dialectical and historical method that limits it to understanding class relations. I will use Marx's analysis of class conflict, but I will also extract his method and apply it to some dimensions of power relations to which he was not sensitive. In this sense I am using Marx's method to expand our present understanding of material relations in capitalism to material relations in capitalist patriarchy.

These relations are illuminated by Marx's theories of exploitation and alienation. Since there has already been much discussion among socialist women and socialist feminists about the importance of the theory of exploitation to understanding woman's oppression, I will mention this only briefly.[3] I will focus on the importance of Marx's dialectical revolutionary ontology as it is presented in his theory of alienation. Although his substantive discussion of alienation applies to women workers in the labor force and in qualified ways to nonpaid domestic workers as housewives, I am particularly interested in his method of analysis. By not reducing the analysis to class and class conflict as expressed in the theory of exploitation, the dialectical method present in the theory of alienation can be extended to the particular revolutionary potential of women. Essentially this means that although the theory of alienation is inclusive of exploitation it should not be reduced to it.[4]

The theory of alienation and its commitment to "species life" in communist society is necessary to understanding the revolutionary capacity of human beings.[5] "Species beings" are those beings who ultimately reach their human potential for creative labor, social consciousness, and social living through the struggle against capitalist society, and who fully internalize these capacities in communist society. This basic ontological structure defines one's existence alongside one's essence. Reality for Marx is thus more than mere existence. It embodies within it a movement toward human essence. This is not a totally abstract human essence but rather an essence we can understand in historical contexts. "Species being" is the conception of what is possible for people in an unalienated society; it exists only as essence in capitalist society.

Without this conception human beings would be viewed as exploited in capitalist relations, but they would not necessarily be understood as potentially revolutionary. Exploitation, without this concept in the theory of alienation, would leave us with an exploited person. But because of the potential of species life in the individual, the exploited worker is also the potential revolutionary. Without the potential of species life we would have Aristotle's happy slaves, not Marx's revolutionary proletariat. And this potential exists in men and women, regardless of their position in the class structure or their relationship to exploitation. The actualizing of this potential, however, is differentiated according to one's class.

With his theory of alienation, Marx is critically probing the nature of capitalism. By capitalism, Marx and Engels referred to the entire process of commodity production. In examining the exploitation inherent in this process, Marx developed his theory of power. Power or powerlessness derives from a person's class position; hence oppression is a result of capitalist organization and is based in a lack of power and control. Through productive labor capitalist society exploits the worker who creates surplus value for the bourgeoisie. The surplus labor, which is inherent in profit, is derived from the difference between the actual and necessary labor time of the worker.

> Productive labor, in its meaning for capitalist production, is wage-labor which, exchanged against the valuable part of capital (the part of the capital that is spent on wages), reproduces not only this part of the capital (or the value of its own labor-power), but in addition produces surplus-value for the capitalist . . . only that wage labor is production which produces capital.[6]

The class structure, which manifests itself in social, political, and cultural forms as well, is economic at its base. Society is divided into the bourgeoisie and the proletariat. The basis of separation and conflict between the two is the relation each one has to the modes of production; hence the proletariat's exploitation, in which surplus value is extracted from their productive labor, is their oppression.

This Marxist indictment of capitalist relations is subsumed into a revolutionary ontology of social and human existence. It posits within each individual a dialectic between essence and existence which is manifested as revolutionary consciousness in society. Both the criticism of class existence as alienating and exploitative and the revolutionary ontology of the theory make Marxist analysis critical to developing a feminist theory which incorporates but moves beyond a theory of class consciousness.

When extended to women, this revolutionary ontology suggests that the possibility of freedom exists alongside exploitation and oppression, since woman is potentially more than what she is. Woman is structured by what she is today—and this defines real possibilities for tomorrow; but what she is today does not determine the outer limits of her capacities or potentialities. This is of course true for the alienated worker. While a worker is cut off from his/her creative abilities s/he is still potentially a creative being. This contradiction between existence and essence lies, therefore, at the base of the revolutionary proletariat as well as the revolutionary woman. One's class position defines consciousness for Marx, but, if we utilize the revolutionary ontological method, it need not be limited to this. If we wish to say that a woman is defined in terms of her sex as well, patriarchal relations define her consciousness and have implications for her revolutionary potential as a result. By locating revolutionary potential as it reflects conflicts between people's real conditions (existence) and possibilities (essence), we can understand how patriarchal relations inhibit the development of human essence. In this sense, the conception of species life points to the revolutionary potential of men and women.

The social relations defining the potential for woman's revolutionary consciousness are more complex than Marx understood them to be. Marx never questioned the hierarchical sexual ordering of society. He did not see that this further set of relations made species life unavailable to women, and hence that its actualization could not come about through the dismantling of the class system alone. Nevertheless, his writings on women are important because of his commitment to uncover the tensions between species life and capitalist alienated forms of social experience for both men and women.

There are partial statements on the family and women's exploitation in *The Economic and Philosophical Manuscripts, The Communist Manifesto, The German Ideology,* and *Capital.* Marx states his position on the bourgeois family in *The Communist Manifesto,* where he sees the family relation as having been reduced to a mere money relation.

> The bourgeois sees in his wife a mere instrument of production. On what foundation is the present family, the bourgeois family, based? On capital, on private gain. . . . The bourgeois claptrap about the family and education, about hallowed co-relation of parent and child, becomes all the more disgusting the more, by the action of modern industry, all family ties among the proletarians are torn asunder, and then children transformed into simple articles of commerce and instruments of labour.[7]

The relations of private property become the mode of exchange. The development of these bourgeois priorities transforms social relations in the family, and, as Marx makes clear in *The German Ideology,* the family, which is seen as the only truly social relationship, becomes a subordinate need.[8] The concerns of private property and possession pervade man-woman relations. In "On the Jewish Question," Marx writes: "The species relation itself, the relation between man and woman, etc., becomes an object of commerce. The woman is bought and sold."[9] The mentality of "having" twists species relationships into those of ownership and domination, and marriage into prostitution. And so in *The Economic and Philosophic Manuscripts* Marx writes:

> Finally, this movement of opposing universal private property to private property finds expression in the animal form of opposing to *marriage* (certainly a *form of exclusive private property*) the *community of women* in which a woman becomes a piece of *communal* and *common* property. . . . Just as woman passes

from marriage to general prostitution, so the entire world of wealth (that is, of man's subjective substance) passes from the relationship of exclusive marriage with the owner of private property to a state of universal prostitution with the community.[10]

Marx saw women's problems as arising from their status as mere instruments of reproduction, and thus he saw the solution in the socialist revolution. In the *Manifesto* he wrote that "the abolition of the present system of production must bring with it the abolition of the community of women springing from that system, i.e., of prostitution, both public and private."[11] The bourgeois family is seen in Marx's writings as an *instrument* of capitalist society, with no dimensions particular unto itself. Woman's oppression is her exploitation in a class society through bourgeois marriage and the family. Woman is perceived as just another victim, undistinguished from the proletariat in general, of the pernicious class division of labor. The sexual division of labor as the sexual definition of roles, purposes, activities, etc., had no unique existence for Marx. He had little or no sense of woman's biological reproduction or maternal functions as critical in creating a division of labor within the family. As a result, Marx perceived the exploitation of men and women as deriving from the same source and assumed that their oppression could be understood in the same structural terms. Revolutionary consciousness is limited to understanding the class relation of exploitation.

There is no reason to doubt, however, that in communist society (where *all* are to achieve species existence) life would still be structured by a sexual division of labor which would entail different life options for men and women. Sex roles would preassign tasks to women which would necessitate continued alienation and isolation. Essence and existence would still not be one. Marx did not understand that the sexual division of labor in society organizes noncreative and isolating work particularly for women. The destruction of capitalism and capitalist exploitation by itself does not insure species existence, i.e., creative work, social community, and critical consciousness for women.

2. Women's Exploitation Throughout History

In *The German Ideology*, Marx and Engels discuss the division of labor in early precapitalist society in familial terms. The first division of labor is the "natural" division of labor in the family through the sex act. The act of child-breeding begins the division of labor.[12] It is through this act that the first appearance of property arises within the family. For Marx and Engels, this is when wife and child become the slaves of the husband.

> This latent slavery in the family, though still very crude, is the first property, but even at this early stage it corresponds perfectly to the definition of modern economists who call it the power of disposing of the labour power of others. Division of labour and private property are moreover identical expressions. . . . [13]

Here are seeds of an early, albeit a crude, insight into the nature of sexual division of labor, although there is no discussion of it as such. What weakens and finally limits the insight is that, for Marx and Engels, this division of labor deriving from the sex act is coincidental and *identical* with the birth of private property—hence, "division of labor and private property are moreover identical expressions."[14] The division of labor has no specific quality of its own, and property arising from a division of labor in the act of procreation is not differentiatied from property arising from the relations of capital. Reproduction and production are seen as one, as they come to be analyzed in relation to the capitalist division of labor in society. There is no notion here that inequalities might arise from the sex act itself. Although reproduction is acknowledged as the first source of the division of labor, it never receives any specific examination. *The German Ideology* presents, then, a skeletal analysis of women's condition as it changes through material conditions.

> The division of labour is at this stage still very elementary and is confined to a further extension of the natural division of labour imposed by the family. The social structure is therefore limited to an extension of the family; patriarchal family chieftains; below them the members of the tribe; finally slaves. The slavery latent in the family only develops gradually.[15]

The division of labor "imposed by the family" is here spoken of as natural, and whether this means "necessary" or "good," it is a division which was accepted by Marx and Engels. Here, then, the division of labor in the family is not viewed as reflective of the economic society which defines and surrounds it—as it is in the later *Communist Manifesto*—but rather at this early historical stage Marx and Engels see the family structuring the society and its division of labor. Marx and Engels' analysis of the family continues: "there develops the division of labour in the sexual act, then that division of labour which develops spontaneously or 'naturally' by virtue of natural predisposition (e.g., physical strength), needs, accidents, etc."[16]

In *The Origin of the Family, Private Property, and the State*, Engels repeated the theme developed in *The German Ideology*: the *"first division of labour is that between man and woman for child-breeding."*[17] The first class antagonism thus arises with the antagonism between man and woman in monogamous marriage, but what this antagonism is based on is never made clear.[18] Engels' claim is that the first class antagonism accompanies (arises with) the antagonism between man and woman. One would not think that the antagonism referred to was one of class. Yet he ultimately spoke of the conflict between man and woman as class conflict; the man represents the bourgeoisie within the family, the wife represents the proletariat.[19] But the bourgeoisie and the proletariat are positions of power deriving from a relation to the economic means of production, not to the sex act of reproduction. By categorizing men and women as classes, the relations of reproduction are subsumed under the relations of production. It is contradictory that Engels acknowledges male-female relations within the family as defining the division of labor in society and yet completely subsumes them under categories of analysis related to reproduction. He offers no explanation that could resolve this dilemma because it stands outside the terms of his analysis.

We have seen that Engels acknowledges that the division of labor emanates from the family to the society. Yet the categories of analysis explaining the slavery of the woman in the family derive entirely from the relations of production. The family comes to be defined by the historical economic modes; it does not itself take part in defining the economy as well as the society, and it is no longer spoken of as a source of the division of labor coincident with economic relations. Economic existence comes to determine the family.[20] Hence, Engels forgot his own analysis of the "first division of labour" and assumed that the family will disintegrate with the elimination of capitalism instead of analyzing how the family itself comes to support an economic mode. Although he acknowledges the problem of woman's existence within the private domestic sphere—outside and opposed to social production—he sees this as reflecting the relations of production rooted in private property. Woman's activity in reproduction (which limits her activity in production) is not seen as problematic.

The family has become a microcosm of the political economy for Engels: "It contains in miniature all the contradictions which later extend throughout society and its state."[21] The man is the bourgeoisie, the woman, the proletariat. What is most interesting is that Engels does not use the categories of male as bourgeoisie and female as proletariat *outside* of the family. There people are assigned class positions according to their relations to the means of production, not their sex. He uses different criteria inside and outside the family to define membership within a class. If these categories were built on like bases of power, the same units of analysis would be applicable both in and out of the family. And if one wants to say that *ultimately* the usage of proletariat/bourgeoisie by Engels within the family is economic, there are evidently still other considerations involved. If this were not so, then he would not have (1) class divisions in the family as bourgeoisie-male/proletariat-female, and (2) class divisions in society in terms of ownership-nonownership of the means of production. Even though, for him, these *ultimately* mean the same thing, what do they reflect *initially* about the relations of the family and capitalism? It would seem that these considerations have to do with power emanating from the sexual differences between men and women in their relations to reproduction. This, however, was not grasped by Engels.

Most of the time Engels works from the simple equation that oppression equals exploitation. Even though Engels recognized that the family conceals domestic slavery, he believed at the same time that there were no differences (in kind) between domestic slavery and the wage-slavery of the husband. They both were derived from capitalism: "The emancipation of woman will only be possible when woman can take part in production on a large social scale and domestic work no longer claims anything but an insignificant amount of her time."[22] The real equality of women would come with the end of exploitation by capital and the transference of private housework to public industry. But given his lack of understanding of the sexual division of labor, even public domestic work would, for Engels, most probably remain woman's work.

In conclusion, the analysis sketched by Marx and Engels in *The German Ideology*, and then further developed by Engels in *The Origin of the Family, Private Property, and the State*, reveals their belief that the family, at least historically, structured the division of labor in society, and that this division of labor reflects the division of labor in the sex act. Initially, the family structure defined the structure of society.

> According to the materialistic conception, the determining factor in history is, in the final instance, the production and reproduction of immediate life. This, again, is of a two-fold character: on the one side, the production of the means of existence, of food, clothing and shelter and the tools necessary for that production; on the other side, the production of human beings themselves, the propagation of the species. The social organization under which the people of a particular historical epoch and a particular country live is determined by both kinds of production; by the stage of development of labour on the one hand and of the family on the other.[23]

This perception is lost, however, in the discussion of the family in capitalist society, for here the family comes to be viewed as just another part of the superstructure, totally reflective of class society, and relations of reproduction become subsumed under the relations of production. The point is not that the family doesn't reflect society, but that through both its patriarchal structure and patriarchal ideology the family and the need for reproduction also *structure* society. This reciprocal relationship, between family and society, production and reproduction, defines the life of women. The study of women's oppression, then, must deal with both sexual and economic material conditions if we are to understand oppression, rather than merely understand economic exploitation. The historical materialist method must be extended to incorporate women's relations to the sexual division of labor and society as producer and reproducer as well as to incorporate the ideological[24] formulation of this relationship. Only then will her existence be understood in its true complexity and will species life be available to her too.

Antithesis: Woman as Sex

1. *Patriarchy and the Radical Feminists*

Although the beginnings of radical feminism are usually considered to coincide with the beginnings of the recent women's liberation movement—around 1969–1970—radical feminism in fact has important historical ties to the liberal feminism[25] of Mary Wollstonecraft, Elizabeth Cady Stanton, and Harriet Taylor Mill, women who spoke of sexual politics long before Kate Millett. These women understood in their own fragmented way that men have power *as men* in a society organized into "sexual spheres." But while they spoke of power in caste terms, they were only beginning to understand the structure of power enforced upon them through the sexual division of labor and society. The claims of these feminists remained reformist because they did not make the necessary connections between sexual oppression, the sexual division of labor, and the economic class structure.

Radical feminism today has a much more sophisticated understanding of sexual power than did these feminist forebears and has thus been able to replace the struggle for the vote and for legal reform with the revolutionary demand for the destruction of patriarchy. It is the biological family, the hierarchical sexual division of society, and sex roles themselves which must be fundamentally reorganized. The sexual division of labor and society expresses the most basic hierarchical division in our society between masculine and feminine roles. It is the basic mechanism of control for patriarchal culture. It designates the fact that roles, purposes, activity, one's labor, are determined sexually. It expresses the very notion that the biological distinction, male/female, is used to distinguish social functions and individual power.[26]

Radical feminists have not only found the analysis of Wollstonecraft, Stanton, and Taylor incomplete, but they have, in much the same way, found the politics and theories of today's left insufficient: existing radical analyses of society also fail to relate the structure of the economic class system to its origins in the sexual class system. Sexual, not economic, power seemed to be central to any larger and meaningful revolutionary analysis. These women were not satisfied with the Marxist definition of power, or with the equation between women's oppression and exploitation. Economic class did not seem to be at the center of their lives.[27] History was perceived as patriarchal, and its struggles have been struggles between the sexes. The battle lines are drawn between men and women, rather than between bourgeoisie and proletariat, and the determining relations are of reproduction, not production.

For radical feminists patriarchy is defined as a sexual system of power in which the male possesses superior power and economic privilege. Patriarchy is the male hierarchical ordering of society. Although the legal-institutional base of patriarchy was more explicit in the past, the basic relations of power remain intact today. The patriarchal system is preserved, via marriage and the family, through the sexual division of labor and society. Patriarchy is rooted in biology rather than in economics or history. Manifested through male force and control, the roots of patriarchy are located in women's reproductive selves. Woman's position in this power hierarchy is defined not in terms of the economic class structure but in terms of the patriarchal organization of society.

Through this analysis, radical feminists bridge the

dichotomy between the personal and the public. Sex as the personal becomes political as well, and women share their position of oppression because of the very sexual politics of the society. The structuring of society through the sexual division limits the activities, work, desires, and aspirations of women. "Sex is a status category with political implications."[28]

2. Shulamith Firestone: Sexual Dialectics

In her book *Dialectic of Sex*, published in 1970, Shulamith Firestone offered a paradigmatic expression of radical feminism. The specific oppression that women experience, she argued, is directly related to their unique biology. Woman's reproductive function is *inherently* central to her oppression; thus, too, is the biological family. According to Firestone, "the sexual imbalance of power is biologically based."[29] Men and women are anatomically different and hence not equally privileged. The domination of one group by another is then derived from this biological male/female distinction.[30] (Although there has been change and development since 1970 among radical feminists, as can be seen in Robin Morgan's new book *Going Too Far,* the unifying thread among them is the concept of sex class as *primary* to understanding the relation of power.)

Firestone's presentation of the idea of a sex class obviously departs from the classical Marxist meaning of class as an economic category denoting a relationship to the means of production. Woman, as a sex, is a class; man is the other and opposing class. This novel idea began the long and important process of trying to articulate the dynamic of sexual power. However, in trying to answer and reject the economic theory of power, as presented by Marxists, she artificially separates the sexual and economic spheres, replacing capitalism with patriarchy as the oppressive system. She fails to move further through an additive or synthesizing perspective because she chooses to deal with sexuality as the key oppression of modern times rather than to view oppression as a more complex reality. It is not that Firestone does not see economic oppression as problematic for women but that she does not view it as the key source of oppression. The either/or formulations about woman's situation stunt the analysis, so that she cannot deal with the complex mix of woman's existence. Dichotomy wins out over woman's complexity. Thus, much as Marxist analysis is not extended to the specificity of women's oppression, Firestone's version of radical feminism cannot understand the full reality or historical specificity of our economic existence. Patriarchy remains a generalized ahistorical power structure.

In this framework the feminist revolution involves the elimination of male privilege through the elimination of sexual distinction itself and the destruction of the biological family as the basic form of social organization. Woman will then be freed from her oppressive biology, the economic independence of women and children will be created, and sexual freedoms not yet realized will develop.

The problem, however, is that woman's body becomes the defining criteria of her existence. It also becomes the central focus in terms of freedom from her reproductive biology. This is a negative definition of freedom—freedom from—where what we need is a positive model of human development— freedom to develop the integration of mind and body. While clearly sexuality is the unique oppression of woman, this does not mean that it encompasses the totality of her situation or that it can express the full dimensions of human potentiality. It says what is different about women, but it doesn't connect woman to the general structure of power. It cannot explain the complexity of power relationships in our society.

There are further problems. Firestone intends to present a synthesis of Marx and Freud. She attempts to do so, however, by negating the social and historical framework of Marx, by treating woman's biology as an atemporal static condition. But inequality is inequality only in a *social context*, while Firestone thinks of it in terms of nature. Women's and men's bodies differ biologically, but to call this an inequality is to impose a *social* assessment on a biological difference.[31] She acknowledges that one cannot justify a discriminatory sex class system in terms of its origin in nature, but one cannot explain it in such terms either.[32] Firestone thus in effect accepts the patriarchal ideology of our own culture, when what is needed is an analysis of how woman's sexuality has been interpreted differently throughout history.

For example, although sex roles existed in feudal society they were experienced differently than in advanced capitalist society because economic and sexual material life were different. Although the nuclear family is precapitalist as well as capitalist, it is actualized in different forms in different societies. To know there are universal elements to women's oppression is important, but it has limited meaning when the specificity of our existence is relegated to the universal. All history may be patriarchal, but this does not mean that the differences between historical periods is not important. It is the specifics which elucidate the general meaning of patriarchal existence. Patriarchy, in this sense, should be understood not merely as a biological system but a political one with a specific history.

Firestone's asocial, ahistorical framework becomes particularly limiting when she discusses technology. It is her view that technology will free woman from her body, through contraception and extrauterine reproduction. Technology is therefore the key to woman's liberation. But although contraception has freed women in important ways, the question remains whether birth control, abortion rights, and so on, will ever be allowed to develop to the degree that would allow woman's role as reproducer to become irrelevant to her social position. Firestone's analysis loses its plausibility when we understand that technology is an intrinsic dimension of a society's power structure. Male ruling-class needs define technological developments; without a change of those in power (and hence of those who define the purposes of technology), technology is an unlikely liberator.[33]

The thrust of Firestone's analysis is to isolate sex oppression from the economic class organization of society although she realizes herself that economic suffering contributes to woman's oppression at least as much as any female ills.[34] She does note that a woman, even when well educated, will not earn as much money as a man. A woman also suffers from this lack of money when she decides to care for children. This in itself should invalidate a totally biological argument for the basis of a revolution needed in the family. Firestone speaks of wanting to relate the structure of the economic class system to its origins in the sexual class system, but she fails to do this. Even if we accept the idea that economic oppression was a basic defense of sexual oppression historically, today the two systems support each other. They are mutually dependent. This relationship only gets distorted when one tries to define it in causal and dichotomized terms. The effect of this dichotomization is the theoretical assertion that sexual oppression is the primary oppression. I do not know what you do with this position politically in a society which superexploits its women within the general context of unemployment and inflation. To say that sexual oppression is primary is to sever the real connections of everyday life. Is this not what Marx did himself by focusing on class exploitation as the primary contradiction? Social reality complicates these theoretical abstractions. It was a consciousness of the incompleteness of the "primary contradiction" syndrome that spawned radical feminism in the first place. Is it not ironic to be plagued by this very same inadequacy once again? Both Shulamith Firestone and, most recently, Robin Morgan have asserted their rejection of Marxist oversimplification of political reality. We need not replace it with radical feminist one-dimensionality. If a commitment to restructuring sexual and class existence is needed then we also need a theory that integrates both.

The connections and relationships between the sexual class system and the economic class system remain undefined in the writings of radical feminism. Power is dealt with in terms of half the dichotomy. It is sexually based; capitalism does not appear within the theoretical analysis to define a woman's access to power. Similarly, interactions between patriarchy as a system of power and woman's biology are also kept separate. Instead of seeing a historical formulation of woman's oppression, we are presented with biological determinism. The final outcome of this dichotomization is to sever the relationship between these conditions and their supporting ideologies. As a result, neither Marxists nor radical feminists deal with the interrelationships between ideas and real conditions sufficiently. If reality becomes segmented, it is not surprising that ideological representations of that reality become severed from the reality as well.

Synthesis: Social Feminism

1. Exploitation and Oppression

Marxist analysis seeks a historical explanation of existing power relationships in terms of economic class relations, and radical feminism deals with the biological reality of power. Socialist feminism, on the other hand, analyzes power in terms of its class origins and its patriarchal roots. In such an analysis, capitalism and patriarchy are neither autonomous systems nor identical: they are, in their present form, mutually dependent. The focus upon the autonomous racial dimensions of power and oppression, although integral to a socialist feminist analysis, falls outside this discussion. As can be seen from the discussion of oppression below, race is viewed as a key factor in defining power, but my discussion focuses only on the relations between sex and class as a first step in moving toward the more inclusive analysis of race.

For socialist feminists, oppression and exploitation are not equivalent concepts, for women or for members of minority races, as they were for Marx and Engels. Exploitation speaks to the economic reality of capitalist class relations for men and women, whereas oppression refers to women and minorities defined within patriarchal, racist, and capitalist relations. Exploitation is what happens to men and women workers in the labor force; woman's oppression occurs from her exploitation as a wage-laborer but also occurs from the relations that define her existence in the patriarchal sexual hierarchy—as mother, domestic laborer, and consumer. Racial oppression locates her within the racist division of society alongside her exploitation and sexual oppression. Oppression is inclusive of exploitation but reflects a more complex reality. Power—or the converse, oppression—derives from sex, race, and class, and this is manifested through both the material and ideological dimensions of patriarchy, racism, and capitalism. Oppression reflects the hierarchical relations of the sexual and racial division of labor and society.

My discussion will be limited to understanding the mutual dependence of capitalism and patriarchy as they are presently practiced in what I have chosen to call capitalist patriarchy. The historical development of capitalist patriarchy can be dated from the mid-eighteenth century in England and the mid-nineteenth century in America. Both of these periods reflect the developing relationship between patriarchy and the new industrial capitalism. Capitalist patriarchy, by definition, breaks through the dichotomies of class and sex, private and public spheres, domestic and wage labor, family and economy, personal and political, and ideology and material conditions.

As we have seen, Marx and Engels saw man's oppression as a result of his exploited position as worker in capitalist society. They assumed that woman's oppression paralleled this. They equated the two when they suggested that domestic slavery was the same, in nature and essence, as wage-slavery. Marx and Engels acknowledged that woman was exploited as a member of the proletariat if she worked in the labor force; if she was relegated to domestic slavery she was seen as a nonwage slave. Capitalism was seen to exploit women, but there was no conception of how patriarchy and capitalism together defined women's oppression. Today, especially with the insights of radical feminism, we see that not only is the equation of exploitation and oppression problematic, but that if we use Marx's own categorization of productive labor as wage labor, domestic slaves are not exploited in the same way as wage slaves. They would have to be paid a wage for this to be true.

The reduction of oppression to exploitation, within Marxist analysis, rests upon equating the economic class structure with the structure of power in society. To the socialist feminist, woman's oppression is rooted in more than her class position (her exploitation); one must address her position within patriarchy—both structurally and ideologically—as well. It is the particular relation and operation of the hierarchical sexual ordering of society within the class structure or the understanding of the class structure within the sexual ordering of society which focuses upon human activity in capitalist patriarchy. They exist together and cannot be understood when falsely isolated. In dealing with these questions, one must break down the division between material existence (economic or sexual) and ideology, because the sexual division of labor and society, which lays the basis for patriarchy as we know it, has both material form (sex roles themselves) and ideological reality (the stereotypes, myths, and ideas which define these roles). They exist in an internal web.

If women's existence is defined by capitalism and patriarchy through their ruling ideologies and institutions, then an understanding of capitalism alone (or patriarchy in isolation) will not deal with the problem of women's oppression. As Juliet Mitchell has written, "the overthrow of the capitalist economy and the political challenge that effects this do not in themselves mean a transformation of patriarchal ideology."[35] The overthrow does not necessitate the destruction of patriarchal institutions either. Although practiced differently in each place, the sexual division of labor exists in the Soviet Union, in Cuba, in China. The histories of these societies have been different, and limitations in the struggle against patriarchy have been defined in terms of the particularities of their cultures. There has been real progress in women's lives, particularly in China and Cuba. But it would be inaccurate to say that a sexual division of labor and society does not exist in these countries. Only recently in Cuba has the sexual division of labor been tackled as a particular problem for the revolution. Patriarchy is crosscultural, then, by definition, though it is actualized differently in different societies via the institutionalizing of sexual hierarchy. The contours of sex roles may differ societally but power has and does reside with the male.

Both radical feminists and socialist feminists agree that patriarchy precedes capitalism, whereas Marxists believe that patriarchy arose with capitalism. Patriarchy today, the power of the male through sexual roles in capitalism, is institutionalized in the nuclear family.[36] Mitchell ties this to the "law of the prehistoric murdered father."[37] In finding the certain root of patriarchy in this mythic crime among men at the dawn of our life as a social group, Mitchell risks discussing patriarchy more in terms of the ideology patriarchy produces, rather than in connecting it to its material formulation in the confrontation between man and woman. She roots the Oedipus complex in the universal patriarchal culture. However, culture is defined for her in terms of an exchange system which primarily exists in ideological form today. For Mitchell, patriarchy precedes capitalism through the universal existence of the Oedipus complex. I contend, however, that patriarchy precedes capitalism through the existence of the sexual ordering of society which derives from ideological and political interpretations of biological difference. In other words, men have chosen to interpret and politically use the fact that women are the reproducers of humanity. From this fact of reproduction and men's political control of it, the relations of reproduction have arisen in a particular formulation of woman's oppression. A patriarchal culture is carried over from one historical period to another to protect the sexual hierarchy of society; today the sexual division of society is based on real differences that have accrued from years of ideological pressure. Material conditions define necessary ideologies, and ideologies in their turn have impact on reality and alter reality. There is a two-way flow: women are products of their social history, and yet women can shape their own lives as well.

For socialist feminists, historical materialism is not defined in terms of the relations of production without understanding its connection to the relations that arise from woman's sexuality—relations of reproduction.[38] And the ideological formulations of these relations are key. An understanding of feminist materialism must direct us to understanding the particular existence of women in capitalist patriarchal society. The general approaches of both Marxists in terms of class and radical feminists in terms of sex obfuscate the reality of power relations in women's lives.

2. Pioneers in Feminist Materialism: de Beauvoir and Mitchell

Simone de Beauvoir confronts the interrelationship between sexuality and history in The Second Sex. While for her "the division of the sexes is a biological fact, not an event in human history,"[39] nevertheless she says "we must view the facts of biology in the light of an ontological, economic, social, and psychological context."[40] She understood that women were defined by men and as such cast in the role of the "other," but she also realizes that the sexual monism of Freud and the economic monism of Engels are inappropriate for the full analysis of woman's oppression.[41] De Beauvoir's initial insights were further developed by Juliet Mitchell, who offered in Woman's Estate a rigorous criticism of classical socialist theory, criticizing it for locating woman's oppression too narrowly in the family.[42] She rejected the reduction of woman's problem to her inability to work,[43] which stresses her simple subordination to the institutions of private property[44] and class exploitation.

Instead, woman's powerlessness in capitalist society is rooted in four basic structures, those of production, reproduction, sexuality, and socialization of children. Woman's biological capacity defines her social and economic purpose. Motherhood has set up the family as a historical necessity, and the family has become the woman's world. Hence, woman is excluded from production and public life, resulting in sexual inequality.

The family under capitalism reinforces woman's oppressive condition. The family supports capitalism by providing a way for calm to be maintained amidst the disruption that is very much a part of capitalism. The family supports capitalism economically by providing a productive labor force and supplying a market for massive consumption.[45] The family also performs an ideological role by cultivating the belief in individualism, freedom, and equality basic to the belief structure of society, although they are at odds with social and economic reality.[46]

Mitchell concludes that by focusing on the destruction of the family alone, woman's situation will not necessarily be substantially altered. For Mitchell "socialism would properly mean not the abolition of the family but the diversification of the socially acknowledged relationships which are forcibly and rigidly compressed into it."[47]

The importance of Mitchell's analysis lies in the fact that she focuses on the powerlessness that women experience because they are reproductive beings, sexual beings, working individuals, and socializers of children—in all the dimensions of their activities. She makes it clear that woman's oppression is based in part on the support the family gives the capitalist system. Power is seen as a complex reality. We are still left, however, with the need to clarify the relationship of the family and the political economy in capitalist patriarchal society. What Mitchell has supplied us with is an understanding of the family in capitalist society.

3. The Sexual Division of Labor and Society in Capitalist Patriarchy: Toward a New Feminist Theory

One of the problems in trying to analyze the interconnections of patriarchy and capitalism is that our language treats the family and the economy as separate systems. The sexual hierarchical division of labor cuts through these two, however. Patriarchy and capitalism operate within the sexual division of labor and society rather than within the family. A sexual division of labor and society that defines people's activity, purposes, goals, desires, and dreams according to their biological sex, is at the base of patriarchy and capitalism. It divides men and women into their respective hierarchical sex roles and structures their related duties in the family domain and within the economy.

This statement of the mutual dependence of patriarchy and capitalism not only assumes the malleability of patriarchy to the needs of capital but assumes the malleability of capital to the needs of patriarchy. When one states that capitalism needs patriarchy in order to operate efficiently one is really noting that male supremacy, as a system of sexual hierarchy, supplies capitalism (and systems previous to it) with the necessary order and control. This patriarchal system of control is thus necessary to the smooth functioning of the society and the economic system and hence should not be undermined. This argument is to underscore the importance of the system of cultural, social, economic, and political control that emanates from the system of male supremacy. To the extent the concern with profit and the concern with societal control are inextricably connected (but cannot be reduced to each other), patriarchy and capitalism become an *integral process;* specific elements of each system are necessitated by the other.

Capitalism uses patriarchy and patriarchy is defined by the needs of capital. This statement does not undermine the above claim that at the same time one system uses the other, it must organize around the needs of the other in order to protect the specific quality of the other. Otherwise the other system will lose its specific character and with it its unique value. To state this as simply as possible one could say that: patriarchy (as male supremacy) provides the sexual hierarchical ordering of society for political control and as a political system cannot be reduced to its economic structure; while capitalism as an economic class system driven by the pursuit of profit feeds off the patriarchal ordering. Together they form the political economy of the society, not merely one or another, but a particular blend of the two. There are problems with this oversimplified statement. It severs relations which exist within both spheres. For instance, capitalism has a set of controls which emanate directly from the economic class relations of society and their organization in the workplace. And it seems to assume a harmony between the two systems at all points. As we move further into advanced capitalism, we can see how uneasy this relationship is becoming. As women increasingly enter the labor force, some of the control of patriarchal familial relations seems to be undermined—the double day becomes more obvious. But the ghettoization of women within the labor force at the same time maintains a system of hierarchical control of women, both sexually and economically, which leaves the sexual hierarchy of the society intact. Deference to patriarchal hierarchy and control is shown in the very fact that the search for cheap labor has not led to a full integration of women into all parts of the labor force. Although women's labor is cheaper, the system of control which maintains both the necessary order of the society and with it the cheapness of women's labor must be protected by segregating women in the labor force. Nevertheless, the *justification* for woman's double day and unequal wages is less well-protected today.

It is important to note the discrepancy between patriarchal ideology and the reality of women's lives. Although all women are defined as mothers (and nonworkers), almost 45 percent of the women in the United States—38.6 millon—work in the paid labor force, and almost all labor in the home. Nearly a quarter of all working women are single; 19 percent are either widowed, divorced, or separated: and another 26 percent are married to men who earn less than $10,000 a year.[48] However, because women are not defined as workers within the ruling ideology, women are not paid for their labor or are paid less than men. The sexual definition of woman as mother either keeps her in the home doing unpaid labor or enables her to be hired at a lower wage because of her defined sexual inferiority. Given unemployment rates, women either do not find jobs at all or are paid at an even lower rate. The sexual division of labor and society remains intact even with women in the paid economy. Ideology adjusts to this by defining women as working mothers. And the two jobs get done for less than the price of one.

All of the processes involved in domestic work help in the perpetuation of the existing society. (1) Women stabilize patriarchal structures (the family, housewife, mother, etc.) by fulfilling these roles. (2) Simultaneously, women are reproducing new workers, for both the paid and unpaid labor force. They care for the men and children of the society. (3) They work as well in the labor force for lesser wages. (4) They stabilize the economy through their role as consumers. If the other side of production is consumption, the other side of capitalism is patriarchy.

Although this sexual division of labor and society antedates capitalism, it has been increasingly institutionalized and specifically defined in terms of the nuclear family because of the needs of advanced capitalism. It now has much more form and structure than it did in precapitalist societies.[49] In precapitalist society, men, women, and children worked together in the home, the farm, or on the land to produce the goods necessary for their lives. Women were procreators and child-rearers, but the organization of work limited the impact of this sexual role distinction. With the rise of industrial capitalism, men were brought out of the home and into the wage-labor economy. Women became relegated to the home and were increasingly viewed by men as nonproductive although many worked in the factories. They came to be seen solely in terms of sex roles. Although women were mothers before industrial capitalism, this was not an exclusive role; whereas, with industrial capitalism, women became housewives. "The housewife emerged, alongside the proletariat—the two characteristic laborers of developed capitalist society."[50] The work that women continued to perform in the home was not conceived of as work. Productive labor was defined as wage labor, labor which produces surplus value—capital.

The conditions of production in society then, define and shape production, reproduction, and consumption in the family. So, too, the family mode of production, reproduction, and consumption affects commodity production. They work together to define the political economy. Within a capitalist patriarchal economy—where profit, which necessitates a system of political order and control, is the basic priority of the ruling class—the sexual division of labor and society serves a specific purpose. It stabilizes the society through the family while it organizes a realm of work, domestic labor, for which there is no pay (housewives), or limited pay (paid houseworkers), or unequal pay (in the paid labor force). This last category shows the ultimate effect on women of the sexual division of labor within the class structure. Their position as a paid worker is defined in terms of being a woman, which is a direct reflection of the hierarchical sexual divisions in a society organized around the profit motive.

The bourgeoisie as a class profits from the basic arrangement of women's work, while all individual men benefit in terms of labor done for them in the home. For men, regardless of class, benefit (although differentially) from the system of privileges they acquire within patriarchal society. The system of privileges could not be organized as such if the ideology and structures of male hierarchy were not basic to the society. It is this hierarchy which protects the sexual division of labor and society along with the artificial needs that have been created through the class system.

The ruling class desire to preserve the family reflects its commitment to a division of labor that not only secures it the greatest profit but that also hierarchically orders the society culturally and politically. Once the sexual division of labor is challenged, particularly in terms of its connection to the capitalist order, one of the basic forms of the organization of work (especially affecting the home, but with wide ramifications for the entire society) will be challenged. This challenge endangers a free labor pool, which infiltrates almost all aspects of living, and a cheap labor pool, as well as the fundamental social and political organization of the society, which is sexual hierarchy itself. The very order and control which derive from the arrangements of power implied in the sexual hierarchy of society will be destroyed.

If we understand that there are basically two kinds of work in capitalist society—wage labor and domestic labor—we can see that we must alter the way we think about workers. What we must do is begin to understand what class means for women. We must not just reexamine the way women have been fit into class categories. We must redefine the categories themselves. We need to define classes in terms of woman's complex reality and her consciousness of that reality.

Presently class categories are primarily male-defined, and a woman is assigned to a class on the basis of her husband's relation to the means of production; woman is not viewed as an autonomous being. According to what criteria is a woman termed middle-class? What does it mean to say that a middle-class woman's life is "easier" than a working-class woman's life when her status is significantly different from that of a middle-class male? What of the woman who earns no money at all (as houseworker) and is called middle-class because her husband is? Does she have the same freedom, autonomy, or control over her life as her husband, who earns his own way? How does her position compare to that of a single woman with a low-paying job?

> Clearly a man who is labeled upper- or middle-class (whatever, precisely, that may mean) has more money, power, security, and freedom of choice than his female counterpart. Most women are wives and mothers, dependent wholly or in part on a man's support, and what the Man giveth, he can take away.[51]

I do not mean by these questions to imply that class labels are meaningless, or that class privilege does not exist among women, or that housewives (houseworkers) are a class of their own. I do mean to say, however, that we will not know what our real class differences are until we deal with what our real likenesses are as women. I am suggesting that we must develop a vocabulary and conceptual tools which deal with the question of differential power among women in terms of their relation to men and the class structure, production and reproduction, domestic and wage labor, private and public realms, etc. Only then will we see what effect this has on our understanding for organizing women. We need to understand our likenesses and differences if we are to be able to work together to change this society. Although our differences divide us, our likeness cuts through to somewhat redefine these conflicts.

A feminist class analysis must begin with distinctions drawn among women in terms of the work they do within the economy as a whole — distinctions among working women outside the home (professional versus nonprofessional), among houseworkers (houseworkers who do not work outside the home and women who are houseworkers and also work outside), welfare women, unemployed women, and wealthy women who do not work at all. These class distinctions need to be further defined in terms of race and marital status. We then need to study how women in each of these categories share experiences with other categories of women in the activities of reproduction, childrearing, sexuality, consumption, maintenance of home. What we will discover in this exploratory feminist class analysis is a complicated and varied pattern, whose multigrid conceptualization mirrors the complexity of sex and class differentials in the reality of women's life and experience.

	Reproduction	Child-rearing	Maintenance of home	Sexuality	Consumption
Unemployed women					
Welfare					
Houseworkers (housewives)					
Working women outside of home— nonprofessional					
Working women outside of home— professional					
Wealthy women who do not work (even in own home)					

This model would direct attention to class differences within the context of the basic relationship between the sexual hierarchy of society and capitalism. Hopefully, the socialist feminist analysis can continue to explore the relationships between these systems, which in essence are not separate systems. Such a feminist class analysis will deal with the different economic realities of women but will show them to be defined largely within the context of patriarchal and capitalist needs. Women as women share like economic status and yet are divided through the family structure to experience real economic class differences. Such an examination should seek to realize woman's potential for living in social community, rather than in isolated homes; her potential for creative work, rather than alienating or mindless work; her potential for critical consciousness as opposed to false consciousness; and, her potential for uninhibited sexuality arising from new conceptions of sexuality.

4. Some Notes on Strategy

What does all of the preceding imply about a strategy for revolution? First, the existing conceptions of a potentially revolutionary proletariat are inadequate for the goals of socialist feminism. Second, there are serious questions whether the potential defined in classical Marxist terms would ever become real in the United States. And, although I think the development of theory and strategy should be interrelated, I see them as somewhat separate activities. Theory allows you to think about new possibilities. Strategy grows out of the possibilities.

This discussion has been devoted to developing socialist feminist theory and I am hesitant to develop statements of strategy from it. Strategy will have to be fully articulated from attempts to use theory. When one tries to define strategy abstractly from new and developing statements of theory, the tendency to impose existing revolutionary strategies on reality is too great. Existing formulations of strategy tend to limit and distort new possibilities for organizing for revolutionary change.

The importance of socialist feminist strategy, to the extent that it exists, is that it grows out of the daily struggles of women in production, reproduction, and consumption. The potential for revolutionary consciousness derives from the fact that women are being squeezed both at home and on the job. Women are working in the labor force for less, and they are maintaining the family system with less. This is the base from which consciousness can develop. Women need to organize political action and develop political consciousness about their oppression on the basis of an understanding of how this connects to the capitalist division of labor. As Nancy Hartsock says: "the power of feminism grows out of contact with everyday life. The significance of contemporary feminism is in the reinvention of a mode of analysis which has the power to comprehend and thereby transform everyday life."[52]

We must, however, ask *whose* everyday life we are speaking about. Although there are real differences between women's everyday lives, there are also points of contact that provide a basis for cross-class organizing. While the differences must be acknowledged (and provide political priorities), the feminist struggle begins from the commonality that derives from the particular roles women share in patriarchy.

Many socialist feminists were radical feminists first. They felt their oppression as women and then, as they came to understand the role of capitalism in this system of oppression, they became committed to socialism as well. Similarly, more and more houseworkers are coming to understand that their daily lives are part of a much larger system. Women working outside the home, both professional and nonprofessional, bear the pressures and anxieties about being competent mothers and caretakers of the home and are becoming conscious of their double day of work.

Male leftists and socialist women often say that women as women cannot be organized because of their isolation in the home and their commitment to their husbands' class. Although cross-class organizing is not possible on all issues because of class conflict among women, it is possible around issues of abortion, health care, rape, child care. Cross-class organizing is worth a serious try if we deal consciously with our class differences and set up priorities in terms of them instead of trying to ignore them. At the same time, the lives of women are remarkably similar given patriarchal controls. We just need to be more conscious of how this works and then structure our political action in terms of it. A strategy to reach all women has never been tried. That its implementation will be difficult goes without saying. But a beginning is already in process as women try to take some control over their lives.

Notes

1. Sheila Rowbotham, in *Women, Resistance, and Revolution* (New York: Pantheon, 1972), makes clear that both the social relations of production and reproduction need to be dealt with in any revolutionary theory.

2. For our purposes dialectics help us focus on the *processes* of power. Hence, in order to understand power one needs to analyze the *relations* that define power rather than treating power as an abstract thing. Any moment embodies the relations of power that define it. The only way to understand what the moment is, is to understand it as a reflection of the processes involved in it. By definition, this requires one to see moments as part of other moments rather than as cut off from each other. Seeing things in separation from each other, as part of either/or options, is the dichotomous thinking of positivism. By trying to understand the elements defining the synthesis of power as it is embodied in any particular moment, one is forced to come to terms with the conflict embodied within it, and hence the dialectical processes of power. See Karl Marx, *Grundrisse*, trans. Martin Nicolaus (New York: Vintage, 1973) and Bertell Ollman, *Alienation: Marx's Conception of Man in Capitalist Society* (New York: Cambridge University Press, 1971).

3. For this discussion see Mariarosa dalla Costa, "Women and the Subversion of the Community" and Selma James, "A Woman's Place" in *The Power of Women and the Subversion of the Community* (Bristol, England: Falling Wall Press, Ltd.); Ira Gerstein, "Domestic Work and Capitalism" and Lise Vogel, "The Earthly Family" in *Radical America* 7 (July–October 1973); Wally Seccombe, "The Housewife and Her Labour under Capitalism," *New Left Review* 83 (January–February 1973); B. Magas, Margaret Coulson, H. Wainwright, "The Housewife and Her Labour Under Capitalism—a Critique" and Jean Gardiner, "Women's Domestic Labour," *New Left Review* 89 (January–February 1975), and, for the latter, in this volume.

4. I do not think the dichotomized view of the early "Hegelian Marx" and the later "materialist Marx" is a helpful distinction. Rather, I think the theories of alienation and exploitation are integrated throughout Marx's work although they are given different priority in specific writings. The *Grundrisse* stands as persuasive proof of this position. See Marx, *Grundrisse* and David McLellan's discus-

sion of the importance of the *Grundrisse* in *Karl Marx, His Life and Thought* (New York: Harper and Row, 1973).

5. For a discussion of species being, see Karl Marx, *The Economic and Philosophic Manuscripts of 1844* (New York: International Publishers, 1964); *The German Ideology* (New York: International Publishers, 1947); "On the Jewish Question," in *Writings of the Young Marx on Philosophy and Society,* ed. Kurt Guddat and Lloyd Easton (New York: Anchor Books, 1967). See also Shlomo Avineri, *The Social and Political Thought of Karl Marx* (New York: Cambridge University Press, 1968); Richard Bernstein, *Praxis and Action* (Philadelphia: University of Pennsylvania Press, 1971); and Ollman, *Alienation.*

6. Karl Marx, *Theories of Surplus Value,* vol. 1 (Moscow: Progress Publishers, 1963), p. 152. See also *Capital,* vol. 1 (New York: International Publishers, 1967).

7. Karl Marx and Friedrich Engels, *The Communist Manifesto* (Chicago: Gateway Press, 1954), pp. 48–49.

8. Marx and Engels, *German Ideology,* p. 17.

9. Marx, "On the Jewish Question," p. 246.

10. Marx, *Economic and Philosophic Manuscripts,* p. 133.

11. Marx and Engels, *Communist Manifesto,* p. 50.

12. Friedrich Engels, *The Early Development of the Family* (a Free Press pamphlet), p. 65. The selection is also the first two chapters of *The Origin of the Family, Private Property, and the State* (New York: International Publishers, 1942).

13. Marx and Engels, *German Ideology,* pp. 21, 22.

14. Ibid.

15. Ibid., p. 9.

16. Ibid., p. 20.

17. Engels, *Origin of the Family,* p. 65. Engels' analysis in *Origin of the Family* differentiates three historical periods—savagery, barbarism, and civilization—in which he traces the evolution of the family.

18. Ibid., p. 66.

19. Marx and Engels, *Communist Manifesto.*

20. See Eli Zaretsky, "Capitalism, the Family, and Personal Life," *Socialist Revolution* 13–14 (January–April 1973): 69–125 and 15 (May–June 1973): 19–71 for a discussion of the historical and economic changes in the family.

21. Engels, *Origin of the Family,* p. 57.

22. F. Engels in *The Woman Question* (New York: International Publishers, 1951), p. 11.

23. Friedrich Engels, *The Origin of the Family, Private Property, and the State*, ed. Eleanor Leacock (New York: International Publishers. 1972), pp. 71–72.

24. Ideology is used in this paper to refer to the ruling ideas of the society. (See Marx and Engels, *German Ideology.*) It is seen as a distortion of reality, protective of existing power arrangements. More specifically, ideology is used to refer to the ideas that protect both male and capitalist power arrangements. Although material conditions often do create the conditions for certain ideologies, ideology and material conditions are in a dialectical relationship. They are both involved in *partially* defining the other. For instance, the "idea" that women are weak and passive is both a distortion of women's capacities and a partial description of reality—a reality *defined by* the ruling ideology.

25. The definition of liberal feminism applies to the reformist understanding of the sexual division of labor. It is a theory which reflects a criticism of the limitations of sex roles but does not comprehend the connection between sex roles and the sexual division of labor and capitalism. Limited by the historical boundaries of the time, early liberal feminists were unable to decipher the capitalist male power structure and instead applauded values which trapped them further in it. They were bound not only by the material conditions of the time (lack of birth control, etc.) but also by a liberal ideology which presented segmented, individualistic conceptions of power.

26. For classical versions of the sexual division of labor see J. S. Mill, *On the Subjection of Women* (New York: Fawcett, 1971) and J. J. Rousseau, *Emile* (London: J. J. Dent & Sons, 1911).

27. Although radical feminism is often called bourgeois by male leftists and socialist women, I think this is simplistic. First, radical feminism itself cuts across class lines in its caste analysis and in this sense is meant to relate to the reality of all women. Hence, in terms of priorities, the theory does not distinguish between working class and bourgeois women, recognizing the inadequacy of such distinctions. Further, the theory has been developed by many women who would be termed "working class." It is inaccurate to say that radical feminists are bourgeois women. The "bourgeois" woman has not really been identified yet in terms of a class analysis specifically pertaining to women.

28. Kate Millett, *Sexual Politics* (New York: Doubleday, 1970), p. 24.
29. Shulamith Firestone, *The Dialectic of Sex* (New York: Bantam Books, 1970), p. 9.
30. Ibid., p. 8.
31. Some people may say that to be stronger is to be more equal, or that inequality exists biologically because men are stronger than women. But this is not Firestone's argument. She argues that it is woman's reproductive role that is at the root of her inequality. Historically, pregnancy made women physically vulnerable, but this is less true today. Firestone does not restrict her thesis to history; she offers it as contemporary analysis.
32. Firestone, *Dialectic of Sex*, p. 10.
33. It is important to know whether technological changes and innovations in birth control methods are tied only to concerns with population control in an era of overpopulation or if they reflect fundamental changes in the way women are viewed in this society. It matters whether women are still viewed as baby machines or not, because these views could come to define technological progress in birth control as nonprogressive.
34. Firestone, *Dialectic of Sex*, p. 8.
35. Juliet Mitchell, *Psychoanalysis and Feminism* (New York: Pantheon, 1974), p. 414. Within the women's movement today there is a varied dialogue in progress on the dimensions and meaning of socialist feminism, and the appropriate questions are still being formulated.
36. Sheila Rowbotham, in *Woman's Consciousness, Man's World* (Baltimore: Penguin, 1973), p. 17, defines patriarchal authority as "based on control over the woman's productive capacity and over her person." Juliet Mitchell, *Psychoanalysis and Feminism*, pp. 407–8, sees patriarchy as defining women as exchange objects based on the exploitation of their role as propagators. Hence, she states, p. 416, that "it is not a question of changing (or ending) who has or how one has babies. It is a question of overthrowing patriarchy."
37. Mitchell, *Psychoanalysis and Feminism*.
38. See Rowbotham, *Women, Resistance, and Revolution*, for the usage of this model of historical materialism in the study of history.
39. Simone de Beauvoir, *The Second Sex* (New York: Bantam, 1952), p. xix.
40. Ibid., p. 33.

41. Ibid., p. 54.
42. Juliet Mitchell, *Women: The Longest Revolution* (a Free Press pamphlet) and *Woman's Estate* (New York: Pantheon, 1974).
43. Mitchell, *Longest Revolution*, p. 4. It has been pointed out that Mitchell herself did not fully understand women's essential role in society as workers. She termed them a marginal or reserve labor force rather than viewing them as necessary to the economy, as domestic laborers as well as wage laborers.
44. Ibid., p. 6.
45. Mitchell, *Woman's Estate*, p. 155.
46. Ibid., p. 156.
47. Mitchell, *Longest Revolution*, p. 28. It is interesting to note that Mitchell in *Psychoanalysis and Feminism*, p. 374, focuses on the relationship *between* families as key to understanding women in patriarchal culture. The relationship between families distinguishes human society from other primate groups. "The legally controlled exchange of women is the primary factor that distinguishes mankind from all other primates, from a cultural standpoint," p. 372. Hence, it is socially necessary for the kinship structure to have exogamous exchange. The psychology of patriarchy that Mitchell constructs is based on the relations of the kinship structure.
48. *Newsweek*, 6 December 1976, p. 69.
49. See Linda Gordon, *Families* (a Free Press pamphlet); A. Gordon, M. J. Buhle, N. Schram, "Women in American Society," *Radical America* 5 (July–August 1971); Mitchell, *Psychoanalysis and Feminism*; Mary Ryan, *Womanhood in America* (New York: Franklin Watts, 1975); R. Baxandall, L. Gordon, S. Reverby, *America's Working Women* (New York: Vintage, 1976); Zaretsky, "Capitalism."
50. Zaretsky, "Capitalism," p. 114.
51. Ellen Willis, "Economic Reality and the Limits of Feminism," *Ms.* 1 (June 1973): 110.
52. Nancy Hartsock, "Feminist Theory and the Development of Revolutionary Strategy" (Johns Hopkins University, unpublished paper), p. 19, and in this book. Portions of this paper appear as "Fundamental Feminism: Process and Perspective," *Quest* 2, no. 2 (Fall 1975): 67–79.

SOME NOTES
ON THE RELATIONS OF
CAPITALIST PATRIARCHY

Zillah Eisenstein

This article attempts to clarify socialist feminism's *method of analysis.* This involves a refocusing and redefinition, by feminism, of the historical Marxian approach. Radical feminist theory can be used to redirect the Marxian method toward understanding the structure of women's oppression, particularly in terms of the sex-class structure, the family, and the hierarchical sexual division of labor and society.[1] One growing school of socialist feminists has been trying to do just this.[2] This integration is based upon a commitment to the transformation of the Marxist method through feminist analysis.[3] The transformed Marxist method recognizes the previously unrecognized sexual spheres of power and the feminist questions require a new understanding of the specific historical processes of power. Juliet Mitchell fails to understand this systhesis when she suggests "we should ask the feminist questions but try to come up with some Marxist answers."[4] This implies a dichotomy between feminism and Marxist analysis, which stunts the analysis of socialist feminism.[5]

Refocusing the Marxist method (as well as its content) via feminism necessitates a reordering of priorities, particularly the question of consciousness in relation to the conditions of society. Questions of consciousness become a part of the discussion of the social reality. Reality itself comes to encompass the relations of class and sex and race. The relations between the private (personal) and public (political) become a major focus having particular consequence for the relations defining sexuality, heterosexuality, and homosexuality. Along with this comes a focus on the importance of ideology. Thus, the dialectic will be self-consciously extended to the relations between consciousness, ideology, and social reality. This new way of viewing things—that society's ideas and people's consciousness are part of the objective social reality and that they operate out of the relations of sex, class, and race—is a product of the feminist assault on the inadequacies of the left, both in theory and practice.

The refocused Marxist methodology means using the theory of social relations to express the relations of capitalist patriarchy.[6] Although this methodology is elucidated through the notion of class society and class conflict in Marx's writing, it is possible to distinguish the theory of social relations from the content given it in existing Marxist analysis. It is important and possible to utilize the method while incorporating and yet moving beyond class analysis. Class analysis is necessary to our understanding but it is not sufficient for our purposes.

Marxist analysis is directed to the study of power. We can use its tools to understand any particular expression of power. That the tools have not been sufficiently used to do so is not an indictment of the analysis but of those who have used it. Marx used his theory of social relations—understanding "things" in their concrete connections—to understand the relations of power in society. Although his analysis was explicated through a discussion of class conflict, his method of analyzing social relations can be used to examine patriarchal struggle as well. This is different, however, from saying we can use the Marxist theory of social relations to answer feminist questions. This would put us back with Firestone's analysis of a materialist history based on biology. Rather, we must use the transformed method to understand the points of contact between patriarchal and class history and to explicate the dialectic between sex and class, sex and race, race and class, and sex, race, and class.

It is impossible to develop an analysis of woman's oppression which has a clear political purpose and strategy unless we deal with reality as it exists. The problem with radical feminism is that it has tried to do this by abstracting sex from other relations of power in society.[7] It is not that radical feminists are unaware of these other relations of power, but they disconnect them. Class and race struggles are necessary for the understanding of patriarchal history; they are not separate histories in practice, although history is often written as if they were. Unless these relations are taken into account, male supremacy is viewed as a disconnected thing, not a process or power relation.

Much of the leftist analysis that spawned radical feminism did not take the commitments of the Marxist method seriously enough to transform it in necessary ways. It refused to continue to probe the question of power in its fullest material and ideological sense. Uniting radical feminism, class analysis, and the transformed Marxist methodology we now must focus upon the processes which define patriarchal and liberal ideology and social existence.

Developing Socialist Feminist Questions

A good starting point for a theory of woman's oppression is with the questions why and how women are oppressed. Juliet Mitchell, in *Psychoanalysis and Feminism*, states:

> It seems to me that "why did it happen" and "historically when" are both false questions. The questions that should, I think, be asked in place of these are: how does it take place in our society? . . . in other words, we can start by asking how does it happen now?[8]

It may be true that the question, "Why did it happen?" is a false question; even if we could find out why it happened then, that might not explain why it happens now; nevertheless, it is still important to ask "Why does it happen now?" Beyond this, to fully elucidate how it happens now one must ask why sexual hierarchy and oppression are maintained. Why and how are connected questions. Either taken in isolation gives us only part of the answer. The question of how directs us to the immediate relations defining existing power arrangements, to the process of oppression. The question of why directs us to these same relations but necessitates our dealing with the existence of patriarchal history as a real force. In this sense both questions are necessary. They elucidate each other by interrelating the specific and yet universal dimensions of male supremacy.

The how and why of woman's oppression has not been integrated in feminist theory. Radical feminism has asked why women are oppressed rather than how the process of power functions. Shulamith Firestone's answer was that woman's reproductive function is inherently central to her oppression. "The sexual imbalance of power is biologically based."[9] Women are defined as reproducers, as a sex class. How women are oppressed is less clearly articulated, and it was Ti Grace Atkinson who began to discuss this. In Atkinson's concept, sex class becomes a political construct. Women are not oppressed because of the biological fact of reproduction, but are oppressed by men who define this reproductive "capacity" as a function. "The truth is that childbearing isn't the function of women. The function of childbearing is the function of men oppressing women."[10] It is society that collapses women's purpose with her biological capacity. Sex class is not biological oppression, it is cultural oppression. The agent of oppression is the cultural and political definition of human sexuality as "heterosexuality." The institutions of family and marriage, and the protective legal and cultural systems which enforce heterosexuality, are the bases of the political repression of women.

Although radical feminists ask why women are oppressed and are now beginning to ask how this comes about, they most often treat history as one piece—as patriarchal history. Although this brings great richness to the radical feminist analysis, by presenting a unifying history for women, we need to understand the particular forms of patriarchy in different historical periods. Otherwise we are left with an abstract rather than concrete history. For instance, patriarchy has had different and yet similar expressions in feudalism and in capitalism. The expression of women's oppression is distinct though related in these two time periods. As Marc Bloch has noted:

The sentimental importance with which the epic [feudal] invested the relations of the maternal uncle and his nephew is but one of the expressions of a system in which the ties of relationship through women were nearly as important as those of paternal consanguinity. One proof of this is the clear evidence from the practices of name giving.[11]

Children could take the name of either father or mother. There seem to have been no fixed rules about this and as a result the family seems to have been unstable as generations switched names. According to Bloch it was this very instability which feudal relations had to address. With the development of capitalism, and its necessarily new forms of economic relations, the family came to be defined more as the source of cultural and social stability. The family calmed the days of early competitive capitalism,[12] whereas feudal relations themselves compensated for the unstable family order.

We must take into account two processes. One is history defined in terms of class—feudal, capitalist, socialist. The other is patriarchal history as it is structured by and structures these periods. For instance, motherhood, housewifery, and the family need to be understood as expressions of patriarchy at various historical moments because they are defined and structured differently in precapitalist and capitalist societies. These historical moments, however, are also part of an historically and culturally continuous reality, which doesn't become concrete and real until it is understood in its particular form. Otherwise it becomes an abstraction and as such, a distorted generalized notion. This is not to disclaim the importance of understanding that patriarchy has an existence which cuts through different class history. Although patriarchy takes on specific qualities at specific moments, it cannot be understood fully, divorced from its universal existence. The universal elucidates the specifics and the specifics give reality to the universal.

If it is true that all social change begins with the leftovers of the previous society, then we must learn exactly what maintains patriarchal hierarchy. Today's matrix of power exists through the particular constraints that capitalism can use to maintain the sexual hierarchy, but at the same time, the relations of capitalist patriarchy derive in part from precapitalist patriarchy, most specifically, feudal patriarchy. Any understanding of the relations of patriarchy has to treat them in their particular historical frame and any statement of the universal or unifying elements becomes an abstraction, albeit a necessary level of abstraction if we are to understand the unifying elements of patriarchal history. Both the specificity and universality of the relations of power must be defined to encompass the particular dynamic of male supremacy.

It is important, in a capitalist society, to understand both the enduring likenesses and differences between feudal patriarchy and capitalist patriarchy. The likenesses are important if we are to try to ensure that they do not continue in a new society. If the capitalist relations of patriarchy are connected to precapitalist forms, we need to challenge the precapitalist elements that are maintained in capitalist society. A ready example is the sexual division of labor. It has been maintained in capitalism and defined in a capitalist context while not specifically deriving from capitalist needs. The maintenance of these precapitalist forms constructs patriarchal history for us. For structuring life in the transition from capitalist patriarchy to feminist socialism, we need a theory of the revolutionary family which no longer accepts the birthmarks of the patriarchal family and sexual hierarchy.[13]

Beginning Notes on the Social Relations of Power

Let us begin with the question of how and why women are exploited and oppressed in capitalist patriarchy.[14] We focus on these questions because understanding women's oppression requires examining the power structures existing in our society. These are the capitalist class structure, the hierarchical order of the masculine and feminine worlds of patriarchy, and the racial division of labor which is practiced in a particular form in capitalism but with precapitalist roots in slavery. Capitalist patriarchy as an hierarchical, exploitative, oppressive system requires racial oppression alongside sexual and class oppression. Women share an oppression with each other; but what they share as sexual oppression is differentiated along class and racial lines in the same way that patriarchal history has always differentiated humanity according to class and race. Clearly, the black woman of American slave society experienced patriarchical oppression, but this experience was complicated by the other power structures to which she was subjected. As a laborer she was allowed no feminine "fragility," as a woman she was "raped" into submission,[15] and as a slave she endured a subhuman status. Instead of seeing sex or class, or race or class, or sex or race, we need to see the process and relations of power. If we direct ourselves to the process of power we can begin to learn how and why we are oppressed, which is the first step in changing our oppression.

None of the processes in which a woman engages can be understood separate from the relations of the society, which she embodies and which are reflected in the ideology of society. For instance, the act of giving birth to a child is only termed an act of motherhood if it reflects the relations of marriage and the family. Otherwise the very same act can be termed adultery, and the child is "illegitimate" or a "bastard." The term "mother" may have a significantly different meaning when different relations are involved—as in "unwed mother." It depends on what relations are embodied in the act. Similarly, what is defined as sexual love and marital bliss in one set of relations is prostitution in another, rape in still another. What one woman does in the home of another, or what she does when hired by a man is seen as domestic work and is paid, but what a woman does as wife or mother in her own home is considered a labor of love, is not defined as work by the society, and is not done for direct wages.

Thus the social relations of society define the particular activity a woman engages in at a given moment. Outside these relations "woman" becomes an abstraction. A moment cannot be understood outside the relations of power which shape it and the ideology which defines, protects, and maintains it. In describing these moments, understanding the ideology of a society becomes crucial because the social relations of capitalist patriarchy are maintained through the ideologies of liberalism, male supremacy, and racism. Here one finds the interpretation of any particular moment that is necessary to the maintenance of capitalist patriarchy.

The Relations of the Family

The family is a series of relations which define women's activities both internal and external to it. Because the family is a structure of relationships which connect individuals to the economy, the family is a social, economic, political, and cultural unit of a society. It is historical in its formation, not a simple biological unit. Like women's roles, the family is not "natural"; it reflects particular relations of the society, particular needs to be filled.

What are some of the relations that define the family? First, woman is a reproducer of children who become workers for the economy and members of the society. She also socializes these children for their roles in the work world and the society as a whole. She labors to feed, clothe, and care for these children, and for her husband. In these capacities, the mother is a domestic laborer within the economy and a nurturer of the social world as well.[16]

Second, within her role in the family woman is a consumer. Consumption is the other side of production.[17] She buys the things the family needs and the economy has to sell. She cares for these goods—by laundering a new dress or preparing a meal. As a consumer, woman is working to select, prepare, and maintain the goods. A woman is importantly intertwined with the economy and society. She is doing what is absolutely necessary for the economy—consuming.

Although motherhood includes the activities we have called domestic labor, it should not be reduced to them. Motherhood should be understood as a more complex reality than domestic labor within the relations of capital—rather, as a patriarchal institution not reducible to any class reality. Domestic labor and housewifery may be the specific capitalist patriarchal statement of motherhood,[18] but we must be careful not to lose the connection to the pre-existing historical notion of mother and all this concept reflects about the relations of male supremacy.

These relations within the family devalue women in the marketplace when they seek employment. In 1970, only 7 percent of American women (as opposed to 40 percent of American men) earned more than $10,000 a year. Stated differently, 93 percent of the American women who worked earned less than $10,000.[19] Woman's labor in the home becomes a liability for finding jobs for pay outside the home. She is paid less in the labor force because of the relations which tie her to the family. Her labor is defined as free or cheap.

We can already see that women are ghettoized in the labor force and that their work there does not challenge the male supremacist organization of society. The influx of women into the lowest ranks of the labor force reflects the patriarchal necessity of male hierarchy for the society at large. Male supremacy is maintained through class hierarchy. This inflexibility is most clearly seen in the contradiction in women's lives—the double day of work. Woman is both worker and mother.

What are the relations which define a woman as mother in the first place? What defines the patriarchal organization of labor? In other words, why are women oppressed as women? The answer often given is that a woman's biology distinguishes her from a man. But even though a woman's relation to reproduction may have initially defined her as the exchange object rather than man,[20] the history of male supremacy and its particular relation to capitalism reflects a series of relations which are not now limited to this unique characteristic. There are a whole series of relations that exist as a result of this definition of woman as reproducer that cannot be "reduced" to their origin. Both cultural and political relations have been defined and redefined to maintain the hierarchy of sexual relations. The initial reason for the hierarchy—perhaps a fear of woman's reproductive capacity, given the lack of biological knowledge of just what it entailed—no longer exists as such. But society still needs a sexual hierarchy because of the way its relations have been structured since then.

If the distinguishing biological characteristic between men

and women is woman's reproductive capacity, then we need to see why and how it is used as part of male supremacist relations, which have constructed a more troublesome system of inequality than the initial source. This is not to understate the importance of understanding woman's biological self as a reproducer, but it is to say that this understanding must entail the political relations which define it at any moment. The relations of production and reproduction, not an abstracted notion of biology, define the relationship woman has to herself and society as a reproductive being. To focus on the fact that woman as reproducer is the universal crosscultural characteristic of male supremacy and therefore the source of the problem is to formulate the problem incorrectly. Looking at this same reality—the control of women by reproduction—does not focus sufficiently on the relations defining reproduction in the society. It is not reproduction itself that is the problem but the relations which define and reinforce it.

Patriarchy has been sustained through the sexual division of labor and society which has been based on a cultural, social, economic usage of woman's body as a vessel of reproduction. Women were exchanged as gifts for what they could bear. Inequalities arose from the mechanism used to celebrate and/or control woman's position as reproducer.[21] Although the systems of exchange have changed, the relations which they produced became part and are still a part (although redefined) of patriarchal history. Because women were often given and were not the givers, because they had no control over the arrangements surrounding their lives, because they often found themselves in new surroundings and ignorant of the ways of the community, women came to experience the exchange system as a system of relations which excluded them from decisions, purposive activity, and control. This exists, although in somewhat different form, in capitalist patriarchal society. Women marry, lose their names, move to new communities when their husbands' jobs necessitate it, feel lonely, and, find it difficult to meet people. And even though the majority of women in lower economic groups work in the labor force, men are treated with priority. Lesbians and other women who choose not to identify closely with a man and conform to the heterosexual norm of marriage, family, and housewife are even more isolated and ostracized. These relations express the priority given men. They define a certain control over the woman's life.

When one looks at relations of reproduction, what one really focuses upon is a system of hierarchical control and ordering which all existing societies have needed and used. Patriarchy as male supremacy has supplied this order, even while the economic organizations of societies change. This is not to imply that patriarchal systems of control have not changed, but they have changed while maintaining their male supremacist structure and without altering the basic impact of male supremacy. During the change from feudalism to capitalism, however, the basic economic class structure and its control system does change.

Because patriarchy is a system of power, it is incomplete to say that men are the oppressors without explaining that they are oppressors because they embody the relations of patriarchy. To speak of individual men as "things," rather than as reflecting the relations of power is to conceive of male power in abstract rather than concrete form. A man as a biological being, were he to exist outside patriarchal relations, would be a hollow shell. In patriarchal history, it is his biology that identifies him with the relations of power. Although some wish to say that men's power is expressed on an individual level through physical strength, I think that this is a true but very limited notion of the power men have in the system of patriarchy. It is rather the relations of sexual hierarchy that allow men to express their power. They have internalized the relations and act upon them daily. A man's sexual power is not within his individual being alone. To destroy patriarchal relations we must destroy the structures of sexual, racial, and class hierarchy partially maintained through the sexual division of labor. If we change the social relations of power, men have to change, because they will no longer have their hierarchical base.

Any of the particular oppressions experienced by women in capitalist patriarchy exhibit relations of the society. As things, they are completely neutral. Abstracted from reality there is nothing innately oppressive about contraception, pregnancy, abortion, childrearing, or affectionate familial relations. However, they all express a very particular oppression for women in this society. If contraceptive methods were devised for both men and women, with a real concern for our health rather than profits, and if abortion was not laden with patriarchal values and did not cost more money than it should, contraception and abortion would be different experiences.[22] If men and women believed that childrearing was a social responsibility, rather than a woman's responsibility, if we did not believe that childhood affection was dependent on privacy rather than intimacy, the "relations" of childrearing would be significantly different. If being pregnant did not involve a woman in patriarchal medical care, if it did not mean having to deal with the relations defining private health care, if it did not mean the loss of pay and the incurrence of financial obligations, and if it meant bringing life into a socialist feminist society, the act of childbirth would take on a wholly different meaning.

Emphasis on the patriarchal experience in capitalist patriarchy reveals, therefore, the relations of power in any particular moment in society. Since life activity in this society is always in process, in process through power relations, we must try to understand the process rather than isolated moments. To understand the process is to understand the way the process may be changed.

Notes

1. See the literature of radical feminism: Ti Grace Atkinson, *Amazon Odyssey* (New York: Links, 1974); Ingrid Bengis, *Combat in the Erogenous Zone* (New York: Alfred Knopf, 1972); Shulamith Firestone, *The Dialectic of Sex* (New York: Bantam, 1970); Kate Millett, *Sexual Politics* (New York: Doubleday, 1970); *Sisterhood Is Powerful*, ed. Robin Morgan (New York: Vintage, 1970) and *Monster* (New York: Vintage, 1972); Red Stockings, *Feminist Revolution* (New York: Red Stockings, Inc., 1975).

2. I am particularly interested in defining the newer and politically more complex portion of socialist feminism rather than any particular sectarian line. This is the position least well articulated at the Socialist Feminist Conference in Yellow Springs, Ohio, summer, 1975: that woman's oppression reflects the problem of capitalism *and* patriarchy. Radical feminism and Marxist analysis are both viewed as necessary elements in the theory.

3. I am indebted to correspondence with Marla Erlien for clarification of this point.

4. Juliet Mitchell, *Women's Estate* (New York: Pantheon, 1971), p. 99.

5. Firestone's analysis is limited by this structural dichotomy. She says she will develop a "materialist history" (Marxist method) based on sex itself (feminist question). In the end she is unable to construct this history because of this dichotomy. Her substitution of sexual oppression for class oppression distorts reality. It limits the possibilities of developing a "real materialism" based on sex and class. See Firestone, *Dialectic of Sex*. Also see Mitchell's discussion of Firestone in *Woman's Estate*.

6. See Bertell Ollman, *Alienation: Marx's Conception of Man in Capitalist Society* (New York: Cambridge University Press, 1971); Karl Marx, *Grundrisse* (New York: Vintage, 1973) and *Capital*, vols. 1 and 3 (New York: International Publishers, 1967).

7. At the same moment that radical feminism suffers from abstraction by dealing insufficiently with economic class reality it is responsible for explicating the "personal" sexual experience, and in this way remedies the earlier abstraction of the Marxist method. For a discussion of this see Nancy Hartsock, "Fundamental Feminism: Process and Perspective," *Quest* 2, no. 2 (Fall 1975): 67–80, and this volume.

8. Juliet Mitchell, *Psychoanalysis and Feminism* (New York: Pantheon, 1974), pp. 364–65.

9. Firestone, *The Dialectic of Sex*, p. 9.

10. Atkinson, *Amazon Odyssey*, p. 5.

11. Marc Bloch, *Feudal Society*, vol. 1 (Chicago: University of Chicago Press, 1961), p. 137. See also Oliver Cox, *Caste, Class and Race* (New York: Monthly Review Press, 1959) and Henri Pirenne, *Economic and Social History of Medieval Europe* (New York: Harvest Books, 1933).

12. See Linda Gordon, *Families* (a New England Free Press pamphlet); A. Gordon, M. J. Buhle, N. Schrom, "Women in American Society,"

Radical America 5 (July–August 1971); Mary Ryan, *Womanhood in America* (New York: Franklin Watts, 1975); Ivy Pinchbeck, *Women Workers and the Industrial Revolution, 1750–1850* (Clifton, N. J.: Augustus Kelly, 1969); Eli Zaretsky, *Capitalism, the Family, and Personal Life* (a *Socialist Revolution* pamphlet).

13. See literature on how socialist countries treat the particularly patriarchal elements of their society: "Women in Transition, *Cuba Review* 4, no. 2 (September 1974); Margaret Randall, *Cuban Women Now* (Toronto: Canadian Women's Educational Press, 1974); Sheila Rowbotham, *Women, Resistance, and Revolution* (New York: Pantheon, 1972); "Women in Vietnam, Chile, Cuba, Dhofar, China and Japan," *Red Rag,* no. 9 (June 1975); Judith Stacey, "When Patriarchy Kowtows: The Significance of the Chinese Family Revolution for Feminist Theory," *Feminist Studies* 2, no. 43 (1975) and in this volume; Hilda Scott, *Does Socialism Liberate Women?* (Boston: Beacon Press, 1974); Linda Gordon, *The Fourth Mountain: Women in China* (a New England Free Press pamphlet).

14. See Sheila Rowbotham, *Woman's Consciousness, Man's World* (Baltimore: Penguin, 1973); Mitchell, *Psychoanalysis and Feminism*; Gayle Rubin, "The Traffic in Women: Notes on the 'Political Economy' of Sex," in *Toward an Anthropology of Women,* ed. Rayna Reiter (New York: Monthly Review Press, 1975).

15. Angela Davis, "Reflections on the Black Woman's Role in the Community of Slaves," *Massachusetts Review* 13, no. 1 and 2 (reprinted from *Black Scholar,* December 1971).

16. See the varied discussions of women's domestic labor: Margaret Benston, *The Political Economy of Women's Liberation* (a New England Free Press pamphlet); Peggy Morton, "Women's Work Is Never Done," in *Women Unite* (Toronto: Canadian Women's Educational Press, 1972); Mariarosa dalla Costa, "Women and the Subversion of the Community" and Selma James, "A Woman's Place" in *The Power of Women and the Subversion of the Community* (a Falling Wall Press, Ltd. pamphlet, 1972); Ira Gerstein, "Domestic Work and Capitalism" and Lise Vogel, "The Earthly Family," *Radical America* 7 (July–October 1973); Wally Seccombe, "The Housewife and Her Labour under Capitalism," *New Left Review* 83 (January–February 1973), with postscript in *Red Pamphlet,* no. 8 (Britain: IMG pub.); B. Magas, H. Wainwright, Maragaret Coulson, "The Housewife and Her Labour under Capitalism—A Critique" and Jean Gardiner, "Women's Domestic

Labor," *New Left Review* 89 (January–February 1975), and, for the latter, this volume.

17. See "Introduction to a Contribution to the Critique of Political Economy," in Karl Marx, *A Contribution to the Critique of Political Economy* (Moscow: Progress Publishers, 1970) for a discussion of the relationship between production and consumption. See also Amy Bridges and Batya Weinbaum, "The Other Side of the Paycheck," in this volume.

18. See Ann Oakley, *Woman's Work* (New York: Pantheon, 1974).

19. Karen Lindsey, "Do Women Have Class?" *Liberation* 20, no. 2 (January–February 1977): 18.

20. I am very much indebted here to the discussion of Rubin, "Traffic in Women."

21. See Rubin, "Traffic in Women"; Mitchell, *Psychoanalysis and Feminism*; and Miriam Kramnick, "Ideology of Motherhood: Images and Myths," paper delivered at Cornell Women's Studies Program, 14 November 1975.

22. Suzanne Arms, *Immaculate Deception* (Boston: Houghton Mifflin, 1975).

FEMINIST THEORY
AND THE DEVELOPMENT OF
REVOLUTIONARY STRATEGY

Nancy Hartsock

A number of writers have detailed problems of the left in America. They have pointed out that it has remained out of touch with large numbers of people, and that it has been unable to build a unified organization, or even to promote a climate in which to debate socialist issues. The left has been criticized for having a prefabricated theory made up of nineteenth-century leftovers, a strategy built on scorn for innovation in politics or for expanding political issues. Too often leftist groups have held that the working class was incapable of working out its own future and that those who would lead the working class to freedom would be those who had memorized the sacred texts and were equipped with an all-inclusive theory that would help them organize the world.

While such a list of criticisms presents a caricature of the left as a whole, it points to a number of real problems,[1] and overcoming them will require a reorientation. Here I can only deal with one aspect of the task: the role of feminist theory and the political practice of the women's movement as a model for the rest of the left.

My thanks to C. Ellison, S. Rose, and M. Schoolman for their suggestions and encouragement, and to the Quest staff who helped me formulate these ideas. Parts of this article appeared in Quest: a feminist quarterly 2, no. 2 (1975), as a critique of the first national socialist feminist conference. In addition, parts were presented in a lecture series in socialist feminism at Ithaca College in the spring of 1977.

I want to suggest that the women's movement can provide the basis for building a new and authentic American socialism. It can provide a model for ways to build revolutionary strategy and ways to develop revolutionary theories which articulate with the realities of advanced capitalism. Developing such a model requires a redefinition of theory in general in the light of a specific examination of the nature of feminist theory and practice, a reanalysis of such fundamental questions as the nature of class, and a working out of the implications of feminist theory for the kinds of organizations we need to build.

Theory and Feminist Theory

Theory is fundamental to any revolutionary movement. Our theory gives us a description of the problems we face, provides an analysis of the forces which maintain social life, defines the problems we should concentrate on, and acts as a set of criteria for evaluating the strategies we develop.[2] Theory has an even broader role, however. As Antonio Gramsci has pointed out, "One can construct, on a specific practice, a theory which, by coinciding and identifying itself with the decisive elements of the practice itself, can accelerate the historical process that is going on, rendering practice more homogeneous, more coherent, more efficient in all its elements, and thus, in other words, developing its potential to the maximum."[3] Thus, theory itself can be a force for change.

At the same time, however, Gramsci proposes that we expand our understanding of theory in a different direction. We must understand that theorizing is not just something done by academic intellectuals but that a theory is always implicit in our activity and goes so deep as to include our very understanding of reality. Not only is theory implicit in our conception of the world, but our conception of the world is itself a political choice.[4] That is, we can either accept the categories given to us by capitalist society or we can begin to develop a critical understanding of our world. If we choose the first alternative, our theory may remain forever implicit. In contrast, to choose the second is to commit ourselves to working out a critical and explicit theory. The political action of feminists over most of the last decade provides a basis for articulating the theory implicit in our practice.[5] Making the theory explicit is difficult but necessary to improve the work feminists are doing.

The Nature of Feminist Theory

Women who call themselves feminists disagree on many things. To talk in such unitary terms about a social movement so diverse in its aims and goals may seem at first to be a mistake. There is a women's movement which appears on television, has national organizations, and is easy for the media to reach and present as representative of feminist thought. But there is a second movement, one harder to find, that is made up of small groups and local organizations whose members work on specific local projects, a movement which came together around the immediate needs of women in a variety of cities, a movement whose energies have gone directly into work for change. It is these groups that form the basis for my discussion of feminist theory. These groups were concerned with practical action—rape crisis centers, women's centers, building women's communities, etc. In coming together as feminists to confront the problems which dominate their lives, women have built a movement profoundly based on practice. Indeed, one of the major tasks for the women's movement is precisely the creation of revolutionary theory out of an examination of our practice.[6]

All these groups share a world view that differs from that of most socialist movements in advanced capitalist countries, and that is at the same time surprisingly close to Marx's world view. It is this mode of analysis, with its own conception of social theory as well as the concrete theories we are developing out of it, that are the sources of feminism's power and the reason I can argue that through our practice, feminists have become the most orthodox of Marxists. As Lukacs argued, orthodoxy in Marxist theory refers exclusively to method.[7]

At bottom, feminism is a mode of analysis, a method of approaching life and politics, a way of asking questions and searching for answers, rather than a set of political conclusions about the oppression of women. Women are applying that method to their own experiences as women in order to transform the social relations which define their existence. Feminists deal directly with their own daily lives—something which accounts for the rapid spread of this movement. Others have argued that socialist feminism must be recognized as a definite tendency within Marxism generally; in contrast, I am suggesting that because feminists have reinvented Marx's method, the women's movement can provide a model for the rest of the left in developing theory and strategy.[8]

The practice of small-group consciousness-raising—with its stress on examining and understanding experience and on connecting personal experience to the structures which define women's lives—is the clearest example of the method basic to feminism. Through this practice women have learned that it was important to build their analysis from the ground up, beginning with their own experiences. They examined their lives not only as thinkers but, as Marx would have suggested, with all their senses.[9] Women drew connections between their personal experiences and political generalities about the oppression of women; indeed they used their personal experience to develop those generalities. We came to understand our experience, our past, in a way that transformed both our experience and ourselves.[10]

The power of the method feminists developed grows out of the fact that it enables women to connect their everyday lives with an analysis of the social institutions which shape them. The institutions of capitalism (including its imperialist aspect), patriarchy, and white supremacy cease to be abstractions; they become lived, real aspects of daily experience and activity. We see the concrete interrelations among them.

All this means that within the feminist movement, an important role for theory has been reemphasized—one in which theorists work out and make "coherent the principles and the problems raised by the masses in their practical activity."[11] Feminism as a mode of analysis, especially when consciousness-raising is understood as basic to that method, requires a redefinition of the concept of intellectual or theorizer, a recasting of this social role in terms of everyday life.

Because each of us is a potential theorist, intellectual, and activist, education comes to have a very different role in the women's movement than it does in the rest of the left today. The kind of political education feminists are doing for themselves differs fundamentally from what I would call instruction, from being taught the "correct political line." Education —as opposed to instruction—is organically connected to everyday life.[12] It both grows out of and contributes to our understanding of it.

Personal and Political Change

"If what we change does not change us/ we are playing with blocks."[13]

Feminist emphasis on everyday life leads to a second area of focus: the integration of personal and political change. Since we come to know the world (to change it and be changed by it) through our everyday activity, everyday life must be the basis for our political work. Even the deepest philosophical questions grow out of our need to understand our own lives.[14] Such a focus means that reality for us consists of "sensuous human activity, practice."[15] We recognize that we produce our existence in response to specific problems posed for us by reality. By working out the links between the personal and the political, and by working out the links between daily life and social institutions, we have begun to understand existence as a social process, the product of human activity. Moreover, the realization that we not only create our social world but can change it leads to a sense of our own power and provides energy for action.

Feminism as a method makes us recognize that human activity also changes us. A fundamental redefinition of the self is an integral part of action for political change.[16]

If our selves are social phenomena and take their meaning from the society of which we are a part, developing an independent sense of self necessarily calls other areas of our lives into question. We must ask how our relationships with other people can foster self-definition rather than dependence and can accommodate our new strengths. That is, if our individuality is the ensemble of our social relations, "to create one's personality means to acquire consciousness of them and to modify one's own personality means to modify the *ensemble* of these relations."[17] Clearly, since we do not act to produce and reproduce our lives in a vacuum, changed consciousness and changed definitions of the self can only occur in conjunction with a restructuring of the social (both societal and personal) relations in which each of us is involved.

Thus, feminism leads us to oppose the institutions of capitalism and white supremacy as well as patriarchy. By calling attention to the specific experiences of individuals, feminism calls attention to the totality of social relations, to the social formation as a whole.[18] A feminist mode of analysis makes it clear that patriarchy, capitalism, white supremacy, forms of social interaction, language—all exist for us as historic givens. Our daily lives are the materialization at a personal level of the features of the social formation as a whole. The historical structures that mold our lives pose questions we must respond to and define the immediate possibilities for change.[19]

Although we recognize that human activity *is* the structure of the social world, this structure is imposed not by individuals but by masses of people, building on the work of those who came before. Social life at any point in time depends on a complex of factors, on needs already developed as well as on embryonic needs—needs whose production, shaping, and satisfaction is a historical process. Developing new selves, then, requires that we recognize the importance of large-scale forces for change as well as that the people we are trying to become—fully developed individuals—can only be the products of history and struggle.[20]

This history and struggle necessitates the creation of a new collectivity closely linked to the creation of new individuals, a collectivity which fundamentally opposes the capitalist concept of the individual. The creation of this new collectivity presupposes the attainment of a "cultural-social" unity through which a multiplicity of dispersed wills, with heterogeneous aims, are welded together with a single aim, on the basis of an equal and common conception of the world, both general and particular, operating in transitory bursts (in emotional ways) or permanently (where the intellectual base is so well rooted, assimilated, and experienced that it becomes passion).[21]

Clearly, we can only transform ourselves by struggling to transform the social relations which define us: changing selves and changed social institutions are simply two aspects of the same process. Each aspect necessitates the other. To change oneself— if individuality *is* the social relations we are involved in—is to change social institutions. Feminist practice reunites aspects of life separated by capitalism and does so in a way which assimilates the intellectual aspect to passion. As Marx said: "The coincidence of the changing of circumstances and of human activity or self changing can be conceived and rationally understood only as *revolutionary practice*."[22] This process of self-changing and growing in a changed world leads us to a sense that our lives are part of a number of larger processes and that all the aspects of our lives must be connected.

The Importance of Totality

By beginning with everyday life and experience, feminism has been able to develop a politics which incorporates an understanding of process and of the importance of appropriating our past as an essential element of political action.[23] We find that we constantly confront new situations in which we act out of our changed awareness of the world and ourselves and in consequence experience the changed reactions of others. What some socialists have seen as static, feminists grasp as structures of relations in process—a reality constantly in the process of becoming something else. Feminist reasoning "regards every historically developed social form as in fluid movement and therefore takes into account its transient nature not less than its momentary existence."[24] This mode of understanding allows us to see the many ways processes are related and provides a way to understand a world in which events take their significance from the set of relationships which come to a focus in them. Thus, we are led to see that each of the interlocking institutions of capitalism, patriarchy, and white supremacy conditions the others, but each can also be understood as a different expression of the same relations.[25]

Since each phenomenon changes form constantly as the social relations of which it is composed take on different meanings and forms, the possibility of understanding processes as they change depends on our grasp of their role in the social whole.[26] For example, in order to understand the increased amount of wage work by women in the United States we need to understand the relation of their work to the needs of capitalism. But we must also look at the conditions of work and the kind of work prescribed for women by patriarchy and white supremacy as different aspects of the same social system. As feminists, we begin from a position which understands that possibilities for change in any area are tied to change occurring in other areas.

Both capitalism and socialism are more than economic systems. Capitalism does not simply reproduce the physical existence of individuals. "Rather it is a definite form of activity of these individuals, a definite form of expressing their life, a definite *mode of life* on their part . . . [and this coincides with] both *what* they produce and *how* they produce."[27] A mode of life is not divisible. It does not consist of a public part and a private part, a part at the workplace and a part in the community—each of which makes up a certain fraction, and all of which add up to 100 percent. A mode of life, and all the aspects of that mode of life, take meaning from the totality of which they form a part.

In part because of shifts in the boundaries between the economic and the political and because of the increasing interconnections between the state apparatus and the economy (through means as varied as public education and government regulation of industry), it becomes even more necessary to emphasize that one can only understand and penetrate, and transform reality as a totality, and that "only a subject which is itself a totality is capable of this penetration." Only a collective individual, a united group of people "can actively penetrate the reality of society and transform it in its entirety."[28]

Feminism and Revolution

If all that I have said about feminism as a method rooted in dealing with everyday life holds true, what is it that makes this mode of analysis a force for revolution? There are three factors of particular importance: (1) The focus on everyday life and experience makes action a necessity, not a moral choice or an option. We are not fighting other people's battles but our own. (2) The nature of our understanding of theory is altered and theory is brought into an integral and everyday relation with practice. (3) Theory leads directly to a transformation of social relations both in consciousness and in reality because of its close connection to real needs.

First, how does a feminist mode of analysis make revolution necessary? The feminist method of taking up and analyzing experience is a way of appropriating reality. Experience is incorporated in such a way that our life experiences become a part of our humanness. By appropriating our experience and incorporating it into ourselves, we transform what might have been a politics of idealism into a politics of necessity. By appropriating our collective experience, we are creating people who recognize that we cannot be ourselves in a society based on hierarchy, domination, and private property. We are acquiring a consciousness which forces us, as Marx put it, "by an ineluctable, irremediable and imperious *distress*—by practical *necessity*—to revolt against this inhumanity."[29] Incorporating, or making part of ourselves, what we learn is essential to the method of feminism.

Second, I argued that a feminist mode of analysis leads to an integration of theory and practice. For feminists, theory is the articulation of what our practical activity has already appropriated in reality. As Marx argued, as struggle develops, theorists "no longer need to seek science in their minds; they have only to take note of what is happening before their eyes and to become its mouthpiece."[30] If we look more closely at the subject about which Marx was writing on this occasion—the British working class—we find that by the time Marx wrote these words that group had already developed theory out of its practice to a considerable degree. A variety of trends had emerged, and ideas about organization and politics had been diffused over a wide area. Isolation from experienced national leadership, and the overimportance of personalities created problems, but the facility with which English working-class people formed associations is impressive. They used a variety of forms taken over from Methodism, friendly societies, trade unions, etc. By the time Marx wrote, it was clear that most people understood that power came from organization.[31]

In looking at history, one is especially struck with the number of false starts, the hesitancy, the backtracking that went into making what we would today recognize as class consciousness. Forming theory out of practice does not come quickly or easily, and it is rarely clear what direction the theory will finally take.

Feminists, in making theory, take up and examine what we find within ourselves; we attempt to clarify for ourselves and others what we already, at some level, know. Theory itself, then, can be seen as a way of taking up and building on our experience. This is not to say that feminists reject all knowledge that is not firsthand, that we can learn nothing from books or from history. But rather than read a number of sacred texts we make the practical questions posed for us in everyday life the basis of our study. Feminism recognizes that political philosophy and political action do not take place in separate realms. On the contrary, the concepts with which we understand the social world emerge from and are defined by human activity.

For feminists, the unity of theory and practice refers to the use of theory to make coherent the problems and principles expressed in our practical activity. Feminists argue that the role of theory is to take seriously the idea that all of us are theorists. The role of theory, then, is to articulate for us what we know from our practical activity, to bring out and make conscious the philosophy embedded in our lives. Feminists are in fact creating social theory through political action. We need to conceptualize, to take up and specify what we have already done, in order to make the next steps clear. We can start from common sense, but we need to move on to the philosophy systematically elaborated by traditional intellectuals.[32]

A third factor in making feminism a force for revolution is that the mode of analysis I have described leads to a transformation of social relations. This is true first in a logical sense. That is, once social relations are situated within the context of the social formation as a whole, the individual phenomena change their meanings and forms. They become something other than they were. For example, what liberal theory understands as social stratification becomes clearer when understood as class. But this is not simply a logical point. As Lukacs has pointed out, the transformation of each phenomenon through relating it to the social totality ends by conferring "reality on the day to day struggle by manifesting its relation to the whole. Thus it elevates mere existence to reality."[33] This development in mass political consciousness, the transformation of the phenomena of life, is on the one hand a profoundly political act and on the other, a "point of transition."[34] Consciousness must become deed, but the act of becoming conscious is itself a kind of deed.

If we grant that the women's movement has reinvented Marx's method and for that reason can be a force for revolution, we need to ask in what specific sense the women's movement can be a model for the rest of the left. At the beginning I outlined a number of criticisms of the left, all rooted in the fact that it has lost touch with everyday life. The contrast I want to draw is one between what Gramsci recognized as "real action," action "which modifies in an essential way both man and external reality," and "gladiatorial futility, which is self-declared action but modifies only the word, not things, the external gesture and not the [person] inside."[35]

At the beginning of this paper I suggested that education took on a new significance for the women's movement because of the role of personal, everyday experience in constructing theory and transforming reality. Feminists are aware that we face the task of building a collective will, a new common sense, and this requires that we must participate in a process of education in two senses. We must, first, never tire of repeating our own arguments and, second, work to raise the general intellectual level, the consciousness of larger numbers of people in order to produce a new and different understanding of everyday life.[36] The women's movement is working at both these tasks—the first by insisting that every woman can reconstruct the more general feminist arguments on her own, the second by turning to the writings of more traditional intellectuals for whatever guidance we may find there.

Marx applied his method systematically to the study of capital. Feminists have not yet really begun systematic study based on the mode of analysis we have developed. Here I can only mention some of the questions which are currently being debated in the women's movement—issues on which there is not yet a consensus but whose theoretical resolution is inseparable from practical, daily, work for change.

Issues for Feminist Theory

The Nature of Class

Marxists have devoted a great deal of attention to the nature of class.[37] Most Marxist theorists agree that there are problems with traditional definitions of class. If to be working class means to have nothing to sell but labor power, then the vast majority of the American population falls within this definition. If to be working class means to contribute directly to the production of surplus value, then far fewer of us fall into that category. A number of modifications of these traditional ideas have been presented. Some writers have argued that there is a "new" working class, that what is important now is the possibility for alliances with sectors of the "new petty bourgeoisie," that knowledge and its possession (science) have become productive forces, or that the working out of the division of mental from manual labor with its attendant ritualization of knowledge is critical to the working out of class boundaries.[38] In this maze of theories about the nature of class under advanced capitalism, a feminist mode of analysis can provide important insights into the nature of class as it structures the concrete existence of groups and individuals.

Because feminists begin from our own experience in a specific advanced capitalist society, we recognize that the lived realities of different segments of society are varied. While it is true that most people have only their labor power to sell (for wages or not), there are real differences in power, privilege, ability to control our lives, and even chances for survival. By focusing on people's daily lives we are learning that our class is not defined by our relationship to the mode of production in the simple sense that if we sell our labor power (for a day or a lifetime) or are part of the family of someone (presumably male) who does, we are working class. Being working class is a way of living life, a mode of life not exclusively defined by the simple fact that we have only our labor power to sell.

Class distinctions in capitalist society are part of a totality, a mode of life which is structured as well by the traditions of patriarchy and white supremacy. Class distinctions in the United States affect the everyday lives of women and men, white and black and Third World people in different ways. A feminist mode of analysis leads us to ask questions which recognize that we already know a great deal about class (in fact, in our daily activity we act on what we know), but need to appropriate what we know to make it into explicit theory.

One's social class is defined by one's place "in the ensemble of social practices, i.e., by [one's] place in the social division of labor as a whole," and for that reason must include political and ideological relations. "Social class, in this sense, is a concept which denotes the effects of the structure within the social division of labor (social relations and social practices)."[39] Feminists writing about class have focused on the structures produced by the interaction of political, ideological, and more strictly economic relations, and have done so from the standpoint of everyday life and activity.

Some of the best descriptions of class and its importance in the women's movement were produced by the Furies, a lesbian/feminist separatist group in Washington, D.C. When the

Furies began, many members of the collective knew very little about the nature of class. But the collective included a number of lower- and working-class women who were concerned about ways middle-class women oppressed them. As one middle-class woman wrote:

> Our assumptions, for example, about how to run a meeting were different from theirs, but we assumed ours were correct because they were easiest for us—given our college educations, our ability to use words, our ability to abstract, our inability to make quick decisions, the difficulty we had with direct confrontations. . . . I learned [that] class oppression was . . . a part of my life which I could see and change. And, having seen the manifestations of class in myself, I better understood how class operated generally to divide people and keep them down.[40]

In the context of working for change, it became clear that

> refusal to deal with class behavior in a lesbian/feminist movement is sheer self-indulgence and leads to the downfall of our own struggle. Middle class women should look first at that scale of worth that is the class system in America. They should examine where they fit on that scale, how it affected them, and what they thought of the people below and above them. . . . Start thinking politically about the class system and all the power systems in this country.[41]

What specifically did the Furies learn when they looked at the way class functioned in daily life? First, they learned the sense in which we have all, no matter what our class background, taken for granted that the "middle class way is *the right way.*" Class arrogance is expressed in looking down on the "less articulate," or regarding with "scorn or pity . . . those whose emotions are not repressed or who can't rap out abstract theories in thirty seconds flat." Class supremacy, the Furies found, is also apparent in a kind of passivity often assumed by middle- and especially upper-middle-class women for whom things have come easily. People who are "pushy, dogmatic, hostile, or intolerant" are looked down on. Advocating downward mobility and putting down those who are not as "revolutionary" is another form of middle-class arrogance. What is critical about all of this is that "middle class women set the standards of what is good (and even the proper style of downward mobility which often takes money to achieve) and act 'more revolutionary than thou' towards those who are concerned about money and the future." Middle-class women retain control over approval. The small, indirect, and dishonest ways of behaving in polite society are also ways of maintaining "the supremacy of the middle class and perpetuating the feelings of inadequacy of the working class."[42]

These accounts of barriers created by class differences within the women's movement lead us toward an understanding of several important points about the nature of class. They lead us to see first that class is a complex of relations, one in which knowledge or know-how is at a premium, and second, at a deeper level, that what is involved in the daily reality of class oppression is the concrete working out of the division between mental and manual labor. Class, especially as it affects the lives of women, is a complex of a number of factors in which political and ideological aspects as well as strictly economic factors play an important role. Theorists have focused too closely on the domination of men by production pure and simple. Looking at the role of class in women's lives highlights the importance of other factors as well, such as the role of family and patriarchal traditions. For both women and men class defines the way we see the world and our place in it, how we were educated and where, and how we act—whether with assurance or uncertainty.[43] The process of production must be seen to include the reproduction of political and ideological relations of domination and subordination. It is these factors that lead to the feelings described as "being out of control," "feeling like you don't know what to do," and feeling that you are incompetent to judge your own performance.[44]

At bottom, people are describing the way it feels to be on the "wrong" side of the division between mental and manual labor. Indeed, the division between mental and manual labor is precisely the concentrated form of class divisions in capitalism.[45] It is critical to recognize that mental labor is the exercise of "political relations legitimized by and articulated to, the monopolization and secrecy of knowledge, i.e. the reproduction of the ideological relations of domination and subordination."[46] Mental labor involves a series of rituals and symbols. And it is always the case that the dominated group either does not know or cannot know the things that are important.[47]

By calling attention to life rather than theory, the women's movement has called attention to cultural domination as a whole—has begun a political analysis that does not take place in isolation from practical activity. By noticing the real differences among women in terms of class—confidence, verbal ability, ease about money, sense of group identity—we are developing new questions about class. While we have barely begun the task of reconstructing the category of class, we are learning that it is important to pay attention to the mechanisms of domination as a whole. By looking at class as a feature of life and struggle, the women's movement has established some of the terms any revolutionary movement must use: Until we confront class as a part of everyday life, until we begin to analyze what we already know about class, we will never be able to build a united and large-scale movement for revolution. In this task, we need to recognize the decisive role of the division between mental and manual labor in all its complexity for the formation of the whole mode of life that is capitalism.

Organizations and Strategies

Feminism, while it does not prescribe an organizational form, leads to a set of questions about organizational priorities. First, a feminist mode of analysis suggests that we need organizations which include the appropriation of experience as a part of the work of the organization itself. We need to systematically analyze what we learn as we work in organizations. While the analysis of our experience in small groups was valuable, we need to develop ways to appropriate our organizational experience and to use it to transform our conception of organization itself. Some feminist organizations are beginning to do this—to raise questions about the process of meetings or about the way work is done and should be done.[48]

Because so many of us reacted to our experience in the

organizations of the rest of the left by refusing to build any organizational structures at all, we have only begun to think about the way we should work in organizations with some structure. We need to build the possiblities for change and growth into our organizations rather than rely on small groups. This means that we need to systematically teach and respect different skills and allow our organizations to change and grow in new directions. We need to use our organizations as places where we begin to redefine social relations and to create new ways of working which do not follow the patterns of domination and hierarchy set by the mode of production as a whole.

A feminist mode of analysis has implications for strategy as well. We can begin to make coalitions with other groups who share our approach to politics. We cannot work, however, with people who refuse to face questions in terms of everyday life or with people who will not use their own experience as a fundamental basis for knowledge. We cannot work with those who treat theory as a set of conclusions to be pasted onto reality and who, out of their own moral commitment, make a revolution for the benefit of their inferiors. A feminist mode of analysis suggests that we must work on issues which have real impact on daily life. These issues are varied—housing, public transportation, food prices, etc. The only condition for coalition with other groups is that those groups share our method. So long as those we work with are working for change out of necessity, because they, like us, have no alternative, there is a real basis for common action.

As we work on particular issues, we must continually ask how we can use these issues to build our collective strength. The mode of analysis developed by the women's movement suggests several criteria with which to evaluate particular strategies. First, we must ask how our work will educate ourselves and others politically, how it will help us to see the connections between social institutions. Second, we must ask how a particular strategy materially affects our daily lives. This involves asking: How does it improve our conditions of existence? How will it affect our sense of ourselves and our own power to change the world? How will a particular strategy politicize people, make people aware of problems beyond individual ones?[49] Third, we must ask how our strategies work to build organizations—to build a collective individual which will increase our power to transform social relations as a whole. Fourth, we must ask how our strategies weaken the institutions which control our lives—patriarchy, white supremacy, and capitalism. Our strategies must work not simply to weaken each of these institutions separately but must attack them on the basis of an understanding of the totality of which they form parts.

In all this, however, we must remember that there is no "ready made, pre-established, detailed set of tactics which a central committee can teach its . . . membership as if they were army recruits."[50] In general, the tactics of a mass party cannot be invented. They are "the product of a progressive series of great creative acts in the often rudimentary experiments of the class struggle. Here too, the unconscious comes before the conscious. . . ."[51]

Most important, a feminist mode of analysis makes us recognize that the struggle itself must be seen as a process with all its internal difficulties. We must avoid, on the one hand, developing a narrow sectarian outlook, and, on the other, abandoning our goal of revolution. We must continue to base our work on the necessity for change in our own lives. Our political theorizing can only grow out of appropriating the practical political work we have done. While the answers to our questions come only slowly and with difficulty, we must remember that we are involved in a continuous process of learning what kind of world we want to create as we work for change.

Notes

1. See, for example, Sylvia Wallace, "The Movement Is Out of Relations with the Working Class," unpublished paper, 1974; Charlotte Bunch, "Beyond Either/Or: Feminist Options," *Quest: a feminist quarterly* 3, no. 1 (Summer 1976).
2. V. I. Lenin, *What Is To Be Done?* (New York: International Publishers, 1929), p. 28.

3. Antonio Gramsci, *Selections from the Prison Notebooks,* trans. Quinton Hoare and Geoffrey Nowell Smith (New York: International Publishers, 1971), p. 365. Gramsci adds that "the identification of theory and practice is a critical act, through which practice is demonstrated rational and necessary and theory realistic and rational."

4. Ibid., p. 327. See also p. 244.

5. I should perhaps note here that I am speaking as a participant as well as a critical observer. The experience I use as a reference point is my own as well as that of many other women.

6. Feminists are beginning to recognize the importance for the movement of conscious theorizing—for critical analysis of what we have been doing for most of the last decade. Among the current issues and problems being reevaluated are the significance of service projects, the importance of leadership, new possibilities for developing organizational structures, and our relationship to the rest of the left.

7. George Lukacs, *History and Class Consciousness* (Cambridge, Mass: M.I.T. Press, 1971), p. 1.

8. On this point, see especially Barbara Ehrenreich, "Speech by Barbara Ehrenreich," *Socialist Revolution* 5, no. 4 (October–December 1975).

9. On this point, compare Karl Marx, *Economic and Philosophic Manuscripts of 1844,* ed. Dirk Struik (New York: International Publishers, 1964), p. 140, and Gramsci, *Selections,* p. 324.

10. This is not to say there have been no problems or that beginning with personal experience always led women to think in larger terms. Some groups have remained apolitical or have never moved beyond the level of personal issues; others have become so opposed to any organizations other than personal organizations that they are immobilized. Problems about the "correct line" are also part of the current debate in the women's movement. On current problems, see Bunch, "Feminist Options."

11. Gramsci, *Selections,* p. 330.

12. Ibid., p. 43.

13. Marge Piercy, "A Shadow Play for Guilt," in *To Be of Use* (Garden City, N.Y.: Doubleday, 1973), p. 17.

14. Gramsci, *Selections,* p. 351.

15. Karl Marx, "Theses on Feuerbach," in Karl Marx and Friedrich Engels, *The German Ideology,* ed. C. J. Arthur (New York: International Publishers, 1970), p. 121. This method also overcomes the

passivity characteristic of much of American life. See, for example, Richard Sennett and Jonathan Cobb, *The Hidden Injuries of Class* (New York: Vintage, 1973), p. 165, and Stanley Aronowitz, *False Promises* (New York: McGraw-Hill, 1973), p. 112.

16. See Gramsci, *Selections*, p. 360. See also Lukacs, p. 19.
17. Ibid., p. 352.
18. See Nicos Poulantzas, *Classes in Contemporary Capitalism* (London: New Left Books, 1975), p. 21.
19. Marx and Engels, *German Ideology*, p. 59.
20. Marx, *Economic and Philosophic Manuscripts*, p. 141. See also Karl Marx, *Grundrisse*, trans. Martin Nicolaus (Middlesex, England: Penguin Books, 1973), p. 162.
21. Gramsci, *Selections*, p. 349.
22. Marx, "Theses on Feuerbach," p. 121. See also Gramsci, *Selections*, pp. 352, 360.
23. See Lukacs, *History*, p. 175.
24. Karl Marx, *Capital*, vol. 1 (Moscow: Foreign Language Publishing House, 1954), p. 20.
25. Marx, *Economic and Philosophic Manuscripts*, p. 119.
26. As Lukacs pointed out, grasping the totality means searching for interrelations. It means elevating the relations among objects to the same status as the objects themselves. (Lukacs, p. 154. See also pp. 8, 10, and 13.)
27. Marx and Engels, *German Ideology*, p. 114.
28. Lukacs, *History*, p. 39.
29. Karl Marx, *Selected Writings in Sociology and Social Philosophy*, trans. T. B. Bottomore (New York: McGraw-Hill, 1956), p. 232.
30. Karl Marx, *The Poverty of Philosophy* (New York: International Publishers, 1973), p. 125.
31. E. P. Thompson, *The Making of the English Working Class* (New York: Vintage, 1963), p. 668.
32. Gramsci, *Selections*, p. 424. See also Marx, "Theses on Feuerbach," p. 122.
33. Lukacs, *History*, p. 22.
34. Ibid., p. 178. See also Gramsci's contention that "for a mass of people to be led to think coherently and in the same coherent fashion about the real present world, is a 'philosophical' event far more important and 'original' than the discovery by some philosophical 'genius' of a truth which remains the property of small groups of intellectuals" (*Selections*, p. 325).
35. Ibid., pp. 225, 307.

36. Ibid., p. 340.
37. The women's movement is debating a number of other important issues: race, lesbianism, power, etc. In this particular context, the role of class seems a useful example. I hardly need to add that what I have to say is simply a very general outline of the directions in which feminist theory can guide our analysis. For a range of approaches to the issue of class see Sennett and Cobb, *Hidden Injuries of Class;* Aronowitz, *False Promises;* Poulantzas, *Classes in Contemporary Capitalism;* C. Wright Mills, *Power, Politics, and People* (New York: Oxford University Press, 1963); T. B. Bottomore, *Classes in Modern Society* (New York: Vintage, 1966); or Richard Parker, *The Myth of the Middle Class* (New York: Liveright, 1972).
38. In addition to the above, see Alain Touraine, *The Post-Industrial Society* (New York: Random, 1971) and Harry Braverman, *Labor and Monopoly Capital* (New York: Monthly Review Press, 1974), esp. part 5.
39. Poulantzas, *Classes,* p. 14.
40. Ginny Berson, "Only By Association," *The Furies* 1, no. 5 (June–July 1972): 5–7.
41. Nancy Myron, "Class Beginnings," *The Furies* 1, no. 3 (March–April 1972): 3.
42. Charlotte Bunch and Coletta Reid, "Revolution Begins at Home," *The Furies* 1, no. 4 (May 1972): 2–3. See also Dolores Bargowski and Coletta Reid, "Garbage Among the Trash," *The Furies* 1, no. 6 (August 1972): 8–9. Some of the essays from the Furies are collected in *Class and Feminism,* ed. Nancy Myron and Charlotte Bunch (Baltimore: Diana Press, 1974).
43. Clearly I disagree with Poulantzas who locates women on the mental side of the mental/manual division of labor. He admits that women tend to occupy the more manual jobs within the hierarchy of jobs on the mental labor side, but as he defines the working class (focusing almost exclusively on employment) the majority of the working class is male. To argue that women are part of the "penumbra around the working class" (p. 319) is to make the mistake Poulantzas himself argued against; it is to refuse to pay attention to political and ideological factors and even to refuse to pay attention to economic factors in any but the narrowest sense. When a woman from a working-class family takes a secretarial job this is hardly enough to make her a part of the petty bourgeoisie.
44. These statements come from Sennett and Cobb, *Hidden Injuries of Class,* pp. 97, 115, and 157. One of the most important effects of

class is to make working-class people doubt they have a legitimate right to fight back.

45. Poulantzas, *Classes*, p. 233.
46. Ibid., p. 240.
47. Ibid., p. 257. Poulantzas correctly calls attention to the fact that there is no technical reason why science should assume the form of a division between mental and manual labor (p. 236). See also Braverman, *Labor and Monopoly Capital*, who documents the history of the increasing separation of the two forms of labor. The separation of mental from manual labor has particularly interesting ramifications where women are concerned, since they have been increasingly excluded from the exercise of technical functions in capitalism. An interesting example is provided by the increasing exclusion of women from the practice of medicine as medicine became a technical skill. (See Hilda Smith, "Ideology and Gynecology in Seventeenth Century England," 1973).
48. Lukacs, *History*, p. 333.
49. More extensive criteria for choosing strategies are presented in Charlotte Bunch, "The Reform Tool Kit," *Quest* 1, no. 1 (Summer 1974).
50. Rosa Luxemburg, "Organizational Questions of Russian Social Democracy," *Selected Writings of Rosa Luxemburg*, ed. Dick Howard (New York: Monthly Review Press, 1971), p. 289.
51. Ibid., p. 293.

MOTHERHOOD, REPRODUCTION, AND MALE SUPREMACY

As we have mentioned, when Engels noted the dual importance for society of production and reproduction he uncovered a key political reality which neither he nor most political analysts since have understood. Most existing discussions of reproduction do not recognize it as a politically necessary aspect of any society that must be organized and ordered along with the other relations of survival. As a result there is no recognition of the political base intrinsic to the biological capacity for reproduction and the societal necessity for it. It has been the particular concern of socialist feminists, including Juliet Mitchell, Sheila Rowbotham, Gayle Rubin, Nancy Chodorow, and Linda Gordon, to remedy this situation.

Nancy Chodorow focuses on mothering as part of the operation of male dominance. Given that both the idea and the reality of motherhood define the activities of most women, Chodorow seeks to explain how motherhood as an institution is reproduced through mothering. Motherhood focuses not only upon the reproduction of children, but also on the reproduction of society: mothering reproduces not only new children but new mothers. This society reproduces the relations of male supremacy and the hierarchical relations necessary to the capitalist marketplace.

In *Woman's Body, Woman's Right*, Linda Gordon showed that a woman's lack of control of reproduction is part of the social relations that define her oppression, and that the struggle for such control has been part of the varied struggle for women's rights and liberation. These relations and struggles must be understood as part of the history of patriarchal, male-supremacist, and/or sex-gender systems. Here Gordon shows that the struggle for control over reproductive capacities is central though not sufficient for the struggle for liberation. She describes the struggle in three stages: (1) nineteenth-century feminism; (2) early twentieth-century feminist socialism; and (3) 1970s feminism. At each stage women have moved toward a fuller understanding of how men control them through control of reproduction. Gordon's basic thesis is that "birth control does not mean population control or birthrate reduction or planned families but reproductive freedom." Reproductive freedom is defined as the control over one's reproductive capacities, not the elimination of biological reproduction. Reproductive self-determination becomes a basic condition for sexual equality and political revolution.

Socialist theory has dealt insufficiently with the reality of women as mothers and radical feminism only begins to probe the question in its full political, economic, and psychoanalytic sense. It has been socialist feminist women who have begun to push the analysis of psychoanalysis to better understand the dynamic involved in the social relations of mothering as it is practiced. Juliet Mitchell was important in opening up this area for analysis, although I think she reinvents the problem of woman's oppression as belonging to the unconscious realm disconnected from real conditions. Nancy Chodorow begins to tackle the question of how the unconscious operates out of a series of conscious realities. If the unconscious were not reinforced daily by the conscious political organization of the society, the unconscious would lose its capacity for reproduction. An analysis of the dynamics of the mind must be integrated with the society which produces, defines, redefines, and reproduces the mind. Socialist feminists have only begun this difficult task; the beginnings are presented in this section.

Related Reading

Bachofen, J. J., *Myth, Religion, and Mother Right: Selected Writings* (Princeton: Princeton University Press, 1967).

Bamburger, Joan, "The Myth of Matriarchy," and Chodorow, Nancy, "Family Structure and Feminine Personality," in *Woman, Culture and Society,* ed. Michelle Rosaldo and Louise Lamphere (Stanford: Stanford University Press, 1974).

Briffault, Robert, *The Mothers: The Matriarchal Theory of Social Origins* (New York: Macmillan, 1931).

Chodorow, Nancy, "Oedipal Asymmetrics and Heterosexual Knots," *Social Problems* (April 1976).

Dinnerstein, Dorothy, *The Mermaid and The Minotaur: Sexual Arrangements and Human Malaise* (New York: Harper & Row, 1976).

Engels, Friedrich, *The Origin of the Family, Private Property and the State* (New York: International Publishers, 1972).

Erikson, Erik H., "Womanhood and the Inner Space," *Identity, Youth, and Crisis* (New York: Norton, 1968).

Freud, Sigmund, "The Passing of the Oedipus Complex. Some Psychological Consequences of the Anatomical Distinction Between the Sexes (1925)," "Female Sexuality (1931)," *Sexuality and the Psychology of Love,* ed. Philip Rieff (New York: Collier Books, 1963).

Mitchell, Juliet, *Psychoanalysis and Feminism* (New York: Pantheon, 1975).

Neumann, Erich, *The Great Mother: An Analysis of the Archetype* (1963; Princeton: Princeton University Press, 1972); *The Origins and History of Consciousness* (1954; Princeton: Princeton University Press, 1970).

Pomeroy, Sarah B., *Goddesses, Whores, Wives and Slaves* (New York: Schocken Books, 1975).

Rubin, Gayle, "The Traffic in Women," in *Toward an Anthropology of Women,* ed. Rayna Reiter (New York: Monthly Review Press, 1975).

Shorter, Edward, *The Making of the Modern Family* (New York: Basic Books, 1975).

MOTHERING, MALE DOMINANCE, AND CAPITALISM

Nancy Chodorow

Women mother. In our society, as in most societies, women not only bear children. They also take primary responsibility for infant care, spend more time with infants and children than do men, and sustain primary emotional ties with infants. When biological mothers do not parent, other women, rather than men, take their place. Though fathers and other men spend varying amounts of time with infants and children, fathers are never routinely a child's primary parent. These facts are obvious to observers of everyday life.

Because of the seemingly natural connection between women's childbearing and lactation capacities and their responsibility for child care, and because of the uniquely human need for extended care in childhood, women's mothering has been taken for granted. It has been assumed to be inevitable by social scientists, by many feminists, and certainly by those opposed to feminism. As a result, the profound importance of women's mothering for family structure, for relations between the sexes, for ideology about women, and for the sexual division of labor and sexual inequality both inside the family and in the nonfamilial world is rarely analyzed.

The material in this paper will appear in revised form in Nancy Chodorow, *Mothering: Psychoanalysis and the Social Organization of Gender* (Berkeley: University of California Press, 1978).

A Note on Family and Economy

Uniquely among early social theorists, Frederick Engels divided the material basis of society into two spheres, that of material production and that of human reproduction.[1] He argued that the two spheres together determined the nature of any particular society. Engels makes clear that he does not think these aspects of social life develop or express themselves in biologically self-evident or unmediated ways, for he equates each with their respective social forms—the production of the means of existence with labor, and the production of people with the family.

Anthropologist Gayle Rubin, in an important recent contribution to the development of feminist theory,[2] pushes further Engels' conception that two separate spheres organize society, and she reforms and expands it in an even more sociological vein. Marx and Marxists, she points out, have convincingly argued two things about any society's organized economic activity, its "mode of production." One is that this activity is a fundamental determining and constituting element (some would say *the* fundamental determining and constituting element) of the society. The second is that it does not emanate directly from nature (is, rather, socially constructed), nor is it describable in solely technological or mechanically economic terms. Rather, a mode of production consists of the technology *and* social organization through which a society appropriates and transforms nature for purposes of human consumption and transforms the experience of human needs to require further manipulations of nature.

Rubin suggests, in an analytic system parallel to this Marxian view, that every society contains, in addition to a mode of production, a "sex-gender system"—"systematic ways to deal with sex, gender, and babies."[3] The sex-gender system includes ways in which biological sex becomes cultural gender, a sexual division of labor, social relations for the production of gender and of gender-organized social worlds, rules and regulations for sexual object choice, and concepts of childhood. The sex-gender system is, like a society's mode of production, a fundamental determining and constituting element of society, socially constructed, and subject to historical change and development. Empirically, Rubin suggests, kinship and family organization form the locus of any society's sex-gender system. Kinship and family organization consist in and reproduce socially organized gender and sexuality.

We can locate features of a sex-gender system and a mode of production in our own society. In addition to assigning women primary parenting functions, our sex-gender system, as all systems to my knowledge, creates two and only two genders out of the panoply of morphological and genetic variations found in infants, and maintains a heterosexual norm. It also contains historically generated and societally more specific features: its family structure is largely nuclear, and its sexual division of labor locates women first in the home and men first outside of it. It is male dominant and not sexually egalitarian, in that husbands traditionally have rights to control wives and power in the family; women earn less than men and have access to a narrower range of jobs; women and men tend to value men and men's activities more; and in numerous other ways that have been documented and redocumented since well before the early feminist movement. Our mode of production is more and more exclusively capitalist.

That our society contains a mode of production and a sex-gender system does not differentiate it from previous societies or from current nonindustrialized societies. The ease with which we can recognize the distinction between the two spheres, however, is a product of our own unique history, during which material production has progressively left the home, the family has been eliminated as a productive economic unit, and women and men have in some sense divided the public and domestic spheres between them. The distinction that we easily draw, however, between the economy ("men's world") and the family ("women's world"), and the analytic usefulness in our separation of the mode of production and the sex-gender system, does not mean that these two systems are not empirically or structurally connected. Rather, they are linked (and almost inextricably intertwined) in numerous

ways. Of these ways, women's mothering is that pivotal structural feature of our sex-gender system—of the social organization of gender, ideology about women, and the psychodynamic
of sexual inequality—that links it most significantly with our
mode of production.

Women's Mothering and the Social Organization of Gender

Women's mothering is a central and defining structural feature of our society's organization of gender, one that it has in
common with all other societies. Over the past few centuries
women of different ages, classes, and races have moved in and
out of the paid labor force as the demand for workers has
shifted and the wage structure varied. Marriage and fertility
rates have fluctuated considerably during this same period.
When there have been children, however, women have cared for
them, usually as mothers in families and occasionally as workers in childcare centers or as paid or slave domestics.

There are few universal statements we can make about the
sociology of the sexes, about the sexual division of labor, about
family structure and practices. Margaret Mead early pointed to
the unexpected malleability and variability of temperaments
between and among the sexes in different societies.[4] Since
then, ethnographic research has confirmed Mead's claim and
has enabled us to extend it to include most of the activities we
normally characterize as masculine or feminine.

This variation is not limitless, however.[5] A few features of
our own sexual division of labor and kinship system remain
which we can tentatively characterize as universal. (Very importantly, all societies do have a sexual division of labor.)
These include women's involvement in routine daily cooking
for their immediate families (festive cooking, by contrast, is
often done by men) and heterosexuality as a sexual norm and
organizational principle of family organization and the structure of marriage. In addition, where hunting of large animals
and war-making take place, these activities are masculine
specializations.

Finally, we find universally that men with full adult status do not routinely care for small children, especially for infants. Women care for infants and children, and when they receive help, it is from children and old people. That women perform primary parenting functions, then, is a universal organizational feature of the family and the social organization of gender. In different periods and societies there are substantial differences in family and kinship structure and in the specific organization and practices of parenting (such as the number of people who provide infant and child care, the family setting in which this is provided, the ideology about mother-infant relationships and about children, whether infants are swaddled, carried on hip, back or breast, kept mainly in cribs, etc.). These variations should not be minimized. At the same time, it is important to keep in mind their common status as variations *within* a sexual and familial division of labor in which women mother. Anthropologists have spoken of the universal, or nearly universal, ways that women's mothering affects other aspects of women's lives, the sexual division of labor, and the ideology and practice of sexual asymmetry in any society. Their insights apply equally to our own society and enrich our understanding of the dynamics of our own social organization of gender.

In all societies there is a mutually determining relationship between women's mothering and the organization of production. Women's work has been organized to enable women to care for children, though childbirth, family size, and child-tending arrangements have also been organized to enable women to work.[6] Sometimes, as seems to be happening in many industrial societies today, women must care for children and work in the labor force simultaneously.

Historically and crossculturally, women's mothering has become a fundamentally determining feature of social organization. Michelle Rosaldo has argued that women's responsibility for child care has led, for reasons of social convenience rather than biological necessity, to a structural differentiation in all societies of a "domestic" sphere that is predominantly women's and a "public" sphere that is men's.[7] The domestic sphere is the sphere of the family. It is organized around mothers and children. Domestic ties are particularistic—based on specific relationships between members—and often intergenerational, and are assumed to be natural and biological. The public sphere is nonfamilial and extra-domestic. Public institutions, activities, and forms of association are defined and recruited normatively, according to universalistic criteria in which the specific relationships among participants are not a factor. The public sphere forms "society" and "culture"—those intended, constructed forms and ideas that take humanity beyond nature and biology. And the public sphere, therefore "society" itself, is masculine.

Societies vary in the extent to which they differentiate the public and the domestic spheres. In small hunter and gatherer bands, for instance, there is often minimal differentiation. Even here, however, men tend to have extra-domestic distribution networks for the products of their hunting, whereas what women gather is shared only with the immediate family.[8]

The structural differentiation between public and domestic spheres has been sharpened through the course of industrial capitalist development, producing a family form centered on women's mothering and maternal qualities. In precapitalist and early capitalist times, the household was the major productive unit of society. Husband and wife, with their own and/or other children, were a cooperative producing unit. A wife carried out her childcare responsibilities along with her productive work, and these responsibilities included training girls—daughters, servants, apprentices—for this work. Children were early integrated into the adult world of work, and men took responsibility for the training of boys once they reached a certain age. This dual role—productive and reproductive—is characteristic of women's lives in most societies and throughout history. Until very recently, women everywhere participated in most forms of production. Production for the home was in, or connected to, the home.

With the development of capitalism, however, and the industrialization that followed, production outside the home expanded greatly, while production within the home declined. Women used to produce food and clothing for the home. Cloth, and later food and clothing, became mass-produced commodities. Because production for exchange takes place only outside the home and is identified with work as such, the home is no longer viewed as a workplace. Home and workplace, once the same, are now separate.[9]

This change in the organization of production went along with and produced a complex of far-reaching changes in the family. In addition to losing its role in production, the family has lost many of its educational, religious, and political functions, as well as its role in the care of the sick and aged. These losses have made the contemporary nuclear family a quintessentially relational and personal institution, the personal sphere of society.[10] The family has become the place where people go to recover from work, to find personal fulfillment and a sense of self. It remains the place where children are nurtured and reared

This split between social production, on the one hand, and domestic reproduction and personal life, on the other, has deepened the preindustrial sexual division of spheres. Men have become less and less central to the family, becoming primarily "bread-winners." They maintained authority in the family for a time, but as their autonomy in the nonfamilial world decreased, their authority in the family itself has declined,[11] and they have become increasingly nonparticipant in family life itself. Psychoanalyst and social theorist Alexander Mitscherlich speaks of "society without the father."[12] Women lost their productive economic role both in social production and in the home.

This extension and formalization of the public-domestic split brought with it increasing sexual inequality. As production left the home and women ceased to participate in primary productive activity, they lost power both in the public world and in their families. Women's work in the home and the maternal role are devalued because they are outside of the sphere of monetary exchange and unmeasurable in monetary terms, and because love, though supposedly valued, is valued only within a devalued and powerless realm, a realm separate from and not equal to profits and achievement. Women's and men's spheres are distinctly unequal, and the structure of values in industrial capitalist society has reinforced the ideology of inferiority and relative lack of power vis-à-vis men which women brought with them from preindustrial, precapitalist times.

At the same time, women's reproductive role has changed.[13] Two centuries ago marriage was essentially synonymous with childrearing. One spouse was likely to die before the children were completely reared, and the other spouse's death would probably follow within five years of the last child's marriage. Parenting lasted from the inception of a marriage to the death of the marriage partners. But over the last two centuries, fertility and infant mortality rates have declined, longevity has increased, and children spend much of their childhood years in school.

Women's Mothering and Ideology about Women

Just as the actual physical and biological requirements of childbearing and child care were decreasing, women's mothering role gained psychological and ideological significance and came increasingly to dominate women's lives, outside the home as well as within it. In this society it is not assumed, as it has been in most societies previously, that women as mothers and wives do productive or income-producing work as part of their routine contribution to their families. The factual basis for this assumption is fast being eroded—as the number of wives and both married and single mothers in the paid labor force soars—but the ideology remains with us. Whatever their marital status and despite evidence to the contrary for both married and unmarried women, women are generally assumed to be working only to supplement a husband's income in nonessential ways. This assumption justifies discrimination, less pay, layoffs, higher unemployment rates than men, and arbitrary treatment. In a country where the paid labor force is more than 40 percent female, many people continue to assume that most women are wives and mothers who do not work. In a situation where almost two thirds of the women who work are married and almost 40 percent have children under eighteen, many people assume that "working women" are single and childless.

The kind of work women do also tends to reinforce stereotypes of women as wives and mothers. This work is relational and often an extension of women's wife-mother roles in a way that men's work is not. Women are clerical workers, service workers, teachers, nurses, salespeople. If they are involved in production, it is generally in the production of nondurable goods like clothing and food, not in "masculine" machine industries like steel and automobiles.[14] All women, then, are affected by an ideological norm that defines them as members of conventional nuclear families.

This ideology is not merely a statistical norm. It is transformed and given an *explanation* in terms of natural differences and natural causes. We explain the sexual division of labor as an outgrowth of physical differences. We see the family as a natural, rather than a social, creation. In general, we do not see the social organization of gender as a product or aspect of social organization at all. The reification of gender, then, involves the removal of all imputation of historicity and all sense that people produce and have produced its social forms.

An ideology of nature that sees women as closer to nature than men, or as anomalies neither natural nor cultural, remains fundamental.[15] In our society, moreover, the particular ideology of nature that defines the social organization of gender generally, and women's lives in particular, bases itself especially upon interpretations and extensions of women's mothering functions and reproductive organs. Historians have described how industrial development in the capitalist United States relegated women to the home and elevated their maternal qualities, as nurturant supporters and moral models for both children and husbands. Ruth Bloch has examined American magazines from the latter part of the eighteenth century to trace the origins of this nineteenth-century ideology.[16] During the late colonial period, magazines assigned no special weight to the role of mother, either in relation to women's other roles or in contrast to the role of father. Women were rational mothers, part of a rational parenting pair, along with their other housewifely duties. Around 1790, however, in conjunction with the growth of increasingly impersonal competitive work engaged in by husbands, a sentimental image of the "moral mother" came to dominate and take over from previously dominant images of women—images Bloch calls the "delicate beauty" and the "rational housewife." The moral mother incorporated some of the traits of her predecessors while giving these new meaning:

> Like the rational housewife, she was capable, indispensable, and worthy of respect. Like the delicate beauty, however, she was wonderfully unlike men, intuitive as opposed to rational, and, therefore, also the subject of sentimental idealizations.[17]

Magazines extolled the involvement and importance of mothers in the production of worthy sons. But they also suggested that women play a similar maternal role for their husbands. Bloch concludes:

> This view of a man's wife as providing him with crucial emotional support fed into a conception of woman as essentially "mother," a role which in the magazines of the 1790s began to receive effusive praise for its indispensable and loving service to the human race.[18]

Thus, the virtues of mother and wife collapsed into one, and that one was maternal: nurturant, caring, and acting as moral model. This rising image of women as mother, moreover, idealized women's sexlessness, pointing further to the assimilation of wife to mother in the masculine psyche.

The moral mother was a historical product. She "provided the love and morality which enabled her husband to survive the cruel world of men."[19] As this world grew crueler with nineteenth-century industrial development, both the image of the moral mother and attempts to enforce it grew as well. Barbara Welter describes its apogee in the "cult of true womanhood."[20] Women's magazines and books expounded upon this cult, and women discussed it in diaries, memoirs, and novels. Bourgeois women of the nineteenth century were expected to be pious, pure, submissive, and domestic—again, to provide a world of contrast to the immoral, competitive world of their husband's work and a place where their own children (more especially their sons) could develop proper moral qualities and character. Because of this, compliance with the requisites of maternal morality was not left to chance. Medical practices defined bourgeois women as sexless and submissive by nature. They explained deviation from this norm (women's resistance and assertions of self) as medically caused. Doctors, upon husbandly suggestion or on their own, extirpated sexual and reproductive organs of women who were too sexual and aggressive and who thereby threatened men's control of women and the careful delineation of sexual spheres.[21]

During the present century the ideology of natural gender differences and of women's natural maternal role has lost some of its Victorian rigidity. The dichotomy between what is social and public, however, and what is domestic and natural takes on ever increasing psychological weight. In a society so thoroughly characterized by, and organized around, socially constructed, universalistic variables (a market in labor, alienation, bureaucratic norms, citizenship, and formal equality of access to the political sphere and before the law), we retain at least one sphere where membership and attribution seem to be entirely independent of social construction. People continue to explain the sexual division of labor and the social organization of gender as an outgrowth of physical differences and to see the family as a natural, rather than a social, creation.

The ideology of women as natural mothers has also been extended within the home. In the last fifty years the average birthrate has fallen, but during this same period studies show that women have come to spend more time in child care.[22] Women in the home used to do productive work and more physical labor along with their mothering. They used to have more children, which meant they were involved in actual physical care and nursing for most of their adult lives. In preindustrial societies, and in traditional communities, children and older people often helped and continue to help in child care. Now homes contain few children, and these children enter school at an early age. They are not available as aides to their mothers.

The Western family has been largely "nuclear" for centuries, in that households have usually contained only one married couple with children. But some of these children could be grown and not married, and households often contained a number of other members—servants, apprentices, boarders and lodgers, a grandparent—as well. The rise of capitalist industrialization has made the household an exclusive parent and small child realm.[23] It has removed men from the household and parenting responsibilities. Infant and child care has become the exclusive domain of biological mothers, who are increasingly isolated from other kin, with fewer social contacts during their parenting time. Participation in the paid labor force does not change this. When women are home, they still have nearly total responsibility for children.

Ironically, biological mothers have come to have more and more exclusive responsibility for child care just as the biological components of mothering have lessened—as women have borne fewer children and bottle feeding has become available. Post-Freudian psychology and sociology has provided new rationales for the idealization and enforcement of women's maternal role, as it has emphasized the crucial importance of the mother-child relationship for the child's development.

This crucial mothering role contributes not only to child development but also to the reproduction of male supremacy. Because women are responsible for early child care and for most later socialization as well, because fathers are more absent from the home, and because men's activities generally have been removed from the home while women's have remained within it, boys have difficulty attaining a stable, masculine gender role identification. They fantasize about and idealize the masculine role, and their fathers and society define it as desirable. Freud first described how a boy's normal oedipal struggle to free himself from his mother and become masculine generated "the contempt felt by men for a sex which is the lesser."[24] Psychoanalyst Grete Bibring argues from her own clinical experience that "too much of mother," resulting from the contemporary organization of parenting and extra-familial work, creates men's resentment and dread of women, and their search for nonthreatening, undemanding, dependent, even infantile women—women who are "simple, and thus safe and warm."[25] Through these same processes, she argues, men come to reject, devalue, and even ridicule women and things feminine. Thus, women's mothering creates ideological and psychological modes which reproduce orientations to, and structures of, male dominance in individual men and builds an assertion of male superiority into the very definition of masculinity.

Women's Mothering and the Reproduction of Capitalism

Women's mothering has traditionally been and continues to be a pivotal feature in the social organization and social reproduction of gender and sexual inequality. In our time it is also pivotal to the reproduction of the capitalist mode of production and the ideology which supports it. To begin with, of course, women, now as always, reproduce the species biologically. But this is a biological universal. In the present context, it is the daily and generational reproduction specific to our contemporary economic system that is of interest.

There are several aspects to reproduction. The capitalist organization of production sustains conditions that ensure a continually expanding labor force whose wages and salaries can maintain its members and their families but are not sufficient to enable them to become capitalists. Legitimating ideologies and institutions—the state, schools, media, families—contribute to the reproduction of capitalism. Finally, workers themselves, at all levels of the production process, are reproduced, both physically and in terms of requisite capacities, emotional orientations, and ideological stances. The family is a primary locus of this last form of reproduction, and women, as mothers and wives, are its primary executors. Women's role and work activities in the contemporary family contribute to the social reproduction specific to capitalism.

With the development of capitalism and the separation of work and family life, women continued to have primary home responsibilities as a heritage from the precapitalist past and as an extension of the domestic-public division found in this earlier period. This did not mean that the factory system and industrialization automatically drew men, and not women, into its labor force: women and children were prominent among the first factory workers. In the United States, most men engaged in agricultural production as the factory system was developing, and in England women and children were a cheaper source of labor than men. Moreover, the first factories produced cloth, which had been previously produced in the home by women. Significantly, however, the development of labor outside the home (a development that would subsequently be reversed)[26] did not affect the division of labor within it. Women of all classes retained, and continue to retain, home responsibilities.

Women, to begin with, are responsible for the daily reproduction of the (by implication, male) adult participant in the paid work world. These responsibilities are psychological and emotional as well as physical: sociologist Talcott Parsons claims that the "stabilization and tension-management of adult personalities" is a major family function.[27] One reading of Parsons' claim is that the family unit, by its very unity, somehow stabilizes and manages the tensions of both adult family members.[28] However, data on mental health and happiness in marriage show the superior mental health of married over single men and single over married women, which suggests that it is only the masculine person (or personality) who benefits psychologically from marriage.[29] A more correct reading then, and one supported by Parsons' view that the wife/mother is her family's "expressive" or "social-emotional" leader, is that the wife/mother does the tension-managing and stabilizing and the husband/father is thereby soothed and steadied.

Socialist-feminist theorists are in substantial agreement with Parsons' statement, but make explicit his implication about differential benefits. Tension-management and stabilization, they suggest, constitute the support necessary to masculine participants in the extra-domestic work world. These participants need such support because their work is alienating and affectless, and would be otherwise unbearable. Women's role in the family, then, serves as an important siphon for work discontent and works to ensure worker stability. It also removes the need for employers themselves to attend to such stability or to create contentedness. Sociologists Peter Berger and Hansfried Kellner put this well:

> The public institutions now confront the individual as an immensely powerful and alien world, incomprehensible in its inner workings, anonymous in its human character. . . . The point, however, is that the individual in this situation, no matter whether he is happy or not, will turn elsewhere for the experiences of self-realization that do have importance for him. The private sphere, this interstitial area created (we would think) more or less haphazardly as a by-product of the social metamorphosis of industrialism, is mainly where he will turn. It is here that the individual will seek power, intelligibility and, quite literally, a name—the apparent power to fashion a world, however Lilliputian, that will reflect his own being: a world that, seemingly having been shaped by himself and thus unlike those other worlds that insist on shaping him, is translucently intelligible to him (or so he thinks); a world in which, consequently, he is *somebody*— perhaps even, within its charmed circle, a lord and master.[30]

The socialist-feminist formulation points us to another important issue. Parsons' focus—and that of other functionalist and psychoanalytically oriented family theorists—on women's social-emotional role, leads us away from noticing that this "role" is work. This affective work, which women's magazines sometimes call ego-building, is one part of that work of women in the home that reconstitutes labor power in capitalist society. This work includes the actual physical labor of housework, which Parsons and other traditional family theorists also ignore. Mariarosa dalla Costa takes the socialist-feminist argument to its extreme and illuminates it through metaphor, if not through reality, in her argument that the home in capitalist society is a factory producing capitalism's most crucial commodity—labor power.[31]

Women also reproduce labor power in their specific role as mothers. Theorists of the Frankfurt Institute for Social Research and Parsonians have drawn on psychoanalysis to show how the relative position of fathers and mothers in the family produces men's psychological commitment to capitalist domination: the internalization of subordination to authority, the development of psychological capacities for participation in an alienated work world, and achievement orientation.[32]

Parsonsians start from the mother's intense, often sexualized, involvement with her male infant. In middle-class American families, where mothers tend not to have other primary affective figures around, a mutual erotic investment between son[33] and mother develops, an investment the mother can then manipulate. She can love, reward, and frustrate him at appropriate moments in order to get him to delay gratification and sublimate or repress erotic needs. This close, exclusive pre-oedipal mother-child relationship first develops dependency in a son, creating a motivational basis for early learning and a foundation for dependency on others. When a mother "rejects" her son or pushes him to be more independent, this behavior, built upon early intense dependency, creates a diffuse need to please and conform outside of the relationship to the mother herself. The isolated husband–absent mother thus creates in sons a personality founded on generalized achievement orientation rather than on specific goal orientations. These diffuse orientations can then be used to serve a variety of specific goals—goals not set by these men themselves.

In an earlier period of capitalist development, individual goals were important for more men, and entrepreneurial achievement as well as worker discipline had to be based more upon inner moral direction and repression. Earlier family arrangements, where dependency was not so salient nor the mother-child bond so exclusive, produced this greater inner direction. "Now," according to Parsons, "the product . . . in demand is neither a staple nor a machine, it is a personality. But, we add, a product in the sense of a highly developed resource, not a product marketed for peer consumption alone."[34] The contemporary family, with its manipulation of dependency in the mother-child relationship, produces a form of " 'labor' [that] has become a mobile resource transferable from one unit to another"[35] and "personal capacities that have become a fully fluid resource for societal functions."[36] The oedipus complex in the contemporary family creates a

" 'dialectical' relationship between dependency, on the one hand, independence and achievement on the other."[37]

Slater extends Parsons' discussion. People who start life with only one or two emotional objects, he argues, develop a "willingness to put all [their] emotional eggs in one symbolic basket."[38] Boys who grow up in American middle-class nuclear families have this experience.[39] Because they received so much gratification from their mother relative as compared to what they got from anyone else, and because their relationship to her was so exclusive, it is unlikely that they can repeat such a relationship. They relinquish their mother as an object of dependent attachment, but, because she was so uniquely important, retain her as an oedipally motivated object to win in fantasy. They turn their lives into a search for success.

This situation contrasts with that of people who have had a larger number of pleasurable relationships in early infancy. These people are more likely to expect gratification in immediate relationships and maintain commitments to more people and are less likely to deny themselves now on behalf of the future. They would not be the same kind of good worker, given that work is defined (as it is in our society) in individualist, noncooperative ways.

Max Horkheimer and theorists of the Frankfurt Institute concern themselves with a similar developmental outcome and focus on the same historical change. Though they implicitly recognize the significance of the mother, they emphasize the decline in the father's role—his distance, unavailability, and loss of authority. They focus on the oedipal relationship of son to father rather than son to mother.

The family has always transmitted orientations to authority. However, the nature of this orientation changed with the structure of authority in the economic world. During the period of early capitalist development more fathers had some economic power. This paternal authority expressed itself in the family as well, and sons, through a classic oedipal struggle, could internalize their father's authority—that is, could internalize bourgeois inner direction and self-motivation and accept

power as it was. As the household became restricted to immediate family members, conditions were set for internalization: "Childhood in a limited family [became] an habituation to
authority."[40] This was an appropriate response to the requirements of wage labor: "In order that they may not despair in the
harsh world of wage labor and its discipline, but do their part,
it is not sufficient merely to obey the pater familias; one must
desire to obey him."[41] Fathers, with the growth of industrialization, became less involved in family life. They did not simply
leave home physically, however. As more fathers became dependent wage laborers, the material base for their familial authority was also eroded. Horkheimer suggests that in reaction
fathers have developed authoritarian modes of acting, but because there is no longer a real basis for their authority there can
be no genuine oedipal struggle. Instead of internalizing paternal authority, sons engage in an unguided search for authority
in the external world. In its most extreme form, this search for
authority creates the characterological foundation for fascism.
More generally, however, it leads to tendencies to accept the
mass ideological manipulation characteristic of late capitalist
society and the loss of autonomous norms or internal standards
as guides for the individual. Contemporary family structure, for
Frankfurt theorists as for Parsons, produces not only manipula-
bility but a search for manipulation.[42]

Thus woman's mothering role and position as primary parent
in the family, and the maternal qualities and behaviors which
derive from it, are central to the daily and generational reproduction of capitalism. Women resuscitate adult workers, both
physically and emotionally, and rear children who have particular psychological capacities which capitalist workers and
consumers require.[43] Most of these connections are historical
and not inevitable. The physical reproduction of workers (both
of men in the work force and of children) must occur, but there
is nothing in the nature of physical reproduction that *requires*
its occurrence in the family. Rather, capitalist development, and
the separation of work from the home, built on precapitalist
forms in a way that has certainly been convenient to capitalists.
People argue that housework as it is currently organized creates

greater profits, since direct market payment for all of a worker's physical requirements and for daycare is unquestionably more expensive than the marginal addition to a worker's salary to "support" his family. Today, moreover, wives continue to do this unpaid work even while earning their own support in the paid labor force. But all this is a question of history, convenience, and profitability. It is not a logical requirement. As more and more women enter the work force, the extra-domestic economic sector may take over more aspects of physical reproduction.[44]

As I have suggested, however, the reproduction of workers is not exclusively or even primarily a physical or physiological question in capitalist society. Capitalist achievement, and properly submissive, organized, and regular work habits in workers, have never been purely a matter of money. Inner direction, rational planning and organization, and a willingness to come to work at certain hours and work steadily, whether or not money is needed that day, certainly facilitated the transition to capitalism. Additional psychological qualities play a major part in late capitalism: specific personality characteristics and interpersonal capacities are appropriate to the bureaucrat, the middle manager, the technician, the service worker, and the white-collar worker. The increasingly nuclear, isolated, neolocal family in which women do the mothering is suited to the reproduction in children of personality commitments and capacities appropriate to these forms of work and domination.

This *internal* connection, rather than a connection of capitalist convenience, is also true of wives' maternal support of husbands and of their denial of threatening (because active) sexuality. Thus, a wife's role draws not only upon the heterosexual (what we might consider specifically "wifely" as opposed to "motherly") elements of ideology about and expectations of women. Sex is undoubtedly a source of masculine self-esteem, and sexual dominance helps a man to take out frustrations encountered on the job and to exercise in his own sphere the control he feels exercised over him.[45] Women's dependent and passive behavior toward their husbands, however, also masks the nurturant controlling that is going on. As long as women continue to provide emotional support and "ego-building" to their husbands, they are mothering them.

The developments I have been discussing gain meaning one from the other. Women's mothering, as a nearly universal feature of family structure, has given particular characteristics to the social organization and valuation of gender as we know it in all societies, and we have inherited our organization of parenting, as well as our sex-gender system, from our precapitalist past. At the same time, particular attributes of the organization and valuation of gender have gained salience in our own society. The organization of gender and male dominance as we experience them are historical products and must be understood historically. Women's mothering has continued to be basic to women's lives and the organization of the family and fundamental to the genesis of ideology about women.

But the development of industrial capitalism has modified this, has given particular meanings to women's mothering and male dominance, and enhanced their significance in particular ways. The same repressions, denials of affect and attachment, rejection of the world of women and things feminine, appropriation of the world of men, identification with the idealized absent father—all a product of women's mothering—create masculinity and male dominance in the sex-gender system and also create men as participants in the capitalist work world.

Women's mothering as a basis of family structure and of male dominance has thus developed an internal connection to the reproduction of capitalism. But while it contributes to the reproduction of sexual inequality, the social organization of gender, and capitalism, it is also in profound contradiction to another consequence of recent capitalist development—the increasing labor force participation of mothers. We cannot predict how or if this contradiction will be resolved. History, ideology, and an examination of industrial countries which have relied on women in the labor force for a longer period and have established alternate childcare arrangements suggest that women will still be responsible for child care, unless we make the reorganization of parenting a central political goal.

Notes

1. Friedrich Engels, *The Origin of the Family, Private Property, and the State*, ed. Eleanor Leacock (New York: International Publishers, 1972).

2. Gayle Rubin, "The Traffic in Women: Notes on the 'Political Economy' of Sex," in *Toward an Anthropology of Women*. ed. Rayna Reiter (New York: Monthly Review Press, 1975).

3. Ibid., p. 168.

4. Margaret Mead, *Sex and Temperament in Three Primitive Societies* (1935; New York: Wm. Morrow).

5. For discussions of the crosscultural sexual division of labor, see *Man the Hunter*, ed. Richard Lee and Irven DeVore (Chicago: Aldine, 1968); Ernestine Friedl, *Women and Men* (New York: Holt, Rhinehart & Winston, 1975); *Woman, Culture and Society*, ed. Michele Rosaldo and Louise Lamphere (Stanford: Stanford University Press, 1974); and Reiter, *Toward an Anthropology of Women*.

6. See Judith K. Brown, "A Note on the Division of Labor by Sex," *American Anthropologist* 72 (1970): 1073–78 and Friedl, *Women and Men*.

7. Michelle S. Rosaldo, "Women, Culture and Society: A Theoretical Overview," in Rosaldo and Lamphere, *Woman, Culture and Society*.

8. Friedl, *Women and Men*.

9. See Alice Clark, *The Working Life of Women in the Seventeenth Century* (1919; Clifton, N.J.: Augustus Kelley); and Robert S. Lynd and Helen Merrell Lynd, *Middletown* (1929; New York: Harcourt Brace, 1959).

10. See Talcott Parsons, "Age and Sex in the Social Structure of the United States" and "The Kinship System of the Contemporary United States," in Talcott Parsons, *Essays in Sociological Theory*, rev. ed. (New York: Free Press, 1954), *Social Structure and Personality* (New York: Free Press, 1964), Parsons and Robert F. Bales, *Family, Socialization and Interaction Process* (New York: Free Press, 1955); Eli Zaretsky, "Capitalism, the Family and Personal Life," *Socialist Revolution* 13–14 (January–April 1973): 69–125; 15 (May–June 1973): 19–70; Peter L. Berger and Hansfried Kellner, "Marriage and the Construction of Reality," in *The Family: Its Structures and Functions*, ed. Rose Laub Coser (New York: St. Martin's Press, 1974).

11. See Grete Bibring, "On the 'Passing of the Oedipus Complex' in a Matriarchal Family Setting," in *Drives, Affects, and Behavior*,

ed. Rudolph M. Loewenstein (New York: International Universities Press, 1953), pp. 278–84; Max Horkheimer, "Authority and the Family," in *Critical Theory* (1936; New York: Seabury, 1975).

12. Alexander Mitscherlich, *Society Without the Father: A Contribution to Social Psychology* (1963; New York: Schocken, 1970).

13. Robert V. Wells, "Demographic Change and the Life Cycle of American Families," *Journal of Interdisciplinary History* 2, no. 2 (1971): 273–82.

14. All my information about women in the labor force is from the U.S. Department of Labor, Employment Standards Administration, Women's Bureau, *1975 Handbook on Women Workers*, Bulletin 297. For a historical study of how clerical work changed as the clerical labor force became female, so that it included much more personal service, coffee-making, etc., see Margery Davies, "Women's Place Is at the Typewriter: The Feminization of the Clerical Labor Force," *Radical America* 8, no. 4 (July–August 1974) and in this volume.

15. See Sherry Ortner, "Is Female to Male as Nature Is to Culture?" in Rosaldo and Lamphere, *Women, Culture and Society*.

16. Ruth Bloch, "Sex and the Sexes in Eighteenth Century Magazines" (1972).

17. Ibid., p. 29.

18. Ibid., p. 31.

19. Ibid., p. 36.

20. Barbara Welter, "The Cult of True Womanhood: 1820–1860," in *The American Family in Social-Historical Perspective*, ed. Michael Gordon (New York: St. Martin's, 1973).

21. See Bernard Barker-Benfield, "The Spermatic Economy of the Nineteenth Century," in Gordon, *The American Family* and Barbara Ehrenreich and Deirdre English, *Complaints and Disorders* (Old Westbury, N.Y.: Feminist Press, 1973).

22. Joann Vanek, *Keeping Busy: Time Spent in Housework, United States, 1920–1970* (1973).

23. See Philippe Aries, *Centuries of Childhood: A Social History of Family Life* (New York: Random, 1965); William Goode, *World Revolution and Family Patterns* (New York: Glencoe Free Press, 1963); Barbara Laslett, "The Family as a Public and Private Institution: An Historical Perspective," *Journal of Marriage and the Family* 35 (1973): 480–92; *Household and Family in Past Time*, ed. Peter Laslett (New York: Cambridge University Press, 1972).

24. Sigmund Freud, "Some Psychical Consequences of the Anatomical

Distinction Between the Sexes," *Standard Edition XIX* (London: Hogarth Press and Institute of Psychoanalysis, 1925), p. 253.

25. Bibring, *Drives, Affects and Behavior*, p. 282.
26. For an excellent discussion of the transition from female to male factory labor as a patriarchal response to the increasing significance of wage labor as a source of income, see Heidi Hartmann, "Capitalism, Patriarchy and Job Segregation By Sex," *Signs* 1, no. 3, part 2 (1976): 137–69, and in this volume.
27. See Parsons and Bales, *Family, Socialization*.
28. For a claim that does not differentiate these functions by gender, see Berger and Kellner in *The Family*.
29. Jessie Bernard, *The Future of Marriage* (New York: Bantam, 1973).
30. Berger and Kellner, in *The Family*, pp. 161–62.
31. Mariarosa dalla Costa, *The Power of Women and the Subversion of the Community* (Bristol, England: Falling Wall Press, 1972).
32. The Frankfurt Institute for Social Research, *Aspects of Sociology* (Boston: Beacon Press, 1972); Max Horkheimer, "Authority and the Family," in *Critical Theory*; Mitscherlich, *Society Without the Father*; Parsons, *Social Structure and Personality*; Parsons and Bales, *Family, Socialization*; Philip Slater, *The Pursuit of Loneliness*, rev. ed. (Boston: Beacon Press, 1976) and *Earthwalk* (New York: Doubleday, 1974).
33. Parsons and his colleagues talk of the "mother-child" relationship. However, they focus on erotic, oedipal attachment as motivating and on the development of character traits which are appropriate to masculine work capacity and not to feminine expressive roles. It is safe to conclude, therefore, that the child they have in mind is male.
34. Talcott Parsons with Winston White, "The Link Between Character and Society," *Social Structure and Personality*, p. 233.
35. Ibid., p. 204.
36. Ibid., p. 233.
37. Ibid., p. 218.
38. Slater, *Earthwalk*, p. 131. See also Slater, *Pursuit of Loneliness*.
39. Again, girls do as well and both genders transfer it to monogamic, jealous tendencies. But Slater is talking about the sexually-toned oedipal/pre-oedipal relationship that is more specific to boys.
40. Horkheimer, in *Critical Theory*, p. 108.
41. Frankfurt Institute, *Aspects*, p. 135.
42. Their accounts do differ but in ways too complex to enter into here. Parsonians tell us more about the genesis of character in

white-collar bureaucrats, professional-technical workers, and managers. Frankfurt theorists focus more on the genesis of character traits in industrial workers.

43. Hidden in most socialist feminist accounts is the fact that women also reproduce *themselves,* physically and psychologically, daily and generationally.

44. This morning (April 10, 1977) the Sunday *New York Times* has a front page article about the increase in eating out and decrease in grocery shopping in recent years.

45. On the ambivalence toward female sexuality in contemporary working-class men, see Lillian Rubin, *Worlds of Pain* (New York: Basic Books, 1976).

THE STRUGGLE FOR REPRODUCTIVE FREEDOM: THREE STAGES OF FEMINISM

Linda Gordon

The contemporary women's liberation movement has again made control of reproduction a political question. Struggling for the right to abortion, criticizing the imperialist imposition of population control programs, and defending people's right to nonreproductive sexual experience, homosexual as well as heterosexual, the feminist program argues that women should have the right to choose parenthood freely.

This essay, written in April–May 1977, is in some ways a bridge, an intermediate process, between two larger works, one finished, one in its beginnings. The essay is based on material in *Woman's Body, Woman's Right: A Social History of Birth Control in America* (New York: Viking, 1976). The essay also contains my first published speculations about the historical development of feminist theory, a topic I am beginning to discuss in another book. The notes in *Woman's Body* should supply enough references for the historical claims made here. One explanatory note is needed, however—my working definition of feminism. It is extremely important to avoid the use of feminism as if it were a moral category, an imprimatur to bestow upon those we agree with. The tendency to use the term in that way is sectarian (like the similar disputes about what is truly socialist, Marxist, or communist) and ahistorical. In the approximately two hundred years of its existence, feminism has already had many varieties and contained sharp oppositions. Many nineteenth-century suffragists, for example, did not believe that full equality between the sexes was desirable; yet not to call them feminists would falsify historical process. By feminism I therefore mean an analysis of women's subordination for the purpose of figuring out how to change it. Despite the breadth of beliefs admitted here, I believe that there has been a fundamental coherence in feminism as a social movement and as a social theory.

Marxists are only just beginning to grapple with these issues. As a theory of capitalist society, Marxism has focused on the relations of production, using a capitalist definition of production—the creation of exchange value. Patterns of male domination in the area of reproduction, not only biological but also the social reproduction of human beings, predate capitalism and are not fully explained by Marxist thought as it exists today. Since sexual relations seem to have been determined to a great extent by considerations about reproduction, Marxist approaches to the roots of sexual domination have been similarly inadequate.

In this article I want to speculate about the conditions that could provide reproductive freedom. These speculations arise from the possibilities made imaginable by the women's liberation movement, which were in turn based on such material possibilities as effective contraception and the heightened productivity of industrial society. In order to see the newness of these possibilities we must look briefly at the history of women's struggle for reproductive self-determination against male domination.

The Suppression of Birth Control

We must begin by rejecting the myth of a prehistorical epoch of sexual freedom. In every known human society sexual activity has been controlled and limited; since we do not know human life outside of society, we do not know human life without some degree of sexual repression. In considering the reproduction issue, we must look at the historical *forms* of sexual repression.

We must also reject the notion that birth control was introduced at a particular historical moment and thereafter began to affect sexual practices. Birth control, like other forms of sexual regulation, is known in most hunting and gathering societies; it seems to have been as generically human a practice as cooking or child socialization. The issue to explain is not the origin of birth control but its suppression and the subsequent struggle for its legalization and improvement.

The suppression of birth control seems to have been coincident with the development of agriculture. There were two primary reasons for this. First, agriculture made labor power more productive and thus made larger populations viable and larger families economically advantageous to their patriarchs. Second, the needs of male supremacy were changing. The accumulation of private property required more exacting regulation of its inheritance, and men were concerned to establish their paternity legally. A ban on birth control helped men enforce monogamy on women.

Thus, the suppression of birth control was a matter of male supremacy as well as economics. Indeed, the two motives were hardly separate, for the wealth produced by increasing agricultural populations was the basis of patriarchal power. As a result, the political struggle for birth control, even women's illicit use of birth control, was a form of resistance not only against nature but also against men.

The organized movement for birth control threatened not just the particular *sexual* subordination of women but also the entire relations between the sexes, or what has been called the sex-gender system. This term is useful because it makes clear that sex and gender are different. Though related, one is biological and the other social. Although gender has proven remarkably constant in history, we have enough evidence of its variability to know that it is within our human capacity to change it. The difficulty is that gender is deeper than "sex roles," it is embedded in the ego itself. In the formation of female gender identity, women's reproductive tasks are extraordinarily important. One of the characteristics of the sex-gender system is that the work of biological reproduction and the reproduction of society and culture through childrearing and family maintenance are both done by women and are so closely connected that they appear identical, as if both were biological attributes of women. Thus when the modern struggle for legal birth control began, antifeminists quickly saw women's demands for control over their biological reproductive processes as a rejection of their social roles as mothers and wives.

Birth control was never obliterated. There was always an underground of birth control technology, both the effective and the ineffective, the practical and the magical, the safe and the dangerous. The effect of the prohibition was to degrade the skill and reduce the safety of the techniques used, as traditional technology was lost and women's confidence and freedom to invent contraceptive techniques were limited by ignorance and shame. Furthermore, urbanization and migration interrupted the transmission of birth control information. The more effective the suppression of contraceptive information, the more frequent the resort to abortion as a primary means of birth control.

Feminism and Sexual Ideology

The struggle for birth control which emerged in the nineteenth century was not directed solely toward the legalization of certain information and technology. It was part of a feminist movement, challenging the subordination of women in sexuality particularly and in the family and society generally. From then on, the birth control movement, even when organizationally autonomous, has always reflected the historical strength and development of feminism.

In the last hundred years there have been three stages in the sexual ideology of the feminists, each of which strongly affected the struggle for reproductive freedom. First, from the mid-nineteenth century to the 1890s, the feminists of the suffrage movement adhered to a sexual ideal which I shall call domesticity; briefly, they believed that sexual activity belonged only within marriage and they were skeptical of its importance in women's lives. Second, in the period near World War I, a new group of feminists, including many men, rejected the antisexual attitudes of the suffragists and associated women's interests with sexual liberation—endorsing amarital sexual activity and, even more important, emphasizing and romanticizing the importance of sexual pleasure. Third, in the 1970s, contemporary feminists have been able to criticize the earlier positions by analyzing the nature of sexual intercourse itself, suggesting that our norms of sexual behavior are distorted by male supremacy, opening to consideration the requirements of women's own sexual pleasure.

In each of these stages the questions of reproductive freedom and sexual freedom were hardly separable. Since we cannot separate these issues nor divide reproductive *goals* from the *process* of their transformation, we must regard this as a history of conflict between social radicals and social conservatives, both sets of views historically specific.

1. Let us begin about the year 1870 and look at what I will call the Victorian sexual system. It is useful to think of it as a system because it was composed of many related parts; it had a fundamental coherence, although, like all such cultural systems, it contained dissidence and contradictions. The feminist reformers who took up the birth control issue shared many convictions with their conservative opponents.

Victorian conservative moralists agreed that the purpose of sexual activity for women should be reproduction, and many denied that women had a sex drive independent of a desire for motherhood. Those who recognized the existence of female sexuality assumed it to be entirely consonant with the satisfaction of men. The relationships that women had with other women, though often passionate, were virtually defined as asexual, making lesbianism practically invisible except as a rare aberration. Enjoying a sharply double standard, rationalized through a notion of separate spheres for the sexes, men simultaneously celebrated (and possibly resented) the chastity of their wives and indulged themselves with prostitutes and other low status women.

By the mid-nineteenth century the same social changes that had created this system threatened its stability. The industrialization of production that had created the separation between men's and women's lives and work, made women's traditional labor degraded, unrewarding, and unappreciated. But while the content of women's work changed, its form remained the same. The changes were not well understood, but were sharply felt. Even today few recognize that housework as we know it was born in advanced industrial society, reflecting the transformation of women who had been manufacturers, farmers, skilled teachers, and healers into small-scale janitors. At the same time, urban life increasingly detached men of all classes from their families and homes into other workplaces.

Responding to these changes, two directly antagonistic social movements developed around the issue of reproduction. On the conservative side, fears of underpopulation, the decline of the family, and the increasing independence of women coalesced into a series of pressures for more rigorous bans on birth control, sex education, and extra-domestic activities among women. In the United States these groups succeeded in enacting the "Comstock" law which prohibited the mailing of obscene material and in then classifying birth control information as obscene; they also secured federal prosecution of several cases under this law. They conducted a propaganda campaign, deliberately confounding contraception with abortion and branding as murder and licentiousness the whole project of birth control.

Contesting the conservative view of reproductive and sexual morality was a powerful feminist movement. It produced a birth control demand, "Voluntary Motherhood," which expressed its principles exactly. The main issue was a woman's right to dignity and autonomy, but it was also implied that willing mothers would be better parents, wanted children better people. The cult of motherhood was thus argued as passionately by feminists as by antifeminists: conservatives argued that motherhood was the basic reason women should stay at home; feminists argued that motherhood was the main reason women needed more power, independence, and respect. These feminists did not urge that women should desert the home, and certainly did not contemplate—as few feminists did until the 1930s—that men should share in domestic work.* Furthermore, by the explicitly sexual content of their birth control ideas, the feminists also endorsed a kind of domesticity. They believed that abstinence, not contraception, was the only

---

*The popularity of matriarchy theory among nineteenth-century feminists suggests a longing for preexisting models of a good society rather than acceptance of the need to define and invent a good society anew. Their exclusive emphasis on suffrage (like the emphasis of later feminists on sexual liberation and birth control) suggests that they were mistaking symptoms and aspects of male supremacy for the whole, that they were unable to comprehend its systematic, coherent, and pervasive forms.

proper form of birth control. They shared the general religious and moral view that sex should be only for reproduction and only within marriage. They were partly motivated by religious and antitechnological feelings, a response to the apparent degradation of women in industrial society. But they also understood contraception not as a tool for a woman's own self-assertion but as a weapon used by men against women: nonreproductive sex appeared to them to be a means for men to escape their responsibility to women.* They saw contraception as a tool of prostitutes and as a potential tool of men in turning women into prostitutes.

The feminists wanted not only voluntary motherhood but also voluntary sex. The nineteenth-century marital system rested, legally as well as in custom, on women's sexual submission to their husbands; refusal of sexual services was grounds for divorce in many states. Feminist insistence on women's right to say no and to justify this on birth control grounds was a fundamental rejection of male dominance in sex. They wanted to end the double standard by imposing chastity on men. Their strong emphasis on women's sisterhood had, at least for us today, sexual implications as well, for they created lasting bonds and passionate loves among women. Interestingly, it was often these voluntary motherhood advocates who simultaneously asserted the existence of female sexual drives. They understood, however, that the discovery of women's own sexual preferences and sensations could not even begin while women were subordinate to men's every sexual whim. Feminist ideas were thus at once antisex and prosex, and feminists were not able to resolve this tension because they did not (or perhaps did not dare) follow women's sexual feelings where they led—to woman-defined kinds of sexual activity not necessarily compatible with conventional heterosexual intercourse.

In their sexual attitudes the nineteenth-century feminists were mainly anti-male. In this respect they were the predecessors of today's radical feminists, not of socialist feminists or

---

*The fact that contraception then was not a commodity but a "home-made" procedure or invention made it less fetishized, its social meaning clear.

liberal feminists. Their critique of the family was a critique of male dominance within it. They did not analyze the family or the sexual division of labor as formations which had become assimilated to capitalism, nor did they perceive that men were not always free agents themselves in these formations. On the other hand, in other aspects of their feminism these activists were often pro-male. Seeing women as victims who had been deprived of the opportunity to realize their full human potential, they saw the male as the human type. This was explicit in the work of a few theorists, especially Charlotte Perkins Gilman, and was implicit in the demands of many other feminists for education and professional work. Feminist thought reflected rapid social changes which were sending women out of their homes into the man's world—into schools, offices, factories, restaurants, theaters, etc. The pro-male point of view made it seem inconceivable that men should do housework and parenting.

In their sexual attitudes, in short, the feminists were defending domesticity, yet their agitation on other questions was encouraging a rejection of domestic life. But celibacy was not a stable alternative for the thousands of single career women at the turn of the twentieth century.

Partly due to the large numbers of non-marrying women, but also because of extensive use of birth control, by the turn of the century birthrate declines in the United States had become highly visible. Between 1905 and 1910 there arose a campaign against "race suicide," whose propagandists protested population decline (having been reared with the mercantilist notion that a healthy nation had to have a growing population), fearing the decline of WASP ruling-class hegemony due to the higher birth rate among Catholic working-class immigrants. Underlying it was an antifeminist backlash, an attack on women's "selfishness," or rejection of domesticity and mothering. (Ironically, the race suicide propaganda let a great many people know of the existence of birth control methods and probably promoted the use of contraception.)

2. Starting in the 1890s a group of feminists, at first mainly European, began to espouse different sexual ideas critical of domesticity. Many were men, such as Havelock Ellis, Edward

Carpenter, later Wilhelm Reich. Men and women alike tended to consider sexual repression as a problem of equal weight for both sexes, though different in nature; and they usually argued that women's liberation would be good for both sexes, that men as well as women suffered from the false sex-gender system, the polarization of sex roles.

In many ways this turn-of-the-century group of feminists took the focus off women and placed it on sex; they tended to view women's subordination as a function of sexual repression, whereas the suffrage movement by and large thought that the distortion of sexual needs and practices was a product of male supremacy.

Certain implications of this sexual-liberation emphasis should be noticed. First, the concern with men's sexual repression tended to mask the fact that men remained the dominant sex, the beneficiaries of the exploitation of women,* and to present men and women as equal victims of a system so abstract that its persistence was inexplicable. In this respect the sexual liberation theorists did not encourage a women's movement. Second, the attack on sexual repression tended inevitably to spotlight the family as the central structure for the perpetuation of repression and to endorse nonmarital sex. Inasmuch as the family was undoubtedly still the main prop of male supremacy in the early twentieth century (and possibly still is), sexual liberation theory was extremely encouraging to the development of a more fundamental challenge to the sex-gender system from a feminist perspective.

Birth control was a very important issue for the sexual-liberation feminists because without it sex could not be separated from the family. They therefore enthusiastically supported and built the birth control movement when it revived in the World War I era. Its reemergence was a response both to the publicity of the race suicide proponents and partly because of

---

*I am purposefully using this word not only in its Marxist sense, referring to the production of surplus value, but also in the common sense usage of being used, ripped off. I do this because I think feminists are correct in perceiving a fundamental similarity between the two forms of exploitation and the alienation from one's labor and one's self that they produce.

the new demographic and sexual situation of women. The urban economy was making smaller families economically possible for professional, business, and working-class women; women were more in the world—working-class women often in the labor force, more privileged women in higher education, the professions, and volunteerism; the requirements of female chastity were weakening for all classes. These developments were all part of the decline of patriarchal power, which had been founded not only on control of women but also on control of families. The entire family structure was being altered by industrial capitalism. The employment of sons and daughters weakened fatherly authority, while the wage labor of the fathers removed them from the home, where they had traditionally exercised authority, and deprived them of the economic and psychic ability to enjoy large families. The uprooting experience of immigration and the impact of individualist liberal ideology also weakened the legitimacy of the patriarchal organization of society. And feminism was itself a product of the frustrations and opportunities presented to women, middle-class women first and most prominently, by the decline of patriarchy.

The organizational impetus for the revived birth control movement came primarily from feminists in the Socialist Party. Their energy was available because so many women were repelled by the conservatism of the suffrage organizations and because socialism was not dealing energetically with any women's issues. They learned the political importance of the birth control issue from the masses, and I use that word advisedly. The experiences of Margaret Sanger and many other birth control organizers show that enormous popular demand virtually forced the issue upon them. Once they began to organize around it, birth control information reached thousands of women previously unexcited by suffrage or other women's rights issues; birth control seemed to them more immediate, more personal, and more tied to class struggle.

The birth control movement of 1914–1920 was a mass movement with leagues in all big cities and many towns. It was a grassroots movement: a few speakers toured nationally, and in the 1920s national organizations arose, but most leagues sprang up locally and autonomously, often initiated by women socialists. People distributed illegal birth control leaflets on the streets, opened illegal clinics, courted arrest in order to use their trials as political forums, and even served time in jail.

This movement should not be seen as some kind of spontaneous revolt of pre-political women. Underlying it was a new radicalism in sexual behavior among many young urban women, influenced by and participating in the feminist sexual-liberation ideology. Their work in birth control was part of an attempt to resolve the contradictions of nineteenth-century feminism which had criticized the family but remained faithful to ideas of permanent monogamy, sex only for reproduction and within marriage.

World War I-era feminist socialists began a critique of the family itself, calling it a prop of bourgeois, male supremacist society, morality, and character structure. In differing degrees these feminists accepted the "sexual revolution"—the normality of divorce; sexual relations before marriage, without ruining a woman's reputation; numerous sexual partners; contraception; and a host of activities previously considered improper, including dating. They thought that enjoyment was a good enough reason for sex and most other activities. They despised so-called bourgeois hypocrisy and paid at least lip service to a single standard of sexual freedom.

In this rejection of domesticity and family-centered sex these early-twentieth-century feminists became, despite their intentions, more pro-male than their predecessors. Their characteristic solution to problems of child care and housework was to propose that women be hired to do those tasks. They were socialists but their proposals, like those of most socialists of their era, were in line with the development of capitalism. And the male was still for them the human type, male culture in most respects human culture. This group of radicals did not fully challenge the sex-gender system either. Redefining the possibilities of the feminine somewhat, they continued to accept a certain view of male gender as permanent.

No feminism prior to the mid-twentieth century analyzed the

full complexities of women's reproductive and sexual imprisonment. But, without bemoaning the loss of something doomed by historical change, we should recognize that nineteenth-century feminist ideas had certain important realizations about women that were lost in the early twentieth century. Feminist thinkers like Elizabeth Cady Stanton, Elizabeth Blackwell, and Charlotte Perkins Gilman understood that women needed a space—physical, psychological, and intellectual—where they were separated from men and insulated from men's demands before they could develop their own sexual feelings, hopes, and theories. Their emphasis on sisterhood and women's solidarity put them in a position of greater fidelity to the masses of women and gave them a strategic sense of the power of women as a collectivity. By contrast, many early-twentieth-century feminists, including birth control leaders like Margaret Sanger and Emma Goldman, had uncritically bought a "sexual" revolution that was really a heterosexual revolution. It drew women out of protected areas, out of women's spaces, into a man's world. It ignored the fact that it is dangerous—physically, emotionally, socially, and economically—for women to indulge in nonmarital sex. Although their sex manuals contributed to sex education and to breaking the chains of prudish ignorance, they steadfastly encouraged women to get sexual pleasure and orgasms from male-oriented intercourse and, by implication, blamed them for frigidity if they could not. Most of them did not believe in the need for an autonomous women's movement. In sexual relations, education, and work they accepted a set-up that placed women *individually* in a man's world, isolated in their danger. Although it was progressive that they urged women to dare, to find the confidence—they didn't say where—to take on men's burdens, their strategy in effect denied women solidarity with other women. Nor did they offer a way to reject women's traditional burdens while assuming men's.

Nevertheless, the birth control movement of the World War I period was a big advance for women. It promoted and finally legalized contraception, and it encouraged partial emergence from sexual constriction. But as part of the heterosexual "sexual revolution," it also created pain, confusion, and loneliness for many women; the transformation out of millennia of subordination cannot be expected to be easy.

The Commoditization of Birth Control, Sex, and Women's Labor

Before we can examine the third stage of feminist sexual ideas we must look briefly at a less optimistic period, from about 1920 to 1965. The decline of the entire left, feminist and nonfeminist, after World War I enervated the birth control movement. Oddly, the power of the Communist Party in the 1930s and early 1940s did not stimulate a feminist revival. But although birth control as a social movement was weakened, birth control as a commodity became legal and widespread. This process occurred in two major stages. First, between 1920 and 1945, the birth control campaign became a professional, male-dominated, centralized, and respectable service project, primarily influenced by elitist and eugenical convictions that the poor should be helped and pacified by having their birth rates lowered. Then, between 1945 and 1960, it became an international population control campaign, ultimately controlled by the United States ruling class through its corporate foundations. These transformations were paralleled by the commercial production and mass marketing of contraceptives and by medical research and development keyed to fertility reduction at all costs, including disregard for health and civil liberties. Birth control is today a commodity and, like all commodities in advanced capitalist society, it is offered to us in such a way that we cannot always distinguish our personal need for the product from the "needs" defined for us by social policy.

With the decline of mass participation, the forward motion the birth control movement had created for women ceased. It is not clear that the increased dissemination of contraception in the United States between 1920 and 1960 created any significant improvement in the lives of most working-class women. The difference between two and ten pregnancies, births, and children is enormous in terms of time and energy. But time and energy are in themselves empty quantities; it is not that the labor of producing children was so unrewarding that reducing it was an automatic gain, and the value of what has replaced this childrearing labor is questionable. Despite smaller families, women seem to spend as many hours on housework and mothering as a century ago. Partly due to smaller families, many more women have entered the labor force and gained at least the promise of independent incomes, but these incomes have been quickly eaten up by family needs, as the inadequecy of men's real wages makes the two-income family increasingly the norm. Employment certainly has not meant intellectual growth for women, as women's jobs are still the worst in pay and working conditions. There are proportionately fewer women in the professions today than in 1920. Furthermore, employment has not relieved most women from exclusive responsibility for reproductive labor and family maintenance. And women as a group—as a gender—continue to be defined mainly by their work in the family.

Despite women's continued social identity with the family, families are in fact dissolving with the rapid increase of divorce and more individualist behavior on the part of all family members. These changes, while perhaps liberating in potential, have in fact rendered people more susceptible to manipulation and have encouraged self-destructive behavior. Sexual health, measured either physically or psychologically, is in some respects deteriorating, as evidenced in spreading venereal disease, rape, and sexual encounters stripped of obligations between people as subjects. The balance between helpful practicality about sex and its dehumanization is a delicate one. Frank discussion of sexual techniques is a needed extension of sex education, a continuation of the best traditions of feminism; but the marketing of sex cookbooks for the "connoisseur" is moving, as commoditization always does, in an antihuman direction by carving up the human experience. Sex thus becomes severed from economic, social, political, and emotional life. Prostitution is providing more sexual services for cash, as in massage parlors and "modeling," or even for barter, as in swinging and in "personal" advertisements for companionship.

At the same time, the commercialization of sexual pleasure and the new norms that make celibacy or sexual restraint seem deviant provide new tools for male chauvinism and the sexist exploitation of women.

3. In the 1970s a revised feminist movement reexamined sex and reproduction politically and reintroduced a libertarian view of both. Women's liberation began where the World War I sex radicals had left off—with a denunciation of the family's role in sexual repression and women's suppression. This denunciation has since been tempered, as we understand how difficult it is to replace the family's supportive functions. But the demystification of the family has allowed a new look at sex and sexual relationships. The romanticism of the sexual-liberation theorists about love and orgasm has been criticized along with the antigenital bias of the suffragists. Contemporary feminists have not only explored new forms of emotional commitments, both long and short term, but have defetishized the sex act itself for the first time in modern history.

The separation of sex from reproduction was not possible, even in imagination, as long as heterosexual intercourse was the definition of the sex act. Changing our view of what constituted proper sexual satisfaction for women has been one of the major historical contributions of the women's liberation movement, its implications most fully expressed in lesbian feminism.

The debunking of the myth of vaginal orgasm was not a sudden breakthrough but a product of a century of agitation that well illustrates a fundamental unity among several waves of feminism. Sex education has been a principal demand of feminists in the United States since the 1840s. The cultural values and physiological information to be offered have changed radically, but all the feminists sought to throw off the blanket of suppression and lies about women's psychological and physiological sexuality. Their goal was the restoration of the legitimacy of female sexual pleasure, though the definition of its proper form changed historically. Since at least the 1870s, feminist groups used forms of "consciousness-raising," discussions among women which revealed the interface between "personal" and "political" problems, sexual problems always looming large among them. Feminist groups have continually attacked, for example, conventional fashions in dress, realizing that the transformation of women into decorations helped to lower their self-esteem and, ironically, stunt their sexual development, keeping them eternally objects and never subjects. Feminists in all periods have emphasized the strength and flexibility of women's bodies as against their beauty, attempting to break the exclusive association of the female body with sexuality; simultaneously, feminists have tried to reintegrate sexuality into full human relationships and fought the commoditization of sex, which required the sacrifice of women as prostitutes to men's distorted sexuality.

There is unity in the feminist tradition, and it is important to see our own historical debts. It is also important to see where we have transcended previous feminism. One vital respect in which mid-twentieth-century feminists have gone further is in avoiding both "blaming-the-victim" analyses (whose action implications are personal struggles to overcome inner obstacles to sexual or other satisfaction) and economic-determinist analyses (whose action implications deny the importance of "personal life" and women's ego structures). The socialist feminist approach of the 1970s has, at its best, encouraged both personal and collective struggle for change. The strategy is to ask for everything, demanding that the society should be structured to allow women to do a little of everything, or at least to have a choice, without faulting women for not being able to do everything.

Contemporary feminism has already significantly improved women's situation, but these improvements have been mainly the result of the process of the struggle itself rather than of specific reforms. Our major gains have been in women's aspirations, self-esteem, and political awareness.

These gains are particularly evident in the structure of family and sexual life. In every historical period one effect of feminism was to raise the status and the opportunities of single women; today the improved position of single women is noticeable. In accomplishing this, feminism's influence has helped married women to challenge their husbands' privileges partly because they had seen the possibility of a life outside marriage. In this respect again the lesbian liberation movement has made possibly the most important contribution to a future sexual liberation. It is not that feminism produced more lesbians. There have always been many lesbians, despite high levels of repression; and most lesbians experience their sexual preference as innate and nonvoluntary. What the women's liberation movement did create was a homosexual liberation movement that politically challenged male supremacy in one of its most deeply institutionalized aspects—the tyranny of heterosexuality. The political power of lesbianism is a power that can be shared by all women who choose to recognize and use it: the power of an alternative, a possibility that makes male sexual tyranny escapable, rejectable—possibly even doomed.

Toward Reproductive Freedom for Women

Growing out of a New Left now several decades old, a socialist women's liberation movement has begun, slowly and erratically, to formulate a program of sexual and reproductive demands. As I write, in the spring of 1977, the women's liberation movement (in contrast to a liberal women's equality movement) appears weakened. Despite the fact that these issues are assuming great political importance in Catholic European countries (notably Italy, Spain, and France) and Third World countries (notably India and parts of Latin America and the Caribbean), the left in the United States is not taking seriously people's longings in these "personal" spheres.

We can identify at least three tasks that such a program must approach. One is the liberation of children from the burden of perpetuating adults' class status and adults' frustrated aspirations from one generation to the next. Another, perhaps the most basic, is the defeat of male supremacy. A third is sexual liberation. The three are intimately connected, but let us look at them one at a time, considering the interconnections as we proceed.

The prohibition on birth control was, as we have seen, related to the defense of class privilege. Today the powers and privileges that can be passed on to succeeding generations through the family are more varied: property, education, confidence, social and political connections. But the essential nature of class divisions is unchanged and depends on the generational passing down of status. Thus in class society children are never individuals and cannot escape the expectations, high or low, attached to their fathers' position. These expectations also distort the reproductive desires and childrearing practices of parents, making it more difficult for them to view their children as individuals.

The interference of class society with reproductive freedom affects not only propertied fathers anxious to perpetuate their power. Poor people frequently assuage their own frustrations by seeking vicarious satisfaction through their children. Women of all classes, denied creative work, achievement or recognition for themselves, live through their children. Childlessness spells not only loneliness but the threat of economic insecurity in old age; while the often subconscious hope for immortality through the family reflects not only the desire to pass on property or prestige but often an emotional need to make a mark as a human being, to feel one's life as significant and lasting. Childrearing seems, deceptively, to offer an area of control, an area in which adults have power to create human value according to their own, not their employers' direction. These factors make children potentially the victims of adults' unsatisfactory lives. They mean that good contraceptive *technology* cannot in itself solve the *social* problem of overpopulation, where it exists, and lack of reproductive freedom.

Beyond these pressures, which all adults feel, male supremacy makes childbearing particularly problematic for women. Children are a source of enormous pleasure and gratification, often the greatest delight in women's lives. Children are beautiful, far more beautiful than most adults, especially in industrial capitalist society where adults are changed by tedious work and insecurity into repressed, cautious, fearful animals.

On the other hand, there are many difficulties of childrearing, especially for poor women and working women in a society that offers little public support for children. Careful weighing of advantages and burdens is hampered by a mythology of motherhood, a series of pronatalist cultural pressures. Childless women often feel like failures, while childless men do not. Girls are socialized from infancy to anticipate motherhood. Women learn to like themselves in mothering roles, which allow them experiences of love and power not easily found in other situations. These maternal attitudes are a part of the female gender, a part of women's very egos.

The motherhood mystique, as opposed to the genuine pleasures of motherhood, serves male supremacy through maintaining a sexual division of labor. At the same time the mystique is used by women to maximize the creative and enjoyable aspects of their lives. Full-time motherhood, when it is possible, is for most women preferable to other job alternatives.

Child care, for all its difficulty, is inherently less alienated and more creative than most other work; it offers a mother at least a semblance of control over her working conditions and goals. Of course much of the skill and creativity of parenthood has been eroded just as most other work in this society has been degraded. Control over child care has been alienated from parents both through socialized institutions such as schools and through commoditization—children's "needs" are mass-produced and sold back to parents in the form of toys, ever higher standards of cleanliness, prescriptive theories of child psychology—all virtually forced on women through high-pressure advertising. Despite this degradation of the work of motherhood, women have not fled from it in disgust but have entered the wage-labor force only out of necessity.

"Falling into motherhood" is the more accurate description on several levels. The unpredictable nature of conception makes pregnancies difficult to schedule. More importantly, inability to choose reflects the lack of decent alternatives. When all the options are bad, it is natural to avoid a decision altogether, leaving events to chance, to nature, to God. It is no wonder that "excess fertility"—births in excess of what the parents themselves say they want—is higher among working-class, poor, and nonwhite women, for they have the fewest desirable alternatives.

A particularly prevalent example of the tendency to respond to a no-win situation by avoiding the semblance of decisions can be seen among young unmarried women. They are not only buffeted by contradictory pressures about motherhood and its alternatives but placed in a double bind by the sexual aspects of male supremacy. Guilt feelings about sex lead many young women, not only Catholics, to the view that contraception is a sin. The secular version of this dogma is that it is wrong to have intercourse without "taking your chances." Pregnancy is a risk that must be taken, a punishment that it is dishonorable to avoid. The pill has diminished this view somewhat because it can be taken routinely every morning, entirely separated from sexual activity. The diaphragm was too difficult for many young women. To carry it with you, to admit to a man that one had a contraceptive device, was to take a responsibility for one's sexual behavior that many young women were not pre-pared for. It is easier and more "normal" for men to be lustful and assertive, for women merely to surrender, to be carried away by a greater force. To acquire and use a diaphragm means that a woman must accept herself as a sexual, heterosexual being, to admit that she plans to continue sexual activity in-definitely. It is easier to deal with guilt about sex by viewing one's adventures as one-time-only slips, promptly repented—over and over.

This is just one side of a double bind. The other side is that women resist the exploitative aspects of the sexual double standard. Women's guilt feelings are not mere relics of a dead morality: they are withdrawals from danger. One's reputation is somewhat safer now in the United States than a generation ago, but men still brag about their conquests. Singleness is frighten-ing to women, while men fear its opposite—trappedness. Wo-men's fear of singleness is not a vestige or a superstitution. Single women are discriminated against and disadvantaged, in comparison both to married women and to single men, socially, economically, and from vulnerability to direct physical danger.

Being without a man is threatening to a woman's very identity, to her self-esteem, because singleness objectively weakens her position. For women, therefore, heterosexual relations are always intense, frightening, high-risk situations which ought, if a woman has any sense of self-preservation, to be carefully calculated. These calculations call for weapons of resistance, which may include sexual denial. One effect of easily accessible contraception has been to deprive women of that weapon. Another weapon is pregnancy itself, for the social ethic that requires marrying and supporting a woman who is pregnant is somewhat stronger, though not thoroughly reliable, than the ethic of loyalty to women as sexual partners. Women get pregnant "accidentally on purpose" as a way of punishing themselves. But they may also be protecting themselves and punishing men. Nothing illustrates better than reproduction that unless women can be free, men will never be. Pregnancy is woman's burden and her revenge.

In these double-bind situations, sexually and economically, "decisions" about childbearing take place with varying levels of ambivalence. Most unplanned pregnancies are partly wanted and partly unwanted. A frequent solution to ambivalence is passivity—not using contraception or using it haphazardly. This is a rational response when no alternative is desirable. Those family planners who speak of irrationality, of women not understanding their own interests, do not themselves understand the problem. Self-determination cannot exist if none of the options is attractive.

We have argued that sexual freedom requires reproductive freedom. We must also recognize the reverse—that reproductive freedom cannot exist without full sexual options. The failings of heterosexual relations to provide women with the love and intimacy we need produces heavy pressures to bear children and heavy pressures on relationships with those children. Population controllers are encountering resistance based in part on the fact that women do not *want* sex to be divorced from reproduction because their sex lives are unsatisfactory otherwise. As patriarchy declines in the advanced industrial countries, it is women who, despite the burdens, want many children. Men's disinterest in children reflects, in part, emptiness created by the male gender identity—fears of responsibility, intimacy, sensuality, and playfulness. But for many women, relations with children have been the most fulfilling in their lives, and this suggests another regrettable emptiness.

Enemies, Overt and Covert

The tendency toward sexual freedom and equality is constantly threatened with deflection, even reversal. These weaknesses are partly due to difficulties within the feminist movement itself. A cross-class movement, feminism has had a tendency to encourage individual success at the expense of collective strategy. Feminists also, as we have seen, isolated particular reforms as panaceas, sexual liberation being one of them. These two faults are connected. Feminists sometimes wandered into utopian experiments, trying to create situations of total equality and freedom by relying on individual wealth, status, and self-confidence. A focus on sexual liberation was understandable because sex seems one of the few areas of human experience still in our own control in an era of totalitarian control over so much else; and because sex is potentially one of the few sources of intense, natural pleasure remaining in an all-commoditized world. But the isolation of "sexual liberation" struggles, while understandable, weakens these very struggles in the long run. Not only does it hold back the development of understanding of the social and economic influences on sexuality, but it fails to challenge the forces which corrupt human sexual potential—class exploitation and male supremacy.

Furthermore, the isolated focus on sexual liberation was seized and manipulated by capitalists in their ever extending search for profits. Sexual pleasure itself, both that produced by individual human beauty and that from caresses, has become commoditized, while the market produces its own, distorted, sexual needs.

Thus the story of the breaking away from Victorian sexual repression over the last century has a double aspect: one of liberation and another of the reimposition of new forms of social control over the human capacity for free and inventive sexual expression. Those two aspects correspond, on the one hand, to the collective and individual rebellions of people, primarily women, against their masters, rebellions represented nowhere more forcefully than in the birth control movement; and, on the other hand, to the economic and political needs of the capitalist system. That the former aspect may yet prove victorious is due in part to the fact that the capitalist economy has developed weakening contradictions within itself.

We are just beginning to perceive the dimensions of the sexual changes produced by this basic restructuring of the labor force. As the expectation that men singly support their families is dissolved, men may lose more of their social power in the family. Increased women's employment means that adult couples, though not necessarily parent-child ties, are losing their economic necessity and women are becoming more reluctant to accommodate themselves to male privileges. Women's growing consciousness of themselves as workers is strengthening their sense of equality with men of their own class and stimulating resistance to their continued sexual exploitation by men.

Male supremacy is now under attack, its traditional supports eroded by capitalism itself, but its beneficiaries are defending it by modifying it to suit new economic conditions. As men once took advantage of the sexual double standard and the enforced chastity of their wives, now they often take advantage of the mythical single standard to belittle and pressure women who resist their sexual preferences. Thus the area of sexual relationships remains now, as it was in the nineteenth century, a major battlefield for feminists.

In this context birth control struggles are but battles, not the whole war. Nevertheless if we insist that birth control does not mean population control or birthrate reduction or planned families, but reproductive freedom, then the issue looms larger. While it is but a piece of a larger social change, it can never be realized until that larger program is a reality. Every one of the conditions that would make reproductive freedom possible— the elimination of hereditary class and privilege, sexual equality, and sexual liberation—is a radical program in itself. From this it follows that reproductive freedom is most likely to be achieved as a rider, so to speak, on the coattails of broad social movements.

The high points of the birth control struggle in the past came with its maximum integration into larger political movements—the exploding "woman movement" in the mid-nineteenth century and the Socialist Party in the 1910s. In the 1970s birth control emerged strong again as a leading demand of the women's liberation movement. Yet relatively little has been gained in the field of birth control. No new male contraceptives have yet been developed; women must still rely primarily on hormonal pills and intrauterine devices, both dangerous. The main achievement has been the legalization of abortion, and this represents a significant victory. It has lowered the price of abortions sharply and made them available in the public clinics and hospitals that poor people must use. But it is a shaky victory and the opposition has not given up. Worse, legal abortions and sterilizations are being forced on poor women, especially nonwhite women.

In the United States in the 1970s two alternative views of reproductive control have emerged to challenge the liberating emphasis of birth control. One is the opposition to abortion, the "right to life" movement. The attribution of human rights to the fetus is not a new idea but repeats nineteenth-century anti-birth control views which, revealingly, confounded abortion with contraception. This is not to deny the existence of moral issues about embryonic life. But right-to-life advocates do not usually fight for "life" in any systematic way. As a social force the movement represents, not Catholics in general, but the threatened Church hierarchy and its right-wing supporters. Right-to-life forces have generally opposed the kinds of social programs which would make abortion less frequent: child care, sex education, contraception, etc. Right-to-lifers are not usually pacifists, though pacifism is the only overall philosophy that could make their position on abortion honorable and consistent. They oppose only the specific forms of "killing" that amount to women's self-defense. They are reacting not merely to a "loosening of morals" but to the whole feminist struggle of the last century; they are defending male supremacy. Often they support it because it is the only system they know which can provide family and social stability, and many right-to-life supporters do not fully understand the implications of their views. Yet many do understand, and even among Catholics many women have rejected the right-to-life position. Opponents of abortion have been repeatedly defeated at the polls—in fact, they have won no elections as of this writing. While the anti-abortion movement often appears strong in working-class neighborhoods, its leadership is always part of the top-down leadership structure administered through the Church and the political party machines. The right to life is not the issue of abortion; the issue is women's rights.

A second form of opposition to reproductive self-determination is population control. The damage it has inflicted on the birth control cause has been the greater because it has been confused with birth control, and because that confusion was based on some shared interests—better and legalized contraception and sterilization.

It is vital that feminists—indeed all who consider themselves democrats—familiarize themselves with the massive evidence against population control programs. First, their purpose is to head off revolutionary change by increasing standards of living, or at least preventing further impoverishment, without a fundamental redistribution of property or reorganization of the relations of production. In this respect, population control is not only antisocialist but antifeminist as well inasmuch as women's suppression is equally located in the social organization of work. Second, despite their intent, population control programs do not improve standards of living; on the contrary, birthrate reductions have historically been an effect, not a cause, of greater prosperity. At best, population control programs, which employ extremely coercive methods, can provoke resistance; at worst they can demoralize people and destroy cultural identity.

Historically *all* reproductive control movements were responses to social unrest created by class inequality and sex inequality. But some in the movements sought to stabilize and justify these inequalities, while others sought to end them. This is the fundamental difference, a difference obscured by the confusion between population control and birth control. It is not the population question itself that divides the two fundamentally opposed movements, and those committed to egalitarian solutions would do well to remain open-minded on the issue of population growth. Among those who have supported birth control in the struggle for equality there is an essential unity of interests between those who have fought primarily for women and those who have fought primarily for the working class. Involuntary childbearing has burdened all women but poor women most, and the sexual inequality that resulted has helped perpetuate other forms of inequality and weakened struggles against them. Reproductive self-determination is a basic condition for sexual equality and for women to assume full membership in all other human groups, especially the working class.

But the working class, like the other classes, has a sexual hierarchy; and Marxists ought to face the fact that the sexual hierarchy has remarkable similarity in all classes—indeed in most cultures. This does not prove that the female gender identity is biologically determined. Nor does it disprove the importance of class struggle. It does, however, show that the sex-gender system is located in patterns of human behavior and human character that are not fully explained by capitalism (or even, possibly, by class society in our current understanding of "class"). Liberation is going to require a struggle against capitalism *and* male supremacy as two connected, but not identical, forms of domination.

SOCIALIST FEMINIST
HISTORICAL ANALYSIS

History lets us understand how things change. To understand the specific forms of women's lives, socialist feminists have found that history must be reconstructed. This is a vast endeavor and the two selections here are representative of such an attempt at reconstruction for one particular time period. Work is in progress to reconstruct the understanding of the development of state formation and how it rewires patriarchy. An incredible amount of work has been done by feminist historians, as will be seen in the list of related reading.

In trying to understand the reality of capitalist patriarchal society, which is the first stage in understanding how it can be changed, it becomes necessary to understand its practice. If the connections between class and sex oppression are to be our focus, we need to know both how these connections defined historical relations and how they have been dealt with historically. How are the relations between sex and class reflected in women's lives? How does the concept "femininity" embrace this connection? How is the connection between sex and class reflected in women's consciousness and in their political struggle? How have male bourgeois historians dichotomized these important relationships?

The articles in this section reveal both the conflicts and the connections between sex and class consciousness among the politically organized nineteenth-century American feminists and the working women of early industrial capitalism. Ellen Dubois' discussion reveals that nineteenth-century feminists had a much more complete understanding of the class realities of their time than either bourgeois or socialist historians have led us to believe. Mary Ryan demonstrates that the development of "femininity" as a defining value for women was related to the more pronounced interconnections between sex and class under industrial capitalism. Although these articles alone do not construct a socialist feminist history, they present a beginning analysis which poses a dialectic between sex and class. We see that the very ideas that define and structure women's lives are connected to changes in the economy and the political needs of the society at the same time that they utilize biological reality. Several of the works which have been important in the ongoing construction of women's history are listed below.

Related Reading

Abbot, Edith, *Women in Industry* (New York: Source Book Press, 1970).

Baxandall, R., S. Reverby, L. Gordon, *America's Working Women* (New York: Random House, 1976).

Braverman, Harry, *Labor and Monopoly Capital* (New York: Monthly Review Press, 1974).

Breines, Wini, "Critique of Woman's Work," *Liberation* 19, no. 5 (July–August 1975).

Dancis, Bruce, "Socialism and Women in the U.S., 1900–1917," *Socialist Review* 27 (January–March 1976).

Davies, Margaret, *Life As We Have Known It, by Cooperative Working Women* (New York: Norton, 1975).

Feminist Studies 3 (Fall 1975), articles from the Berkshire Conference.

Flexner, Eleanor, *Century of Struggle: The Woman's Rights Movement in the United States*, rev. ed. (Cambridge, Massachusetts: Harvard University Press, 1975).

Gordon, A., M. J. Buhle, N. Schram, "Women in American Society," *Radical America* 5 (July-August 1971).

Gordon, Linda, *Woman's Body, Woman's Right: A Social History of Birth Control in America* (New York: Viking, 1976).

Guttman, Herbert, *The Black Family in Slavery and Freedom* (New York: Pantheon, 1976).

Hartman, Mary S. and Lois Banner, eds., *Clio's Consciousness Raised: New Perspectives on the History of Women* (New York: Harper & Row, 1974).

Laslett, Peter, *The World We Have Lost* (New York: Scribner, forthcoming).

Oakley, Ann, *Woman's Work, the Housewife Past and Present* (New York: Pantheon, 1974).

O'Neill, William, ed., *Women at Work* (New York: Quadrangle, 1972).

Pinchbeck, Ivy, *Women Workers and the Industrial Revolution, 1750–1850* (Clifton, N.J.: Augustus Kelley, 1969).

Quick, Paddy, "Rosie the Riveter: Myths and Realities," *Radical America* 9, no. 4–5 (July-October 1975): 115–33.

Rowbotham, Sheila, *Hidden from History* (New York: Pantheon, 1975).

Ryan, Mary, *Womanhood in America* (New York: Franklin Watts, 1975).

Schreiner, Olive, *Women and Labor* (New York: Johnson Reprint, 1972).

Westheimer, Barbara Mayer. *We Were There: The Story of Working Women in America* (New York: Pantheon, 1977).

Westin, Jean, *Making Do: How Women Survived the 30's* (Chicago: Follett, 1976).

Withorn, Ann, "The Death of CLUW," *Radical America* 10, no. 2 (March–April 1976).

THE NINETEENTH-CENTURY WOMAN SUFFRAGE MOVEMENT AND THE ANALYSIS OF WOMEN'S OPPRESSION

Ellen DuBois

What is the political significance of studying the history of the feminist movement? Not, I think, to identify revolutionary ancestresses or petty bourgeois leaders whose errors we can blame for our current oppression. We study the past to learn how to think about the present, to understand how change happens, to see how history creates and restrains the possibilities for people to intervene deliberately in it and change its course. We study the history of radicalism to understand why certain social movements take a particular character in particular periods, to learn how to locate political radicalism in history. Ultimately, we study history so that we can understand the history of which we are a part, and the changes we may be able to bring to it.

This paper is a brief survey of the history of the woman suffrage movement from 1865 to 1875, the decade after the Civil War. There are two major points I want to make about the feminism of this movement. First, I want to assert the basic radicalism of its politics. Suffragists were led by the facts of women's lives to begin to analyze and imagine radical changes in the two major systems that structured women's oppression: capitalism and male supremacy. Second, I want to locate the limits of the radicalism of the woman suffrage movement in the particular social conditions of nineteenth-century women's lives—specifically, the nature of the sexual division of labor

---

This paper is a slightly modified version of a lecture given as part of the lecture series in socialist feminism at Ithaca College in the spring of 1976.

and of women's total dependence on marriage. My object is to situate the woman suffrage movement in its own historical context so that its radicalism can be appreciated and its failures understood.

From one perspective, suffragism in the years immediately following the Civil War was a very radical movement. Its leaders—especially Elizabeth Cady Stanton and Susan B. Anthony—cooperated with Victoria Woodhull and William Sylvis, free love advocates, with the labor movement, and even with the First International. In order to understand the nature of woman's oppression and the possibility of her emancipation, suffragists found themselves drawn more and more toward the most advanced aspects of nineteenth-century political thought. They identified and criticized capitalism as a major source of woman's oppression, addressed themselves to the position of working women, spoke out boldly against the sexual double standard and exploitation of women, and were beginning to identify marriage and the family—even more than political disfranchisement—as the basic source of woman's oppression. Such a politics deserves to be called radical, both because of the breadth to which it aspired and the particular positions it took.

The Reconstruction years were a very active period for reform in general. Even the boldest of abolitionists had not expected the abolition of slavery in their life times, and yet it had happened. This unleashed radical energies and radical visions. If a reform movement could help to liberate an entire race from slavery, then nothing was beyond political agitation, beyond deliberate social change. Particular postwar forces further encouraged suffragists in radical directions. Congressional battles over the Fourteenth and Fifteenth amendments led them to dissolve their twenty-year alliance with the antislavery movement, which freed them from its domination and was followed by a tremendous explosion of theoretical energy. This rapid development can be seen in the pages of the independent feminist journal *The Revolution,* which Stanton and Anthony edited from 1868 to 1870.

At the same time, the suffragists began to acquire a constituency among American women. This is the period in which suffragism began to take on the character of a social movement—ultimately, although not until much later, to become a mass one. On the one hand, this process of organizing a constituency helped suffrage leaders develop theoretically by connecting the movement to the needs and concerns of non-political American women. On the other hand, the acquisition of a constituency acted to restrain the sexual and economic radicalism to which suffragists were otherwise inclining. The objective social conditions of women's lives in the mid-nineteenth century, their dependence on marriage and the sexually segregated nature of the labor force, constituted the basic framework within which suffragism had to develop.

Suffragists and Capitalism

In the antebellum period, woman suffragists, like other reformers associated with abolitionism, had very little to say about industrial capitalism, the oppression of workers, or the potential power of the labor movement. Their focus was on chattel slavery and on the ruling class of the South. In fact abolitionists—among them such woman suffrage pioneers as Susan B. Anthony and Lucy Stone—seemed to have resented the connections that labor leaders tried to make between chattel and wage-slavery as a diversion from the primary task of eliminating black slavery. (It is only fair to add that labor spokespeople were not foremost in the antislavery ranks and seemed at least as frightened by the possible competition of freed black workers as of the slavocracy's encroachments on liberty.) In addition, woman suffrage leaders were rarely from the ranks of wage-earners. Some, like Stone and Anthony, were the daughters of small farmers. Others, most notably Stanton, were the children of considerable wealth. The daughter of a major New York landholder, Stanton wrote of her early ideas about poverty: "We believed that all these miserable one-sided arrangements were as much in harmony with God's laws as the revolutions of the solar system; and accepted the results with pious indignation."

What suffragists wrote and said about capitalism in the years immediately after the Civil War stands in stark contrast to this. They admitted that there was antagonism between labor and capital and unequivocably took the part of labor. *The Revolution* covered labor activities, particularly laboring men's conventions in New England and New York. Many of the political and theoretical issues that were of pressing concern to labor leaders—currency reform, land policy, and the formation of a new labor-based reform party—received a great deal of attention from the journal's editors. Its position on the 1868 presidential elections, about which male abolitionists were excessively partisan, was that neither the Democrats nor the Republicans had anything to offer. Anthony wrote, "Both major parties are owned body and soul by the Gold Gamblers of the Nation, and so far as the honest working men and women of the country are concerned it matters very little which succeeds." This clearly reflects the impact of the labor movement and of a working-class perspective.

A speech that Elizabeth Cady Stanton delivered in 1868, entitled "On Labor," further illustrates that suffragists were learning the basic principles of labor reform from its leaders.[1] In this speech Stanton reversed her prewar position and asserted the essential identity of chattel and wage-slavery:

> I find that the same principle degrades labor as upheld slavery. The great motive for making a man a slave was to get his labor or its results for nothing. When we consider that the slave was provided with food and clothes and that the ordinary wages of the laborer provide his bare necessities, we see that in a money point of view they hold the same position. And the owner of one form of labor occupies no higher moral status than the other, because the same motive governs in both cases.

Furthermore, she began the speech with an endorsement of strikes as a method of testing workers' "numbers and purpose" and as a "link in the chain of their final triumph." When we remember that not only did most middle-class reformers consider strikes an illegitimate tactic, but that the issue occasionally divided the ranks of labor itself, we see how much Stanton and other suffragists' economic thought had progressed.

Most of Stanton's speech condemned the suffering of the masses of workers under capitalism. She described for her audience, particularly those "in the full enjoyment of all the blessings that wealth can give" (among which she was clearly included), the conditions of the poor.

> Look around you in the filthy lanes and by-streets of all our cities, the surging multitudes ragged, starving, packed in dingy cellars and garrets where no ray of sunshine or hope ever penetrates, no touch of light or love to cheer their lives. Look in the factories and workshops where young and old work side by side with tireless machines from morn til night, through all the days, the weeks, the months, the years that make up the long sum of life, impelled by that inexorable necessity that knows no law, toil or starvation. . . . Look what these unfortunates suffer in our jails, prisons, asylums; look at the injustice in our courts, for when men must steal or starve, theft may be a virtue that might give the poor man bail as dollars do the rich, for in the scale of justice motive might sometime outweigh the crime. Let us look deep down into the present relations of the human family and see if the conditions of different classes cannot be more fairly established. Under all forms of government, about seven-tenths of the human family are doomed to incessant toil, living in different degrees of poverty, from the man who hopes for nothing but daily bread for himself and family, to the one who aims at education and accumulation. The filth, the squalor, the vice in the conditions and surroundings of the poor are apparent to most careless observers, but the ceaseless anxiety and apprehension of those evils yet to come that pervade all alike in the ascending scale from the lowest to the fortunate few who live on the labor of others add to the sum of human misery an unseen element of torture that can never be measured or understood.

This is very moving prose, but not that unusual: such descriptions were appearing with increasing frequency in the pages of respectable, socially aware magazines and newspapers. The suffering worker was beginning to replace the suffering slave as a staple of liberal social criticism.

In "On Labor" Stanton said more than that the masses suffered from poverty. She also said that they created the wealth which had been stolen from them to make a few very rich. "Is it right that many should be clothed in rags, while the few shine in garments that the poor have woven, in the jewels they have dug from the mines of wealth?" she asked. This was a material, rather than a moral, critique of the uneven distribution of wealth. Such an analysis reflected the labor theory of wealth that was generally held by nineteenth-century working people. They understood that if something useful had been produced, labor had produced it. This contention reflected the experience of skilled workers whose perspective and power predominated. They were proud of their economic worth. They—and their employers—knew that without their skills, knowledge, and experience, production could not proceed.

This is what attracted suffragists to the labor movement and to its critical perspective on capitalism. Stanton, Anthony, and others took the part of labor not out of pity for the workers' suffering but out of appreciation for labor's strength. A recognition of the dignity of work and the economic power of skilled labor pointed toward the potential of organized labor as a *political* force, as a source of social change. Stanton wrote in *The Revolution* in 1868, "The one bow of promise we see in the midst of this general political demoralization that all our thinking men deplore today is the determined defiant position of the laboring classes," to which she added, so that we recall the feminist impulse behind all of this political reaching-out, "and the restless craving of women for noble and more serious purposes in life."

From this general perspective on the labor movement, the suffragists developed an interest in working women. Anthony in particular hoped to be able to build what she called "a great movement of working women for the vote." Suffragists gave considerable attention to the low wages, restricted labor market, abysmal working conditions, and general economic vulnerability of wage-earning women. They contended that the ballot would remedy these evils, particularly by increasing the working woman's power during strikes, and they usually argued that working women needed the vote more than other women. But they did not see the working woman primarily as a victim. Instead, they saw her as the woman of the future, as an indication of the direction that woman's development as a sex should take toward emancipation. Unlike the rest of the nineteenth-century working woman's defenders, the suffragists believed that women belonged in the labor force and that an ultimate solution to the working woman's oppression was not to return her to her domestic enclave. They championed the working woman on the basis of what they perceived as her strengths, her craft, competence, and productive capacities. Above all, they saw the working woman as aspiring to an honorable independence, which was, after all, what they hoped for from enfranchisement.

All of the characteristics that the suffragists looked for in working women—competence, skill, contribution to the social product, equality with and independence from men—were characteristics of the skilled worker, whose presence and strength shaped the labor movement of the time. For a brief but significant period, Stanton and Anthony worked closely with a group of New York City working women, typesetters. Together, suffragists and typesetters formed a Working Women's Association, an organization that lasted about a year.[2]

The typesetters with whom suffragists allied were very rare among women. They were skilled workers in a field—printing—dominated by male labor. This unique position lay at the center of their feminist impulse and their alliance with the suffragists. The overwhelming majority of working women were much less skilled, earned much less money, and, most importantly, were herded into a very few all-women industries—garment and textile manufacturing, and domestic work. Such women lacked the very thing that was the nineteenth-century worker's source of dignity, pride, and sense of self-worth, and which suffragists hoped would provide the basis for working women's feminism, a skill. Put another way, the feminist vision of independence and equality with men had little meaning for women whose wages did not even reach the subsistence level and who had no male coworkers with whom they could demand equality. The skilled, women wage-earners around whom Anthony imagined building a suffrage movement simply did not exist in appreciable numbers. It was this firm division of the labor market into male and female sectors and the incredibly depressed character of the female sector, that most restrained suffragists.

Rather than women wage-earners, the suffragists found that their demand for the vote and their vision of female independence attracted middle-class women, either those imprisoned in an enforced domesticity or renegades from ladydom who were independent business women, professionals, or artists. Such women formed the major constituency of the suffrage movement until well into the twentieth century, when suffragists once again turned to wage-earning women and the feminist potential among them.

Suffragists and Male Supremacy

We can see similar conflicting impulses for and against the radicalization of suffragists' analysis with respect to the issue of male supremacy, and particularly the sexual oppression of women. In the prewar suffrage movement, demands for basic legal rights, the need to establish the seriousness of women's protests, and the presence of significant numbers of male supporters on feminist platforms preempted any serious examination of heterosexuality, or, as the nineteenth century called it, "the social question." Woman's suffrage leaders were themselves divided on the advisability of a public investigation into the "social question," although the majority of them, under the leadership of Stanton, were probably inclined to make such an open investigation.

The break with abolitionists and the founding of *The Revolution* opened new vistas for suffragists. They began to write extensively about the "social question." Whereas the prewar woman suffrage movement hesitated to advocate even liberalized divorce laws, in its first year *The Revolution* published articles on abortion, prostitution, female physiology, sex education, cooperative housekeeping, and the social arrangements of the Oneida community. The positions taken by *Revolution* writers varied. Sometimes, for instance, they condemned the high number of abortions women were having as evidence of their frivolity; at other times they expressed sympathy with women forced because of economic and social inequality into pregnancies they had not invited or did not want. What is important, however, is that all these questions were discussed, with the goal of understanding which social and sexual arrangements would work to women's greatest benefit. *The Revolution*, in other words, was committed to developing a feminist position on the social question. Most often, *Revolution* articles identified the problem as the sexual double standard and called for a militant attack on it. For instance, in an article on prostitution, Sarah Norton suggested that the police "turn their attention to reforming the opposite sex. . . . Prostitution will cease when men become sufficiently pure to make no demand for prostitutes. In any event, the police should treat both sexes alike."

Soon suffragists moved their critique of the double standard out of the pages of *Revolution* and into more public forums. From 1868 to 1871 Stanton and Anthony organized a series of mass meetings around current sexual scandals, in order to generate a public feminist presence on such issues. The first case, in 1868, was that of Hester Vaughn, a young English immigrant who had been tried and found guilty of infanticide in Pennsylvania. Vaughn had emigrated from England on the promise of marriage, but when she arrived in Philadelphia she found her fiancé married to another woman. Unable to find any other work, she became a domestic servant. After a few months she was seduced by her employer, became pregnant, and was dismissed. She took a room alone, gave birth unattended, and was discovered three days later with her dead infant by her side. She was tried, found guilty, and sentenced to death, the presiding judge remarking that the crime of infanticide had become so prevalent that "some woman must be made an example of." Suffragists organized a mass meeting and distributed free tickets to working women, many of whom came.

The Vaughn case allowed suffragists to demonstrate the connections between the economic, social, and political dimensions of women's oppression. They particularly pointed to the double sexual standard that fixed all blame on Vaughn, first for her illegitimate pregnancy and then for the death of her infant. "What a holocaust of women and children we offer annually to the barbarous customs of our present type of civilization, to the unjust laws that make crimes for women that are not crimes for men," Stanton wrote angrily.

The McFarland/Richardson case followed the Vaughn affair by a year. Daniel McFarland fatally shot Albert Richardson because Richardson was planning to marry McFarland's ex-wife, whom he had so abused that she had divorced him. Abby McFarland married Richardson on his deathbed, Henry Ward Beecher officiating, and most of official New York was incensed at her daring. Stanton, Anthony, and *The Revolution* supported her. Stanton wrote in the journal that Abby McFarland Richardson was like a fugitive slave who has "escaped from a discordant marriage. This wholesale shooting of wives' paramours should be stopped," Stanton insisted. "Suppose women should decide to shoot their husbands' mistresses, what a wholesale slaughter of innocents we should have of it!" McFarland was tried for murder, found innocent on grounds of insanity, and then given custody of his twelve-year-old son. Stanton and Anthony organized another mass meeting of women to protest both the verdict and the custody decision. From the podium Stanton contended that the major issue was whether a husband had the "right of property in the wife"— that is, whether he could compel her to have sexual intercourse at any time. Stanton argued that Abby Richardson's rejection of this "legalized prostitution" had led to her divorce, and she concluded that "even divorce helps to educate other wives similarly situated into higher ideas of purity, virtue, and self-respect." Certainly a far cry from 1860, when the issue of liberalized divorce was kept off the woman suffrage platform.

In addition to these public forums, Stanton brought her forthright analysis of sexual corruption to women in a more direct form. For several years, starting in 1869, she held small meetings—what we might call consciousness-raising sessions—on "marriage and maternity." During the seven or eight months of every year in which she was lecturing around the country, she would speak to mixed audiences on suffrage in the evenings and to women-only audiences in the afternoons on "the new science of marriage and motherhood." She and Anthony even held such a meeting among Mormon women in Salt Lake City, for which offense they were not allowed to return to Utah for many years. She reported that women responded very enthusiastically to these meetings, where she probably urged them to resist intercourse if it was for their husbands' satisfaction.

By 1870 Stanton had moved beyond a simple condemnation of the sexual double standard and of "legalized prostitution"—unconsenting sexual relations within marriage. She had begun to argue that men's sexual power was the basic source of women's oppression; she came quite close to calling for a feminist attack on marriage. At an unusual, sexually mixed meeting in New York City at which she discussed women's sexual oppression within the marriage institution, she stated, somewhat threateningly: "The men and women who are dabbling with the suffrage movement for women should be at once warned that what they mean logically if not consciously in all they say is next social equality, and next freedom, or in a word free love, and if they wish to get out of the boat, they should for safety sake get out now, for delays are dangerous." Stanton was not the only woman thinking along such lines. Paulina Wright Davis, a long-time feminist activist from Rhode Island, wrote in 1870: "Although equality in education and in industrial avocations may and will be regulated by the ballot, the social relations and rights will not be; they underlie even the ballot, and will only be regulated by purifying the moral sentiment."

Exactly what Stanton and other sexual radicals among the suffragists were putting forward as a program is not clear. At the McFarland/Richardson meeting Stanton urged that women sever unsatisfactory marriage relations by divorce, but later she cautioned against haste in remarriage as "indelicate and indecent." At times, she seemed more to urge women to reject legal marriage than to reform it. This is what the nineteenth century called "free love."

When Stanton's critique of marriage reached this level, her

audience began to fall away. A too-public focus on the "compulsory adulteries of the marriage bed," and a call to women to leave it, alienated the women who, at the private parlor talks on marriage and maternity, had responded so enthusiastically. Anthony found that a group of Dayton, Ohio, women whom she was trying to organize "took up the cudgels" in defense of marriage when she criticized the absolute physical control it gave husbands over their wives. At the founding convention of the National Woman Suffrage Association in 1869, new recruits reported that they had "heard people back home say that when women endorsed woman suffrage they endorsed Free Loveism," and asked for a resolution repudiating it. Similarly, at a national meeting of suffragists a year later, the audience refused to resolve in favor of "women's sole and absolute rights over her own person."

How do we understand this reluctance to commit themselves openly to say in public what they admitted in private about the extent of women's sexual degradation in marriage? To begin with, we must appreciate the number of external obstacles between these women and freedom, how few spiritual and material resources they had and the opposition they knew they would face, however timid their efforts. When a small group of Dubuque, Iowa, housewives formed a woman suffrage club in 1869 and concentrated on getting someone to give a July 4 address on woman's right to the ballot, both local and Chicago newpapers called them "radicals" and "free-thinkers." Another group of midwest women had to work several months to win the right to hold offices in a free library association in which they had only been allowed to be members. Like Chinese women less than three decades ago, these women faced the incredibly long road to full freedom with their feet bound.

To end the explanation for nineteenth-century woman's sexual and domestic conservatism here, however, would be inadequate. That would leave us with the mistaken impression that building a social movement is always a conservatizing process, in which leaders with a radical vision have to battle their followers' timidity and acceptance of prevailing ideas. The history of American radicalism is full of examples to the contrary, of the rank and file being more radical and daring than its leadership. What is important here is the particular social conditions of the potential membership of the movement at a specific moment in history. Most nineteenth-century women had no alternative to marriage. They could not support themselves through wage labor. The absence of reliable contraception made celibacy or extramarital pregnancy the sexual consequences for a woman who abandoned the institution of marriage. Lacking any real options, women were frequently hostile to what they saw as attacks on the institution of marriage and much more likely to defend than to attack it. The call to the first woman suffrage convention in Iowa in 1870 identified the organizers as "mothers, wives, daughters who believe that the marriage bond is to the social, what the Constitution is to the political union." It seemed to Mary Livermore, an important suffragist who joined the movement in 1869, that "the majority of women will always, as the world stands, be wives, mothers, and mistresses of homes."

Ultimately, it was the conditions of women's lives— specifically their dependence on marriage and the sexual division of labor—that determined the shape of nineteenth-century suffragism. We should understand the inability of nineteenth-century feminists to develop solutions adequate to the oppression of women less as a failure of their political imagination or boldness than as a reflection of the state of historical development of capitalism and of male supremacy.

By the same token, the twin axes of woman's oppression are currently in an advanced state of collapse and present contemporary feminists with great revolutionary possibilities. Marriage and the family, to which nineteenth-century women clung, are economically under siege, sexually dysfunctional, and emotionally overloaded. We are certainly no longer tied to them as the only way to organize our personal and social lives. The expansion of capital has transformed women into permanent members of the labor force and is homogenizing the work of all of us into a single level of nonskill. Its continued ability to function without major problems is in doubt.

Thinking about the history of feminism is the same as placing ourselves, our oppressions, and our capacity for liberation in historical perspective. Then we are in a better position to make use of the political prospects with which history presents us.

Notes

1. For the entire text of this speech, see Ellen DuBois, "On Labor and Free Love: Two Unpublished Speeches of Elizabeth Cady Stanton," *Signs: Journal of Women in Culture and Society* 1 (1975): 257–68.
2. The story of the Working Women's Association is discussed in Alma Lutz, "Susan B. Anthony for the Working Woman," *Boston Public Library Quarterly* 11 (1959): 33–43; and Israel Kugler, "The Trade Union Career of Susan B. Anthony," *Labor History* 2 (1961): 90–100.

FEMININITY AND CAPITALISM IN ANTEBELLUM AMERICA

Mary P. Ryan

It is a fundamental assumption of socialist feminism that the status of women and the mode of production are intimately intertwined within the dialectic of history. Yet concepts like femininity and capitalism have seldom been joined together by an historical link that is more precise than the weak conjunction "and" which appears in the title of this paper. For analytic purposes, the integral social process that occurs at the juncture between women and economics can be viewed from three aspects. Femininity, first of all, designates a constellation of ideas found in every society which ascribes certain traits of character almost exclusively to women and conspires to dichotomize the human personality according to sex. More than the mere superstructure of sexual inequality, femininity signifies a complex cultural and psychological process whereby females prepare to assume the status of the second sex. In other words, femininity does not stand alone but is always rooted in a second universal structure of societies: the division of labor, power, and privilege by sex. Third, and finally, this sexual differentiation of personality and society evolves in tandem with the organization of material life, of which capitalism represents only one historical stage.

Throughout human history and across a wide span of cultures femininity has continuously replicated the political pattern of male dominance. The universality of patriarchy, how-

This article was first presented as a lecture in the socialist feminism lecture series at Ithaca College in the spring of 1975.

ever, coexists with countless variations in the contours of femininity and in the sexual division of labor itself. Consequently, it is only within a specific historical system that the relationship between ideals of womanhood and the mode of production can be tightly and accurately linked. This paper examines one such historical case, the relationship between femininity and capitalism during the early stages of American industrialization, roughly between the third and seventh decades of the nineteenth century. Antebellum America is a particularly appropriate period in which to explore these relationships because it was then that femininity began to acquire its infamous mystique. This antebellum prototype of the feminine mystique prepared women to assume a specific set of social and economic roles, one of which was most fully actualized within petty bourgeois households. In putting the tenets of femininity into practice, this class of women played a strategic part in the development of American capitalism.

The substantiation of this thesis will entail, first, an account of the development of the American economy between 1820 and 1860 and, second, a description of the concept of femininity in that period. The connection between the two will consist of an inferred relationship between popular ideas, social behavior, and economic organization; it will not be much more precise than that lamentable conjunction "and." This method is particularly inadequate because it fails to identify the active participation of women in their own history, and might even leave the impression that women were compliant victims of vulgar economic determinism. This mistaken notion cannot be fully dispelled until historians have completed the difficult research necessary to review the development of capitalism from woman's perspective. The rough outlines of such a history will be suggested at the end of this discussion.

The first European settlers in North America carried an array of feminine stereotypes into the new world—images of the "weaker vessel," seductive Eve, and the loose-tongued town gossip—as well as prescriptions for female meekness and wifely obedience. The central feature, however, was the injunction to be a helpmeet, a sturdy, orderly, and industrious farmer's wife. This mode of femininity was well adapted to the exigencies of frontier survival and the ardor of woman's role as mistress of the early American farmhouse. The home economy of the seventeenth century consigned women to obedience to a resident patriarch but at the same time integrated her into a common sphere of subsistent agricultural production. Accordingly, early American culture expended few words and little energy propagating refined distinctions between the masculine and feminine personality. The American economy resembled precapitalist subsistence for only a few generations, however, and it had given way to a system of commercial markets by the time of the Revolution. Before the nineteenth century, nonetheless, a few gilded volumes attesting to the charms of the fashionable lady were the only suggestions of a new definition of femininity.[1]

It was not until the 1830s that male and female temperament became the object of widespread interest. In this period male and female characters became expressed in the familiar antinomies: rational/emotional, aggressive/passive, courageous/timid, strong/delicate, and so forth. This epic event in the history of femininity coincided with America's swift advance toward industrial capitalism. The antebellum years were the most rapid period of industrialization in American history: the proportion of industrial production doubled every decade from 1820 to 1860. This formative era of American capitalism had some distinctive features. First, most manufacturing was conducted in small production units, with the average manufactory containing only twelve employees as late as the 1850s. Even in New York City the typical firm employed less than thirty workers. At the same time the fully mechanized, steam-powered production of textiles and of iron made it possible for a single capitalist to amass the labor power of hundreds under one factory roof. In other words, small-scale independent production flourished alongside the massive routinized factories of large capitalists. Large-scale textile and metal production often grew beside small, artisan shops. In Providence, Rhode Island, for example, the number of smiths, bakers, carriage makers, and carpenters was increasing at the rate of 50 percent per decade in the 1840s.[2] In the largest productive sector, agriculture, the family farm, a small enterprise, provided the backbone of this economic development. At the same time, the small production unit became increasingly dependent on capital investment in technology, be it a reaper or machine tools, and more closely tied to a competitive national market by way of railroads and canals. These small-scale capitalists included the majority of antebellum households.

These small-scale capitalists gradually usurped productive roles from the family economy—often from their own wives. The production of soap, candles, and medicine was transferred to shops on Main Street, transforming use values into commodities and converting female labor into male jobs. The expanding consumer market and the changed location of production created an isolated home environment for the wives and daughters of the petty bourgeoisie and established the precondition for a new femininity.[3]

The social relations which surrounded the petty bourgeois home were characterized above all else by uncertainty and movement. Antebellum geographical mobility was gargantuan, even by contemporary standards. Whether in a northeastern city or on the midwestern frontier, Americans were likely to see between 50 and 80 percent of their neighbors disappear every decade. Social and occupational mobility appears to have been equally pervasive. In Boston, for example, residents changed their jobs at an unprecedented rate and were as apt to plummet downward economically as rise toward riches.[4] If the case of Poughkeepsie, New York, is at all representative, the American small businessmen occupied a most precarious status. In that city three of every five businessmen failed within a period of four years.[5]

Structural changes in the economy often threatened independent artisans with obsolesence as their crafts became mechanized and their productive roles were usurped by unskilled laborers. Enterprising farmers feared losing their farms and their livelihoods, given price fluctuations in the grain market or the vicissitudes of land speculation. The economy was punctuated with depressions. Full recovery from the panic of

1837 was not achieved until the mid-1840s—only to be followed by another devastating depression in the 1850s.

One antebellum writer offered this list of the disruptive and anxiety-provoking conditions of the period. "The fluctuating state of our population, the alterations in commercial affairs to which the country has been especially subjected, the sudden and unexpected reverses in fortune which have been witnessed in every section of the union, the mania for land speculation." These words were penned by one Margaret Coxe in a book with the revealing title, *Claims of the Country on American Females*. This book, and many others like it, called upon women to counteract the instability of the period. They recited a litany of feminine virtues which comprised the "cult of true womanhood": piety, purity, submissiveness, and domesticity. The last term actually subsumes all the rest, for "true women" seldom wandered from the private space of the home.[6]

Although admonished never to desert their home stations, women were also assured, by a popular dictum called "women's influence," that they had great power in society at large: "The influence of woman is not circumscribed by the narrow limits of the domestic circle. She controls the destiny of every community. The character of society depends as much on the fiat of woman as the temperature of the country on the influence of the sun." The use of the metaphors of sun and stream was the favorite literary mode for conveying women's influence, but some writers were not above less genteel language. Margaret Coxe called women "national conservatives in the largest sense," and a San Francisco editor called them "God's own police." The literature was quite clear that the female virtues had a subtly coercive function—to provide stability and order amid the tensions and disruptions of industrialization.[7]

Femininity was thus put forth as a unique method of insuring social order. Unlike the police force, penitentiaries, and asylums that emerged in the same period, women's conservative influence would be lodged in the individual personality, would infiltrate all of America, and would station itself in homes across the land. But if this peculiar method of keeping the peace was to function well, masses of women had to be enrolled in a vast decentralized army. The recruitment campaign was conducted by a thriving publishing industry, one of the most rationalized and highly developed enterprises of the period. Publishing had become a $12-million business by 1850, as shrewd and self-made men like the Harper brothers of New York produced books in a highly mechanized process and sent them speeding through the nation by rail. The bulk of the profits for such publishers came from women's literature; ladies magazines, domestic fiction, and didactic volumes on marriage, housekeeping, and childrearing. The popular woman's literature of the nineteenth century was one point at which capitalist enterprise and femininity met.[8]

The American woman was initiated into femininity at an early age and escorted step by step into womanhood. Before the nineteenth century, sex differentiation between girls and boys was relatively muted. Seventeenth-century literature about children, as well as their games and portraits, made only minor distinctions between the sexes. Even when sexual display became more fashionable among the upper classes in the eighteenth century, distinctions in dress and behavior between boys and girls remained relatively imprecise. The etchings of children which illustrated nineteenth-century publications, however, tell a very different story. These ideal boys and girls differ drastically in their attire, posture, and the objects they are portrayed with. The boys are attired in dark pantaloons and play with dogs while their pastel-attired sisters sit quietly fondling dolls and flowers. The literary invocations on proper child development are even more didactic. For example, the widely popular poet Lydia Sigourney wrote a girl's reading book in 1830 designed to "combine with the accomplishment of reading sentiments that are feminine in their character." These sentiments included passivity, gentleness, and altruism and were often traits of characters such as the little girl who was "so quiet and affectionate, looking like a dove." In other reading books little girls were admonished to "make it your duty to please" and repeatedly advised that "a happy wife and mother is undoubtedly the happiest of all womankind."[9]

As the American girl approached adolescence and young

womanhood, her attention was focused on the ideal home and toward the selection of the mate who would install her there. Literary instructions on mating contained rudimentary instructions—avoid drunks, roués, and gigolos—and above all else, marry only for love. In so doing the young woman would fulfill her peculiarly feminine identity, for "a woman's nature feeds on love. Love is its life." The ubiquitous and euphoric quality of love is seldom defined. It appears in the soliloquies of heroines, such as the following: "Ever since I first thought of it at all, though I can't remember when that was, I have always said I would never marry a man I was not willing to die for." In this bit of dialogue, love paraded as a kind of sacrifice to the death. Another heroine conceived of love as the wish "to have my woman's will bent in glad humility before a stronger mind." The male complement to this sentiment was described in the same novel as follows: "I feel a sort of unratified right of property in her" or "I wish to control her destiny."[10] The immensely popular sentimental novels of the 1850s are replete with such hair-raising expressions of romantic femininity, and include these essential ingredients: love is central to female identity; it matures in adolescent fantasies and expresses itself in intense emotional attractions with sacrificial overtones; and it culminates in subordination to a male in the bonds of matrimony. Such a romantic view of femininity had some crude sociological functions. It served as an inducement to marry, as alliances arranged by parents disappeared. Second, the extravagances of romantic love assisted paragons of femininity in leaping the widening gap between the sexes and agreeing to share bed and board with a strange masculine personality. Third, the scheme of sexual politics that underlay this rendition of love served as psychological preparation for the subordination that was to mark a woman's married life.

Whatever its function, the romantic euphoria quickly dissipated after marriage or, as one heroine put it, descended from "the tropic to the temperate zones," from "adoration to friendship." At this point in the female life cycle a woman's love became manifest in the day-to-day services she rendered her spouse. The duties of the loving wife were endlessly described in housekeeping manuals and magazine articles. They came in answer to this pointed question: "How is the head of the household to be made comfortable when he returns from those toils by which the household is maintained?" The proper response was envisioned by one male writer as follows: "Your wants are all anticipated, the fire is burning brightly, the clean hearth flashes under the joyous blaze; the old elbow chair is in its place; if trouble comes upon you she knows that her voice, beguiling you with cheerfulness, will lay aside your fear."[11] Such images of wifely service clearly entail extensive female labor, not only the housekeeping chores that maintained this warm domestic refuge but also the stores of emotional energy expended in comforting and cheering the weary breadwinner.

The writers of the period regarded such services as more than private matters. As femininity became installed in home after home, they reasoned, it assumed crucial social significance. First of all, good wives would assuage all the alienation men confront in the work force and then send them back refreshed into the competitive fray. Second, a wife would save her husband from any temptation to drink, gamble, or carouse, which might distract him from capitalistic enterprise and forfeit his family's comfort. At the same time, an army of ideal wives would restrain competitive excesses. As one writer put it: "If all is well at home we need not watch him at the market. One will work cheerfully for small profit if he be rich in the love and society of the home."

The methods of maintaining this wifely control were appropriately feminine—subtle and loving manipulation. The preferred practice was demonstrated by one of T. S. Arthur's model wives, Mrs. Penrose. When her husband attempted a rendezvous with some nefarious businessmen in a local tavern, Mrs. Penrose playfully announced, " 'You are my prisoner, I will not let you go!' And she twined her arms around his forehead. As she desired it so it was." The wife's mission was also taken to a psychosexual level. As G. F. Barker-Benfield has pointed out, her Victorian disdain for sexuality repressed excessive male lust and reduced excessive expenditures of se-men, both of which were judged destructive to health, offensive to bourgeois frugality, and detrimental to the national economy. The ultimate reward for all these womanly services to mate and nation was described as follows: "When removed from the turmoil of life or wounded in spirit a husband can open to you his whole soul, unbosoming his sorrow as on a mother's breast, assured of encouragement and sympathy. Then indeed, you are happy you have achieved the highest aspiration of the faithful wife."[12]

Such a view of femininity has bizarre ramifications: that a wife's greatest satisfaction is to provide a maternal bosom for her spouse, to be a nurturing, asexual mother. True women submitted to intercourse only for the purpose of procreation, that is, to reach that apex of nineteenth-century femininity, motherhood. This most hallowed aspect of femininity, like romantic and matrimonial love, was new. As late as the 1830s, childrearing was believed to be the obligation of both parents. Fathers' books advised men of their patriarchal responsibility to oversee the educational and moral training of their children and to supervise the vocational instruction and occupational placement of their sons. Such ideas were soon swept away, however, in a chorus of praise for motherhood. Countless mothers' books and mothers' magazines proclaimed "what a delightful office the creator has made for the female. What love and tenderness can equal that existing in the mother for her offspring." Motherhood was touted as woman's "one duty and function, that alone for which she was created." For the first time childhood socialization, and not merely the physical care of infants, was subsumed under the concept of motherhood. The new obligations entailed a more complete regimen of physical care for infants and children, including elaborate control over hygiene, diet, and clothing, as well as an introduction to the arcana of teething, constipation, and masturbation. The physical care of children, nonetheless, was clearly secondary to the mother's surveillance of her child's moral development. *Godey's Lady's Magazine* called women "those builders of the human temple who lay the foundation for an eternity of glory or of shame." It was the "empire" of the mother to maintain "entire, perfect, dominion over the unformed character of her infant."[13]

To fulfill this awesome responsibility American women were instructed in a childrearing method called gentle nurture, which promised that by exercising control over the child's emotions, the mother could weld her offspring to lifelong compliance with the virtues of propriety, diligence, self-control, and conscientiousness. Even a nursing infant was believed to comply with these directives rather than lose the love and warmth of the mother on whom he or she was so deeply dependent. As the child grew to adolescence and made forays outside the maternal nest, he or she would carry a mother's value system deep within. When young men and women were set loose amid the temptations of the adult world, the monitoring image of the mother would deter them from any act that could wound a being who had expended a lifetime of love and devotion on their behalf. Women were to implant in the character of the next generation the same strict standards and sober habits they monitored in their husbands.[14]

Antebellum theories of childrearing left a deep imprint on the personality of woman, as the following quotation illustrates: "Her right to the child's first love, her intuitive discernment of its desires and impulses, her tact in discovering the minutest shades of temperament, her skill in forming the heart to her purpose, are proofs both of the mother's prerogative and the divine power whence it emanates."[15] The notions of female intuition and emotional sensitivity appear in the context of an evolving female social role. The stereotyped traits of womanhood were useful social skills equipping females to divine and direct the course of child development. This female social role was devised at the point when children were no longer assured of inheriting the status and occupation of their parents, be it on the farm or in the artisan's shop. Explicit socialization was required to prepare the mobile children of the petty bourgeoisie for an uncertain future in a fluid and changing social structure, to train them to morality and righteousness when far from the sight of their parents. Thus, at least according to antebellum romantic literature, femininity formed a vital link between the private world of the home and the world of work. The women who adopted and expanded the roles of wife and mother accommodated two generations of Americans, their husbands and sons, to the occupational exigencies of the capitalist system.

These spouses, sons, and daughters inhabited a distinctive but precarious class position, somewhere in the vague, evanescent social history of the emerging middle class. Each generation saw advances in large-scale production and distribution and the consequent depletion of the ranks of petty commodity producers and small merchants. By the end of the nineteenth century the majority of Americans no longer held their own productive property, whether farm, a craftsman's tools, or a shopkeeper's merchandise. In short, the petty bourgeoisie of the antebellum era was being steadily absorbed into the ranks of wage-earners and salaried employees.[16] Those who held the more affluent positions in this occupational structure—clerks, professionals, business agents—measured their respectability, their "middle class" status, increasingly in private and consumptive terms: in their manners, reputations, and model home lives. These cultural measures of gentility, as well as the material accoutrements of middle-class status—the neat cottages, ornate parlors, and healthy, well-groomed children— were testimony to the work of housewives. These products of woman's work were as sure a sign of middle-class status as was a white-collar job. A woman's labor in the role of mother also encroached upon the male role of determining the class position of children. A son's social status was no longer determined solely by the inheritance of his father's property but also by what Dun and Bradstreet called "character and reputation," clearly products of maternal socialization. In other words, women could shape the personalities of their sons and daughters in such a way as to propel the middle-class family into a second generation. All this is only to suggest that femininity may have forged one last link with capitalism: it designates the important role of housewives and mothers in the formation of the American middle class.

Were females merely puppets of domestic writers, easily manipulated into assuming their serviceable but secondary roles in industrial society? How did the women themselves see it? To assume this social-historical vantage point, it is necessary to consider the economic position of women in the late eighteenth and early nineteenth century. Agriculture was becoming an increasingly commercial enterprise, trade was expanding, and the occupational structure was diversifying, but the opportunities for advancement were open only to those with the right to hold, control, and alienate property—that is, to adult men. At the same time, commodity production was absorbing the basic functions of women in the household economy, including the manufacture of cloth. Such dislocations led many women, often in the wake of revivals, to create a panoply of benevolent and reform societies. In countless missionary associations, orphan societies, and charities, women took on broadened and dignified roles in the changing society. Furthermore, it was often in such collective, self-directed activities that women formulated some of the tenets of true womanhood. As early as 1815, maternal associations were meeting to explore methods of childrearing, well before the mass production of manuals on the subject. Women's temperance associations and moral reform societies also antedated the popular injunction that females purify and control their husbands and sons through domestic moral guardianship.[17] Finally, it was women who penned the bulk of the domestic literature we have referred to, beginning with the sentimental poems that inundated early nineteenth-century newspapers and extending to the best-selling novels of the 1850s. Women themselves then played a large part in constructing the feminine characteristics and accompanying social roles granted their sex in this new system of sexual differentiation.

Although these developments may appear to us as a forerunner of the feminine mystique, they should be considered in the light of the options available to women within the constraints of history. Whatever its pernicious legacy, antebellum femininity offered the women of that era a personal sense of value and social usefulness. The doctrine of women's influence contained within it both honorific rewards and a promise of social power, as well as the possibility of avoiding a male world that was by all accounts brutally intimidating. Under the guise of domestic retirement, women formed supportive alliances with one another. In addition, the cult of true womanhood accorded a modicum of release and occasional escape from the contradictions of sexism. The very literature that inculcated femininity provided cathartic outlets for the tensions inherent in it. Anxiety about one's fate in the marriage market could be relieved by the happy ending of a romantic novel, while animosity toward the male object of that romantic pursuit was disguised in portrayals of insipid, villainous, or crippled heroes. At times women's literature employed cynicism and satire. For example, women might laugh their predicaments away with Sarah Payson Willis. Under the pen name of Fanny Fern, Willis wrote essays on such subjects as "How to Manage Husbands," wherein she called men "pussycats" to be controlled by such devices as this: "Give him a twitch backwards when you want him to go forwards." Fanny Fern captured the contradictions of woman's removal from the productive sphere when she described marriage as "the hardest way on earth of getting a living."[18]

At the same time writers such as these, by virtue of adopting a feminine pose and addressing a female audience, gained a professional literary status which was unprecedented in the history of their sex. Other women wielded the standard of feminine altruism in such a way as to create impressive social and economic enterprises. For example, one tiny band of women in Boston cared for 10,000 families and expended $22,000 in charity in its thirty-year history. The Female Guardian Society of New York sheltered 2,000 women and more than 1,500 children in a five-year period.[19] Such female enterprise was on a scale that rivaled the work of many male capitalists.

Rather than act out the saccharine postulates of femininity, antebellum women found ways of achieving comfort in their narrow roles and opportunities to manipulate and broaden their horizons. It is wrong to portray the female sex as passive mimics of male-directed capitalism. In fact, we must entertain the notion that women played a central and self-directed role in the formation of that system. Furthermore, some antebellum women consciously confronted the contradictions of femininity. America's first women's movement was inaugurated in the middle of this period, just as the concept of femininity was being elevated. The events at Seneca Falls in 1848 suggest a further twist in the relationship between femininity and industrial capitalism. Once the position of women had been fully articulated, particularly in the form of a stereotype, it became possible to see the full extent of sexual inequality and to assault it. That the women's movement has continued and has repeatedly fallen short of even its bourgeois goals demonstrates the tenacity of femininity and the centrality of the female domestic roles in the structure of advanced capitalism.

It has been argued that the essential features of modern femininity were formulated in antebellum America, directly around the predicament of small entrepreneurs and petty capitalists during the early stages of industrial capitalism. This femininity was originally quite remote from the working center of fully industrial capitalism, the proletariat. Yet by the 1850s this class had reached sizeable proportions, and thus must come within the purview of any analysis of femininity. This labor force was not supplied, however, by the primary audience to the antebellum literature of femininity, white native-born American women. By 1860 Yankees were far outnumbered by immigrants in the ranks of unskilled factory workers, and after this date white native American women rarely entered the labor force. In some cases, such as the textile industry, immigrant women constituted the majority of the industrial labor force. Women, coming from such places as Ireland and French Canada, took up the factory posts once filled by Yankee mill girls and carried forward a central female role in this vital sector of industrializing capitalism. They are representative of a sizeable, direct, female contribution to the labor power that propelled American industrial growth.

It would be a mistake, however, to categorize working-class women simply, or even primarily, in terms of female membership in the proletarian work force. Only one in five women were gainfully employed outside the home during the nineteenth century, a figure which probably represented an overall decline in female production since the days of the home economy.[21] The largest portion of women workers, moreover, found employment as domestic servants, that is, labored in homes rather than in factories. Furthermore, almost all these women would retire from the paid labor force upon marriage, and if they supplemented family income they did so by remaining at home to take in washing, keep boarders, or do piecework. Thus, although immigrant women and/or the wives of the working class were clearly more accustomed to breadwinning and familiar with industrial conditions of employment than the wives and daughters of the petty bourgeoisie, the interruption of their work upon marriage and the domestic nature of their gainful employment disqualify them from permanent membership in the proletariat.[22]

Distinctly womanly services were in demand even at the lowest rungs of the class structure, where women met the personal needs of other workers, their husbands, sons, and daughters. It is unlikely that such social functions were performed in the manner and under the conditions of petty-bourgeois femininity. The limited monetary resources of a working-class woman often necessitated the substitution of physical labor for the purchasing power of the middle-class homemaker. For example, the working-class housewife would raise her own livestock and concoct her own home remedies long after her middle-class counterpart had become accustomed to relying on the grocer and druggist to meet these needs. Likewise, the reproductive role of women was more burdensome physically in the household of the working class. The high birthrate of immigrant working-class women, consistently well above that of middle-class wives, testifies to arduous female labor in producing the additional wage-earners which sustained lower-class families.[23] Yet the structural similarity between working-class and middle-class womanhood outweighs these incidental differences. The fact remains that the women of both classes maintained a distinctly female relationship to industrial capitalism. The wives of bank cashiers and factory operatives alike played out their crucial nineteenth-century roles at the periphery of industrial production, outside the cash nexus, and without wages.

In the shadows of domesticity, however, women performed myriad social and economic services which neither the husband's wages nor the employer's capital were able or willing to provide. The work that went into decorating a middle-class home or scouring a tenement kitchen adumbrates the still hidden history not only of women but also of the capitalistic system. Whatever the class position of American males, their daily power to labor and to reproduce another generation of workers depended on partnership with women. To the extent that females in both classes provided these services to male breadwinners they gave shape to a common set of social relations. Several terms have been employed to categorize this process, among them the reproduction of labor power, the mode of reproduction, the social relations of the sexes.[24] Any one of these phrases identifies an extensive sphere of private, domestic, and female activity, which, while outside the productive sector, was essential to capitalistic industrialization. So in closing, let me offer one last nineteenth-century title for women. It appeared in The Ladies Wreath for 1852 and described the relationship between femininity and industrial capitalism by simply calling women "the manufacturers of society."

Notes

1. Roger Thompson, Women in Stuart England and America: A Comparative Study (London: 1974), pp. 8–12; Mary P. Ryan, Womanhood in America (New York: Franklin Watts, 1975), chs. 1 and 2.

2. Howard P. Chudacoff, The Evolution of American Urban Society (Englewood Cliffs, N.J.: Prentice-Hall, 1975), pp. 51–52.

3. Neil McKendrick, "Home Demand and Economic Growth: A New View of the Role of Women and Children in the Industrial Revolution," in Historical Perspectives: Studies in English Society and Thought, ed. Neil McKendrick (London, 1974), pp. 152–210.

4. Peter R. Knights, "Population, Turnover, Persistence and Residential Mobility in Boston, 1830 to 1860," in *Nineteenth-Century Cities*, ed. Richard Sennett and Stephen Thernstrom (New Haven: Yale University Press, 1969), p. 264.

5. Clyde Griffen and Sally Griffen, "Family and Business in a Small City, Poughkeepsie, New York, 1850–1880," *Journal of Urban History* (May 1975): 317–37.

6. Margaret Coxe, *The Claims of the Country on American Women* (Columbus, 1942), p. 13; Barbara Welter, "The Cult of True Womanhood, 1820–1860," *American Quarterly* 18. no. 162 (1966): 151–74.

7. Michael Gordon and M. Chaples Bernstein, "Mate Choice and Domestic Life in the Nineteenth-Century Marriage Manual," *Journal of Marriage and the Family* (November 1970): 670; Roger W. Lothchin, *San Francisco, 1846–1856: From Hamlet to City* (New York: Oxford University Press, 1976), p. 256.

8. Laurence C. Wroth and Rollo G. Silver, "Book Production and Distribution from the American Revolution to the War Between the States," in *The Book in America*, ed. Hellmut Lehman-Haupt (New York, 1951).

9. Lydia Maria Child, *The Mother's Book*, 5th ed. (New York, 1849), pp. 161–62; Lydia H. Sigourney, *The Girls' Reading Book* (New York, 1837), p. 6; Catherine M. Sedgwick, *Means and Ends* (Boston, 1839), p. 16.

10. Catherine Maria Sedgwick, *Clarence* (Philadelphia, 1830), p. 152; Marion Harland, *Alone* (New York, 1856), p. 81.

11. Donald Mitchell, *Dream Life* (New York, 1907), p. 181.

12. *The Mother's Assistant and Young Ladies' Friend* 13, no. 3: 77; Lydia Sigourney, *Letters to Young Ladies* (New York, 1838), p. 74; Timothy Shay Arthur, *What Can a Woman Do?* (New York, 1858), p. 87; G. F. Barker-Benfield, "The Spermatic Economy: A Nineteenth Century View of Sexuality," in *The American Family in Social Historical Perspective*, ed. Michael S. Gordon (New York: St. Martin's Press, 1973), pp. 336–72.

13. Lydia Sigourney, *Letters to Mothers*, 6th ed. (New York, 1846), p. vii; Ruth E. Finley, *The Lady of Godey's, Sarah Josepha Hale* (Philadelphia, 1931), p. 128.

14. Ann Kuhn, *The Mother's Role in Childhood Education* (New Haven: Yale University Press, 1947); Mary P. Ryan, "American Society and the Cult of Domesticity, 1830–1860" (Ph.D. diss., University of California, Santa Barbara, 1971), ch. 2.

15. Sigourney, *Letters to Mothers*, p. 32.

16. Peter Gabriel Filene, *Him/Her Self: Sex Roles in Modern America* (New York, 1974), pp. 73–74.

17. The active role of women in the creation of femininity and sex roles is the subject of the author's current research on the history of women and the family in nineteenth-century Utica, New York. See, for example, "A Woman's Awakening: Evangelical Religion and the Families of Utica, New York, 1800 to 1840," forthcoming, *American Quarterly*.

18. Helen Waite Papashvily, *All the Happy Endings* (New York, 1956); Sarah Payson Willis, *Fern Leaves from Fanny's Portfolio* (Buffalo, N.Y., 1853), pp. 363, 384.

19. Keith Medler, "Ladies Bountiful: Organized Women's Benevolence in Early Nineteenth-Century America," *New York History* (July 1967): 231–54.

20. Frank L. Mott, "Portrait of an American Mill Town: Demographic Response in Mid-Nineteenth Century Warren, Rhode Island," *Population Studies* (March 1972): 156; Daniel J. Walkowitz, "Working-Class Women in the Gilded Age: Factory, Community, and Family Life among Cohoes, New York Cotton Workers," *Journal of Social History* (Summer 1972): 464–90.

21. Eric Richards, "Women in the British Economy Since About 1700: An Interpretation," *History* (October 1974): 337–57.

22. Laurence Glasco, "The Life Cycles and Household Structure of American Ethnic Groups," *Journal of Urban History* (May 1975): 339–63. Virginia Yans McLaughlin, "Patterns of Work and Family Organization: Buffalo Italians," *Journal of Interdisciplinary History* (Autumn 1971): 299–314; Mary Catherine Mattis, "The Irish Family in Buffalo, New York, 1855–1875" (Ph.D. diss., Washington University, 1975), pp. 136–40.

23. Joan W. Scott and Louise Tilly, "Women's Work and the Family in Nineteenth-Century Europe," *Comparative Studies in Society and History* (January 1975): 36–64.

24. Renate Bridenthal, "The Dialectics of Production and Reproduction in History," *Radical America* (March–April 1976): 3–11; Joan Kelly-Gadol, "The Social Relation of the Sexes, Methodological Implications of Women's History," *Signs* (Summer 1976): 808–24; "Women in Struggle," *NACLA Newsletter* 6, no. 10 (December 1972).

CAPITALIST PATRIARCHY
AND FEMALE WORK

Instead of narrowly defining female work as work located only in the labor force, which is true of both liberal and Marxist definitions, socialist feminists, as we have seen, also recognize women's domestic labor as work essential for society. Socialist feminism thus recognizes that female work encompasses the activities of production, reproduction, and consumption. Women who work within the wage-labor force (production) also work within the home (nonwage production, reproduction, consumption); women who are not part of the wage-labor force still work in the home. Understanding that much of women's activity is work enables us to see how and why it is integrated into society. In a society organized around work, we need to view women's activities as they relate to this reality.

In this section we examine female work as activity which is necessary to the smooth operation of the economy and society. First, reproduction of children is demanded by the need of any society to reproduce itself, and capitalist patriarchal societies need new workers. Second, production is necessary to produce material goods. In capitalist patriarchal societies commodity production is the source of both profit and wages. Third, consumption is necessary in a commodity system because that is the way one obtains the goods one needs. Hence, female work encompasses the relations of woman's activity in these three spheres for socialist feminists.

Discussions of female work in capitalist patriarchy have often reduced it to the question of whether or not domestic labor is directly exploited labor creating surplus value. If so,

then women can be considered the proletariat and hence potentially revolutionary because of their direct relation to capital.
However, it is my position that the question of whether women
are oppressed as proletarians does not hinge on whether
domestic labor can be squeezed into the preexisting categories
of wage labor, surplus value, and "productive" work. Rather,
woman's revolutionary potential emanates from the very nature
and organization of the work *as domestic work*—both in its
patriarchal and in its capitalist elements. To the degree domestic
labor is a sexual organization of economic existence it is a
cross-class reality that affects all women. This is the feminist,
political concern which is left out of much of the discussion of
domestic labor when the preexisting analytical categories of
class take priority.

Whether we consider domestic labor the production of use
values (as Margaret Benston does) or the maintenance and
reproduction of labor power (Peggy Morton) or the product of
surplus value (Mariarosa dalla Costa) or as nonproductive labor
(Ira Gerstein) or as privatized work (Karl Marx), it is unpaid
work that is sexually assigned. Domestic labor—the work necessary
to the maintenance of the home—involves production, consumption, reproduction, and maintenance of labor power. It is
the work of bringing children into the world and trying to raise
them within the home (i.e., cooking, cleaning, laundering, loving, mothering). Domestic labor is indispensable to the operation of capitalist patriarchal society *as it now exists*. It is socially necessary labor. It may be "indirectly" productive in that
it maintains the laborer. It may well be, as Lise Vogel has said,
the indispensable complement of wage labor. Wally Seccombe
has pointed out that one cannot understand the truly *deceptive*
nature of wages in capitalist society unless one realizes that
they are payment both for work done by the individual in the
labor force *and* by his domestic counterpart. Women's work is
the other side of men's work. One then only sees half of reality
if one examines workers outside the home, as wage slaves. The
other half is the domestic slave. And this analysis applies to
married men and to women who work both in the paid labor
force and in the home.

I have listed below the many articles that have formed the debate over the nature of domestic labor. Of the many possibilities, I have chosen to reprint Jean Gardiner's article because it raises some of the most probing questions for the domestic labor issue. She wrote this as a criticism of Wally Seccombe's "The Housewife and Her Labour Under Capitalism." She criticizes his distortion of the "unique" qualities of female work. This article, however, does not deal explicitly with the patriarchal base of domestic labor, and with the fact that as domestic laborers women are partially mothers. As such, motherhood is not discussed as integral to the formulation and practice of domestic labor.

Heidi Hartmann, in "Capitalism, Patriarchy, and Job Segregation by Sex," and Margery Davies, in "Woman's Place Is at the Typewriter," talk in more detail about the other side of the double day in their discussion of women in the labor force. They show how the sexual division of labor is not limited to the realm of the household but is definitive in the wage-labor sphere as well. Women carry the household with them into the marketplace. Amy Bridges and Batya Weinbaum, in "The Other Side of the Paycheck," complete the construction of the female worker with their discussion of women as consumers. They argue that the category "consumer" is misleading in that it mystifies the work involved in the very process of shopping, buying, preparing, mending, etc. Most consumer goods require and involve work before they can be used. The consumer is also a worker because she maintains the needed relationship between production and consumption; as such she is necessary to capitalist patriarchal society. Again, the authors do not explicitly develop the patriarchal prerequisites to the need of capital, but they do explore the specific reality of capitalist priorities in female work and activity as it is presently practiced.

Related Reading

Benston, Margaret. "The Political Economy of Women's Liberation," *Monthly Review* (September 1969), reprinted in *Voices from Women's Liberation*, ed. L. B. Tanner (New York: New American Library, 1971).

Braverman, Harry, *Labor and Monopoly Capital* (New York: Monthly Review Press, 1974).

Capitalism and the Family, a *Socialist Revolution* pamphlet (San Francisco: Agenda Publishing, 1976).

Dalla Costa, Mariarosa, *The Power of Women and the Subversion of the Community* (Bristol, England: Falling Wall Press, 1972).

Ehrenreich, Barbara and Deidre English, "The Manufacture of Housework," *Socialist Revolution* 5, no. 26 (October–December 1975).

Gerstein, Ira, "Domestic Work and Capitalism," *Radical America* 7, nos. 4 and 5 (July–October 1973). The entire volume is devoted to women's labor.

Houseworker's Handbook, c/o Leghorn & Warrior, Women's Center, 46 Pleasant Street, Cambridge, Mass. 02139.

Howe, Louise Kapp, *Pink Collar Workers* (New York: G. P. Putnam's Sons, 1977).

James, Selma, *A Woman's Place* (Bristol, England: Falling Wall Press).

Magas, B., H. Wainwright, Margaret Coulson, " 'The Housewife and Her Labour under Capitalism'—A Critique," *New Left Review* 89 (January–February 1975): 59–71.

Morton, Peggy, "Women's Work Is Never Done," *Women Unite* (Toronto: Canadian Women's Educational Press, 1972).

Seccombe, Wally, "The Housewife and Her Labour under Capitalism," *New Left Review* 83 (January–February 1973).

Stover, Ed, "Inflation and the Female Labor Force," *Monthly Review* 26, no. 8 (January 1975).

Tepperman, Jean, "Organizing Office Workers," *Radical America* 10, no. 1 (January–February 1976): 3–23. See also her book, *Not Servants, Not Machines* (Boston: Beacon Press, 1976).

The Women's Work Project, *Women in Today's Economic Crisis* (Union for Radical Political Economics pamphlet).

Vogel, Lise, "The Earthly Family," *Radical America* 7, nos. 4 and 5 (July–October 1973).

Zaretsky, Eli, "Socialist Politics and the Family," *Socialist Revolution* 19 (January–March 1974): 83–99.

———, "Capitalism, the Family and Personal Life," *Socialist Revolution* 1–2, 3, nos. 13–14, 15 (1973).

WOMEN'S DOMESTIC LABOR

Jean Gardiner

This contribution to current debates about the political economy of housework has two specific objectives.[1] First, it presents a critique of Wally Seccombe's article "The Housewife and Her Labour under Capitalism" in New Left Review in 1973.[2] Second, it looks at two questions currently under discussion among Marxist feminists concerning women's domestic labor. Why have housework and child care, in modern industrial capitalist societies such as Britain, continued to such a great extent to be the responsibility of women and organized on a private family basis? What are the pressures working for or against fundamental change in the economic role of women within the family in the current phase of British capitalism? Since Seccombe does not himself attempt to answer these questions, it may not be immediately obvious why they should be linked to a critique of his article. However, it is his failure to relate the theory of women's domestic labor to questions such as these, which are of key political importance to socialists in the women's movement, that forms the basis of this critique—rather than the existence of internal inconsistencies or obscur-

This article originally appeared in New Left Review 89 (January–February 1975): 47–58. It was a slightly rewritten version of a paper presented to the Women and Socialism Conference in Birmingham, England, in September 1974. The ideas expressed in the paper, although written by an individual, are to a very great extent the product of collective discussion in the London Political Economy of Women Group.

ity in his arguments themselves. I shall begin by summarizing and criticizing the core of Seccombe's article, which concerns the role of women's domestic labor in value creation. There will then follow a more general examination of Seccombe's political and theoretical framework, which is counterposed to the approach of socialist feminists. This will lead into discussion of why women's domestic labor has retained such importance in the reproduction and maintenance of the labor force. In conclusion, I shall look at the possible pressures currently working for or against change in the role of domestic labor.

Domestic Labor and Value Creation

One aspect of Seccombe's article that is to be welcomed is that it reflects a growing recognition by Marxists outside the women's liberation movement of the need to consider the productive aspect of women's role in the family, and the economic and not just ideological function of the proletarian family in capitalist society. From this recognition Seccombe goes on to ask what role domestic labor plays in the creation of value and to see how this is linked to the general mystification of the wage system.

First, in discussing how the wage form obscures domestic labor's relation to capital, Seccombe concentrates on showing how this is one aspect, not previously discussed by Marxists, of the more general way elucidated by Marx, in which the wage form obscures the relation of labor to capital. For Marx argued that while the wage appeared to pay for the labor actually performed by the worker, in fact it paid only for the labor going to the reproduction and maintenance of the laborer, i.e., for labor power and not for labor. This left the laborer performing part of his labor unpaid, which was the source of surplus value. Seccombe goes on from this to argue that a part of the wage specifically reflects the value created by the housewife's domestic labor in reproducing and maintaining the worker (and his "substitutes" in the next generation). This is the part of the wage that goes to maintaining and reproducing the housewife (and her "substitutes").

This approach is based on what Seccombe refers to as "a consistent application of the labour theory of value to the reproduction of labour power itself—namely, that all labour produces value when it produces any part of a commodity that achieves equivalence in the market place with other commodities." The argument runs through a number of stages. First, because commodities bought with the male worker's wages are not in a finally consumable form and housework is neccessary to convert the commodities into regenerated labor power, this labor performed by the housewife is one part of the total labor embodied in the worker, the other part being the labor embodied in commodities bought with the wage. This point is straightforward and uncontroversial, once one accepts that domestic labor is a neccessary component of the labor required to maintain and reproduce labor power. The problem arises when we go on from here to ask what the connection is between domestic labor performed and the value of labor power; and whether and how it is possible to measure the contribution of domestic labor in value terms.

Seccombe's opinion is that the neccessary labor of the housewife is realized, when labor power is sold, as a part of its value. In doing this he draws an analogy between petty commodity production and domestic labor. Petty commodity production is the form of production where individuals work separately and independently in a self-employed capacity to produce different goods and services for exchange through the market. He gives the example of a shoemaker and a tailor. This form of production has in common with domestic labor that it is individual and privatized.

Marx, in expounding the labor theory of value in the first volume of *Capital*, first applied it in fact to precapitalist petty commodity production. He argued that under this form of production, although it is not socialized, the terms on which commodities are exchanged will be determined by the different amounts of labor embodied in them. I do not wish here to enter into the question of to what extent the labor theory of value does operate under petty commodity production, but first to note that the assumption on which its operation is based is that labor is mobile between different occupations. For the argument goes as follows. If the shoemaker were not rewarded equally for his labor as the tailor, he would pack up his business and go into tailoring, or at least persuade his sons to do that.

It seems misleading to apply this same analysis to housework where women do not, in any straightforward sense, have the option of moving to another occupation. Women are tied through marriage to housework and housework is therefore not comparable to other occupations. Therefore, there appears to be no mechanism for the terms of the sale of labor power to be determined by the domestic labor performed in its maintenance and reproduction.

Seccombe then goes on to argue that although the labor theory of value can be applied to domestic labor, the law of value does not operate upon it. By this he means that only labor working directly for capital, i.e., wage labor but not domestic labor, is subject to the pressure for constantly improved productivity because of the competition operating between capitalists. This explains the technological backwardness and privatization of housework.

What Seccombe really means when he says that the value that the housewife creates is realized as one part of the value labor power achieves as a commodity when it is sold, becomes clearer in the following section, when he talks about the wage transaction. Here the wage is seen to be divided into two parts, one part (A) sustaining the wage laborer (and his "substitutes") and one part (B) sustaining the domestic laborer (and her "substitutes"). Moreover, "the value of B is equivalent to the value domestic labour creates." Thus, in saying that the housewife creates value which is realized as part of the value of labor power, Seccombe is actually arguing that the part of the husband's wage packet going to the wife (and her "substitutes") provides a measure of the domestic labor performed by her in reproducing the man's labor power. What he has done is to jump from an analysis of petty commodity production, where the producer receives from the sale of commodities the equivalent of labor performed, to capitalist production and the wage transaction. But while he argues that the wage laborer does not receive back the full value he creates, merely the value of his labor power, he presents the value created by the domestic laborer as actually determined by the value she receives from her husband's wage packet. Thus the mystification of the wage form which Seccombe exposes and rejects in the case of wage labor is then applied unquestioningly to domestic labor.

In support of this argument, Seccombe quotes Marx on unproductive workers rendering a personal service (such as cooks, seamstresses, etc): "This does not prevent the value of the services of these unproductive labourers being determined in the same (or analogous) way as that of the productive labourers: that is, by the production costs involved in maintaining or producing them." Here Marx, in referring to "the value of the services" of unproductive and productive laborers, cannot mean the value created by this labor (as Seccombe obviously understands him to mean). He must mean the value of their labor power. Otherwise he would be contradicting his own theory of the role of productive labor in the creation of value.

If the value housewives create is in fact equal to the value they receive from their husbands' wage packets, capital neither gains nor loses, in terms of surplus value, from domestic labor. According to the analysis, therefore, there are no apparent economic reasons why capital would wish to retain domestic labor. Seccombe does not in fact raise this question, but instead takes the existence of domestic labor under capitalism as a given. It is, of course, the case that the law of value (see above) does not operate directly on domestic labor. Once a woman is a full-time housewife, capital is in no way concerned about the productivity of her labor. However, the question of whether or not women are full-time housewives or full- or part-time wage workers is clearly of interest to capital and subject to the requirements of capitalist accumulation ruling at a particular time. Although Seccombe recognizes that there is nothing inherent in housework and child care that should prevent it from being socialized, he offers only a circular argument to explain its privatization. Because it has not been socialized it remains privatized: "Precisely because there exists no continual impetus to reorganize domestic labour to improve its efficiency, it is the one labour process which has not been socialized, though there is nothing inherent in the work itself that would prevent it from being so.''

Another reason why Seccombe's theoretical approach is misleading is that it fails to show how the role of domestic labor may become more significant from the point of view of capital in a crisis. In fact, there is a striking gap between his discussion of labor value and his political conclusions, which recognize how in a time of crisis (such as the present) housewives bear the major burden of working-class loss of real income and are forced to work harder in the home to stretch the reduced wages coming in. Yet the implications of his theoretical analysis are that a reduction in wages going to the wife would reflect a reduction in the value created by her domestic labor, which seems either a meaningless or an incorrect conclusion.

A final implication of Seccombe's analysis is that the economic relationship between husband and wife is one of equal exchange; that the value of the wife's services is equal to the value she receives from her husband's wage packet. This fails to recognize in any way the effects of the wife's economic dependence on her husband and the power relations within the family. If housewives are bound by marriage contract and by many ideological pressures to performing services for their husbands; if within marriage they are economically dependent on their husbands' wages and outside marriage in an inferior bargaining position within the labor market; what then is the mechanism by which equal exchange between husbands and wives can be established?

Political Implications

At this point it seems appropriate to look specifically at general aspects of Seccombe's theory which can be criticized from the viewpoint of socialist feminists. There are three criticisms that can be made, all of which have already been touched on in the previous section.

The first point is Seccombe's failure to recognize sexism in the relations between working-class men and women. He does refer to the economic dependence of the housewife on her husband and the authority it gives the man, as well as to the private nature of the division of the wage between husband and wife. However, he does not go on to discuss the resultant power relations within the family, but rather draws the conclusion that housewives' consciousness of class oppression and ability to join in the struggle against it will be limited. For he argues that the housewife's atomization and lack of any direct relation with capital will cause her to see her husband as the oppressor instead of capital: "She rebels as an isolated individual to the immediate detriment of her husband and children and her actions do not contest the relations of capital directly." Not only does this provide a highly debatable generalized picture of working-class women's consciousness, since it ignores all the factors leading women to identify with the class position of their husbands; it also implies that women's awareness of sexism is more a product of their isolation and political back-wardness than a perception of the oppressive relationships which they experience.

The second criticism that can be made relates to the way Seccombe situates his own theory and political conclusions in relation to orthodox Marxism. As already pointed out, Sec-combe argues that the way in which the wage form obscures domestic labor's relation to capital is one aspect of the general way in which, as Marx showed, the wage form obscures the relation of labor to capital. Thus he emphasizes the need to integrate domestic labor into Marx's theory rather than asking whether a more radical reappraisal of Marx's theory is neces-sary in the light of feminist critiques. Moreover, his characteri-zation of his own theory is highly misleading, since in arguing that domestic labor creates value he is adopting a definition of value that seems rather nonorthodox from a Marxist point of view. As far as his political conclusions are concerned it is clear that what concerns him is whether housewives can make a "contribution to the advancement of the class struggle" and not how working-class women can find ways of collectively struggling against their specific class and sex oppression, or how the male proletariat can learn from women's struggles. It is disturbing that some of the content of socialist feminist debate can be so easily reabsorbed into prefeminist political perspectives.

The third criticism concerns Seccombe's general lack of historical perspective in discussing the family and women's domestic labor in capitalism. He does discuss how the development from feudalism to capitalism brought about fundamental changes; but for the period since then he offers only a static picture (except for recognizing in passing the continued erosion of the family's "vitality and autonomy" under capitalism, through the transfer to the state of major responsibility for education). He does refer to the updating of domestic technology through purchase of labor-saving devices, but regards this as irrelevant to the organization of labor in the home. In reality, many changes have occurred since the rise of capitalism affecting the role of women's domestic labor: e.g., changes in women's paid employment, decline in family size and infant mortality, improvements in housing, the development of the welfare state, mass production of consumer products like prepared food and clothing. Furthermore, if we are to have any notion of how the current feminist movement relates to tendencies in capitalism and of how to direct our struggles, it is essential for us to understand how past changes in the role of women in the family have occurred, and to recognize that the current situation is by no means a static one.

Why Has Domestic Labor Been Maintained?

The character of domestic labor under capitalism has two important aspects. First, a historical prerequisite of the capitalist mode of production was that the domestic family economy of workers ceased to be self-sufficient and self-reproducing. The capitalist mode of production could only develop once the mass of producers had been deprived of independent means of subsistence and were thus dependent on selling their labor power for a wage. Thus domestic labor lost its independent economic basis. But dependence on wages has never meant that workers' needs are in fact all satisfied through the purchase of commodities. Thus the second aspect of women's domestic labor is that at all stages of capitalist development it has played an essential although changing role in meeting workers' needs.

Therefore, capitalism developed out of feudalism through workers becoming dependent on the wage system, but has never provided totally for workers' needs through commodity production, instead retaining domestic labor to carry out an important part of the reproduction and maintenance of labor power. There are three possible reasons why this should be the case. (1) It may be more profitable in a strict economic sense from the point of view either of capital as a whole or of dominant sections of capital. (2) The socialization of all services currently performed in the home might so alter the nature of those services that they would cease to meet certain needs, especially emotional needs. (3) Any further erosion of domestic labor might undermine ideological aspects of the family (e.g. authoritarianism, sexism, individualism) which are important in maintaining working-class acceptance of capitalism. I shall look at each of these possible reasons in turn.

Economic Factors

A number of economic factors need to be taken into account in considering whether it might or might not be profitable from the point of view of capital for housework and child care to be socialized. These can be broadly summarized within the following three categories of problems facing capitalists: (1) the overall level of wages that capitalists have to pay workers; (2) the availability of a labor force that is adequate both quantitatively and qualitatively; (3) the expansion of markets for capitalist commodities.

First, let us look at the problem of wages or the value of labor power. Marx wrote that "the value of labour power is determined, as in the case of every other commodity, by the labour time necessary for the production and consequently also the reproduction of this special article."[3] Seccombe interprets this as meaning that the value of labor power includes the value of labor performed by the housewife. However, it in fact seems clear that Marx was confining his analysis of consumption in the working-class family to consumption of commodities. This is because his was an analysis of a pure capitalist mode of production, in which the only productive relations were those of wage labor working for capital. Thus I shall take the value of labor power to refer to the value of commodities purchased by the wage and consumed by the worker's family. This gives us a definition of necessary labor or value as that portion of labor performed in commodity production which goes to workers' consumption via wages, and a definition of surplus labor or value as that portion of labor performed in commodity production which is unpaid and goes to profits for capitalist accumulation or consumption.

This implies that necessary labor is not synonymous with the labor embodied in the reproduction and maintenance of labor power once one takes account of domestic labor. To put the argument in a different way, the overall standard of living of workers is not determined just by the wage bargain between capital and labor, as it appears to be in Marx's analysis, but also by the contribution of domestic labor. Likewise the role of the state through taxation and social spending needs to be taken into account.

What this approach implies is that the value of labor power is not determined in any straightforward sense by the historically determined subsistence level of the working class. If one accepts that there is, at any given time, a historically determined subsistence level, this level can be achieved by varying the contributions to it of commodities purchased out of wages on the one hand and domestic labor performed by housewives on the other. Thus, at a given level of subsistence and a given level of technology, necessary labor may in fact be a variable.

This approach clearly has implications also for the determination of the rate of surplus value. In Marx's analysis of capital, the rate of surplus value was determined by the dual struggle between wage labor and capital: (1) the labor extracted from workers in the capitalist production process; (2) the wage bargain between wage labor and capital. In fact, because of the role of domestic labor, the variability of the price level and the intervention of the state via taxation and social spending, the struggle over the surplus is also conducted at other levels, no less important from a capitalist viewpoint although considerably less organized, from the point of view of labor. The contribution which domestic labor makes to surplus value is one of keeping down necessary labor to a level that is lower than the actual subsistence level of the working class. For example, it could be argued that it is cheaper for capital to pay a male worker a wage sufficient to maintain, at least partially, a wife who prepares meals for him, than to pay him a wage on which he could afford to eat regularly at restaurants. This seems intuitively to be the case, although it appears to conflict with the argument that if housework were socialized the resulting savings in labor time should substantially cheapen the process. The important point here is that the savings in labor time are only one aspect of socialization. The other is that work which as housework is not paid for as such (the wife's remuneration out of her husband's wage packet often being kept to a minimum, because it is not seen as hers by right) becomes wage work, commanding payment in accordance with what is generally expected in the labor market.

Thus, very great savings in labor time are probably necessary for the socialization of housework not to entail rises in the value of labor power. (This does not, of course, imply that socialization would never occur if it did entail rises in the value of labor power, since there are a number of other factors discussed below which may influence this.) It may, in fact, be the case that many of the services which have remained domestic tasks are actually not subject to major savings in labor time. For example, adequate socialized preschool child care requires a minimum of one adult to five children, without taking account of administrative and ancillary workers. If one compares this with the average family with its 2.5 children to one woman, one gets a rough estimate of no more than a 50 percent saving of labor.

Thus in terms simply of the overall level of wages, there appear to be pressures working against the socialization of housework and child care from a capitalist viewpoint. However, the remaining two types of economic factors suggested above as relevant would seem to push in the opposite direction. The first of these is the availability of an adequate labor force. Pressure for socialization of housework and child care might spring from a recognition by capital that it will be unable to recruit sufficient women workers without taking responsibility, directly or through the state, for performing some of the tasks previously carried out by women in their families. A rather different aspect of this problem is that socialization of child care might also arise for educational reasons, i.e., from pressure to influence the quality of the labor force in the next generation.

The third related economic factor concerns adequate markets for capitalist production. Production of commodities for workers' consumption is clearly one important area of capitalist expansion. Capitalists are not always preoccupied with the need to hold down wages, since at certain periods rising wages can act as a stimulus to capitalist accumulation as a whole. During such a phase of capitalist development, therefore, socialization of housework might occur in response to capital's search for new areas of expansion. This clearly happened for example, in the fifties and sixties in Britain with the expansion of convenience foods.

If we now attempt to put together the different economic arguments related to socialization of housework, two different possible interpretations emerge. On the one hand, there may be conflicting pressures on capital as a whole, so that different pressures will dominate at different phases of capitalist development (i.e., depending on whether there is economic crisis and stagnation or expansion and rising productivity and employment). On the other hand, there may be conflicting pressures amongst capitalists, e.g., between those who require an expanding female labor force or whose profitability is related to sales of consumption goods to workers and those whose major concern is to hold down wages. (This may or may not reflect a genuine conflict of interests among capitalists; it may merely be perceived as a conflict by individual capitalists who are incapable of recognizing the long-term interests of capital as a whole.) However, it is important to stress that the two interpretations are not mutually exclusive, as I shall discuss more fully below.

Thus one can find economic arguments both to explain the retention of domestic labor under capitalism and to suggest the possibility of changes in its role in connection with subsequent developments in capitalism. I shall now turn briefly to the other two sets of reasons put forward as possible explanations why domestic labor has retained its importance.

Psychological Factors

The first of these concerns the nature of the services provided by domestic labor and the impossibility of producing genuine substitutes in the form of commodities. This also raises the question of the way male workers specifically benefit from women's role in the home. For an important component of the use values produced by women in the family is the direct personal relationships within the family on which they are based. It is arguable that the emotional content of many of the tasks a wife performs for her husband is as important to him as their practical purpose. Thus a man who was deprived of his wife's services, while being provided with additional wages sufficient to purchase commodity substitutes, might feel immeasurably worse off and indeed highly discontented. This is not to say that the family currently satisfies all of men's emotional needs, but rather that there are very few ways in which these needs can be satisfied outside it in capitalist society. Certainly our image of what socialism would be like does not eliminate domestic work, but rather poses it as a cooperatively shared activity rather than the sole responsibility of women.

Ideological Factors

The other possible explanation concerns the ideological role of the family. It is possible that any further erosion of domestic labor might undermine the notion of the independent family, responsible for its own survival and competing with other families toward that end. It is also possible that socialization of preschool child care might reduce competitiveness, individualism, and passive acceptance of authoritarianism. In addition, eliminating domestic labor further might undermine male domination, sexual divisions within the working class, and women's passivity, all of which contribute to the political stability of capitalist society. However, changes in ideology occur in a highly complex way and certainly not just in response to changes in production. The whole area of ideology needs far more consideration than I can give it here.

Conflicting Economic Pressures

As was pointed out above, different economic pressures will be operating in different phases of capitalist development, and these will influence whether housework and child care remain domestic or become socialized. This can be illustrated in the following way. In a situation of economic stagnation like the current one in Britain, when the overall rate of investment and economic growth is very low, the state will attempt to hold down wages and workers' consumption as a whole and to encourage investment and exports by giving profit incentives to business. This will have the following implications with respect to the socialization of housework and child care.

1. The state will be attempting to minimize the level of its social spending, redirecting resources as much as possible out of workers' consumption into industrial investment. Therefore, it is unlikely that the state will expand childcare facilities or other substitutes for domestic labor.

2. Although capitalists producing workers' consumption commodities will be attempting to maintain their markets, capitalists generally will be trying to hold down wages. The overall effect of this will be to reduce the profitability of the capitalists producing for workers' consumption and possibly to redirect capital into areas where state intervention or other factors are raising profitability, e.g., exports. Because of this, it is unlikely that capital will be attracted during such a period into production for workers' consumption, including capitalistic socialization of housework or child care.

3. Commodity production which represents a direct sub-

stitution for domestic labor, like convenience foods, may be an area of workers' consumption which is especially subject to decline in a period of crisis, because there will be pressure on housewives to substitute their own labor for commodities in order to stretch the wage further. It is interesting to note, for example, that in 1971, a year of very high unemployment and acceleration in the rise of food prices, convenience food sales fell by 5 percent while seasonal food sales rose by 4 percent, a dual reversal of long-term trends up to that point.[4]

4. Although in a period of stagnation there may be individual areas of shortage of female labor (e.g., nurses), setting up pressures on individual employers to provide nurseries or other facilities, overall shortage of labor is unlikely to be a major problem because of the relatively high level of unemployment.

If we now turn to a situation of economic growth, with a high rate of investment and rapid rise in output per head accompanied by a strong balance of payments, there would be more likelihood of further socialization taking place.

1. It would be possible for both workers' consumption of commodities and state social spending to rise without reducing profitability.

2. Capital would be attracted into new areas of production for workers' consumption which rising wages would make profitable.

3. Rising wages might be a prerequisite of rapid growth, if it was necessary to win acceptance by the workers of new techniques and new ways of organizing labor on which growth might be dependent (e.g., shift work).

4. Likewise, if capital required more women to do full-time work or shift work or simply needed larger numbers of women workers, socialized child care might be a prerequisite.

Conclusion

I have argued that Seccombe's theoretical approach to women's domestic labor can be criticized in the following major ways. His view that it is consistent with Marx's value theory to say that domestic labor creates value which is equivalent to the amount of the male worker's wage going to reproduce and maintain the domestic laborer is based on an incorrect analogy with petty commodity production. His theory of domestic labor is ahistorical, since it does not in any way confront the question of how the role of domestic labor has been modified since the rise of capitalism, or why it has been retained in the form that it has under capitalism. The theory implies an equal exchange between the wage-working husband and the housewife, obscuring both the unequal power position within the family which derives from the economic dependence of the wife and the nonequivalence of what actually gets exchanged, i.e., personal services on the part of the wife for money commodities on the part of the husband. The theory also leads to empirically ridiculous conclusions, e.g., that the less a wife receives from her husband's wage packet the less she contributes to the creation of value. Finally, Seccombe's theoretical approach denies any validity in their own right to the kind of questions being raised by the feminist movement and is based instead on concern over whether housewives can make a "contribution to the class struggle."

In attempting to pose an alternative approach to the role of domestic labor, I have argued that domestic labor does not create value on the definition of value which Marx adopted, but does nonetheless contribute to surplus value by keeping down neccessary labor, or the value of labor power, to a level that is lower than the actual subsistence level of the working class. This being the case, at a time of economic crisis such as the present, when a major requirement for capital is to hold down the level of wages, domestic labor performs a vital economic function and further socialization of housework or child care would be detrimental from a capitalist point of view. However, other pressures (e.g., the need for women wage workers or the need to expand markets for workers' consumption) might lead to further socialization of housework and child care in a period of capitalist expansion. What I have not dealt with here are ways in which political campaigns deriving from the women's movement and labor movement could influence what might actually happen. But I hope that the analysis contributes to providing a framework within which debates about political strategy can be placed.

Notes

1. Published contributions to these debates include Margaret Benston, "The Political Economy of Women's Liberation," *Monthly Review* (September 1969), reprinted in *Voices from Women's Liberation*, ed. L. B. Tanner (New York: New American Library, 1971); Peggy Morton, "Women's Work Is Never Done," *Leviathan* (May 1970); Sheila Rowbotham, *Woman's Consciousness, Man's World* (Baltimore: Penguin, 1973); John Harrison, "Political Economy of Housework," *Bulletin of the Conference of Socialist Economists* (Spring 1974).
2. Wally Seccombe, "The Housewife and Her Labour under Capitalism," *New Left Review* 83 (January–February 1973).
3. Karl Marx, *Capital*, vol. 1 (Moscow: Progress Publishers, 1961), p. 170.
4. The National Food Survey.

THE OTHER SIDE OF THE PAYCHECK: MONOPOLY CAPITAL AND THE STRUCTURE OF CONSUMPTION

Batya Weinbaum and Amy Bridges

I

The housewife is central to understanding women's position in capitalist societies. Marxists expected that the expropriation of production from the household would radically diminish its social importance.[1] In the face of the household's continuing importance, Marxists have tried to understand it by applying concepts developed in the study of production.[2] Yet obviously, the household is not like a factory, nor are housewives organized in the same way as wage laborers.

As Eli Zaretsky has written, the housewife and the proletarian are the characteristic adults of advanced capitalist societies.[3] Moreover, households and corporations are its char-

This article originally appeared in *Monthly Review*, July–August 1976. It was subsequently presented as part of the lecture series in socialist feminism at Ithaca College in the spring of 1977.

Many people read earlier drafts and provided important criticisms and insights. Our discussions with friends have furthered our understanding, and we would like to thank Carol Benglesdorf, Carol Brown, Maarten deKadt, Rosalind Feldberg, David Gold, Sherry Gorelick, Heidi Hartmann, Ira Katznelson, Paula Manduca, Alice Messing, Laurie Nisonoff, Rosalyn Petchesky, Frances Piven, Adam Przeworski, Ann Marie Traeger, and Nancy Wiegersma for their help. Discussions of this paper at the various places it was presented have also been helpful, and we would like to acknowledge the Womens Studies College of SUNY Buffalo, Chicago URPE, Northeast Regional URPE, Boston University Sociology Colloquium, and Marxist Feminist Groups I and II for providing forums for us to discuss these ideas.

acteristic economic organizations. Just as the socialization of production has not abolished the housewife, so accumulation has not abolished the economic functions of the household. Harry Braverman has demonstrated how the accumulation process creates new occupational structures, and he has documented the expansion of capital's activity to new sectors. We will argue that these developments also change the social relations of consumption, an economic function which continues to be structured through the household and performed by women as housewives.

We will show how capital organizes consumption work for housewives, drawing them out of the household and into the market. The changing relations of consumption work require more time to be spent outside the house and create a context in which housewives develop their own political perspectives on capitalist society. In particular, the context of housewives' political consciousness will be found in the contradictions between their work in the market and their role in the home. We think that this aspect of women's activity provides a perspective for viewing women's work inside the home and women as wage laborers, about which a great deal has recently been written. We will argue that capital makes contradictory demands on women's energies, structuring conflicts for individual women and structuring conflicts between housewives and wage laborers in the market. These arguments require an understanding of capitalism in which we can locate consumption, which is the purpose of the next section.

II

In every society, people must have food, clothing, and shelter in order to live. In capitalist society, production of these necessities is organized for private profit, and people must acquire the things they need for survival by buying commodities. Therefore, as capital expropriates production from households, it also expands market relations. These, like production relations, are "definite relations that are indispensable and independent of [our] will."[4] The obvious consequence of monopoly ownership of the means of production is monopoly ownership of commodities and the necessity of *purchasing* the means of life.

Insofar as capitalist production is reconciled with social needs, this happens in the market. In a society of small, independent producers, sellers brought their products to the market for exchange. Only in the market would they discover if their product filled a social need. Since producers worked independently, rather than coordinating their activities, the outcome was chancy. If the product was salable, its price (money in the pocket of the producer) placed constraints on the producer's ability to fill his or her needs. So the "social character of each producer's labor" only showed itself "in the act of exchange,"[5] and the market was the place where private production and socially determined needs were—more or less—reconciled.

In advanced capitalist society, the organization of production as a whole retains anarchic characteristics, but large-scale production makes the "social" character of production apparent in the workplace. And "markets" are not organized for individuals to exchange their products. Rather, selling is an activity organized by capital—increasingly, by large-scale capital replacing "Ma and Pa" stores. Yet just as the small producer measured the "social worth" of his product by its price, so wage laborers largely measure their social worth by the size of their paycheck.[6] And just as the price (small) producers received for their products place constraints on the ability to meet needs, so income constrains access to commodities. Thus the relation of private production to social needs continues to be evident in the market: consumption via the market is the other side of the paycheck. Just as in all societies people work while in capitalist societies people labor,[7] so in all societies people reproduce themselves, but in capitalist societies they consume. In capitalist societies, the market serves as the bridge between the production of things and the reproduction of people.

The reproduction of people happens in the household. By this we mean simply that the household is the place where people's needs for food, rest, shelter, and so on are met. Of course the household is not a self-sufficient unit containing resources to meet these needs. Household members must enter the labor market to exchange their labor power for wages, and they must also go out to exchange wages for needed goods and services. Most households are made up of families, in which men are the primary wage earner and women are responsible for consumption. In the labor market men confront capital in the form of their employers; in the market for goods and services women confront capital in the form of commodities. This sexual division of labor is not absolute: increasing numbers of women work for wages, and many men participate in consumption work.[8] However these roles are divided, household survival requires participation in exchange relations.

Yet the contradiction between private production and social needs remains. Capitalist accumulation creates its own necessities: the reserve army of labor is the clearest expression of capital's needs, which contradict and take precedence over people's needs for their own reproduction. By saying the market is the bridge between private production and social needs, we draw attention to the fact that people must express "effective demand" to get what they need (they must have money). Of course, effective demand is not a matter of choice, for income is determined by position in the class structure. Thus consumption is always a function of class, and when we say that capitalist production is reconciled with social needs, this is always with the recognition that this reconciliation is imperfect under capitalism.

While the market provides the setting for the reconciliation of private production and socially determined need, that reconciliation is primarily the work of women. Women are responsible for "nurturance," and while nurturance requires many kinds of activity, in its concrete aspects it can only be accomplished through the careful management of income. Consumption (purchasing goods and services for household members) is the first step in this task, and it is the housewife's responsibility for nurturance which conditions her confrontation with capital in the form of commodities. Thus the work of consumption, while subject to and structured by capital, embodies those needs—material and nonmaterial—most antagonistic to capitalist production; and the contradiction between private production and socially determined needs is embodied in the activities of the housewife.

III

Consumption is the work of acquiring goods and services. This work is the economic aspect of women's work outside the paid labor force, and we term women doing this work "consumption workers." The term is not meant to imply that women in this role are themselves wage laborers, but it is used to emphasize that what they are doing is work.[9] As already explained, given housewives' responsibility for the home, consumption work is part of the attempt to reconcile production for profit with socially determined needs. In addition, consumption work involves a set of relations between housewives as consumption workers on the one hand and wage laborers in stores and service centers on the other. We will examine consumption work from the point of view of the housewife and then look at relations between consumption workers and wage laborers in the market.

Ellen Willis was the first leftist to write about "consumerism" as work necessitated by capital and to insist that understanding "consumerism" as neurotic is simply sexist.[10] Other writers have been more likely to see women as consumers trying to "compensate" for being cut off from socially organized labor by buying things![11] As the means of production have been progressively expropriated from the household, and as capitalists produce conmodities which can be more economically bought than made there,[12] the sphere of the market and the necessity for finding things we need there expands. The main impetus to consumption work is not a psychological need to express creativity through purchasing (though keeping a family going on what most people earn is indeed a creative undertaking, with its own gratifications). The force behind consumption work is the need to reconcile consumption needs with the production of commodities.

Housewives' work, therefore, cannot be understood if we see women as simply "sweeping with the same broom in the same kitchen for centuries."[13] And while many men are accustomed to saying that "women are their own boss" and can arrange their work as they will, a careful examination of housewives' work shows that capital and the state set quite a schedule for them. Leaving aside the fact that young children are demanding and insistent taskmasters, the hours of the husband's work, the time the children must be in school, and for households that live from week to week (which is *most* households) the day of the shopping, are not determined by the housewife herself. Housewives must work in relation to schedules developed elsewhere, and these schedules are not coordinated with each other. Housewives are expected to wait for weeks for installations and repairs, to wait in lines, to wait on the phone. Changes in the distribution network and the expansion of services demand physical mobility within this less-than-flexible series of schedules. The increase in the number of services as well as shopping centers means housewives spend more time travelling between centers than in producing goods or services. The centralization of shopping centers and services may make distribution more efficient, but at the expense of the housewife's time.[14] The consumption worker, unlike the wage laborer, has no singular and obvious antagonist, but many antagonists: the state, the supermarket, the landlord, etc.

Examination of consumption work also requires analysis of the division of labor between paid and unpaid workers in shopping centers. Relations of production in these sectors reappear in a corresponding structure of consumption work. Here the consumption worker frequently plays an important part in affecting productivity. Ben Seligman illustrates this mechanism with the example of retail food centers:

> It is sometimes argued that gross margins have gone up since the 1950s because modern supermarkets' methods shift the burden of services to the housewife. No longer is a human clerk available to advise her as to which product represents the superior buy; the clerk has been transformed into the "materials handler," stamping prices on canned goods, and the only information he is able to

impart concerns the location of the canned beans. In effect, the housewife now performs services that at one time were paid for by the retailer. In Switzerland an effort has even been made to have supermarket customers punch their own cash registers (it has not met with success). The housewife performs more and more tasks—searching the shelves, grinding the coffee, filling the basket—and contributes to the upward drift of the margins because she is not reimbursed for her services. Of course, she ought to be paid in the form of lower prices, but in the present course of events, that seems unlikely.[15]

The same holds true in retailing, health, education, and other service industries:

In the supermarket and the laundromat, the consumer actually works, and in the doctor's office the quality of medical history the patient gives may influence significantly the productivity of the doctor. Productivity in banking is affected by whether the clerk or the customer makes out the deposit slip—and whether it is correctly made out or not. Thus the knowledge, experience, honesty, and motivation of the consumer affect service production.[16]

Capital, therefore, demonstrates this ability to increase its own profit by rearranging the labor process and working conditions of shopping and service centers. Those employed there find their work increasingly reduced to detail labor; those who shop for services do the walking, the figuring, the comparing, and sometimes even the services themselves (as when auto drivers fill their own gas tanks). Each center has its own rules of behavior and performance. Both those who are employed and those who are shopping or seeking services suffer a speedup.

As we have indicated, consumption work is not just buying "things," but also buying services. Just as it has become more economical to buy many things than to make them (bread, clothing, chicken soup), so "the care of humans for each other has become institutionalized,"[17] and households have become increasingly dependent on securing services from the state and through the market. The expansion of services has been undertaken both by the state (education, welfare, prisons, old age homes) and by capital (some medical services, some old age homes, insurance, banks, fast-food chains, laundries, hairdressers). Together, and with the absence of reasonable alternatives, they render households increasingly dependent on a proliferation of widespread centers.

This transition is most vividly demonstrated in changes in the organization of medical services. At an earlier stage of capitalism, doctors could carry a bag of tools to make house calls. The doctor who now relies on an array of testing equipment can only provide medical care in hospitals and clinics, and housewives must bring family members to them. Indeed, there, as in other service centers, the housewife is little more than a detail laborer, lacking access to expertise to judge the quality of what she gets, power to choose what she will purchase, or the ability to replace the service with a self-organized counterpart. Even the women's health movement, for example, while it can provide many kinds of routine care, has barely begun to appropriate the expertise of the medical profession and rework medical science to be more useful to women.

At times, particular developments in the accumulation process draw more women into the paid labor force. At present, the expansion of the service sector and of clerical work,[18] in conjunction with the fall of real wages among men, pushes increasing numbers of women into the labor force. Just as consumption work requires increasing time and energy,[19] fewer women are able to provide that time and energy. While capital enters new arenas of activity, it continues to organize them in an anarchic rather than a socially coordinated way. The needs of capital are contradictory, therefore, in regard to its demands for women's time. Worse, in a recession public funding for services declines, and work we are increasingly ill-equipped to perform is pushed back into the home. Daycare centers close;[20] schools go to double sessions (making it harder to coordinate children's school hours with parents' work hours); Mayor Daley even encourages neighborhood vegetable gardens! Since women are usually both the consumption workers and the wage laborers in the distribution of goods and services, it is especially clear that capital shifts between paying and not paying for the same work. The wage laborers in the commercial and service sectors have strikebreakers perpetually at their door. Capitalist organization pits cashiers and shoppers, nurses and patients, teachers and parents against each other.

There are, of course, class differences in the work of "housewives." Ruling-class women need not concern themselves directly with reproduction on a daily basis, though they do have a particular role in the reproduction of capitalist class relations. Charity activities, for example, smooth the rough edges of capitalism and help legitimate the social system as a whole.[21] Our sketch of housewives' work is most representative, we believe, for working-class and so-called middle-class women. We may, however, make some distinctions between them. More income gives middle-class women freedom from the more degrading aspects of consumption work (they can have their groceries delivered). These women may also make consumption a "creative" activity and a means of self-expression. This is no doubt the basis for the idea that *all* women engage in consumption for its psychological benefits. Finally, middle-class women take upon themselves the responsibility for organizing others' consumption, through voluntary organizations.[22] Working-class housewives more often participate in the wage-labor force, thereby taking on a second job. Lower income makes consumption a complex survival task. Women who are dependent on the state for support obviously spend more time obtaining both goods and services from civil bureaucracies than other women do; in addition, the commodities available to them are overpriced and of poor quality, largely because of the neighborhoods in which they live.[23] Thus, capital constructs consumption work for women in complex ways: capital organizes the distribution of income to the household, and this largely determines the distribution of households into neighborhoods; at the same time, capital organizes distribution of particular goods and services to particular areas.

We have argued that consumption work is structured by the state and by capital, and that this work is alienating and exhausting. The reproduction of labor in *capitalist* societies requires that the products and services produced with a view to profit be gathered and transformed so that they may meet socially determined needs. In this situation, it is not clear what kinds of reorganization will take place. Certainly, ideas for the reorganization of consumption work on a social basis have been around for a long time (cf. Charlotte P. Gilman, *Women and Econonics*). Yet the reorganization of consumption work and services to living labor on the part of capital and/or the state can hardly be expected to result in humanized social services. The experiences of and proposals for state-run child care are a case in point, that the profusion of goods and services under capitalism results in increased dehumanization.

There is nothing in shopping, or going for health care or education *per se* that must be alienating and tiring. After all, for centuries the market was the site of social interaction and a time for holiday. It is housewives' responsibility for "nurturance" on one hand, and the impossibilities of helping other human beings be healthy and creative within the constraints of the present system on the other, that create the incredible tensions of the practice of consumption work.[24] As Roz Petchesky says:

> It's the connection between the shit private production provides in the market and the miracles women are supposed to perform with it inside the family that's really the key. The cutting edge of consumption work isn't procuring but taking up the slack—trying to maintain goods designed for obsolescence; trying to prepare nourishing meals out of vitamin-depleted, over-processed foods . . . trying to encourage and tutor kids that the schools doom to failure.[25]

For all her efforts, the housewife lacks the social power to provide what she feels is best for her family. It is consumption work on one hand, and the ends which it is supposed to serve on the other, which form the network from which housewives' perspective on society is developed.

IV

How has this perspective been organized in practice?[26] In the first instance, consumption work leads to specific areas of political activity: for example, housing. As explained by an organizer in a Boston tenants' union: "The majority of workers in the tenant movement are women. An explanation for this is that tenants' unions are an area where women can be aggressive and take on an active leadership role because we are spending a great deal of time where we live and know the people we live with."[27] Similarly, boycott activities, militant responses to inflation (especially of food prices), and community struggles (often directed against state policies) are areas in which women play important, if not predominant, roles.[28]

But more generally, the dispersed organization of consumption workers, prey to many capitalists as well as to the state, seems conducive to recognition of the oppressiveness and exploitation of capitalism as a system. During the Brookside miners' strike, the miners' wives not only supported the demands of their husbands but also made more radical and far-reaching demands, insisting on food stamps, boycotting and picketing stores, protesting antistrike propaganda and harassment of strikers' children in the schools. Their practice as housewives demonstrated to them that not just the workplace but the whole city was dominated by the mine owners, and their political activity demonstrated this to the community.[29] In cities where the ruling class is more immediately diverse, this perspective is more complicated, but it still underlies many of women's non-workplace struggles.

Women's activity in revolutionary times may flow from activities ordinarily engaged in, which take on more political meaning during political upheavals.[30] In Portugal since the overthrow of the fascist regime, women in working-class neighborhoods have formed tenant committees to take over buildings for dwelling units and for community service facilities. These tenant committees have survived their initial activities and remain a basic organizational form in urban communities.[31] Similarly, Chilean women were active in the construction of distribution networks before the coup in Chile. During the *Unidad Popular* government, one of the most severe problems was shortages, creating difficulties in food distribution. These problems were in part engineered by rebellious small merchants threatened by socialism and in part by cattle-growers who slaughtered their herds rather than relinquish them to expropriating cooperatives. These induced shortages and distribution difficulties led to the formation of *Juntas de Abastecimientos* (JAPs) or Prices and Supplies Committees, which were a spontaneous popular response and succeeded in reducing the need for rationing. Housewives played a dominant role in neighborhood groups representing both mass organizations and local retailers. Their task was to ensure fair distribution of consumer goods. In the first month of their existence, 450 JAPs were formed in Santiago, Chile's major city. The committees incorporated 100,000 households and more than 600,000 people. Within a few months, 20 percent of the country's beef consumption was distributed through the committees.[32]

Marxists have been too hasty to see community-based struggles as reformist. A struggle is not necessarily progressive because it is in a factory, or reformist because it is outside it. If leftists have, until recently, been indifferent to community and consumerist politics, this is in part for a good reason: however progressive these struggles may be as agitational or educational activity, ultimately struggles outside production cannot *alone* constitute a revolutionary strategy. And many community-based struggles have *not* been progressive. Yet to ignore these struggles altogether is unfortunate for several reasons. Demands for control, while they may be accommodated, threaten bourgeois hegemony and serve as a practice in self-management, an important component in the socialist alternative. At the same time, they have a positive education function in demonstrating the possibilities of organized action and revealing the constraints on political activity within capitalism. Moreover, community and household-based demands insist that production and provision of services be oriented to social needs and in this way embody values antithetical to capitalist production. They call attention to this society's inability to provide for its people. These demands also embody values upon which a socialist society must be built, that society be organized to meet social needs.[33] Finally, as in the case of the Brookside women, housewives' political activity may come from the recognition that not idiosyncratic malfunction, but the organization of society as a whole, is antagonistic to their needs and interests.

A capitalist society creates many social places from which to view capital: places in production and services (machinist, social worker), places in communities (housewife), places isolated from communities (Wall Street). It follows from the nature of capitalist societies that individuals in many *different* social places may discover that society is not organized for them but against them. Clearly, there are no places whose occupants are automatically revolutionaries. One of our tasks as Marxists is to investigate the perspectives on capitalist societies which are provided by these different social places. We can only do this if our understanding embraces not only capitalist production itself but also recognizes how capitalist production shapes society as a whole, and shapes the practices of people in particular places as well. We have shown some of the ways capital structures consumption work, organizing the daily practice of housewives, on which their understanding of society is based.[34] The organization of a revolutionary class requires the joining of those perspectives antagonistic to capital, and forging a vision of society collectively organized to meet social needs.

Notes

1. Marx, Engels, Lenin, and Bebel, for example, recognized that women were oppressed in the family. They thought women's liberation and the possibility of healthy relations between men and women would result when the family ceased to be the basic economic unit of society. Within capitalism, men and women would become wage laborers, as the production responsibilities of the household became socialized. With the abolition of private property, services could be socialized as well, and men and women would be free to form personal relations free of economic functions.

2. In their emphasis on work done inside the household, and understood as "production," most Marxist-feminist work could be included: Paddy Quick, Peggy Morton, Mariarosa dalla Costa, Margaret Benston, Juliet Mitchell, etc. We recognize that housewives prepare goods for use by family members, but our emphasis is not on housework as a kind of "production." Rather, we argue that

housewives' activity is largely a reflection of the fact that *capital* organizes the manufacture of goods and provision of services.

3. Eli Zaretsky, "Capitalism, the Family, and Personal Life," *Socialist Revolution* 1–2, 3, nos. 13–14, 15 (1973).

4. Karl Marx, preface to "A Contribution to the Critique of Political Economy" in Karl Marx and Friedrich Engels, *Selected Works in One Volume* (New York: International Publishers, 1968), p. 182.

5. Karl Marx, *Capital*, vol. I (New York: International Publishers, 1967), pp. 107–8. See also the *Grundrisse*, ed. Martin Nicolaus (New York: Vintage, 1973), p. 225. Marx discusses the market in chs. 2 and 3 of *Capital* and in various places in the *Grundrisse*.

6. See *Grundrisse*, trans. David McClellan (New York: Harper and Row, 1971), p. 66: "In capitalist societies, the individual's power over society and his association with it is carried in his pocket." For money as a measure of social worth, see *Capital*, vol. 1, p. 133.

7. Cf. Engels' distinction between work and labor, *Capital*, vol. 1, p. 186, n. 1. Here Engels writes that the labor process has two aspects: ". . . in the simple labor-process, the process of producing use-values, it is *work*; in the process of creation of value it is *labor*."

8. We are not making an argument here about the relation of capital to the sexual division of labor. See Heidi Hartmann and Amy Bridges, "The Unhappy Marriage of Marxism and Feminism: Towards a More Progressive Union."

9. See n. 7.

10. Ellen Willis, " 'Consumerism' and Women," *Notes from the Third Year*, reprinted in *Woman in Sexist Society*, ed. Vivian Gornick and Barbara K. Moran (New York: New American Library, 1972), pp. 658–65.

11. Mariarosa dalla Costa, *The Power of Women and the Subversion of the Community* (Bristol, England: Falling Wall Press, 1971), p. 43.

12. See Harry Braverman, *Labor and Monopoly Capital* (New York: Monthly Review Press, 1974), p. 281, and chs. 13 and 16, *passim*.

13. Dalla Costa, *Power of Women*, p. 36.

14. Centralization of service distribution is economical for capital and the state, but not the best way to provide services, since the services become less accessible. So, for example, when The Woodlawn Organization drew up a plan for Woodlawn Model Cities, an important element was the proposal for neighborhood service centers which would be accessible and would distribute *all* services. Only hospital facilities would be centrally located.

15. B. Seligman, "The Higher Cost of Eating," in *Economics of Dissent* (New York: Quadrangle, 1968), p. 229.
16. Victor Fuchs, *The Service Economy* (New York: Columbia University Press, 1968).
17. Braverman, *Labor and Monopoly Capital*, p. 279.
18. Ibid., chs. 15 and 16.
19. Capital also increases time spent on women's work done inside the house. See H. Hartmann, "Capitalism and Women's Work in the Home: 1900–1930" (Ph.D. diss., Yale University, 1974). See also Walker, "Homemaking Still Takes Time," *Journal of Home Economics* 61 (1969), pp. 621–22.
20. R. Petchesky and K. Ellis, "Children of the Corporate Dream," *Socialist Revolution* 12 (November–December 1972).
21. See G. William Domhoff, *The Higher Circles* (New York: Random House, 1971), ch. 2: "The Feminine Half of the Upper Class."
22. See, for example, Robert S. and Helen M. Lynd, *Middletown* (Cambridge, Mass.: Harvard University Press, 1959) or John R. Seeley et al., *Crestwood Heights* (Toronto: University of Toronto Press, 1956).
23. See David Caplovitz, *The Poor Pay More* (New York: Free Press, 1962).
24. Although our discussion of consumption work has focused on the monopoly capital stage, at places where monopoly capital penetrates prior economic modes, the tension of changes in consumption is also sharp. For example, the purchase and use of powdered milk marketed by international agribusiness corporations in the Third World has led to deaths and/or deformities of infants who would have been better off with their mothers' milk, given impure water supply and the need for natural antibodies in the mothers' lactate system. See *Formula for Malnutrition*, CIC Brief, April 1975, available for 60¢ from the Interfaith Center on Corporate Responsibility, Room 566, 475 Riverside Drive, NYC. In the nineteenth century, the demands of capitalist production had the same effect: women workers in England, unable to go home to nurse their babies, gave the babies "Godfrey's cordial," a narcotic which kept the infants asleep but often killed them. See *Capital*, vol. 1, p. 395.
25. Personal communication to the authors.
26. There is little space for examples, but see Edith Thomas, *The Women Incendiaries* (New York: George Braziller, 1966); Alice Bergman, *Women in Vietnam* (San Francisco, 1974); *The Chilean*

Road to Socialism, ed. J. Ann Zammit and Gabriel Palma (Austin, Texas: University of Texas Press, 1973).

27. Barry Brodsky, "Tenants First: FHA Tenants Organize in Massachusetts," *Radical America* 9, no. 2 (1975), p. 41.

28. Women also played important roles in organizations created by (or against) the War on Poverty. See J. D. Greenstone and Paul E. Peterson, *Race and Authority in Urban Politics* (New York: Russell Sage, 1973); F. F. Piven and R. Cloward, *Regulating the Poor* (New York: Pantheon, 1971).

29. Ann Marie Traeger and Weinbaum, unpublished interviews, August 1974.

30. Edith Thomas comments: "The 'political' activity of women, then, appeared first in these various consumers' cooperatives and this follows tradition. Women are much closer to everyday realities than men are. Feeding the family is a part of their age-old role. The price of bread has been their business for centuries. Thus, before seeking to involve themselves in truly political activity, they tried to attend to 'the administration of things,' upon which they could act directly. It is from this angle that the most aware women among them thought to have a hold on the social reality. But that was obviously only one aspect of the question" (*The Women Incendiaries*, p. 14).

31. Interview with Pacifica Radio correspondent, May 1975.

32. *The Chilean Road to Socialism*, ed. Zammit and Palma, p. 89.

33. The consequences of leaving consumption organized through the household under socialism even after production has been socialized are discussed in Weinbaum, "The Curious Courtship of Women's Liberation and Socialism: Perspectives on the Chinese Case," in the second special issue on the political economy of women, *Review of Radical Political Economics*, Spring 1976.

34. It should be obvious that we are not arguing that all housewives are politically active, much less revolutionary. Just as wage laborers may feel "inadequate" because their earnings are low or because they are not promoted (see Jonathan Cobb and Richard Sennett, *The Hidden Injuries of Class* [New York: Vintage, 1973]), so housewives may internalize contradictions which are structural. Our emphasis is counter to the current understandings that housewives by nature of their "place" are conservative. For this view, see Zeitlin's book on Cuba, in the preparation of which he didn't interview women because "everyone knows" that women haven't played a role in revolution.

CAPITALISM, PATRIARCHY, AND JOB SEGREGATION BY SEX

Heidi Hartmann

The division of labor by sex appears to have been universal throughout human history. In our society the sexual division of labor is hierarchical, with men on top and women on the bottom. Anthropology and history suggest, however, that this division was not always a hierarchical one. The development and importance of a sex-ordered division of labor is the subject of this paper. It is my contention that the roots of women's present social status lie in this sex-ordered division of labor. It is my belief that not only must the hierarchical nature of the division of labor between the sexes be eliminated, but the very division of labor between the sexes itself must be eliminated if women are to attain equal social status with men and if women and men are to attain the full development of their human potentials.

The primary questions for investigation would seem to be, then, first, how a more sexually egalitarian division became a less egalitarian one, and second, how this hierarchical division of labor became extended to wage labor in the modern period. Many anthropological studies suggest that the first process,

A slightly longer version of this article appeared in Signs 1, no. 3, part 2 (Spring 1976). I would like to thank many women at the New School for Social Research for sharing their knowledge with me and offering encouragement and debate: in particular, Amy Hirsch, Christine Gailey, Nadine Felton, Penny Ciancanelli, Rayna Reiter, and Viana Muller. I would also like to thank Amy Bridges, Carl Degler, David Gordon, Fran Blau, Grace Horowitz, Linda Gordon, Suad Joseph, Susan Strasser, and Tom Victorisz for helpful comments.

sexual stratification, occurred together with the increasing productiveness, specialization, and complexity of society: for example, through the establishment of settled agriculture, private property, or the state. It occurred as human society emerged from the primitive and became "civilized." In this perspective capitalism is a relative latecomer, whereas patriarchy,[1] the hierarchical relation between men and women in which men are dominant and women are subordinate, was an early arrival.

I want to argue that, before capitalism, a patriarchal system was established in which men controlled the labor of women and children in the family, and that in so doing men learned the techniques of hierarchical organization and control. With the advent of public-private separations such as those created by the emergence of state apparatus and economic systems based on wider exchange and larger production units, the problem for men became one of maintaining their control over the labor power of women. In other words, a direct personal system of control was translated into an indirect, impersonal system of control, mediated by society-wide institutions. The mechanisms available to men were (1) the traditional division of labor between the sexes, and (2) techniques of hierarchical organization and control. These mechanisms were crucial in the second process, the extension of a sex-ordered division of labor to the wage-labor system, during the period of the emergence of capitalism in Western Europe and the United States.

The emergence of capitalism in the fifteenth to eighteenth centuries threatened patriarchal control based on institutional authority as it destroyed many old institutions and created new ones, such as a "free" market in labor. It threatened to bring all women and children into the labor force and hence to destroy the family and the basis of the power of men over women (i.e., the control over their labor power in the family).[2] If the theoretical tendency of pure capitalism would have been to eradicate all arbitrary differences of status among laborers, to make all laborers equal in the marketplace, why are women still in an inferior position to men in the labor market? The possible answers are legion; they range from neoclassical views that the

process is not complete or is hampered by market imperfec-
tions to the radical view that production requires hierarchy
even if the market nominally requires "equality."[3] All of these
explanations, it seems to me, ignore the role of men—ordinary
men, men as men, men as workers—in maintaining women's
inferiority in the labor market. The radical view, in particular,
emphasizes the role of men as capitalists in creating hierarchies
in the production process in order to maintain their power.
Capitalists do this by segmenting the labor market (along race,
sex, and ethnic lines among others) and playing workers off
against each other. In this paper I argue that male workers have
played and continue to play a crucial role in maintaining sexual divisions in the labor process.

Job segregation by sex, I will argue, is the primary mechanism in capitalist society that maintains the superiority of men
over women, because it enforces lower wages for women in the
labor market. Low wages keep women dependent on men because they encourage women to marry. Married women must
perform domestic chores for their husbands. Men benefit, then,
from both higher wages and the domestic division of labor.
This domestic division of labor, in turn, acts to weaken women's position in the labor market. Thus, the hierarchical
domestic division of labor is perpetuated by the labor market,
and vice versa. This process is the present outcome of the
continuing interaction of two interlocking systems, capitalism
and patriarchy. Patriarchy, far from being vanquished by
capitalism, is still very virile; it shapes the form modern
capitalism takes, just as the development of capitalism has
transformed patriarchal institutions. The resulting mutual ac-
commodation between patriarchy and capitalism has created a
vicious circle for women.

My argument contrasts with the traditional views of both
neoclassical and Marxist economists. Both ignore patriarchy, a
social system with a material base. The neoclassical economists
tend to exonerate the capitalist system, attributing job segregation to exogenous *ideological* factors, like sexist attitudes. Marxist economists tend to attribute job segregation to capitalists,
ignoring the part played by male workers and the effect of

centuries of patriarchal social relations. In this paper I hope to redress the balance. The line of argument I have outlined here and will develop further below is perhaps incapable of proof. This paper, I hope, will establish its plausibility rather than its incontrovertability.

The first part of this paper briefly reviews evidence and explanations offered in the anthropological literature for the creation of dominance-dependence relations between men and women. The second part reviews the historical literature on the division of labor by sex during the emergence of capitalism and the Industrial Revolution in England and the United States. This part focuses on the extension of male-female dominance-dependence relations to the wage-labor market and the key role played by men in maintaining job segregation by sex and hence male superiority.

Anthropological Perspectives on the Division of Labor by Sex

Some anthropologists explain male dominance by arguing that it existed from the very beginning of human society. Sherry Ortner suggests that indeed "female is to male as nature is to culture."[4] According to Ortner, culture devalues nature; females are associated with nature, are considered closer to nature in all cultures,[5] and are thus devalued. Her view is compatible with that of Rosaldo,[6] who emphasizes the public-private split, and that of Lévi-Strauss, who assumes the subordination of women during the process of the creation of society.

According to Lévi-Strauss, culture began with the exchange of women by men to cement bonds between families—thereby creating *society*.[7] In fact, Lévi-Strauss sees a fundamental tension between the family (i.e., the domestic realm in which women reside closer to nature) and society, which requires that families break down their autonomy to exchange with one another. The exchange of women is a mechanism that enforces the interdependence of families and that creates society. By analogy, Lévi-Strauss suggests that the division of labor between the sexes is the mechanism which enforces "a reciprocal state of dependency between the sexes."[8] It also assures heterosexual marriage. "When it is stated that one sex must perform certain tasks, this also means that the other sex is forbidden to do them."[9] Thus the existence of a sexual division of labor is a universal of human society, though the exact division of the tasks by sex varies enormously.[10] Moreover, following Lévi-Strauss, because it is men who exchange women and women who are exchanged in creating social bonds, men benefit more than women from these social bonds, and the division of labor between the sexes is a hierarchical one.[11]

While this first school of anthropological thought, the "universalists," is based primarily on Lévi-Strauss and the exchange of women, Chodorow, following Rosaldo and Ortner, emphasizes women's confinement to the domestic sphere. Chodorow locates this confinement in the mothering role. She constructs the universality of patriarchy on the universal fact that women mother. Female mothering reproduces itself via the creation of gender-specific personality structures.[12]

Two other major schools of thought on the origins of the sexual division of labor merit attention. Both reject the universality, at least in theory if not in practice, of the sex-ordered division of labor. One is the "feminist-revisionist" school which argues that we cannot be certain that the division of labor is male supremacist; it may be separate but equal (as Lévi-Strauss occasionally seems to indicate), but we will never know because of the bias of the observers which makes comparisons impossible. This school is culturally relativist in the extreme, but it nevertheless contributes to our knowledge of women's work and status by stressing the accomplishments of females in their part of the division of labor.[13]

The third school also rejects the universality of sex-ordered division of labor but, unlike relativists, seeks to compare societies to isolate the variables which coincide with greater or lesser autonomy of women. This school, the "variationist," is subdivided according to the characteristics members emphasize: the contribution of women to subsistence and their control over their contribution, the organization of tribal versus state societies, the requirements of the mode of production, the emergence of wealth and private property, the boundaries of the private and public spheres.[14] They suggest that increased sexual stratification occurs along with a general process of social stratification (which at least in some versions seems to depend on and foster an increase in social surplus—to support the higher groups in the hierarchy).

The work in this school of anthropology suggests that patriarchy did not always exist, but rather that it emerged as social conditions changed. Moreover, men participated in this transformation. Because it benefited men relative to women, men have had a stake in reproducing patriarchy. Although there is a great deal of controversy among anthropologists about the origins of patriarchy, and more work needs to be done to establish the validity of this interpretation, I believe the weight of the evidence supports it. In any case, most anthropologists agree that patriarchy emerged long before capitalism, even if they disagree about its origins.

In England, the formation of the state marks the end of Anglo-Saxon tribal society and the beginning of feudal society. Throughout feudal society the tendencies toward the privatization of family life and the increase of male power within the family appear to strengthen, as does their institutional support from church and state. By the time of the emergence of capitalism in the fifteenth through eighteenth centuries, the nuclear, patriarchal peasant family had become the basic production unit in society.[15]

The Emergence of Capitalism and the Industrial Revolution in England and the United States

The key process in the emergence of capitalism was primitive accumulation, the prior accumulation that was necessary for capitalism to establish itself.[16] Primitive accumulation was a twofold process which set the preconditions for the expansion of the scale of production: first, free laborers had to be accumulated; second, large amounts of capital had to be accumulated. The first was achieved through enclosures and the removal of people from the land, their subsistence base, so that they were forced to work for wages. The second was achieved through both the growth of smaller capitals in farms and shops amassed through banking facilities, and vast increases in merchant capital, the profits from the slave trade, and colonial exploitation.

The creation of a wage-labor force and the increase in the scale of production that occurred with the emergence of capitalism had in some ways a more severe impact on women than on men. To understand this impact let us look at the work of women before this transition occurred and the changes which took place as it occurred.[17] In the 1500s and 1600s, agriculture, woolen textiles (carried on as a by-industry of agriculture), and the various crafts and trades in the towns were the major sourses of livelihood for the English population. In the rural areas men worked in the fields on small farms they owned or rented and women tended the household plots, small gardens and orchards, animals, and dairies. The women also spun and wove. A portion of these products were sold in small markets to supply the villages, towns, and cities, and in this way women supplied a considerable proportion of their families' cash income, as well as their subsistence in kind. In addition to the tenants and farmers, there was a small wage-earning class of men and women who worked on the larger farms. Occasionally tenants and their wives worked for wages as well, the men more often than the women.[18] As small farmers and cottagers were displaced by larger farmers in the seventeenth and eighteenth centuries, their wives lost their main sources of support, while the men were able to continue as wage laborers to some extent. Thus women, deprived of these essential household plots, suffered relatively greater unemployment, and the families as a whole were deprived of a large part of their subsistence.[19]

In the 1700s, the demand for cotton textiles grew, and English merchants found they could utilize the labor of the English agricultural population, who were already familiar with the arts of spinning and weaving. The merchants distributed materials to be spun and woven, creating a domestic industrial system which occupied many displaced farm families. This putting-out system, however, proved inadequate. The complexities of distribution and collection and, perhaps more important, the control the workers had over the production process (they could take time off, work intermittently, steal materials) prevented an increase in the supply of textiles sufficient to meet the merchants' needs. To solve these problems, first spinning, in the late 1700s, and then weaving, in the early 1800s, were organized into factories. The textile factories were located in the rural areas, at first, in order both to take advantage of the labor of children and women, by escaping the restrictions of the guilds in the cities, and to utilize waterpower. When spinning was industrialized, women spinners at home suffered greater unemployment, while the demand for male handloom weavers increased. When weaving was mechanized, the need for handloom weavers fell off as well.[20]

In this way, domestic industry, created by emerging capitalism, was later superseded and destroyed by the progress of capitalist industrialization. In the process, women, children, and men in the rural areas all suffered dislocation and disruption, but they experienced this in different ways. Women, forced into unemployment by the capitalization of agriculture more frequently than men, were more available to labor, both in the domestic putting-out system and in the early factories. It is often argued both that men resisted going into the factories because they did not want to lose their independence and that women and children were more docile and malleable. If this was in fact the case, it would appear that these "character traits" of women and men were already established before the advent of the capitalistic organization of industry, and that they would have grown out of the authority structure prevailing in the previous period of small-scale, family agriculture. Many historians suggest that within the family men were the heads of households, and women, even though they contributed a large part of their families' subsistence, were subordinate.[21]

We may never know the facts of the authority structure within the preindustrial family, since much of what we know is from prescriptive literature or otherwise class biased, and little is known about the point of view of the people themselves.

Nevertheless, the evidence on family life and on relative wages and levels of living suggests that women were subordinate within the family. This conclusion is consonant with the anthropological literature, which describes the emergence of patriarchial social relations along with early societal stratification. Moreover, the history of the early factories suggests that capitalists took advantage of this authority structure, finding women and children more vulnerable because of familial relations and the changes in agriculture which left them unemployed.[22]

The transition to capitalism in the cities and towns was experienced somewhat differently than in the rural areas, but it tends to substantiate the line of argument just set out: men and women had different places in the familial authority structure, and capitalism proceeded in a way that built on that authority structure. In the towns and cities before the transition to capitalism a system of family industry prevailed: a family of artisans worked together at home to produce goods for exchange. Adults were organized in guilds, which had social and religious functions as well as industrial ones. Women and men generally performed different tasks: the men worked at what were considered more skilled tasks, the women at processing the raw materials or finishing the end product. Men, usually the heads of the production units, had the status of master artisans. Women usually belonged to their husbands' guilds, but they did so as appendages: girls were rarely apprenticed to a trade and thus rarely became journeymen or masters. Married women participated in the production process and probably acquired important skills, but they usually controlled the production process only if they were widowed (when guilds often gave them the right to hire apprentices and journeymen). Young men may have married within their guilds (i.e., the daughters of artisans in the same trade). In fact, young women and girls had a unique and very important role as extra or casual laborers in a system where the guilds prohibited hiring additional workers from outside the family; undoubtedly they learned skills which were useful when they married.[23] Nevertheless, girls appear not to have been trained as carefully as boys were and, as adults, not to have attained the same status in the guilds.

Although in most trades men were the central workers and women the assistants, other trades were so identified by sex that family industry did not prevail.[24] Carpentry and millinery were two such trades. Male carpenters and female milliners both hired apprentices and assistants and attained the status of master craftspersons. According to Alice Clark, although some women's trades, such as millinery, were highly skilled and organized in guilds, many women's trades were apparently difficult to organize because the skills could not be easily monopolized. All women, as part of their home duties, knew the arts of textile manufacturing, sewing, food processing, and to some extent, trading.[25]

In the seventeenth and eighteenth centuries the family industry system and the guilds began to break down, faced by a demand for larger output. Capitalists began to organize production on a larger scale, and production became separated from the home. Women were excluded from participation in the industries as they no longer took place at home, where married women apparently tended to remain to carry on their domestic work. Yet many women out of necessity sought work in capitalistically organized industry as wage laborers. When women entered wage labor they appear to have been at a disadvantage relative to men. First, as in agriculture, there was already a tradition of lower wages for women (in the previously limited area of wage work). Second, women appear to have been less well trained then men and obtained less desirable jobs. And third, they appear to have been less well organized.

Because I think the ability of men to organize themselves played a crucial role in limiting women's participation in the wage-labor market, I want to offer some evidence to support the assertion that men were better organized and some plausible reasons for their superiority in this area. I am not arguing that men had greater organizational abilities at all times and all places, or in all areas or types of organization, but that they did in England during this period, particularly in the area of economic production. As evidence of their superiority, we have the guilds themselves, which were better organized among men's trades than women's, and in which, in joint trades, men had superior positions—women were seldom admitted to the hierarchical ladder of progression. Second, we have the evidence of the rise of male professions and the elimination of female ones during the sixteenth and seventeenth centuries. The medical profession, male from its inception, established itself through hierarchical organization, the monopolization of new, "scientific" skills, and the assistance of the state. Midwifery was virtually wiped out by the men. Brewing provides another example. Male brewers organized a fellowship, petitioned the king for monopoly rights (in exchange for a tax on every quart they brewed), and succeeded in forcing the numerous small-scale brewers to buy from them.[26] Third, throughout the formative period of industrial capitalism, men appear to have been better able to organize themselves as wage workers. And, as we shall see below, as factory production became established men used their labor organizations to limit women's place in the labor market.

In ascertaining why men might have had superior organizational ability during this transitional period, we must consider the development of patriarchal social relations in the nuclear family, as reinforced by the state and religion. Since men acted in the political arena as heads of households and in the households as heads of production units, it seems likely that they would develop more organizational structures beyond their households. Women, in an inferior position at home and without the support of the state, would be less able to do this. Men's organizational knowledge, then, grew out of their position in the family and in the division of labor. Clearly, further investigation of organizations before and during the transition period is necessary to establish the mechanisms by which men came to control this public sphere.

Thus, the capitalistic organization of industry, in removing work from the home, served to increase the subordination of women, since it increased the relative importance of the area of men's domination. But it is important to remember that this domination was already established and that it clearly influenced the direction and shape that capitalist development took. As Clark has argued, with the separation of work from the home men became less dependent on women for industrial production, while women became more dependent on men economically. English married women, who had supported themselves and their children, became the domestic servants of their husbands. Men increased their control over technology, production, and marketing, as they excluded women from industry, education, and political organization.[27]

When women participated in the wage-labor market, they did so in a position as clearly limited by patriarchy as it was by capitalism. Men's control over women's labor was altered by the wage-labor system, but it was not eliminated. In the labor market the dominant position of men was maintained by sex-ordered job segregation. Women's jobs were lower paid, considered less skilled, and often involved less exercise of authority or control.[28] Men acted to enforce job segregation in the labor market; they utilized trade-union associations and strengthened the domestic division of labor, which required women to do housework, child care, and related chores. Women's subordinate position in the labor market reinforced their subordinate position in the family, and that in turn reinforced their labor-market position.

The process of industrialization and the establishment of the factory system, particularly in the textile industry, illustrate the role played by men's trade-union associations. Textile factories employed children at first, but as they expanded they began to utilize the labor of adult women and of whole families. While the number of married women working has been greatly exaggerated,[29] apparently enough married women had followed their work into the factories to cause both their husbands and the upper classes concern about home life and the care of children. Neil Smelser has argued that in the early factories the family industry system and male control could often be maintained. For example, adult male spinners often hired their own or related children as helpers, and whole families were often employed by the same factory for the same length of working day.[30] Technological change, however, made this increasingly difficult, and factory legislation which limited the hours of children, but not of adults, further exacerbated the difficulties of the "family factory system."

The demands of the factory laborers in the 1820s and 1830s had been designed to maintain the family factory system,[31] but by 1840 male factory operatives were calling for limits of eight hours of work a day for children between nine and thirteen, and forbidding the employment of younger children. According to Smelser this caused parents difficulty in training and supervising their children, and to remedy it male workers and the middle and upper classes began to recommend that women, too, be removed from the factories.[32]

The upper classes of the Victorian Age, the age that elevated women to their pedestals, seem to have been motivated by moral outrage and concern for the future of the English race (and for the reproduction of the working class): "In the male," said Lord Shaftesbury, "the moral effects of the system are very sad, but in the female they are infinitely worse, not alone upon themselves, but upon their families, upon society and, I may add, upon the country itself. It is bad enough if you corrupt the man, but if you corrupt the woman, you poison the waters of life at the very fountain."[33] Engels, too, appears to have been outraged for similar reasons: "we find here precisely the same features reappearing which the Factories' Report presented,—the work of women up to the hour of confinement, incapacity as housekeepers, neglect of home and children, indifference, actual dislike to family life, and demoralization; further the crowding out of men from employment, the constant improvement of machinery, early emancipation of children, husbands supported by their wives and children, etc., etc."[34] Here, Engels has touched upon the reasons for the opposition of the male workers to the situation. Engels was apparently ambivalent about whose side he was on, for, while he often seems to share the attitudes of the men and of the upper classes, he also referred to the trade unions as elite organizations of grown-up men who achieved benefits for themselves but not for the unskilled, women, or children.[35]

That male workers viewed the employment of women as a

threat to their jobs is not surprising, given an economic system where competition among workers was characteristic. That women were paid lower wages exacerbated the threat. But why their response was to exclude women rather than to organize them is explained not by capitalism, but by patriarchal relations between men and women: men wanted to assure that women would continue to perform the appropriate tasks at home.

Engels reports an incident which probably occurred in the 1830s. Male Glasgow spinners had formed a secret union: "The Committee put a price on the heads of all blacklegs [strikebreakers] . . . and deliberately organized arson in factories. One factory to be set on fire had women blacklegs on the premises who had taken the places of men at the spinning machines. A certain Mrs. MacPherson, the mother of one of these girls, was murdered and those responsible were shipped off to America at the expense of the union."[36] Hostility to the competition of young females, almost certainly less well trained and lower paid, was common enough. But if anything, the wage work of married women was thought even less excusable.

In 1846 the *Ten Hours' Advocate* stated clearly that they hoped for the day when such threats would be removed altogether: "It is needless for us to say, that all attempts to improve the morals and physical condition of female factory workers will be abortive, unless their hours are materially reduced. Indeed we may go so far as to say, that married females would be much better occupied in performing the domestic duties of the household, than following the never-tiring motion of machinery. We therefore hope the day is not distant, when the husband will be able to provide for his wife and family, without sending the former to endure the drudgery of a cotton mill."[37] Eventually, male trade unionists realized that women could not be removed altogether, but their attitude was still ambivalent. One local wrote to the Women's Trade Union League, organized in 1889 to encourage unionization among women workers: "Please send an organizer to this town as we have decided that if the women here cannot be organized they must be exterminated."[38]

The deplorable situation of women in the labor market was explained in a variety of ways by British historians and economists writing in the early twentieth century. Some accepted the logic of the male unions that women belonged at home if possible and men's wages should be increased. Ivy Pinchbeck, for example, stated: "the industrial revolution marked a real advance, since it led to the assumption that men's wages should be paid on a family basis, and prepared the way for the more modern conception that in the rearing of children and in homemaking, the married woman makes an adequate economic contribution."[39] Others argued that this system would only perpetuate women's low economic status. Examining the literature from this period (especially the Webb-Rathbone-Fawcett-Edgeworth series in the *Economic Journal*) is important because it sets the framework for nearly all the explanations of women's position in the labor market that have been used since. In addition, this literature tends to support the argument, delineated in this paper, that job segregation was detrimental to women and that male unions tended to enforce it.

Several writers who focused on job segregation and noncompeting groups as the central mechanism discussed the actions of male unionists as well. Sidney Webb offered as a justification for the lower wages women received the explanation that they rarely did the same grade of work, even when engaged in the same occupation or industry. He cited cigar making, where men made fancy cigars and women made cheap ones requiring less skill.[40] Yet he also acknowledged the role male unions played in preventing women from gaining skills and admitted the possibility that, even for equal work, women received lower wages.[41]

Millicent Fawcett argued that equal pay for equal work was a fraud since women had been kept from obtaining equal skills and their work (at the same jobs) was, in fact, not equal.[42] The essence of trade-union policy, she felt, was to exclude women if they were less efficient and, furthermore, to keep them less efficient.[43] As Eleanor Rathbone put it in 1917, male union leaders will support equal pay as "an effective way of maintaining the exclusion of women while appearing as the champions of equality between the sexes." Many of the followers, she thought, "are obviously rather shocked in their hearts at the idea of a woman earning a man's pay."[44]

Rathbone also considered seriously the different family responsibilities of women. They are a reality, she insisted; men do support their families more often than women do, and men want sufficient money to do this. But she did not necessarily agree with this arrangement; she simply acknowledged that most people considered it "a fundamental part of the social structure":

> The line of argument I have been following usually either irritates or depresses all women who have the interests of their own sex at heart, because it seems to point to an impasse. If the wages of men and women are really based upon fundamentally different conditions, and if these conditions cannot be changed, then it would seem . . . that women are the eternal blacklegs, doomed despite themselves to injure the prospects of men whenever they are brought into competition with them. . . . If that were really so, then it would seem as if men were justified in treating women, as in practice they have treated them—as a kind of industrial lepers, segregated in trades which men have agreed to abandon to them, permitted to occupy themselves in making clothes or in doing domestic services for each other, and in performing those subsidiary processes in the big staple trades, which are so monotonous or unskilled that men do not care to claim them.[45]

World War I, however, had raised women's expectations, and women were not likely to go back to their place willingly— even though the male unions had been promised that the women's jobs were only temporary—especially since in addition to their wages, married women whose husbands were at war received government allowances according to family size. Rathbone wrote: "the future solution of the problem is doubtful and difficult, and . . . it opens up unpleasant possibilities of class antagonism and sex antagonism; . . . for women especially it seems to offer a choice between being exploited by capitalists or dragooned and oppressed by trade unionists. It is a dismal alternative."[46] She recommended the continuation of allowances after the war because they would insure that families would not have to rely on men's wages, that women who stayed at home would be paid for their work, and that women in the labor market could compete equally with men since their "required" wages would not be different. By 1918, Fawcett also thought equal pay for equal work a realizable goal. Advancement in the labor market required equal pay in order not to undercut the men's wages. The main obstacles, she argued, were the male unions and social customs. Both led to overcrowding in the women's jobs.[47]

In 1922, F. Y. Edgeworth formalized Fawcett's job segregation and overcrowding model; job segregation by sex causes overcrowding in female sectors, which allows men's wages to be higher and forces women's wages to be lower than they would be otherwise. Edgeworth agreed that male unions were the main cause of overcrowding.[48] He argued that men *should* have an advantage because of their family responsibilities, and the corollary, that since women do not have the same family responsibilities as men, and may even be subsidized by men, their participation will tend to pull wages down. And he seemed to suggest that equal competition in the job market would result in lower wages even for single women vis-à-vis single men, because women required 20 percent less food for top efficiency. In this last, Edgeworth was simply taking seriously what many had remarked upon—that women have a lower standard of living than men and are willing to work for less.[49] Edgeworth concluded that restrictions on women's work should be removed but that, since unfettered competition would probably drag down the wages of men for the reasons noted above, men and families should be compensated for their losses due to the increased participation of women.[50]

The main explanation the English literature offers for lower wages is job segregation by sex, and for both lower wages and the existence of job segregation it offers several interdependent explanations: (1) the exclusionary policies of male unions, (2) the financial responsibility of men for their families, (3) the willingness of women to work for less (and their inability to get more) because of subsidies or a lower standard of living, and (4) women's lack of training and skills. The English historical literature strongly suggests that job segregation by sex is patriarchal in origin, rather longstanding, and difficult to eradicate. Men's ability to organize in labor unions—stemming perhaps from a greater knowledge of the technique of hierarchical organization—appears to be key in their ability to maintain job segregation and the domestic division of labor.

Turning to the United States experience provides an opportunity, first, to explore shifts in the sex composition of jobs, and, second, to consider further the role of unions, particularly in establishing protective legislation. The American literature, especially the works of Edith Abbott and Elizabeth Baker,[51] emphasizes sex shifts in jobs and, in contrast to the English literature, relies more heavily on technology as an explanatory phenomenon.

Conditions in the United States differed from those in England. First, the division of labor within colonial farm families was probably more rigid, with men in the fields and women producing manufactured articles at home. Second, the early textile factories employed young single women from the farms of New England: a conscious effort was made, probably out of necessity, to avoid the creation of a family labor system and to preserve the labor of men for agriculture.[52] This changed, however, with the eventual dominance of manufacture over agriculture as the leading sector in the economy and with immigration. Third, the shortage of labor and dire necessity in colonial and frontier America perhaps created more opportunities for women in nontraditional pursuits outside the family; colonial women were engaged in a wide variety of occupations.[53] Fourth, shortages of labor continued to operate in women's favor at various points throughout the nineteenth and twentieth centuries. Fifth, the constant arrival of new groups of immigrants created an extremely heterogeneous labor force, with varying skill levels and organizational development and rampant antagonisms.[54]

Major shifts in the sex composition of employment occurred in boot and shoe manufacture, textile manufacture, teaching, cigar making, and clerical work.[55] In all of these, except textiles, the shift was toward more women. New occupations opened up for both men and women, but men seemed to dominate in most of them, even though there were exceptions. Telephone operating and typing, for example, became women's jobs.

In all of the cases of increase in female employment, the increases were partially stimulated by a sharp rise in the demand for the service or product. During the late 1700s and early 1800s, domestic demand for ready-made boots went up because of the war, a greater number of slaves, general population expansion, and the settling of the frontier. Demand for teachers increased rapidly before, during, and after the Civil War as public education spread. The demand for cheap machine-made cigars grew rapidly at the end of the nineteenth century. The upward shift in the numbers of clerical workers came between 1890 and 1930, when businesses grew larger and became more centralized requiring more administration, distribution, transportation, marketing, and communication.

In several cases the shift to women was accompanied by technical innovations, which allowed increased output and sometimes reduced the skill required of the worker. By 1800, bootmakers and shoemakers had devised a division of labor which allowed women to work on sewing the uppers at home. In the 1850s, sewing machines were applied to boots and shoes in factories. In the 1870s, the use of wooden molds, rather then hand bunching, simplified cigar making, and in the 1880s, machinery was brought in. And in clerical work, the typewriter, of course, greatly increased the productivity of clerical labor. The machinery introduced in textiles—mule spinners—was traditionally operated by males. In printing, where male unions were successful in excluding women, the unions insisted on staffing the new linotypes.[56]

The central purposes of subdividing the labor process, simplifying tasks, and introducing machines were to raise production, to cheapen it, and to increase management's control over the labor process. Subdivision of the labor process ordinarily allowed the use of less skilled labor in one or more subportions of the task. Cheapening of labor power and more control over labor were the motive forces behind scientific management and earlier efforts to reorganize labor.[57] Machinery was an aid in the process, not a motive force. Machinery, unskilled labor, and women workers often went together.

In addition to greater demand and technical change, often a shortage of the usual supply of labor contributed to a change in the labor force. In textiles, for example, in the 1840s the young New England farm women were attracted to new job opportunities for middle-class women, such as teaching. Their places in the mills were taken by immigrants. In boots and shoes the increased demand could not be met by the available trained shoemakers. And in clerical work, the supply of high-school educated males was not equal to the increase in demand. Moreover, in clerical work in particular the changes that occurred in the job structure reduced its attractiveness to men—with expansion, the jobs became deadends—while for women the opportunities compared favorably with their opportunities elsewhere.[58]

Cigar making offers ample opportunity to illustrate both the opposition of male unionists to impending sex changes in labor-force composition in their industries and the form that opposition took: protective legislation.[59] Cigar making was a home industry before 1800, when women on farms in Connecticut and elsewhere made rather rough cigars and traded them at village stores. Early factories employed women, but they were soon replaced by skilled male immigrants whose products could compete with fancy European cigars. By 1860, women were only 9 percent of the employed in cigar making. This switch to men was followed by one to women, but not without opposition from the men. In 1869, the wooden mold was introduced, and so were Bohemian immigrant women (who had been skilled workers in cigar factories in Austria-Hungary).[60] The Bohemian women, established by tobacco companies in tenements, perfected a division of labor in which young girls (and later their husbands)[61] could use the molds. Beginning in 1873 the Cigarmakers International Union agitated vociferously against home work, which was eventually restricted (for example, in New York in 1894). In the late 1880s machinery was introduced into the factories, and women were used as strikebreakers. The union turned to protective legislation.

The attitude of the Cigarmakers International Union toward women was ambivalent at best. The union excluded women in 1864 but admitted them in 1867. In 1875 it prohibited locals from excluding women but apparently never imposed sanctions on offending locals.[62] In 1878 a Baltimore local wrote Adolph Strasser, the union president: "We have combatted from its incipiency the movement of the introduction of female labor in any capacity whatever, be it bunch maker, roller, or what not."[63] Lest these ambiguities be interpreted as national-local conflicts, let Strasser speak for himself: "We cannot drive the females out of the trade, but we can restrict their daily quota of labor through factory laws. No girl under 18 should be employed more than eight hours per day; all overwork should be prohibited. . . ."[64]

Because women are unskilled workers, it may be erroneous to interpret this as animosity to *women* per se. Rather it is the fear of the skilled for the unskilled. Yet male unions denied women skills, while they offered them to young boys. This is quite clear in the case of printing.[65]

Women had been engaged as typesetters in printing from colonial times. It was a skilled trade but required no heavy work. Abbott attributed the jealousy of the men in the trade to the fact that it was a trade "suited" to women. In any case, male unions seem to have been hostile to the employment of women from the beginning. In 1854 the National Typographical Union resolved not to "encourage by its act the employment of female compositors."[66] Baker suggests that the unions discouraged girls from learning the trade, and so women learned what they could in nonunion shops or as strikebreakers.[67] In 1869, at the annual convention of the National Labor Union, of which the National Typographical Union was a member, a struggle occurred over the seating of Susan B. Anthony, because she had allegedly used women compositors as strikebreakers. She had, she admitted, because they could learn the trade no other way.[68] In 1870 the Typographical Union charted a women's local in New York City. Its president, Augusta Lewis, who was also corresponding secretary of the National Typographical Union, did not think the women's union could hold out for very long, because, although the union women supported the union men, the union men did not support the union women: "It is the general opinion of female compositors that they are more justly treated by what is termed 'rat' foremen, printers, and employers than they are by union men."[69] The women's local eventually folded in 1878.

Apparently, the general lack of support was successful from the men's point of view, for, in 1910, Abbott claimed that: "Officers of other trade unions frequently refer to the policy of the printers as an example of the way in which trade union control may be successful in checking or preventing the employment of women."[70] The Typographical Union strongly backed equal pay for equal work as a way to protect the men's wage scale, not to encourage women. Women who had fewer skills could not demand, and expect to receive, equal wages.[71]

Unions excluded women in many ways, not the least among them protective legislation.[72] In this the unions were aided by the prevailing social sentiment about work for women, especially married women (work was seen as a social evil which, ideally, should be wiped out[73]) and by a strong concern on the part of "social feminists" and others that women workers were severely exploited because they were unorganized.[74] The social feminists did not intend to exclude women from desirable occupations but their strategy paved the way for this exclusion, because to get protection for working women they argued that women, as a sex, were weaker than men and more in need of protection.[75] Their strategy was successful in 1908 in *Muller v. Oregon*, when the Supreme Court upheld maximum-hours laws for women, saying:

> The two sexes differ in structure of body, in the capacity for long-continued labor particularly when done standing, the influence of vigorous health upon the future well-being of the race, the self-reliance which enables one to assert full rights, and in the capacity to maintain the struggle for subsistence. This difference

justifies a difference in legislation and upholds that which is designed to compensate for some of the burdens which rest upon her.[76]

In 1916 in *Bunting v. Oregon* Brandeis used virtually the same data on the ill effects of long hours of work to argue successfully for maximum-hours laws for men as well as women. *Bunting* was not, however, followed by a spate of maximum-hours laws for men, the way *Muller* had been followed by laws for women. In general, unions did not support protective legislation for men, although they continued to do so for women. Protective legislation, rather than organization, was the preferred strategy only for women.[77]

The effect of the laws was limited by their narrow coverage and inadequate enforcement, but despite their limitations, in those few occupations where night work or long hours were essential, such as printing, women were effectively excluded.[78] While the laws may have protected women in the "sweated" trades, women who were beginning to get established in "men's jobs" were turned back.[79] Some of these women fought back successfully, but the struggle is still being waged today along many of the same battle lines. As Ann C. Hill argued, the effect of these laws, psychically and socially, has been devastating. They confirmed woman's "alien" status as a worker.[80]

Throughout the above discussion of the development of the wage-labor force in England and the United States, I have emphasized the role of male workers in restricting women's sphere in the labor market. Although I have emphasized the role of men, I do not think that of employers was unimportant. Recent work on labor-market segmentation theory provides a framework for looking at the role of employers.[81] According to this model, one mechanism which creates segmentation is the conscious, though not necessarily conspiratorial, action of capitalists; they act to exacerbate existing divisions among workers in order to further divide them, thus weakening their class unity and reducing their bargaining power.[82] The creation of complex internal job structures is itself part of this attempt. In fact, the whole range of different levels of jobs serves to obfuscate the basic two-class nature of capitalist society.[83] This model suggests, first, that sex segregation is one aspect of the labor-market segmentation inherent in advanced capitalism and, second, capitalists have consciously attempted to exacerbate sex divisions. Thus, if the foregoing analysis has emphasized the continuous nature of job segregation by sex—present in all stages of capitalism and before[84]—and the conscious actions of male workers, it is important to note that the actions of capitalists may have been crucial in calling forth those responses from male workers.

Historically, male workers have been instrumental in limiting the participation of women in the labor market. Male unions have carried out the policies and attitudes of the earlier guilds, and they have continued to reap benefits for male workers. Capitalists inherited job segregation by sex, but they have quite often been able to use it to their own advantage. If they can supersede experienced men with cheaper women, so much the better; if they can weaken labor by threatening to do so, that's good, too; or, if failing that, they can use those status differences to reward men, and buy their allegiance to capitalism with patriarchal benefits, that's okay too.[85]

But even though capitalists' actions are important in explaining the current virility of sex segregation, labor-market segmentation theory overemphasizes the role of capitalists and ignores the actions of workers themselves in perpetuating segmentation. Those workers in the more desirable jobs act to hang onto them, their material rewards, and their subjective benefits.[86] Workers, through unions, have been parties to the creation and maintenance of hierarchical and parallel (i.e., separate but unequal) job structures. Perhaps the relative importance of capitalists and male workers in instituting and maintaining job segregation by sex has varied in different periods. Capitalists during the transition to capitalism, for example, seemed quite able to change the sex composition of jobs—when weaving was shifted to factories equipped with power looms women wove, even though most handloom weavers had been men, and mule spinning was introduced with male operators even though women had used the earlier spinning jennies and water frames.

As industrialization progressed and conditions stabilized somewhat, male unions gained in strength and were often able to preserve or extend male arenas. Nevertheless, in times of overwhelming social or economic necessity, occasioned by vast increases in the demand for labor, such as in teaching or clerical work, male capitalists were capable of overpowering male workers. Thus, in periods of economic change, capitalists' actions may be more instrumental in instituting or changing a sex-segregated labor force—while workers fight a defensive battle. In other periods male workers may be more important in maintaining sex-segregated jobs; they may be able to prevent the encroachment of, or even to drive out, cheaper female labor, thus increasing the benefits to their sex.[87]

Conclusion

The present status of women in the labor market and the current arrangement of sex-segregated jobs is the result of a long process of interaction between patriarchy and capitalism. I have emphasized the actions of male workers throughout this process because I believe that emphasis to be correct. Men will have to be forced to give up their favored positions in the division of labor—in the labor market and at home—both if women's subordination is to end and if men are to begin to escape class oppression and exploitation.[88] Capitalists have indeed used women as unskilled, underpaid labor to undercut male workers, yet this is only a case of the chickens coming home to roost—a case of men's cooptation by and support for patriarchal society, with its hierarchy among men, being turned back on themselves with a vengeance. Capitalism grew on top of patriarchy; patriarchal capitalism is stratified society par excellence. If nonruling-class men are to be free they will have to recognize their cooptation by patriarchal capitalism and relinquish their patriarchal benefits. If women are to be free, they must fight against both patriarchal power and capitalist organization of society.

Because both the sexual division of labor and male domination are so long standing, it will be very difficult to eradicate them and impossible to eradicate the latter without the former. The two are now so inextricably intertwined that it is necessary to eradicate the sexual division of labor itself in order to end male domination.[89] Very basic changes at all levels of society and culture are required to liberate women. In this paper, I have argued that the maintenance of job segregation by sex is a key root of women's status, and I have relied on the operation of society-wide institutions to explain the maintenance of job segregation by sex. But the consequences of that division of labor go very deep, down to the level of the subconscious. The subconscious influences behavior patterns, which form the micro underpinnings (or complements) of social institutions and are in turn reinforced by those social institutions.

I believe we need to investigate these micro phenomena as well as the macro ones I have discussed in this paper. For example, it appears to be a very deeply ingrained behavioral rule that men cannot be subordinate to women of a similar social class. Manifestations of this rule have been noted in restaurants, where waitresses experience difficulty in giving orders to bartenders, unless the bartender can reorganize the situation to allow himself autonomy; among executives, where women executives are seen to be most successful if they have little contact with others at their level and manage small staffs; and among industrial workers, where female factory inspectors cannot successfully correct the work of male production workers.[90] There is also a deeply ingrained fear of being identified with the other sex. As a general rule, men and women must never do anything which is not masculine or feminine (respectively).[91] Male executives, for example, often exchange handshakes with male secretaries, a show of respect which probably works to help preserve their masculinity.

At the next deeper level, we must study the subconscious— both how these behavioral rules are internalized and how they grow out of personality structure.[92] At this level, the formation of personality, there have been several attempts to study the production of gender, the *socially* imposed differentiation of humans based on biological sex differences.[93] A materialist interpretation of reality, of course, suggests that gender production grows out of the extant division of labor between the sexes, and, in a dialectical process, reinforces that very division of labor itself.[94] In my view, because of these deep ramifications of the sexual division of labor we will not eradicate sex-ordered task division until we eradicate the socially imposed gender differences between us and, therefore, the very sexual division of labor itself.

In attacking both patriarchy and capitalism we will have to find ways to change both society-wide institutions and our most deeply ingrained habits. It will be a long, hard struggle.

Notes

1. I define patriarchy as a set of social relations which has a material base and in which there are hierarchical relations between men, and solidarity among them, which enable them to control women. Patriarchy is thus the system of male oppression of women. Gayle Rubin argues that we should use the term "sex-gender system" to refer to that realm outside the economic system (and not always coordinate with it) where gender stratification based on sex differences is produced and reproduced. Patriarchy is thus only one form, a male dominant one, of a sex-gender system. Rubin argues further that patriarchy should be reserved for pastoral nomadic societies as described in the Old Testament where male power was synonymous with fatherhood. While I agree with Rubin's first point, I think her second point makes the usage of patriarchy too restrictive. It is a good label for most male-dominant societies. See Gayle Rubin, "The Traffic in Women," in *Toward an Anthropology of Women*, ed. Rayna Reiter (New York: Monthly Review Press, 1975). Muller offers a broader definition of patriarchy "as a social system in which the status of women is defined primarily as wards of their husbands, fathers, and brothers," where wardship has economic and political dimensions. See Viana Muller, "The Formation of the State and the Oppression of Women: A Case Study in England and Wales," mimeographed (New York: New School for Social Research, 1975), p. 4, n. 2. Muller relies on Karen Sacks, "Engels Revisited: Women, the Organization of Production, and Private Property," in *Woman, Culture, and Society*, ed.

Michelle Rosaldo and Louise Lamphere (Stanford: Stanford University Press, 1974). Patriarchy as a system between and among men as well as between men and women is further explained in a draft paper, "The Unhappy Marriage of Marxism and Feminism: Towards a New Union," by Amy Bridges and Heidi Hartmann.

2. Marx and Engels perceived the progress of capitalism in this way, that it would bring women and children into the labor market and thus erode the family. Yet despite Engels' acknowledgment in *The Origin of the Family, Private Property, and the State* (New York: International Publishers, 1972), that men oppress women in the family, he did not see that oppression as based on the control of women's labor, and, if anything, he seems to lament the passing of the male-controlled family. See his *The Condition of the Working Class in England* (Stanford: Stanford University Press, 1968), esp. pp. 161–64.

3. See Richard C. Edwards, David M. Gordon, and Michael Reich, "Labor Market Segmentation in American Capitalism," draft essay, and the book they edited, *Labor Market Segmentation* (Lexington, Mass.: D.C. Heath, 1975) for an explication of this view.

4. Sherry B. Ortner, "Is Female to Male as Nature Is to Culture?" *Feminist Studies* 1, no. 2 (Fall 1972): 5–31. "The universality of female subordination, the fact that it exists within every type of social and economic arrangement, and in societies of every degree of complexity, indicates to me that we are up against something very profound, very stubborn, something that cannot be remedied merely by rearranging a few tasks and roles in the social system, nor even by rearranging the whole economic structure" (pp. 5–6).

5. Ortner specifically rejects a biological basis for this association of women with nature and the concomitant devaluation of both. Biological differences "only take on significance of superior/inferior within the framework of culturally defined value systems" (ibid., p. 9). The biological explanation is, of course, the other major explanation for the universality of female subordination. I, too, deny the validity of this explanation and will not discuss it in this paper. Female physiology does, however, play a role in supporting a cultural view of women as closer to nature, as Ortner argues persuasively, following de Beauvoir (ibid., pp. 12–14). Ortner's article was reprinted in *Woman, Culture, and Society* in slightly revised form.

6. Michelle Z. Rosaldo, "Woman, Culture, and Society: A Theoretical Overview," in *Woman, Culture, and Society.*

7. Claude Lévi-Strauss, "The Family," in Man, Culture and Society, ed. Harry L. Shapiro (New York: Oxford University Press, 1971).

8. Ibid., p. 348.

9. Ibid., pp. 347–48. "One of the strongest field recollections of this writer was his meeting, among the Bororo of central Brazil, of a man about thirty years old; unclean, ill-fed, sad, and lonesome. When asked if the man was seriously ill, the natives' answer came as a shock: what was wrong with him?—nothing at all, he was just a bachelor. And true enough, in a society where labor is systematically shared between men and women and where only the married status permits the man to benefit from the fruits of woman's work, including delousing, body painting, and hair-plucking as well as vegetable food and cooked food (since the Bororo woman tills the soil and makes pots), a bachelor is really only half a human being" (p. 341).

10. For further discussion of both the universality and variety of the division of labor by sex, see Melville J. Herskovits, Economic Anthropology (New York: W. W. Norton, 1965), esp. ch. 7; Theodore Caplow, The Sociology of Work (New York: McGraw-Hill, 1964), esp. ch. 1.

11. For more on the exchange of women and its significance for women, see Rubin in Toward an Anthropology.

12. Nancy Chodorow, Family Structure and Feminine Personality: The Reproduction of Mothering (Berkeley: University of California Press, forthcoming). Chodorow offers an important alternative interpretation of the Oedipus complex. See her "Family Structure and Feminine Personality" in Woman, Culture, and Society, as well as her article in this volume.

13. Several of the articles in the Woman, Culture, and Society collection are of this variety. See particularly Collier and Stack. See also Ernestine Friedl, "The Position of Women: Appearance and Reality," Anthropological Quarterly 40, no. 3 (July 1967): 97–108.

14. For an example of one particular emphasis Ruby Leavitt states: "The most important clue to woman's status anywhere is her degree of participation in economic life and her control over property and the products she produces, both of which factors appear to be related to the kinship system of a society" (Ruby B. Leavitt, "Women in Other Cultures," in Women and Sexist Society, ed. Vivian Gornick and Barbara K. Moran [New York: New American Library, 1972], p. 396). In a historical study which also seeks to address the questions of women's status, Joanne McNa-

mara and Suzanne Wemple ("The Power of Woman through the Family in Medieval Europe: 500–1100," *Feminist Studies* 1, nos 3–4 [Winter–Spring 1973]: 126–41) emphasize the private-public split in their discussion of women's loss of status during this period.

15. Both Christopher Hill and Lawrence Stone describe England during this period as a patriarchal society in which the institutions of the nuclear family, the state, and religion were being strengthened. See Christopher Hill, *Society and Puritanism* (New York: Schocken Books, 1964), esp. ch. 13; Lawrence Stone, *The Crisis of the Aristocracy, 1558–1641*, abr. ed. (New York: Oxford University Press, 1967), esp. ch. 11. Recent demographic research verifies the establishment of the nuclear family prior to the Industrial Revolution. See *Household and Family in Past Time*, ed. Peter Laslett (Cambridge: Cambridge University Press, 1972).

16. See Karl Marx, "The So-called Primitive Accumulation," in *Capital*, 3 vols. (New York: International Publishers, 1967), 1, pt. 8; Stephen Hymer, "Robinson Crusoe and the Secret of Primitive Accumulation," *Monthly Review* 23, no. 4 (September 1971): 11–36.

17. This account relies primarily on that of Alice Clark, *The Working Life of Women in the Seventeenth Century* (New York: Harcourt, Brace & Howe, 1920). Her account is supported by many others, such as B. L. Hutchins, *Women in Modern Industry* (London: G. Bell & Sons, 1915); Georgiana Hill, *Women in English Life from Medieval to Modern Times*, 2 vols. (London: Richard Bentley & Son, 1896); F. W. Tichner, *Women in English Economic History* (New York: F. P. Dutton, 1923); Ivy Pinchbeck, *Women Workers and the Industrial Revolution, 1750–1850* (London: Frank Cass, 1930; reprinted 1969).

18. Women and men in England had been employed as agricultural laborers for several centuries. Clark found that by the seventeenth century the wages of men were higher than women's and the tasks done were different, though similar in skill and strength requirements (Clark, *Working Life*, p. 60). Wages for agricultural (and other work) were often set by local authorities. These wage differentials reflected the relative social status of men and women and the social norms of the time. Women were considered to require lower wages because they ate less, for example, and were expected to have fewer luxuries, such as tobacco (see Clark, *Working Life*, and Pinchbeck, *Women Workers*, throughout for substantiation of

women's lower standard of living). Laura Oren has substantiated this for English women during the period 1860–1950 (see n. 49).

19. The problem of female unemployment in the countryside was a generally recognized one which figured prominently in the debate about poor-law reform, for example. As a remedy, it was suggested that rural families be allowed to retain small household plots, that women be used more in agricultural wage labor and also in the putting-out system, and that men's wages be adjusted upward. See Pinchbeck, *Women Workers*, pp. 69–84.

20. See Stephen Marglin, "What Do Bosses Do? The Origins and Functions of Hierarchy in Capitalist Production," *Review of Radical Political Economics* 6, no. 2 (Summer 1974): 60–112, for a discussion of the transition from putting out to factories. The sexual division of labor changed several times in the textile industry. Hutchins writes that the further back one goes in history, the more was the industry controlled by women. By the seventeenth century, though, men had become professional handloom weavers, and it was often claimed that men had superior strength or skill—which was required for certain types of weaves or fabrics. Thus, the increase in demand for handloom weavers in the late 1700s brought increased employment for men. When weaving was mechanized in the factories women operated the power looms, and male handloom weavers became unemployed. When jenny and waterframe spinning were replaced by mule spinning, supposedly requiring more strength, men took that over and displaced women spinners. A similar transition occurred in the United States. It is important to keep in mind that as a by-industry, both men and women engaged in various processes of textile manufacture, and this was intensified under putting out (see Pinchbeck, *Women Workers*, chs. 6–9).

21. See E. P. Thompson, *The Making of the English Working Class* (New York: Vintage Books, 1963); Clark, *Working Life*; and Pinchbeck, *Women Workers*.

22. In fact, the earliest factories utilized the labor of poor children, already separated from their families, who were apprenticed to factory owners by parish authorities. They were perhaps the most desperate and vulnerable of all.

23. Hutchins, *Women in Modern Industry*, p. 16. See also Olive J. Jocelyn, *English Apprenticeship and Child Labor* (London: T. Fisher Unwin, 1912), pp. 149–50, on the labor of girls, and Clark, *Working Life*, ch. 5, on the organization of family industry in towns.

24. The seventeenth century already found the crafts and trades sex divided. Much work needs to be done on the development of guilds and the sexual division of labor and on the nature of women's organizations. Such work would enable us to trace more accurately the decline in women's status from the tribal period, through feudalism, to the emergence of capitalism.

25. Clark, *Working Life.*

26. See Clark, *Working Life,* pp. 221–31, for the brewers, and pp. 242–84, for the medical profession.

27. Ibid., ch. 7. Eli Zaretsky, "Capitalism, the Family, and Personal Life," *Socialist Revolution* 1–2, 3 (1973), follows a similar interpretation of history and offers different conclusions. Capitalism exacerbated the sexual division of labor and created the *appearance* that women work for their husbands; in reality, women who did domestic work at home were working for capital. Thus according to Zaretsky the present situation has its roots more in capitalism than in patriarchy. Although capitalism may have increased the consequence for women of the domestic division of labor, surely patriarchy tells us more about why men didn't stay home. That women worked for men in the home, as well as for capital, is also a reality.

28. William Lazonick argues in his dissertation, "Marxian Theory and the Development of the Labor Force in England" (Ph.D. diss., Harvard University, 1975), that the degree of authority required of the worker was often decisive in determining the sex of the worker. Thus handloom weavers in cottage industry were men because this allowed them to control the production process and the labor of the female spinners. In the spinning factories, mule spinners were men because mule spinners were required to supervise the labor of piecers, usually young boys. Men's position as head of the family established their position as heads of production units, and vice versa. While this is certainly plausible, I think it requires further investigation. Lazonick's work in this area (see ch. 4, "Segments of the Labor Force: Women, Children, and Irish") is very valuable.

29. Perhaps 25 percent of female textile factory workers were married women (see Pinchbeck, *Women Workers,* p. 198; Margaret Hewitt, *Wives and Mothers in Victorian Industry* [London: Rockliff, 1958], pp. 14 ff.). It is also important to remember that factories were far from the dominant employer of women. Most women worked as domestic servants.

30. Neil Smelser, *Social Change and the Industrial Revolution*

(Chicago: University of Chicago Press, 1959), chs. 9–11. Other researchers have also established that in some cases there was a considerable degree of familial control over some aspects of the work process. See Tamara Hareven's research on mills in New Hampshire, "Family Time and Industrial Time: The Interaction between Family and Work in a Planned Corporation Town, 1900–1924," *Journal of Urban History* 1, no. 3 (May 1975): 365–89. Michael Anderson, *Family Structure in Nineteenth Century Lancashire* (Cambridge: Cambridge University Press, 1971), argues, based on demographic data, that the "practice of allowing operatives to employ assistants, though widespread, can at no period have resulted in a predominantly parent-child pattern of employment" (p. 116). Also see Amy Hirsch's treatment of this question in "Capitalism and the Working Class Family in British Textile Industries during the Industrial Revolution," mimeographed (New York: New School for Social Research, 1975).

31. "[The factory operatives'] agitation in the 1820's and 1830's was one avenue taken to protect the traditional relationship between adult and child, to perpetuate the structure of wages, to limit the recruitment of labourers into industry, and to maintain the father's economic authority" (Smelser, *Social Change*, p. 265). Lazonick ("Marxian Theory") argues that the workers main interests were not in maintaining their familial dominance in industry but in maintaining their family life outside industry. According to Smelser, agitation before 1840 sought to establish equal length days for all workers, which would tend to maintain the family in the factory, whereas after 1840 male workers came to accept the notion that married women and children should stay at home.

32. The question of the motives of the various groups involved in passing the factory acts is indeed a thorny one. Women workers themselves may have favored the legislation as an improvement in their working conditions, but some undoubtedly needed the income longer hours enabled. Most women working in the mills were young, single women who perhaps benefited from the protection. Single women, though "liberated" by the mills from direct domination in their families (about which there was much discussion in the 1800s), were nevertheless kept in their place by the conditions facing them in the labor market. Because of their age and sex, job segregation and lower wages assured their inability to be completely self-sufficient. Ruling-class men, especially

those associated with the larger firms, may have had an interest in factory legislation in order to eliminate unfair competition. Working-class and ruling-class men may have cooperated to maintain men's dominant position in the labor market and in the family.

33. Mary Merryweather, *Factory Life*, cited in *Women in English Life from Medieval to Modern Times* 2:200. The original is recorded in *Hansard Parliamentary Debates*, 3d ser., House of Commons, 7 June 1842.
34. Friedrich Engels, *The Condition of the Working Class in England in 1844* (Stanford: Stanford University Press, 1968), p. 199.
35. Ibid., p. xv.
36. Friedrich Engels, *The Condition of the Working Class in England*, p. 251.
37. Smelser, *Social Change*, p. 301. Similarly, Pinchbeck quotes from a deputation of the West Riding Short-Time Committee which demands "the gradual withdrawal of all females from the factories" because "home, its cares, its employments, is woman's true sphere." Gladstone thought this a good suggestion, easily implemented by appropriate laws, e.g., "forbidding a female to work in a factory after her marriage and during the life-time of her husband" (*Women Workers*, p. 200, n. 3, from the *Manchester and Salford Advertiser* [8, 15 January 1842]).
38. Quoted in G. D. H. Cole and Raymond Postgate, *The Common People, 1746–1946*, 4th ed. (London: Methuen, 1949), p. 432.
39. Pinchbeck, *Women Workers*, pp. 312–13. The history of the emergence of capitalism and the Industrial Revolution clearly shows that the "family wage" is a recent phenomenon. Before the late 1800s, it was expected that working-class (and earlier, middle- and upper-class) married women would support themselves. Andrew Ure, a manufacturer, wrote in 1835: "Factory females have also in general much lower wages than males, and they have been pitied on this account with perhaps an injudicious sympathy, since the low price of their labour here tends to make household duties their most profitable as well as agreeable occupation, and prevents them from being tempted by the mill to abandon the care of their offspring at home. Thus Providence effects its purposes with a wisdom and efficacy which should repress the short-sighted presumption of human devices" (*The Philosophy of Manufacturers* [London: C. Knight, 1835], p. 475). The development of the family wage is discussed in somewhat

greater detail in Heidi Hartmann, "Capitalism and Women's Work in the Home, 1900–1930" (Ph.D. diss., Yale University, 1974). More work needs to be done on this concept.

40. Sidney Webb, "The Alleged Differences in the Wages Paid to Men and Women for Similar Work," *Economic Journal* 1, no. 4 (December 1891): 639.

41. "The competition between men and women in industry is, indeed, not so much a direct underselling in wages as a struggle to secure the better paid kinds of work" (ibid., p. 658).

42. Millicent G. Fawcett, "Mr. Sidney Webb's Article on Women's Wages," *Economic Journal* 2, no. 1 (March 1892): 173–76.

43. In her review of *Women in the Printing Trades*, ed. J. Ramsay MacDonald (*Economic Journal* 14, no. 2 [June 1904]: 295–99), Fawcett wrote that a trade union in Scotland "decided that women must either be paid the same rates as men or got rid of altogether" (p. 296). She cites "the constant and vigilant opposition of Trades Unions to the employment and the technical training of women in the better paid and more skilled branches of trade" (p. 297). As one example, she cites the London Society of Journeymen Bookbinders who tried to get the highly skilled job of laying gold leaf—a woman's job—assigned to the male union members.

44. Eleanor F. Rathbone, "The Remuneration of Women's Services," *Economic Journal* 27, no. 1 (March 1917): 58.

45. Ibid., pp. 62, 63.

46. Ibid., p. 64.

47. Millicent G. Fawcett, "Equal Pay for Equal Work," *Economic Journal* 28, no. 1 (March 1918): 1–6.

48. "The pressure of male trade unions appears to be largely responsible for that crowding of women into comparatively few occupations, which is universally recognized as a main factor in the depression of their wages" (F. Y. Edgeworth, "Equal Pay to Men and Women for Equal Work," *Economic Journal* 32, no. 4 [December 1922]: 439).

49. While this reasoning may sound circular, I believe it is quite valid. As Marx said, wages are determined by the value of the socially necessary commodities required to maintain the worker, and what is necessary is the product of historical development, of customs of comfort, of trade union activity, etc. (*Capital* 1:171). Laura Oren has examined the literature on the level of living of working-class families and found that, indeed, within the family, women have less food, less leisure, and less pocket money ("The Welfare of

Women in Laboring Families: England, 1860–1950," *Feminist Studies* 1, nos. 3–4 [Winter–Spring 1973]: 107–25). That women, like immigrant groups, can reproduce themselves on less, and have for centuries, is a contributing factor in their lower wages.

50. Edgeworth's conclusions are typical of those of neoclassical economists. In furthering Fawcett's analysis he further abstracted from reality. Whereas Fawcett had realized that women were not less efficient than men, and Rathbone had argued similarly, Edgeworth clung to the notion that men deserved more and sought to justify it theoretically. He opposed family allowances, also with neoclassical reasoning, because they would raise taxes, discourage investment, encourage the reproduction of the poorer classes, and remove the incentive for men to work. Edgeworth reports the comment of a lady-inspector: "I almost agree with the social worker who said that if the husband got out of work the only thing that the wife should do is to sit down and cry, because if she did anything else he would remain out of work" ("Equal Pay," p. 153).

51. Edith Abbott, *Women in Industry* (New York: Arno Press, 1969); Elizabeth F. Baker, *Technology and Woman's Work* (New York: Columbia University Press, 1964).

52. See Abbott, *Women in Industry*, esp. ch. 4.

53. Ibid., ch. 2.

54. These antagonisms were often increased by employers. During a cigarmakers strike in New York City in 1877, employers brought in unskilled native American girls. By printing on the boxes, "These cigars were made by American girls," they sold many more boxes of the imperfect cigars than they had expected to (ibid., p. 207).

55. This summary is based on Abbott and is substantiated by both Baker and Helen L. Sumner, *History of Women in Industry in the United States*, 1910, United States Bureau of Labor, *Report on Condition of Women and Child Wage-Earners in the United States* (Washington, D.C.: Government Printing Office, 1911), vol. 9.

56. Baker and Abbott rely heavily on technological factors coupled with biological sex differences as explanations of shifts in the sex composition of jobs. Increased speed of machines and sometimes increased heaviness are cited as favoring men, who are stronger and have longer endurance, etc. Yet often each cites statistics which indicate that the same types of machines are used by both sexes, e.g., mule spinning machines. I would argue that these

perceived differences are merely rationalizations used to justify the current sex assignment of tasks. Social pressures were powerful mechanisms of enforcement. Abbott gives several examples of this. A woman had apparently learned the mule in Lawrence and went to Waltham when mules were introduced there. She had to leave, however, because according to a male operative: "The men made unpleasant remarks and it was too hard for her, being the only woman" (*Women in Industry*, p. 92). And: "Some of the oldest employees in the New England mills to-day [1910] say they can remember when weaving was so universally considered women's work that a 'man weaver' was held up to public ridicule for holding a 'woman's job'" (ibid., p. 95).

57. See Harry Braverman, *Labor and Monopoly Capital* (New York: Monthly Review Press, 1974), esp. chs. 3–5.

58. Elyce J. Rotella, "Occupational Segregation and the Supply of Women to the American Clerical Labor Force, 1870–1930" (paper presented at the Berkshire Conference on the History of Women, Radcliffe College, 25–27 October 1974). Despite the long-standing recognition of job segregation and shifts in sex composition, there are surprisingly few studies of the process of shifting. In addition to Rotella for clerical workers there is Margery Davies, "Woman's Place Is at the Typewriter," *Radical America* 8, no. 4 (July–August 1974): 1–28 and in this volume. Valerie K. Oppenheimer discusses the shift in elementary teaching in *The Female Labor Force in the United States* (Berkeley: Institute of International Studies, University of California, 1970). Abbott and Baker also discuss several shifts.

59. This account is based primarily on Abbott, *Women in Industry*, ch. 9, and Baker, *Technology*, pp. 31–36.

60. According to Abbott, Samuel Gompers claimed the Bohemian women were brought in for the express purpose of strikebreaking (*Women in Industry*, p. 197n.).

61. Bohemian women came to America first, leaving their husbands behind to work on the fields. Their husbands, who were unskilled at the cigar trade, came over later (ibid., p. 199).

62. In 1877 a Cincinnati local struck to exclude women and was apparently successful. The *Cincinnati Inquirer* said: "The men say the women are killing the industry. It would seem that they hope to retaliate by killing the women" (ibid., p. 207).

63. Baker, *Technology*, p. 34.

64. John B. Andrews and W. D. P. Bliss, *History of Women in Trade*

Unions in *Report on Condition of Woman . . .,* vol. 10. Although the proportion of women in cigar making did increase eventually, in many other manufacturing industries the proportion of women decreased over time. Textiles and clothing are the outstanding examples (see Abbott, *Women in Industry,* p. 320, and her "The History of Industrial Employment of Women in the United States," *Journal of Political Economy* 14 [October 1906]: 461–501). Sumner, cited in U.S. Bureau of Labor Statistics, Bulletin 175, concluded that men had taken over the skilled jobs in women's traditional fields, and women had to take unskilled work wherever they could find it (p. 28).

65. This account is based primarily on Abbott and Baker. The hostility to training women seems generalizable. The International Molders Union resolved: "Any member, honorary or active, who devotes his time in whole or in part to the instruction of female help in the foundry, or in any branch of the trade shall be expelled from the Union" (Gail Falk, "Women and Unions: A Historical View," mimeographed [New Haven, Conn.: Yale Law School, 1970]. Published in somewhat shortened form in *Women's Rights Law Reporter* 1 [Spring 1973]: 54–65).

66. Abbott, *Women in Industry,* pp. 252–53.

67. Baker, *Technology,* pp. 39–40.

68. See Falk, "Women and Unions."

69. Eleanor Flexner, *Century of Struggle* (New York: Atheneum Publishers, 1970), p. 136.

70. Abbott, *Women in Industry,* p. 260.

71. Baker observed that the testimony on the Equal Pay Act in 1963 was about evenly divided between those emphasizing women's needs and those emphasizing the protection of men (*Technology,* p. 419).

72. Falk noted in "Women and Unions" that unions used constitutional exclusion, exclusion from apprenticeship, limitation of women to helper categories or nonladder apprenticeships, limitation of proportion of union members who could be women, i.e., quotas, and excessively high fees. Moreover, the craft unions of this period, pre-1930, had a general hostility toward organizing the unskilled, even those attached to their crafts.

73. Such a diverse group as Caroll Wright, first U.S. Labor Commissioner (Baker, *Technology,* p. 84), Samuel Gompers and Mother Mary Jones, traditional and radical labor organizers, respectively (Falk, "Women and Unions"), James L. Davis, U.S. Secretary of

Labor, 1922 (Baker, p. 400), Florence Kelley, head of the National Consumers League (Hill), all held views which were variations of this theme. (Ann C. Hill, "Protective Labor Legislation for Women: Its Origin and Effect," mimeographed [New Haven: Yale Law School, 1970], parts of which have been published in Barbara A. Babcock, Ann F. Freedman, Eleanor H. Norton, and Susan C. Ross, *Sex Discrimination and the Law: Causes and Remedies* [Boston: Little, Brown, 1975], a law text which provides an excellent analysis of protective legislation, discrimination against women, etc.)

74. William O'Neill characterized those women who participated in various reform movements in the late nineteenth and early twentieth centuries "social feminists" to distinguish them from earlier feminists like Stanton and Anthony. The social feminists came to support women's rights because they thought it would help advance the cause of their reforms; they were not primarily interested in advancing the cause of women's rights (*Everyone Was Brave* [Chicago: Quadrangle Books, 1969], esp. ch. 3). William H. Chafe, *The American Woman* (New York: Oxford University Press, 1972), also provides an excellent discussion of the debate around protective laws.

75. What was achievable, from the legislatures and the courts, was what the social feminists aimed for. Because in *Ritchie v. People* (155 Ill. 98 [1895]), the court had held that sex alone was not a valid basis for a legislature to abridge the right of an adult to contract for work and, thus, struck down a maximum-hours law for women, and because a maximum-hours law for baking employees had been struck down by the U.S. Supreme Court (Lockner), advocates of protective labor legislation believed their task would be difficult. The famous "Brandeis Brief" compiled hundreds of pages on the harmful effects of long hours of work and argued that women needed "especial protection" (see Babcock et al., *Sex Discrimination*).

76. Ibid., p. 32.

77. In 1914 the AFL voted to abandon the legislative road to reform. See Hill, "Protective Labor Legislation."

78. Some states excluded women entirely from certain occupations: mining, meter reading, taxicab driving, core making, streetcar conducting, elevator operating, etc. (ibid.).

79. These conclusions are based on Hill, ibid., and are also supported by Baker, *Technology*.

80. At the same time that women were being excluded from certain skilled jobs in the labor force and otherwise protected, the home duties of women were emphasized in popular literature, through the home economics movement, in colleges and high schools, etc. A movement toward the stabilization of the nuclear family with one breadwinner, the male, is discernible. See Hartmann, "Capitalism and Women's Work."

81. Edwards, Gordon, and Reich, *Labor Market Segmentation,* use labor-market segmentation to refer to a process in which the labor market becomes divided into different submarkets, each with its own characteristic behaviors: these segments can be different layers of a hierarchy or different groups within one layer.

82. Michael Reich's thesis, "Racial Discrimination and the White Income Distribution" (Ph.D. diss., Harvard University, 1973), sets forth this divide-and-rule model more thoroughly. In the labor-market-segmentation model there is another tendency toward segmentation in addition to the divide-and-rule mechanism. It arises out of the uneven development of advanced capitalism, i.e., the process of creation of a core and a peripheral economy. In fact, in the Edwards, Gordon, and Reich view, labor-market segmentation only comes to the fore under monopoly capitalism, as large corporations seek to extend control over their labor markets.

83. Thomas Vietorisz, "From Class to Hierarchy: Some Non-Price Aspects on the Transformation Problem" (paper presented at the Conference on Urban Political Economy, New School for Social Research, New York, 15–16 February 1975).

84. The strong divisions of the labor market by sex and race that existed even in the competitive phase of capitalism call into question the dominance of labor homogenization during that phase—as presented by Edwards, Gordon, and Reich.

85. Capitalists are not always able to use patriarchy to their advantage. Men's ability to retain as much of women's labor in the home as they have may hamper capitalist development during expansive phases. Men's resistance to female workers whom capitalists want to utilize also undoubtedly slows down capitalist advance.

86. Engels, Marx, and Lenin all recognized the *material* rewards the labor aristocracy reaps. It is important not to reduce these to *subjective* benefits, for then the problems arising out of intraclass divisions will be minimized. Castles and Kosack appear to make this error (see their "The Function of Labour Immigration in Western European Capitalism," *New Left Review,* no. 73 [May–June 1972]: 3–12, where references to Marx et al. can be found).

87. David Gordon suggested to me this "cyclical model" of the relative strengths of employer and workers.

88. Most Marxist-feminist attempts to deal with the problems in Marxist analysis raised by the social position of women seem to ignore these basic conflicts between the sexes, apparently in the interest of stressing the underlying class solidarity that should obtain among women and men workers. Bridges and Hartmann's draft paper (n.1) reviews this literature.

89. In our society, women's jobs are synonymous with low-status, low-paying jobs: "we may replace the familiar statement that women earn less because they are in low paying occupations with the statement that women earn less because they are in *women's jobs*. . . . As long as the labor market is divided on the basis of sex, it is likely that the tasks allocated to women will be ranked as less prestigious or important, reflecting women's lower social status in the society at large" (Francine Blau [Weisskoff], "Women's Place in the Labor Market," *American Economic Review* 62, no. 4 [May 1972]: 161).

90. Theodore Caplow, *The Sociology of Work* (New York: McGraw-Hill, 1964), pp. 237 ff., discusses several behavioral rules and their impact. Harold Willensky, "Women's Work: Economic Growth, Ideology, Structure," *Industrial Relations* 7, no. 3 (May 1968): 235–48, also discusses the implication for labor-market phenomena of several behavioral rules.

91. "The use of tabooed words, the fostering of sports and other interests which women do not share, and participation in activities which women are intended to disapprove of—hard drinking, gambling, practical jokes, and sexual essays of various kinds—all suggest that the adult male group is to a large extent engaged in a reaction *against* feminine influence, and therefore cannot tolerate the presence of women without changing its character entirely" (Caplow, *Sociology of Work*, p. 239). Of course, the lines of division between masculine and feminine are constantly shifting. At various times in the nineteenth century, teaching, selling in retail stores, and office work were each thought to be totally unsuitable for women. This variability of the boundaries between men's jobs and women's jobs is one reason why an effort to locate basic behavioral principles would seem to make sense—though, ultimately, of course, these rules are shaped by the division of labor itself.

92. Caplow based his rules on the Freudian view that men identify freedom from female dominance with maturity, i.e., they seek to escape their mothers.
93. See Rubin (n. 1) and Juliet Mitchell, *Feminism and Psychoanalysis* (New York: Pantheon, 1974), who seek to recreate Freud from a feminist perspective. So does Shulamith Firestone, *The Dialectic of Sex* (New York: Bantam, 1971).
94. For example, the current domestic division of labor in which women nurture children profoundly affects (differentially) the personality structures of girls and boys. For a non-Freudian interpretation of this phenomenon, see Chodorow (n. 12).

WOMAN'S PLACE IS AT THE TYPEWRITER: THE FEMINIZATION OF THE CLERICAL LABOR FORCE

Margery Davies

A large proportion of the recent historical research about women in the labor force has focused on industrial workers, using their specific factory experiences as a model for viewing the class as a whole. On the other hand, relatively little attention has been given to clerical workers. This is surprising: in 1968 for example, over 40 percent of women in the U.S. labor force were employed as clerical and sales workers, while only 16.5 percent were employed in the industrial work force.[1] This essay is a contribution to a discussion aimed first at clarifying the role of a "secretarial proletariat," and second at broadening the definition of the working class to include other than those in industrial production. In particular, there are millions of low-level clerical workers, most of them women, who form an important segment of the working class.

The essay is historical in scope and focuses on the feminization of the clerical labor force. Women now form the majority of the clerical work force, but this was not always the case. How did women enter and come to dominate clerical work? How did the ideology with respect to women office workers change? What are the connections between a sexual segmentation of the clerical labor force and hierarchical relations in the office? The first step in answering these questions is to look at the nineteenth-century office.[2]

Two of the basic characteristics of nineteenth-century offices in the United States are that they were small and staffed almost

This article was originally published in *Radical America* 8, no. 4 (July–August 1974).

exclusively by men.³ Census data for 1870, for example, show that out of 76,639 office workers in the United States, women numbered only 1,869; men were 97.5 percent of the clerical labor force.⁴ With the exception of a few banks, insurance companies, and governmental branches, most offices in the United States prior to the Civil War usually contained about two or three clerks. This is not surprising, since most capitalist firms were also relatively small until the last decades of the nineteenth century. For example, in "Bartleby" Herman Melville described a Wall Street lawyer's office of the 1850s which consisted of the lawyer, three copyists, and an errand boy.⁵

The small size of offices at this time meant that the relationship between employer and employee tended to be very personalized. The clerks worked under the direct supervision, and often the direct eyesight, of their employers. Although the tasks of a clerk were generally well defined—the job of the copyists in "Bartleby" was to transcribe legal documents—they were often asked to do numerous other tasks. It was clearly the employer who set the limits of the clerk's job—there was no question of the clerk being ruled by the inexorable pace of a machine.

The personal benevolence of an employer could go a long way toward making the hierarchical relations within an office more tolerable. An employer who spoke nicely to his clerks, let them leave early if they were feeling sick, or gave them a Christmas goose helped to create working conditions against which the clerks were not likely to rebel. By treating his clerks with kindness or politeness, a paternalistic employer was also likely to be able to get them to work harder.

This personalization of the work relationship in the nineteenth-century office lies at the root of the phenomenon of employees being "devoted to the firm." A clerk who spent forty or fifty years working for the same small office of an insurance company did not necessarily work so long and so hard out of a belief in the importance of promoting that particular company's kind of insurance. The source of his devotion was much more likely the network of personal relations he had built up in the office over the years. It was probably more important to the employee to "produce" a good working relationship with his boss, with whom he was in constant contact, than to produce, for example, improvements in the insurance company's filing system. Needless to say, that good working relationship no doubt depended in part on the employee producing improvements in the filing system. But whether the employee cared more about the selling of insurance or his personal relationship with his employer, the end result tended to be the same: the clerk became a "devoted employee of the firm" who was not likely to rebel or go out on strike.

Not all clerks in the nineteenth-century office spent all their working days in clerical positions. A clerkship also served as an apprenticeship for a young man who was "learning the business" before he moved on to a managerial position. These were often nephews, sons, or grandsons of the firms's managers and owners. Most clerks, however, ended up with gold watches, instead of managerial posts, in return for their years of devoted service. Thus, the clerks in an office at any particular time came from different class backgrounds and were likely to have very different occupational futures.

Political-Economic Changes

In the last few decades of the nineteenth century, American corporations underwent a period of rapid growth and consolidation. These changes, which marked the rise of modern industrial capitalism, had been signalled by development in banks, insurance companies, and public utilities; they had spread to manufacturing enterprises by the turn of the century.[6] As business operations became more complex, there was a large increase in correspondence, record-keeping, and office work in general. This expansion created a demand for an expanded clerical labor force. In 1880 there were 504,454 office workers who constituted 3 percent of the labor force; by 1890 there were 750,150 office workers.[7] The number of office workers has been increasing ever since. (See Table 2) In order to fill the need for clerical workers, employers turned to the large pool of educated female labor.

As early as the 1820s women had been receiving public high school educations. Worcester, Massachusetts opened a public high school for girls in 1824; Boston and New York City did so in 1826.[8] In 1880, 13,029 women graduated from high school in the United States, as compared to only 10,605 men. The figures for 1900 show an even greater disparity: 56,808 female high school graduates and 38,075 male.[9]

Until the end of the nineteenth century, schools were the main place of employment for these educated women. The feminization of elementary and secondary teaching had taken place with the introduction of compulsory public education and consequent increase in teaching jobs. In 1840 men were 60 percent of all teachers and in 1860 they made up only 14 percent.[10] Women were hired in education because they were a cheap replacement for the dwindling supply of male teachers. "As Charles William Eliot observed some years after the feminization of primary school teaching was largely completed: 'It is true that sentimental reasons are often given for the almost exclusive employment of women in the common schools; but the effective reason is economy. . . . If women had not been cheaper than men, they would not have replaced nine tenths of the men in American public schools.' "[11]

But teaching was about the only job that drew on the pool of educated female labor in substantial numbers. The "professions"—law, medicine, business, college teaching—both excluded women and did not employ large numbers of people. The 1890 census, for instance, counted only 200 women lawyers.[12] Social work was still the preserve of moral reformers like Jane Addams; the growth of social work as an occupation with government funding did not come until the twentieth century. Nursing was beginning to employ some women by the end of the nineteenth century: in 1900 there were 108,691 nurses and midwives, although only 11,000 of them had become graduate nurses and achieved professional status.[13]

In the last decades of the nineteenth century, the situation was, then, the following. There were more women than men graduating from high school every year. These women constituted a pool of educated female labor which was being drawn upon only by elementary and secondary schools. Consequently, there were literally thousands of women with training that qualified them for jobs that demanded literacy, but who could not find such jobs. Excluded from most of the professions, these women were readily available for the clerical jobs that started to proliferate at the end of the nineteenth century. The expansion and consolidation of enterprises in the 1880s and 1890s created a large demand for clerical labor; the large pool of educated female labor constituted the supply.

Women Enter the Office

Prior to the Civil War there were no women employed in substantial numbers in any offices, although there were a few women scattered here and there who worked as bookkeepers or as copyists in lawyers' offices.[14] During the Civil War, however, the reduction of the male labor force due to the draft moved General Francis Elias Spinner, the U.S. treasurer, to introduce female clerical workers into government offices. At first women were given the job of trimming paper money in the Treasury Department, but they gradually moved into other areas of clerical work. The experiment proved successful and was continued after the war. Commenting upon this innovation in 1869, Spinner declared "upon his word" that it had been a complete success: "Some of the females [are] doing more and better work for $900 per annum than many male clerks who were paid double that amount."[15] At the time, men clerks were being paid from $1200 to $1800 per year.[16]

Despite this start, it was not until the 1880s that they began to pour into the clerical work force. In 1880, the proportion of women in the clerical labor force was 4 percent; in 1890 it had jumped to 21 percent. By 1920, women made up half of the clerical workers: 50 percent of all low-level office workers (including stenographers, typists, secretaries, shipping and receiving clerks, office machine operators, and clerical and kindred workers not elsewhere classified) were women. In 1960, 72 percent of them were (see Table 2). This tremendous increase in the number of women office workers has changed the composition of the female labor force. In 1870, less than 0.05 percent of the women in the labor force were office workers; by 1890 1.1 percent were. In 1960, 29.1 percent of all women in the labor force were office workers.

The Treasury's precedent facilitated the entrance of women into the clerical labor force; the prejudices against women working in offices had already started to deteriorate by 1880. A second factor that eased women into the office was the invention of the typewriter. By the 1890s the typewriter had gained widespread acceptance as a practical office machine.[17]

Various American inventors had been working on "writing machines" since the 1830s. They had generally been thought of as crackpots by capitalists and the general public alike. But by the early 1870s, an inventor named Christopher Latham Sholes had managed to produce a fairly workable machine. The Remington family, which had manufactured guns, sewing machines, and farm machinery, bought the rights to start making typewriters. They did not sell well at first. People bought them out of curiosity for their own private use, but it was not until the last two decades of the nineteenth century that businesses began to buy the machines in large quantities.

It seems fairly clear that it was not until businesses began to expand very rapidly that employers saw the usefulness of a mechanical writing machine. Changes in the structure of capitalist enterprises brought about changes in technology: no one was interested in making the typewriter a workable or manufacturable machine until its utility became clear. But the typewriter also gave rise to changes in office procedure. Writing was faster; the increase in correspondence and record-keeping was caused in part by the existence of the machine. For example, Robert Lincoln O'Brien made the following comment in the *Atlantic Monthly* in 1904:

> The invention of the typewriter has given a tremendous impetus to the dictating habit. . . . This means not only greater diffuseness, inevitable with any lessening of the tax on words which the labor of writing imposes, but it also brings forward the point of view of the one who speaks.[18]

The typewriter also facilitated the entrance of women into the clerical labor force. Typing was "sex-neutral" because it was a new occupation. Since it had not been identified as a masculine job, women who were employed as typists did not encounter the criticism that they were taking over "men's work." In fact, typing soon became "women's work"; in 1890, 63.8 percent of the 33,418 clerical workers classified as stenographers and typists were women; by 1900, that proportion had risen to 76.7 percent. The feminization of low-level clerical work proceeded extremely rapidly.

It is important to determine why women wanted to become office workers. Most women at the end of the nineteenth century probably worked out of economic necessity. This holds true for the unmarried single woman of middle-income origins as well as for the immigrant working-class woman, single or married, who worked to keep her family from starving.

Clerical work attracted women because it paid better than did most other jobs women could get. In northeastern American cities clerical wages were relatively high: domestic servants were paid $2 to $5 a week, factory operatives, $1.50 to $8, and department store salesgirls, $1.50 to $8, whereas typists and stenographers could get $6 to $15.[19]

Clerical work also enjoyed a relatively high status. A woman from a middle-income home with a high school education was much more likely to look for clerical work than for work as a house servant or as a factory girl making paper boxes, pickles, or shoes. Clerical positions were coveted by working-class women who usually could find work only in sweatshops, factories, or department stores.

Despite the fact that women were pouring into offices at the end of the nineteenth century, they still met with disapproval. An engraving of 1875 shows a shocked male government official opening the door on an office that has been "taken over by the ladies."[20] The women are preening themselves before a mirror, fixing each other's hair, reading *Harper's Bazaar*, spilling ink on the floor—in short, doing everything but working. The engraving makes women working in an office seem ludicrous: women are seen as frivolous creatures incapable of doing an honest day's work.

Table 1

Stenographers and Typists by Sex, 1870–1930

	Total	Male	Female	% Female
1870	154	147	7	4.5%
1880	5,000	3,000	2,000	40.0%
1890	33,400	12,100	21,300	63.8%
1900	112,600	26,200	86,400	76.7%
1910	326,700	53,400	263,300	80.6%
1920	615,100	50,400	564,700	91.8%
1930	811.200	36.100	775.100	95.6%

Source: Alba M. Edwards, *Comparative Occupational Statistics for the United States, 1870–1940.* Published as part of Volume IV of the Report on Population of the 16th Census of the United States, Washington, D.C., 1943, Tables 9 and 10. Figures for 1880 on are to the nearest hundred.

Outright contempt was not the only negative reaction. Bliven cites the following passage from *The Typewriter Girl,* a novel by Olive Pratt Rayner whose heroine is an American typist fallen on hard financial times in London:

Three clerks (male), in seedy black coats, the eldest with hair the color of a fox's, went on chaffing one another for two minutes after I closed the door, with ostentatious unconsciousness of my insignificant presence. . . . The youngest, after a while, wheeled around on his high stool and broke out with the chivalry of his class and age, "Well, what's your business?"

My voice trembled a little, but I mustered up courage and spoke. "I have called about your advertisement. . . . "

He eyed me up and down. I am slender, and, I will venture to say, if not pretty, at least interesting looking.

"How many words a minute?" he asked after a long pause.

I stretched the truth as far as its elasticity would permit. "Ninety-seven," I answered. . . .

The eldest clerk, with the foxy head, wheeled around, and took his turn to stare. He had hairy hands and large goggle-eyes. . . . I detected an undercurrent of double meaning. . . . I felt disagreeably like Esther in the presence of Ahasuerus—a fat and oily Ahasuerus of fifty. . . . He perused me up and down with his small pig's eyes, as if he were buying a horse, scrutinizing my face, my figure, my hands, my feet. I felt like a Circassian in an Arab slavemarket. . . . [21]

The overtones of sexuality are hard to miss. The implication seems to be that a decent girl is risking her morality if she tries to invade the male preserve of the office. Whether or not such sensationalism was backed up by many instances of seduction or corruption, the message seems clear: the office was a dangerous place for a woman of virtue.

Even in 1900, some people counseled women to leave the office and return to their homes, where they rightfully belonged. The editor of the *Ladies' Home Journal*, Edward Bok, gave just such advice in the pages of his magazine in 1900:

> A business house cannot prosper unless each position has in it the most competent incumbent which it is possible to obtain for that particular position. And, although the statement may seem a hard one, and will unquestionably be controverted, it nevertheless is a plain, simple fact that women have shown themselves naturally incompetent to fill a great many of the business positions which they have sought to occupy. . . . The fact is that not one woman in a hundred can stand the physical strain of the keen pace which competition has forced upon every line of business today.[22]

The Shift in Ideology

Sixteen years after Bok used the pages of the *Ladies' Home Journal* to admonish women to return home, another writer in the same magazine not only took for granted the fact that women worked in offices but also found that certain "feminine" qualities were particularly suited to clerical work. "The stenographer plus" was described by Harry C. Spillman:

> I should describe the equipment of the ideal stenographer as follows: Twenty percent represents technical ability—that is, the ability to write and read shorthand and to typewrite rapidly and accurately; thirty percent equals general information—that is, education other than that in shorthand and typewriting; and the last and most important fifty percent I should ascribe to personality. . . .
>
> There are two kinds of personality—concrete and abstract: the one you can see, the other you can feel. The concrete side is that which the stenographer sees when she looks in the mirror. The stenographer who wins must look good—not in the sense that she

must be beautiful, for dividends are never declared on pink cheeks and classic features; but she should make the very most of her personal equipment. . . .

That other kind of personality—the abstract kind—is the more important element in the stenographer's equipment, for it involves her temperament. Thousands of stenographers stay in mediocre positions because they lack the ability to adapt their conduct to those fixed principles of harmony and optimism which must prevail in all big undertakings.[23]

Fortune magazine, in a series of unsigned articles on "Women in Business," carried the argument a step further and equated secretaries with wives:

The whole point of the whole problem, in other words, is that women occupy the office because the male employer wants them there. Why he wants them there is another question which cannot be answered merely by saying that once there they take to the work very nicely. It is doubtless true that women take to the work nicely. Their conscious or subconscious intention some day to marry, and their conscious or subconscious willingness to be directed by men, render them amenable and obedient and relieve them of the ambition which makes it difficult for men to put their devotion into secretarial work. But that fact only partially explains the male employer's preference. It indicates that women and by virtue of some of their most womanly traits are capable of making the offices a more pleasant, peaceful, and homelike place. But it does not indicate why the employer desires that kind of office rather than an office full of ambitious and pushing young men intent upon hammering their typewriters into presidential desks. To get at that problem pure speculation is the only tool.

One might well speculate somewhat as follows: the effect of the industrial revolution was the dedomestication of women. . . . In the process the upper-class home, as the upper-class home was known to the Victorians, disappeared. The male was no longer master in his own dining room and dreadful in his own den nor did a small herd of wives, daughters, and sisters hear his voice and tremble. He was, on the contrary, the more or less equal mate of a more or less unpredictable woman. And he resented it.

He resented the loss of his position. He regretted the old docility, the old obedience, the old devotion to his personal interests. And finding himself unable to re-create the late, lost paradise in his home he set about re-creating it in his office. What he wanted in the office was not the office mistress described at least fifty-two times a year by American short-story writers. His very pretty and very clever and very expensive wife was already mistress enough and to spare. What he wanted in the office was something as much like the vanished wife of his father's generation as could be arranged—someone to balance his checkbook, buy his railroad tickets, check his baggage, get him seats in the fourth row, take his daughter to the dentist, listen to his side of the story, give him a courageous look when things were blackest, and generally know all, understand all. . . .

Whether or not any such speculative explanation of the male desire for a female office is sound there can be no doubt that the desire exists and that it is the male employer who is chiefly responsible for the female secretary.[24]

In 1900, the *Ladies' Home Journal* warned women that they could not stand the physical strain of working in a fast-paced business office. But by 1916 the *Journal* was comparing the faithful female secretary to some heavenly body who "radiated the office with sunshine and sympathetic interest." It had not taken very long for the ideology to shift and for people to accept the presence of women in offices. Bok had argued in 1900 that women, by virtue of their "nature," were unsuited to the office. But only a few years later, the *Journal* came close to arguing that the "natural" temperament of women made them good stenographers. And by 1935, *Fortune* had concocted a full-fledged historical justification for the assertion that "woman's place was at the typewriter."

Women, so the argument went, are by nature adaptable, courteous, and sympathetic—in a word, passive. This natural passivity makes them ideally suited to the job of carrying out an endless number of routine tasks without a complaint. Furthermore, their docility makes it unlikely that they will aspire to rise very far above their station. Thus their male boss is spared the unpleasant possibility that his secretary will one day be competing with him for his job.

The image of the secretary as the competent mother-wife who sees to her employer's every need and desire was a description which most fitted a personal secretary. Here certain "feminine" characteristics ascribed to the job of personal secretary— sympathy, adaptability, courtesy—made women seem the natural candidates for the job. Not all clerical workers were personal secretaries. For the large proportion of clerical workers who were stenographers, typists, file clerks, and the like, another ideological strain developed, emphasizing the supposed greater dexterity of women. These workers were seldom assigned to one particular boss, but instead constituted a pool from which any executive could draw as he wished. In the case of these low-level clerical workers, personal characteristics such as sympathy and courtesy seemed less important. Dexterity—the ability to do work quickly and accurately—was much more important. Not long after the typewriter began to be used as a matter of course in business offices, people started to argue that women, endowed with dextrous fingers, were the most fitting operators of these machines. Elizabeth Baker states that "women seemed to be especially suited as typists and switchboard operators because they were tolerant of routine, careful, and manually dextrous."[25]

Women's Place in the Office Hierarchy

Whether it was for the warmth of their personalities or the dexterity of their fingers, women came to be viewed as "natural" office workers. Why did this ideology develop?

The ideology is obviously connected to the feminization of the clerical labor force. If women were employed in large numbers in offices, then it was not surprising that an ideology justifying their presence there developed. Women were originally employed in offices because they were cheaper than the available male labor force. As corporations expanded at the end of the nineteenth century, they were forced to draw on the pool of educated females to meet their rapidly increasing demand for clerical workers. But the expansion of capitalist firms did not entail a simple proliferation of small, "nineteenth-century" offices. Instead, it meant a greatly expanded office structure,

Table 2
Feminization of the Clerical Labor Force

		Bookkeepers, accountants, and cashiers	Messengers, errand and office boys and girls[1]	Stenographers, typists, and secretaries	Shipping and receiving clerks	Clerical and kindred workers[3]	Office machine operators
1870	total	39,164[4]	7,820[6]			29,655[7]	
	female	893[5]	46			930[8]	
	% female	2%	.6%			3%	
1880	total	75,688[9]	12,447			64,151[10]	
	female	4,295[9]	228			2,315[10]	
	% female	6%	2%			4%	
1890	total	160,968	45,706			219,173[7]	
	female	28,050	1,658			45,553[7]	
	% female	17%	4%			21%	
1900[2]	total	257,400	63,700			357,100	
	female	74,900	3,800			104,400	
	% female	29%	6%			29%	
1910	total	491,600	95,100			1,034,200	
	female	189,000	6,400			386,800	
	% female	38%	7%			37%	
1920	total	742,000	99,500			2,092,000	
	female	362,700	8,100			1,038,400	
	% female	49%	8%			50%	

1930	total	940.000	79.500	2.754.000			36.200
	female	487.500	5.100	1.450.900			32.100
	% female	52%	6%	53%			89%
1940	total	931.300	60.700	1.174.900	229.700	1.973.600	64.200
	female	475.700	3.000	1.096.400	9.100	702.500	55.100
	% female	51%	5%	93%	4%	36%	86%
1950	total	—	59.000	1.629.300	297.400	2.354.200	146.200
	female	—	10.600	1.538.000	20.700	1.252.900	120.300
	% female	—	18%	94%	7%	53%	82%
1960	total	—	63.200	2.312.800	294.600	3.016.400	318.100
	female	—	11.200	2.232.600	25.000	1.788.700	236.400
	% female	—	18%	96%	8%	59%	74%

1. Messengers, errand and office boys and girls includes "telegraph messengers" through 1900.
2. Figures from 1900 on are rounded off to the nearest hundred.
3. Not elsewhere classified.
4. Census figures estimated and 374 added because of undercount in 13 southern states.
5. Census figures estimated and 2 added because of undercount in 13 southern states.
6. 70 added because of undercount in 13 southern states.
7. Partly estimated and 494 added because of undercount in 13 southern states. Figures do not include "Abstractors, notaries, and justices of peace," classified in 1940 in the group "clerical workers."
8. Partly estimated and 6 added because of undercount in 13 southern states. Figures do not include "Abstractors, notaries, and justices of peace," classified in 1940 in the group "clerical workers."
9. Estimated.
10. 1890 and 1900 data partly estimated and 1880 data entirely estimated. Figures do not include "Abstractors, notaries, and justices of peace," classified in 1940 in the group "clerical workers."

Sources: For 1870–1940: Janet M. Hooks. Women's Occupations through Seven Decades, U.S. Department of Labor, Women's Bureau, Bulletin #218 (Washington, D.C.: GPO. 1947), Table IIA: Occupations of Women Workers, 1870–1940; Table IIB: Occupations of All Workers, 1870–1940.
For 1950–1960: Bureau of the Census, Census of Population, United States Summary (Washington, D.C.: GPO, 1960), Table 201: Detailed Occupation of the Experienced Civilian Labor Force, by Sex, for the United States: 1960 and 1950.

with large numbers of people working in a single office. No longer were some of the clerks, in effect, apprenticing managers. The expanded structure, on the contrary, brought with it a rapid growth of low-level, deadend jobs.

By 1920 over 90 percent of the typists and stenographers in the United States (see Table 1) were women—whose "natural" docility and dexterity made them the ideal workers for these jobs. By harping upon the docility of the female character, writers like Spillman in the *Ladies' Home Journal* provided a convenient rationalization for women's position on the bottom of the office hierarchy.

It is important to point out that differentiating office workers by sex is not the same as dividing them into groups distinguished, say, by eye color. The sexual division of labor in the office—where men hold the majority of managerial positions and women fill the majority of low-level, clerical jobs—is strengthened by the positions men and women hold outside the office.

When the ideology of passive female labor first manifested itself in the early twentieth century, the United States was, by and large, a patriarchal society. Patriarchal relations, in which men made decisions and women followed them, were carried over into the office. These patriarchal social relations meshed very conveniently with office bureaucracies, where the means by which workers were told what to do was often an extremely personalized one. For although the number of clerical workers was large, they were often divided into small groups of five or six typists, stenographers, or file clerks directly accountable to one supervisor. And since that supervisor was usually a man and those clerical workers women, it is easy to see how patriarchal patterns would reinforce the office hierarchy.

The segmentation of the office work force by sex thus promoted a situation where a docile mass of clerical workers would follow without rebellion the directives of a relatively small group of managers. The ideology that women were naturally suited to those jobs can be seen as an important buttress of the hierarchical office structure.

Notes

1. U. S. Department of Labor, Women's Bureau, 1969 Handbook of Women Workers, Women's Bureau Bulletin 294 (Washington: Government Printing Office, 1969), p. 90.

2. Concrete information about female office workers is not easy to find. In a comprehensive bibliographical Guide to Business History (1948), Henrietta Larson points out that "it is significant that the works dealing with the subject [office management] are concerned largely with 'systems' and machines—the office worker has been left in neglected obscurity" (pp. 771–72).

   There are a few analytical studies of office workers, the most notable of which are David Lockwood's The Blackcoated Worker and C. Wright Mills' White Collar: The American Middle Classes (New York: Oxford University Press, 1956). Grace D. Coyle focuses on women in offices and the kind of work they do in "Women in the Clerical Occupations," The Annals of the American Academy of Political and Social Science 143 (May 1929); Fortune published a series of articles on "Women in Business" in 1935; the Women's Bureau of the U. S. Department of Labor has issued a number of bulletins on office workers. In addition, there is quite a long list of books addressed to women which tell them how to be better secretaries: the main point of these manuals seems to be that women should be certain to please their (male) bosses and that they should be neat and accurate about any number of office tasks. And dotted throughout the prominent women's magazines are articles about the "business woman."

   Finally, there are some fictional works which provide a certain amount of insight into office work. "Bartleby" (1856) by Herman Melville is set in a Wall Street lawyer's office of the 1850s and describes the men who work there as copyists; Alice Adams (1921) by Booth Tarkington is about the daughter of a white-collar employee who is forced to give up her hopes of joining the upper-class social clique in town, accept her own middle-class status, and finally climb the "begrimed stairway" of the local business college in preparation for becoming a "working girl."

   But all in all there is very little information about the history of female clerical workers. However, there are bits and pieces of evidence, upon which this essay is based.

3. For the purposes of this discussion the term "nineteenth-century office" will be used to describe those office structures which

existed prior to the widespread monopolization and bureaucratization of capitalist corporations, a process which was well
underway in the United States by the end of the nineteenth century. "The modern office" will be used to describe the structures
which developed after that bureaucratization. The description of
the nineteenth-century office which follows is based primarily on
Lockwood's *The Blackcoated Worker* and on Mills' *White Collar.*
4. Janet M. Hooks, *Women's Occupations Through Seven Decades,*
Women's Bureau Bulletin 218 (Washington: Government Printing
Office, 1947), Tables IIA and IIB.
5. Herman Melville, "Bartleby," in *The Piazza Tales* (1856; Garden
City: Doubleday, 1961).
6. See Alfred Chandler, *Strategy and Structure* (Cambridge, Mass:
M.I.T. Press, 1962). See also Stephen Hymer, "The Multinational
Corporation and the Law of Uneven Development" in *Economics
and the World Order,* ed. Jagdish Bhagwati (New York: Macmillan Company, 1972).
7. Bureau of the Census, Department of Commerce and Labor, Special Report of the 12th Census, *Occupations at the 12th Census*
(Washington, D.C., 1904). Data is for "number of persons engaged
in specified occupations." "Office workers" includes bookkeepers
and accountants; clerks and copyists; and stenographers and
typewriters (typists).
8. Elizabeth Faulkner Baker, *Technology and Women's Work* (New
York: Columbia University Press, 1964), p. 57. Baker argues that
girls were given high school educations because the number of
women teachers was increasing: "Men were being attracted by
business opportunities and skilled trades, and the phenomenal
growth of public schools created an alarming shortage of teachers.
. . . But relief from the scarcity of male teachers of course required that girls as well as boys be taught" (p. 57). However, the
fact that so many girls got high school educations in the
nineteenth century still seems rather surprising; unfortunately,
recent analysts of the rise of mass education in the United States
do not remark upon it. See Michael Katz, *The Irony of Early
School Reform* (Cambridge, Mass.: Harvard University Press,
1968) or Samuel Bowles, "Unequal Education and the Reproduction of the Social Division of Labor," *Review of Radical Political
Economics* (Winter 1971). For more information about the history
of women's education, see also Thomas Woody, *A History of
Women's Education in the United States* (New York, 1929).

9. Data for high school graduates from Federal Security Agency, Office of Education, *Biennial Survey of Education.* Cited in the *Statistical Abstract of the United States* (1952), p. 121. One possible explanation for the fact that more women than men were graduating from high school is the following: in the case of working-class men and women, the boys left school to work. The money they could earn was badly needed by their families. But if girls entered the factory labor force, their wages would be considerably lower than those of their brothers. This fact, coupled with attitudes that men were the more important bread-winners and that woman's place was in the home, may have resulted in working-class girls staying in school longer than their brothers. At any rate, it is clear that figures on high school graduates must be broken down by class, and probably also by ethnic group, before the disparity between male and female high school graduates can be adequately explained.

10. Katz, *Irony of Early School Reform*, p. 58.

11. Ibid., p. 58.

12. Robert W. Smuts, *Women and Work in America* (New York: Columbia University Press, 1959).

13. Baker, *Technology and Women's Work*, pp. 62–63.

14. Helen L. Sumner, *History of Women in Industry in the United States* (61st Congress, 2nd session, U.S. Senate Document 645; Bureau of Labor, 1911), p. 239.

15. "Women in Business: I," *Fortune* 12 (July 1935): 53.

16. Ibid., p. 53.

17. The following account of the development of the typewriter is based on Bruce Bliven, Jr., *The Wonderful Writing Machine* (New York: Random House, 1954).

18. Ibid., p. 134.

19. Smuts, *Women and Work*, p.90. It is very difficult to find statistics about clerical wages at the end of the nineteenth century broken down by sex; Bliven and Smuts do not cite sources for their wage statistics.

20. The engraving is reproduced in Bliven, *Wonderful Writing Machine*, p. 73.

21. Bliven, *Wonderful Writing Machine*, pp. 75–76. Bliven gives no date for *The Typewriter Girl*, but the context of his argument leads to the conclusion that the novel was a late nineteenth-century potboiler.

22. Edward Bok, "The Return of the Business Woman," *Ladies' Home*

Journal (March 1900): 16. I am indebted to Elaine Wethington of the University of Michigan at Ann Arbor and her unpublished manuscript, "The Women's Magazines and the 'Business Woman,' 1890–1919" for this reference. Wethington notes that Bok did not shrink from also pointing out that office work was the "best paid and most respectable employment for young women"; he was quite happy to have his magazine reflect opposing opinions in order not to alienate any of its one million subscribers. Wethington's paper is extremely useful as a source for articles about office workers in the prominent American women's magazines.

23. Harry C. Spillman, "The Stenographer Plus," *Ladies' Home Journal* (February 1916): 33.

24. "Women in Business: II," *Fortune* 12 (August 1935): 55. It is interesting to speculate why *Fortune* published its defense of women in the office in 1935. It is possible that during the Depression there was some criticism of the employment of women as clerical workers when unemployment rates for men, the traditional breadwinners, were so high.

25. Baker, *Technology and Women's Work*, p. 74.

PATRIARCHY IN REVOLUTIONARY SOCIETY

Since socialist feminist analysis postulates the existence of patriarchy (via a hierarchical sexual division of society) before the historical development of capitalism, it is absolutely necessary to be self-conscious about what happens to the sexual organization of society with the destruction of capitalism. It is a historical and political reality that the revolutionary reorganization of production in the Soviet Union, China, and Cuba did not entail a parallel revolutionary reorganization of the sexual hierarchy. Particularly on this score the revolutions have been incomplete.

Carollee Bengelsdorf and Alice Hageman, and Margaret Randall, discuss the very specific commitments being made to restructure the sexual division of labor in Cuba. There is increasing recognition of the double work day there, and the government is trying to institutionalize a new division of labor between the sexes through legal codes. However, to the degree that Cuba insists on a repressive stance on the question of homosexuality one wonders if the full roots of patriarchy can be destroyed. For the real destruction of the sexual division of labor, the power of heterosexuality must be challenged, and Cuba will have to reevaluate the relationship between the cultural and political definition of sexuality as heterosexual and the sexual ordering of society as patriarchal. I think Bengelsdorf and Hageman overstate the case when they write "the major structures that guaranteed the oppression and the exploitation of women have been destroyed" in Cuba. Although woman's economic exploitation has been addressed through the Cuban Revolution, I think woman's oppression rooted in the patriarchal structuring of society remains, although it is being challenged.

Judith Stacey, in "When Patriarchy Kowtows: The Significance of the Chinese Family Revolution for Feminist Theory," discusses the fundamental and important changes in the lives of women in revolutionary China, while at the same time assessing the continuation of patriarchal hierarchical organization. There is little criticism in China of the double day of work for women, a double day that takes on a different form than in the United States because of the social organization of daycare.

The belated struggle against patriarchy in socialist countries is the newest form of socialist feminist struggle. There are no examples of an *integrated* revolutionary struggle against class and sex oppression at the inception of revolution. We can only speculate that if these forces are combined in the *initial* struggles of revolution, there will be a more successful attempt at creating human liberation. We need to put it to the test of history.

Related Reading

Bobroff, Anne, "The Bosheviks and Working Women, 1905–1920," *Radical America* 10, no. 3 (May–June 1976).

Croll, Elizabeth, *The Women's Movement in China, 1949–1973* (Anglo-Chinese Education Institute, 1974).

Davin, Delia, *Woman-Work* (New York: Oxford University Press, 1976).

Eisen-Bergman, Arlene, *Women of Vietnam* (San Francisco: People's Press, 1974).

Gordon, Linda, *The Fourth Mountain: Women in China* (New England Free Press pamphlet).

Katz, N. and N. Diamond, *Fragments from a Lost Diary and Other Short Stories* (Boston: Beacon Press, 1973).

O'Sullivan, Sue, "The Moon for Dinner, Changing Relations . . . Women in China" (London: Backdov Pamphlets, 1974).

Randall, Margaret, *Cuban Women Now and the Afterword* (Toronto: Canadian Women's Educational Press, 1974).

Rubenstein, Dale Ross, *How the Russian Revolution Failed Women* (New England Free Press pamphlet).

Scott, Hilda, *Does Socialism Liberate Women?* (Boston: Beacon, 1976).

"Women Hold Up Half the Sky," reprints from *Peking Review* and *China Reconstructs* (Peking, Yenan Books).

"Women in Chile," NACLA Report, no. 6 (September 1975).

"Women in Transition," *Cuba Review*, no. 2 (September 1974).

"Women in Vietnam, Chile, Cuba, Dhofar, China and Japan," *Red Rag*, no. 9 (June 1975).

EMERGING FROM UNDERDEVELOPMENT: WOMEN AND WORK IN CUBA

Carollee Bengelsdorf and Alice Hageman

Colonialism and neocolonialism, by definition, must impose distortions both upon the structures of the subjugated society and upon the minds and persons of those who live within it. If the class structure that exists in any colonized society is perverted to reflect the interests of the colonizer, so too, the patriarchal structure is similarly distorted. The manner in which imperialism has traditionally employed the patriarchal structure of victim countries for its own purposes is a study that remains to be undertaken. If, however, we can accept the notion that "woman is the most deformed product of class based society," then the situation of women in colonized and neocolonized society is even more deformed, even more complex.[1]

That complexity is the heritage of women in revolutionary Cuba. That the coming of the revolution, the systematic destruction of economic and political structures neocolonialism had set up to support itself, has meant a profound change in the lives of women in Cuba is beyond doubt. One has only to look at the statistics and to think what free health care, free education, free housing, and a legal system shaped by and growing

This is a revised and updated version of the authors' article by the same title which appeared in *Cuba Review* 4, no. 2. Parts of it were also presented in the lecture series in socialist feminism at Ithaca College in the spring of 1975. The authors wish to thank Jean Grossholtz for her critical reading and crucial comments and Marifeli Ferez Stable for the analysis provided in her article "Toward the Emancipation of Cuban Women," forthcoming in *Latin American Perspectives*.

out of the people's specific needs would mean in our own lives. One has only to talk to any forty-year-old Cuban woman, to watch her eyes as she discusses the difference between her life before 1959 and her life now as she describes her pride in what she and her neighbors have seen come to pass around them, shaped by their own hands and their own efforts. One has only to spend time with any twenty-year-old Cuban woman to understand that she is completely free of areas of conflict (the anxiety of economic dependence on a man, for example) which we ourselves will never totally overcome.

That oppression still exists is also beyond doubt, it is obvious in almost every aspect of a Cuban woman's life. The same woman who drives a tractor or studies at a sugar engineering school must daily confront the possessive imposition of a dozen commenting males every time she walks down the street. A National Heroine of Labor, who has cut more than a million pounds of sugarcane, will worry about the shape and condition of her fingernails. The anniversary of the attack on Moncada, the attack that launched the final phase of the Cuban revolutionary struggle, is still celebrated with something resembling a beauty contest to choose the female "star" of the celebration and her court.

A socialist society is, by its very definition, a transitional society: it is the period during which the vestiges of the class structure of its predecessor are to be destroyed. And in an underdeveloped country like Cuba, it must be, as well, the period during which the material abundance upon which communism is based is created. But the oppression that continues to exist in Cuba is not simply the result of the transition to socialism in an underdeveloped country. The Cuban experience demonstrates to us, in practice, that the systematic destruction of the bases of capitalism does not, in and of itself, spell the end of the patriarchal nexus that sustained these bases. It demonstrates, in human terms, the complexity of the process of rooting out the paraphernalia of patriarchy. And it demonstrates, as well, that only when the fundamentals of capitalism are gone can a frontal attack on the oppression of women be launched. In the pages that follow, we attempt to examine closely the changes which have taken place in one aspect of women's lives: their participation in the labor force.[2]

In 1969 and 1970, during the period of the ten-million-ton sugar harvest, billboards and walls throughout the island proclaimed, in bold letters, "Women: The Revolution within the Revolution!" and "The Revolution of Women Is Greater than the Revolution Itself." These posters were part of a massive effort, spearheaded by the Federation of Cuban Women (FMC), to encourage women to incorporate themselves into the labor force. The posters, and more fundamentally the effort itself, reflected many complementary streams of thought and action in the Cuban revolutionary process.

There was and is a labor shortage in Cuba. During the 1970 harvest it was abundantly clear that every available pair of hands was essential. Yet the purpose of the harvest was not simply to amass ten million tons of sugar: none of the great mobilizations undertaken since the revolution has had one single goal. The purpose of this effort, on another level, was precisely to use the harvest to begin drawing women out of their homes into the workplaces in great numbers. Why? Here, some central assumptions of the Cuban revolutionary process become clear.

Cuba is still fighting its way out of underdevelopment. In this battle to create material abundance, its chief resource is its people. A woman, or any human being in Cuba, cannot feel fully a part of that society unless she is actively engaged, physically and mentally, in the hard, daily, collective struggle to conquer underdevelopment. Nor can she overcome a kind of personal underdevelopment if her life is bound by the four walls of her home, or even the broader confines of her neighborhood. The Cubans hold to a fundamental belief, emerging out of practice, that human beings can realize themselves only through work, creative and productive, only through using and developing the capacities which lie within them. Under socialism, Che wrote, work acquires "a new condition." It is through work, through "a contribution to the life of the society in which he is reflected . . . that man achieves total awareness of his social being, which is equivalent to his full realization as a human being."[3] Women make up 49 percent of the population in Cuba. The revolution cannot succeed in creating material abundance and transforming human consciousness unless women are fully integrated into its effort to create new people and a new society. Women must grow with the revolution, or both the Cuban Revolution and Cuban women will suffer.

The barriers to this societal and individual realization have been formidable, and they are not all in the past. They encompass not only the historical position of Cuban women prior to the revolution but also the material fact of underdevelopment and the persistence of attitudes deeply embedded in colonial and neocolonial society, attitudes held by both men and women.

The misery and deprivation Cuban women suffered both within the work force and outside it prior to the revolution were part of the misery suffered by the society as a whole. Throughout the country in 1958 more than 600,000 people, or 28 percent of the labor force, were unemployed or underemployed.[4] They formed a permanent shifting supply of labor for the large, foreign-owned companies that dominated the island's economy.

According to the 1953 census, only one out of seven women worked outside her home. Those who did acted out of necessity. The wives and daughters of the unemployed and underemployed, of workingmen and *campesinos*, worked when the survival of their families depended upon it. The jobs they could get were extremely limited. Women in pre-revolutionary Cuba, as elsewhere in the capitalist world, filled the lowest ranks in the reserve labor army. Indeed, women first entered the industrial labor force only with the demise of slavery. As Cuban ethnologist Fernando Ortiz noted:

> It was at the end of the Ten Years' war that a woman went to work in a Havana factory for the first time; it was the cigarette factory La Africana . . . . From that time on women came to form a part of the factory proletariat. As slavery, which was abolished in 1880,

was giving its last gasps, industrial greed, unable to depend on slave labor any longer, but unwilling to pay the salaries of free men, created the feminine proletariat, which is cheaper.[5]

In 1953, the major industrial sectors open to female employment were tobacco (where women constituted 35 percent of the workers) and textiles (where women were 46 percent).[6] Many women—70,000—could only land jobs as domestic workers. These women were paid between five and thirty pesos a month (a peso was equivalent to a dollar).

As a result of low wages, domestic work was often the prelude to prostitution. C. Wright Mills has reported the observation of one Cuban revolutionary that

> nobody knows how many of our sisters were whores in Cuba during the last years of the Batista tyranny. In Havana [in 1957] there were some 270 overcrowded brothels, there were dozens of hotels and motels renting rooms by the hour, and there were over 700 bars congested with *meseras*—or hostesses—the first step towards prostitution. There were about 12 *meseras* to each bar, and they each earned from the bar about $2.25 a day. The employers and the Government grafter each got about $52 a day out of it.[7]

Maintaining a reserve labor army required little educational input. Women, at the lowest rank of this army, required even less. The level at which education was provided to women insured that they would not move out of their designated roles. The 1953 census records that more than one out of five women could neither read nor write: in rural areas, this figure jumped to two out of five. One third of ten-year-old girls were not in school at the time of the census, and only one in a hundred women over twenty-five had any university education.

Colonialism and neocolonialism had equipped women to be uneducated servants in their own homes and in the homes of others. Women who rebelled against their fate, who incorporated themselves into the long revolutionary process, helped to bring down this structure of exploitation and oppression. But it was only with the destruction of the old economic and political order, beginning on a countrywide scale in 1959, that the possibility for concrete change in the position of all women began to emerge.

Women in Cuba entered the revolution as persons who had been doubly exploited: as workers and as women. The pre-revolutionary heritage left women with several specific handicaps with regard to work. Their level of education and training was minimal. Ancient taboos instructed them to remain at home; the *calle*, or street, was considered the man's province and the *casa*, or home, the woman's place. Finally, there was an assumption that all work related to house and children had to be done by women.

During the first five years of the revolution, from 1959 to 1963, much attention centered on overcoming the effects of this double exploitation. Efforts to raise women's level of general knowledge, basic skills, and political consciousness led to the development of new programs.[8] Some 20,000 maids attended the special Schools for the Advancement of Domestic Servants, which were established in Havana in 1960; many went on to staff childcare centers. Others took night school general education courses, which included shorthand and typing, and full-time day courses preparing for specific tasks in administration or commerce. The Ana Betancourt School for Peasant Girls brought thousands of women from remote areas of Cuba to Havana for a year to learn sewing skills and basic education.

Although some women were trained during this period for traditionally non-female jobs, such as bus driving, women in general were channeled into areas and types of work historically associated with women. These efforts, however, cannot be dismissed out of hand. The revolution was concentrating scarce resources and much effort into altering, as quickly as possible, the lives of those women who were most exploited. Nor could it be expected, given existing prejudices, that women or their families would have readily accepted radically different types of jobs. Nonetheless, the patterns of sexual division in the labor force were not fundamentally challenged in those early years.

By the mid 1960s, the goal of providing women with basic

education was close to being accomplished. The Ana Betancourt School was transformed in 1963 to a nine-grade, unified school. The Schools for Domestic Servants were supplanted by educational programs operated by the FMC on the basis of one's neighborhood rather than one's pre-revolutionary occupation. During this same period, the old structures of discrimination in the entire educational system were being systematically torn down, providing access for women who had always been at home to training and knowledge to which few, if any, could have aspired prior to the revolution. During the Literacy Campaign of 1961, which reduced the rate of illiteracy from 23 percent to 3.7 percent, 56 percent of those who learned to read and write were women. Women were then encouraged to go on with their studies. Girls who, prior to the revolution, could have aspired to little more than basic literacy skills were incorporated into the educational system at every level. By 1970, women composed 49 percent of Cuba's elementary school students, 55 percent of high school students, and 40 percent of students in higher education.[9]

The creation in 1964 of a Secretary of Production in the FMC marked a shift in emphasis. As the means to provide disadvantaged women with basic education and/or new skills became increasingly widespread, systematic efforts were undertaken to incorporate women into the labor force. Although there was some slow but steady progress in this area throughout the 1960s, it was through preparations for the 1970 harvest that a quantitative change in the orientation toward women and work took place.

During the period 1969–1970, hundreds of thousands of women participated as volunteers in the countrywide mobilization. For some, this was their first work outside the home; for others, the experience provided the bridge between working outside the home on a temporary basis and being incorporated into the labor force on a full-time basis. From 1969 on, revolutionary leaders planned to recruit some 100,000 women into the labor force each year.

At the beginning of the 1970s, the assumption behind this effort to vastly increase the recruitment of women was made clear: eventually, all women would be drawn out of their homes into socially productive work. This expectation was articulated in the vagrancy law, which went into effect in March 1971. It is worth quoting relevant sections of the law:

Article 1: All citizens who are physically and mentally fit have the social duty to work.

Article 2: All men from 17 through 60 and all women from 17 through 55 are presumably physically and mentally fit to work.

Article 3: All male citizens of working age who are fit to work and are not attending any of the schools in our national system of education but who are completely divorced from any work center are guilty of the crime of loafing.

The law stops short of making it a crime if women do not work, but its direction is clear and the discussions it provoked made this obvious. *Granma* of 14 March 1971 reported that during the discussions of the law, one of the changes proposed, but not adopted, was "that it be applied to single women who neither work nor study." Some work centers recommended that the full weight of the law be applied to women.

By the early 1970s, the female Cuban labor force could be characterized by several traits. First, it had grown enormously in number. In 1974, women comprised 25.3 percent of the total work nor study." Some work centers recommended that the full involved in salaried work outside the home.[10] Seventy percent of Cuban women workers had joined the labor force in the years following the triumph of the revolution.

Second, women tended to be concentrated in those sectors in which they had generally worked before: in particular, education, health, administration, and light industry.[11] By and large then, much of the work women were doing could be seen as an extension of female functions within the home. There were, of course, exceptions. A great deal of publicity was given to women who worked in jobs that were traditionally men's work, such as cane cutting. Yet the sexual division of labor received reinforcement on several levels. In certain areas, such as daycare, what had been necessity in the early days of the revolution was escalated to the level of theory. The fact that all those who worked daily in direct contact with children were women began to be given a "scientific" justification: children needed female nurturing. It was "only natural" that those who principally cared for children in daycare centers should be women.

The sexual division of labor received the force of law with Resolutions 47 and 48 issued by the Ministry of Labor in 1968. The resolutions reserved some 500 job categories specifically for women and prohibited women from entering an equal number of professions. The resolutions were justified by revolutionary leaders on several bases. Essentially, it was argued that they worked to counter prejudices against hiring women by assuring them that certain areas of work would be open to them. At the same time, at the critical ten-million-ton harvest time, they released men to do other, presumably more physically taxing, jobs in other areas of the economy. It was further asserted by some that the resolutions helped psychologically to facilitate women's entry into the work force by reassuring them that they would not be asked to do certain types of work. Whatever the justification, at least one effect of Resolutions 47 and 48 was to underline and strengthen notions of a "natural" sexual division of labor.

Finally, although women were leaving their houses and entering the labor force in greater numbers, they were also leaving the labor force and returning to their homes at an alarming rate. For example, during the last three months of 1969, 140,000 women were incorporated into the labor force. Some 110,000 of these women were still working at the end of 1969. This represented a net gain, however, of only 27,000 for that period, since at the same time 80,000 other women had left work.[12] For the entire period from 1969 to 1974, it has been estimated that more than 700,000 women had to be recruited into the labor force in order to achieve a net gain of just under 200,000 women workers (see Table 1).[13]

One reason for this high dropout rate is that vestiges of the old *casa/calle* taboo have not been completely eradicated. At the Thirteenth Congress on Cuban Workers in November 1973, Fidel pointed out that

> it costs a lot to train a nurse! It costs a lot of money to train a teacher! All those years—elementary school, high school. And what a need we have for teachers! But if a young man made a good

Table 1

Entrance and Stability of Women in the Labor Force

Year	Number of women entering the work force	Net increase	Decrease
1969	106,258	25,477	
1970	124,504	55,310	
1971	86,188	—	63,174[1]
1972	130,843	37,263	
1973	138,437	72,279	
1974	127,694	69,748	
Total	713,924	196,903	

1. This figure does not represent women workers who have left the labor force in 1971 only, but is rather an accumulation of data since 1967. In 1971 an accounting of all women who had left the labor force was made and definitive records gathered by the National Bank of Cuba.
Source: "Sobre el Pleno Ejercicio de la Igualdad de la Mujer," *Tesis y Resoluciones: Primer Congreso del Partido Comunista de Cuba* (Havana: DOR, 1976), p. 574.

salary, and he married the teacher, he told her: "Don't go to work, we don't need the money." And the country lost a good teacher. Lost a good nurse. Of course, when the country lost the teacher or the nurse it wasn't only for economic reasons, it's all the residual male chauvinism and supermanism and all those things that are still a part of us.

But as a more widespread phenomenon, the fluctuation in women's work patterns must be traced to the existence of a "second shift." Some women have interpreted Fidel's assertion in 1966 that "women in a social revolution should be doubly revolutionary" to mean that they should assume the dual role of worker and housekeeper, and in fact proudly describe themselves as "double revolutionaries." Others have become discouraged or overcome by fatigue and have left their jobs. In a plastic shoe factory near Havana, for example, many women had stopped work; their main complaint was depression. Their husbands refused to help with the housework, and they were worried about the care their children were receiving.[14]

Despite the drive to increase the number of women in the work force, it is clear there had been no corresponding effort to get men into the kitchen. Although there were disparate references over the years to the issue of responsibilities in the home by the (overwhelmingly male) revolutionary leadership, there was no real challenge to the assumption that laundry, cooking, and care of children were exclusively women's work. The expectation held firm that women would be relieved of the "thousand unimportant trivialities" to the extent that the state could take on and collectivize those responsibilities.[15] In conditions of underdevelopment, this has inevitably meant a de facto "second shift" for most women who work. Given the scarcity of resources, the full services necessary to relieve women of household tasks simply could not be immediately provided.

The situation became even more obvious with an examination of leadership ranks, both in the workplace and in the vanguard and mass organizations. In the workplace, it was apparent that if women had to pick up children at daycare centers, pick up the shopping or the laundry, get home to cook dinner and take care of other household chores, they would have difficulties staying extra hours in their workplace to attend assemblies or betterment courses or do voluntary work. Interim measures, such as the decision taken at the Thirteenth Congress of the Cuban Trade Union to automatically award working mothers a labor of merit, do not in any way get at the heart of the problem.[16] Women workers have had less chance both to develop and to display attitudes and skills that lead to promotion to leadership positions. These difficulties are amply demonstrated by the number of women in leadership positions, even in sectors of the economy where women are concentrated. Table 2 reveals that in none of the nine major sectors employing women does the percentage of females in leadership positions come near matching the percentage of women working in that sector.

Within the branches of various industries, there is also consistent underrepresentation of women in leadership positions. In the Ministry of Light Industries, for example, women make up 77.6 percent of the workforce in the branches producing

Table 2

Distribution of Female Workers in the Labor Force

Bodies	Percent of female labor force	Percent female leadership
Minsap (Ministry of Public Health)	64	31.5
Mined (Ministry of Education)	58	40.0
Cubatabaco	53	8.1
Minil (Ministry of Milk Processing Industries)	41	20.4
Init (National Tourism Institute)	41	15.7
MINCIN (Ministry of National Trade)	36	26.6
MINAL (Ministry of Food Industries)	18	5.8
INRA (National Institute of Agranar Reform)	9	1.9
Minaz (Ministry of Sugar)	7	3.3

Source: *Memories: Second Congress of Cuban Women's Federation* (Havana: Editorial Orbe, 1975), p. 19.

ready-made articles. Yet they comprise only 51.9 percent of the leadership in these branches. In Graphic Arts, 24.6 percent of the work force and only 7.9 percent of the leadership are women.[17]

The Communist Party in Cuba makes the fundamental decisions about the direction of the revolution. The difficulties women have in entering and remaining in the work force, and then in fully participating in their work centers, greatly inhibit their chances for becoming party members and therefore participating, at the highest levels, in critical decision-making. The party in Cuba represents, as the Cubans see it, the vanguard of the working class, the great majority of the population. Its members are those judged to have the highest degree of revolutionary "consciencia." Therefore, it is in the workplaces that potential party members in Cuba are nominated. Clearly, if 25.3

percent of the work force is women, the possibility for female party membership reflecting the total female population is already limited. And if women workers are limited in their ability to engage fully in their workplaces, it is unlikely that party membership will reflect even that numerical strength in the work force. And indeed, only 13.23 percent of party militants are women.[18]

When the leadership ranks of the vanguard organizations are examined, an even more severe disproportion is evident (see Table 3). In the party, 2.9 percent of the municipal national leadership is female. There are no women members in the political bureau, nor in the secretariat, the two bodies which carry on the daily work of the party. Out of 112 Central Committee members, five are women (four of the twelve alternates are women).[19]

It may be supposed that the disproportional underrepresentation of women, both as members and as leaders, would be less in the Young Communists' League (the UJC), since most members were born into the revolution and formed within its structures, rather than within the structures of the past. It is indeed

Table 3

Percentage of Female Leaders in the Party, the UJC,
and the Mass Organizations[1]

Level	PCC[2]	UJC[3]	CTC[4]	CDR[5]	ANAP[6]
Municipal	2.9	22	24	7	16.38
Regional	4.1	7	21	7	0.76
Provincial	6.3	7	15	3	1.19
National	5.5	10	7	19	2.04

1. These figures were compiled before the new administrative reorganization went into effect. It eliminates the regional level, rationalizes the size of the municipalities, and expands the number of provinces from 6 to 14.
2. PCC (Cuban Communist Party) 13.23 percent women.
3. UJC (Communist Youth Organization) 29 percent women.
4. CTC (Confederation of Cuban Workers) 25.3 percent women.
5. CDR (Committees for the Defense of the Revolution) 50 percent women.
6. ANAP (National Association of Small Farmers) percentage not available.
Source: "Sobre el Pleno Ejercicio de la Igualdad de la Mujer," p. 585.

less, but the organization is still dominated by men: some 29 percent of UJC members are women; women comprise 22 percent of the municipal leadership and 10 percent of the national leadership. And in the mass organizations, the situation is much the same. Even in the neighborhood organizations—the CDRs, which are formed from those who reside in a delimited area—women make up 50 percent of the membership but comprise only 7 percent of the municipal CDR leadership and 19 percent of the national leadership.

Problems with the promotion of women to leadership positions are evident even within the Federation of Cuban Women (the FMC). When promotion involves a change of residence, especially in the case of married women, a whole series of difficulties have arisen, which have, according to party sources, proved "truly unsolvable." These problems stem from the inability of husband, or family, or husband's work center to take seriously the importance of the work of the women in question.[20]

In an attempt to understand more precisely the reasons for this high underrepresentation of women among the leaders of every important organization in the society, a survey was taken, under the auspices of the Confederation of Cuban Workers (CTC), in 211 work centers throughout the country. In all, 5,168 workers, both men and women, were asked to cite the major factors inhibiting greater female participation.[21] Some 85.7 percent cited women's domestic obligations as a chief factor. (It is interesting to note that 51.5 percent saw the "low cultural level" of women as a factor. Yet, according to calculations made for the Party Congress, women workers in Cuba have achieved, on the average, a higher educational level than men.[22])

It follows logically that when it came to nominating and electing candidates to the newly organized governmental structures, women would be underrepresented. The new structures were set up first in the province of Matanzas in 1974. The percentage of women nominated, in meetings of neighbors, was 7.6, the percentage elected was 3. When women in Matanzas were asked whether they would have been willing to serve if elected, 54.3 percent said no. The majority cited "domestic tasks and care of children and husband" as the fundamental obstacle.[23]

The revolution has not been unconcerned about these problems. In the workplace, various structures have been created to ease both the objective and subjective tensions associated with the shift from *casa* to *calle*. Organizations or sections of organizations have emerged since 1969 whose purpose is to confront the problem of keeping women in the workplace. In 1969, the Feminine Front was incorporated into the trade union structure. At the end of that year, "Rescue Commissions" in various workplaces were set up through the joint effort of the CTC, the Ministry of Work, and the FMC. These commissions have the responsibility for providing help, both material and psychological, to women who have been assigned low positions in their workplaces because of their educational level. In November 1970 the Incorporation and Permanence Commission, composed of representatives from the party, the Ministry of Work, the CTC, and the FMC, was established with activities aimed, as well, at achieving permanency among women in the labor force.[24]

Moreover, the number and variety of facilities serving the families of working women have steadily increased in quantity and variety. By 1974 there were 642 daycare centers in operation, caring for more than 55,000 children. The number of centers is as yet insufficient. The economic plan for 1976-1980 contains provisions for the construction of some 400 more daycare centers, which will allow for a capacity of 150,000 children.[25] Even this will not meet the level of need. Places in daycare centers are allotted solely to the children of working women. In 1973 only 16 percent of these children could be accommodated, and there was a waiting list of 19,000.[26]

The majority of women who work and whose children do not yet have access to daycare make use of various extended-family type structures: grandmothers, other women relatives, or close women friends who do not work. In some of those rural areas where daycare centers are not readily available, women themselves have organized "guerrilla daycare." Groups of women either rotate the responsibility for caring for children or assign one among them to take the responsibility, so that the rest would be free to participate in agricultural labor.

The *Plan Jaba,* or Shopping Bag Plan, grants any member of the family of a woman who works priority service at her local grocery store, as long as there are no able-bodied adults in that family who are neither working nor studying. By 1974, 144,934 families of working women were benefiting from the plan. Families have two options. They can choose the "predispatch" plan, which means they drop off a list at their local store in the morning and pick up their groceries that evening. Or they can opt for "immediate dispatch," which means the person doing the shopping has the right to go to the front of the line at each counter. The *Plan Jaba* was organized and is run by FMC members, that is by women, and is constantly subject to revisions. Every two or three months, CDRs hold community control meetings to criticize and suggest changes in public services, including the *Plan Jaba.*

Increasing numbers of workplaces are offering laundry services to their workers. Laundry service suggests more than machines and soapsuds. It implies the construction of buildings, the provision of trucks to transport the laundry, and the employment of workers to operate the service. Although the quality of service is constantly improving, smooth operations are still difficult, especially outside Havana. In Santiago, for example, the time from delivery to return can range up to five, or ten, or even fifteen days, largely due to shortages of vehicles for transport. In a society where no one has a closet full of clothes, a laundry service that might take fifteen days doesn't eliminate laundry from housework, and therefore from women's work.

Working women are offered preferential access to a variety of other goods and services. Special days solely for working women are part of the regular *libreta,* or ration book, schedule. These are days when new selections of goods go on sale; therefore, working women receive first choice. One often passes store windows containing goods marked "these articles only for sale to working women." Stores are open throughout the day and evening, so women can shop independent of working hours.

More and more refrigerators, pressure cookers, and small appliances that aid in housework are being distributed through the unions in workplaces, with priority given to working women. Working women receive preferential access to dry cleaners, shoe stores, tailors, hairdressers, and medical appointments, thereby further reducing the amount of time they must spend waiting in line.

Efforts have also been made to facilitate accessibility to the workplace, to reduce the distance women must travel. New housing projects have constructed, or have plans to construct, easily accessible work centers predominantly for women. A plastic shoe factory staffed by 400 workers, 245 of whom are women, has been built next to the José Martí District in Santiago; 85 percent of the 245 women workers live in José Martí. A textile factory to be operated primarily by women is in the process of construction at the new city of Alamar.

Several considerations emerge clearly from an examination of these efforts. First, there is no question that the revolution is committed to providing, as quickly as possible, the facilities to relieve as much of the individualized burden of housework. But the necessary material resources have been extremely limited. For example, at the beginning of the 1970s, the Cubans launched major campaigns to construct new houses and new schools. The results are already impressive. By 1974, housing for 13,000 people at the new city of Alamar had been built, and 150 schools in the countryside were in operation. But these projects draw heavily on physical resources, such as cement or heavy equipment, the same resources necessary to build daycare centers or laundries. The housing shortage is severe. Schools in the countryside provide the setting for a more revolutionary socialization of the next generation, both men and women. How can one say that more daycare centers now, or better laundry services now, should have higher priority?

Moreover, while the collectivization of household tasks in the public sector is necessary and potentially liberating, as long as women continue to bear the overwhelming burden of the remaining chores, the fact that they may now go to the head of the grocery line hardly solves the problem. As long as the notion holds that the state is freeing *women* from this work rather than *people*, those tasks that remain uncollectivized inevitably rest in women's hands and on their shoulders. Furthermore, if these old ideas about what is women's responsibility are not rooted out and destroyed, the people who do those household chores the state has assumed are likely to be women. In this way, collectivization of tasks reinforces rather than destroys a sexual division of labor.

In this context, the recent series of events and undertakings with regard to the position of women takes on particular significance. These events seem to indicate that the revolutionary leadership (still overwhelmingly male) has made a qualitative leap, and, for the first time, has begun a concerted nationwide campaign at the grass roots level against some of the most fundamental aspects of the heritage of patriarchy. The first major related event concerned Resolutions 47 and 48. At the 1973 Thirteenth Congress of the Cuban Trade Union organization, it was stated that neither women nor men should be kept from doing any sort of work required by the revolution (within the limits of considerations of health), and that, therefore, the resolutions should be "reconsidered." This position was reemphasized at the National Congress of the Women's Federation (the FMC), in December of the following year. The FMC issued a call for a study of Resolution 48, the resolution which prohibited woman from occupying certain jobs:

> We consider that the concept "prohibition" implies discrimination both for men and for women; thus we propose, in the case of such jobs, that the conditions and risks entailed be explained to the woman and that the decision be hers as to whether or not she will occupy the job.[27]

The major systematized thrust of efforts, however, has centered upon the issue of the "second shift." The issuance of the Family Code in the summer of 1974 must be examined in this framework. The Family Code states clearly and unequivocally, that in homes where both partners work, both must share equally the responsibility for tasks related to the household and to the raising of children. It thereby gives the force of law to the notion of shared responsibility.

But the significance of the code has wider dimensions as well. In Cuba, every law proposed is first discussed and modified in meetings of each of the mass organizations, both in the workplace and in the neighborhoods, before it goes into effect. According to various accounts, discussions of the Family Code were interesting for what did not get said, as well as what did. No men stood up to object to the parts that stipulate equal responsibility in the home. This, of course, does not mean that all Cuban men agreed with it. What it does mean is that men recognized publically the social justice of the provisions, even if, in their private lives, they had no intention of abiding by them. The Family Code became law on International Women's Day, 1975. A reading of those sections which deal with equal responsibility in the household and with regard to children is now standard procedure at marriage ceremonies.

At the same time that the Family Code was being considered, women throughout Cuba were organizing for the 1974 FMC Congress, mentioned above. This effort involved innumerable discussions of issues related to women in the labor force. Out of these discussions came a number of suggestions for expanding and improving upon services the state has assumed, which do not intrinsically challenge the notion of the second shift. The Congress' resolutions call for:

1. Increasing the participation of women workers in qualification and requalification courses, by setting up classes during working hours without detriment to salary.
2. Broadening and improving laundry and dry cleaning facilities.
3. Broadening the system of sales to women and studying the opening and closing hours of commercial stores.
4. Increasing the number of factories which produce made-to-order clothes.
5. Developing plans for the production of prepared and semiprepared food.
6. Implementing four- and six-hour shifts and other special work schedules where economic considerations allow.[28]

But at a more fundamental level, the FMC Congress reasserted firmly and repeatedly the necessity for an end to the second shift, for a sharing of household responsibilities: "It is a job for the entire society to solve or to share the problems and difficulties which obstruct the total incorporation of women . . ."[29] Its resolutions included proposals for joint action with the trade unions and other mass organizations in order to fight what were phrased as "comfortable attitudes" with respect to the distribution of domestic chores in the home.[30]

By far the strongest statement that the revolution *must* achieve *full* equality between men and women comes out of the First Congress of the Cuban Communist Party, in December 1975. The document dealing with women states unequivocally that "in practice, the full equality of women does not yet exist . . . ," that "a fundamental battle must be waged in the realm of consciousness, because it is there that the backward concepts which lock us in the past continue to subsist."[31]

The document further brings to public attention the surveys cited above dealing with women in the work force and women in relation to leadership positions which reveal the depth of the problem and, in their very statement, the depth of the Cuban leadership's understanding of the problem. The Party Congress resolutions generally reassert and elaborate those issued at the FMC Congress the previous year. But the party firmly recognizes, as well, the refusal of men to participate fully in the execution of household and child care chores as a major manifestation of backward concepts. It asserts that "it is a revolutionary duty, in the unescapable present, to achieve an equable distribution of unavoidable household chores."[32]

What conclusions can we draw about the present position of women workers in Cuba? Some are clear and apply generally to all women in Cuba. First and most fundamentally, the enormity of the contrast between woman's fate in pre-revolutionary Cuba, and her possibilities in post-1959 Cuba must be stressed. Without question, the major structures that guaranteed the oppression and exploitation of women have been destroyed. This is manifested in many ways; its visual image is reflected in any schoolroom, any work center, any meeting, on any street. The fact that the number of divorces in Cuba rose from 2,500 in 1958 to 25,000 in 1970 gives a succinct indication of one enormous change: women are no longer locked into the prison of an oppressive marriage by economic necessity.[33]

What is clear, as well, about women in Cuba is that contradictions continue to exist. The national, structured attack on sexism, as related to women's ability to work, really began only in the past few years. Far too little time has elapsed to make more than tentative statements about where things stand, but there are various indications of directions and problems. Humor is often an excellent index of the effectiveness of a given measure, and since 1974, many funny stories, often highly defensive in nature, have made the rounds in Cuba. One such story is told of a party member (male) who agreed, after much resistance, to share part of the burden of housework. He consented to do the laundry, on the condition that his wife take it outside to hang up—so that his neighbors would never know.

On another level, members of the most recent (1977) Venceremos Brigade reported that women are indeed approaching mass organizations to which they belong, most particularly the FMC and the CTC, to seek aid in getting their husbands to abide by the Family Code's decree of equal responsibility in the house. There are no accounts of women taking their husbands to court for failure to comply with the code, an action which theoretically became possible with enactment of the Family Code as law. However, a survey attempting to discover the total number of hours women worked was conducted among 251 women workers in April 1975—one month after the Family Code became law. As reported at the Party Congress, the survey found that women worked in their work centers and in their homes an average of thirteen hours daily, Monday through Friday, and eleven and a half hours on the weekends "owing to the accumulation of domestic tasks."[34] Clearly, the problem had not just disappeared with the issuing of the Family Code.

Further, the Cubans continue to assert a "scientific" biological differentiation between men and women, a sort of reasoning which has historically been cause and/or justification for the sexual division of labor. Fidel Castro, in his speech to the closing of the FMC congress, explained why it was that women should be treated with what he called "proletarian courtesy": "It is true with women, and must be so with women because they are physically weaker and because they have tasks and functions and human responsibilities that the man does not have."[35] The general acceptance in Cuba of this biological determinism has been reflected and continues to be reflected within the work force.

Its most recent, and perhaps most controversial incarnation, comes in the form of the Resolution 40, issued by the Ministry of Labor (MINTB) in June 1976, at the conclusion of their study of Resolutions 47 and 48. The new resolution restricts women from taking some 300 types of jobs (instead of 500). The justification given cites reasons of the health of women—this despite the FMC's call for it to be each woman's own choice. The list contains some jobs in which there is scientific evidence of potential danger to women who intend to bear children but not to men (at least as far as research has gone). Work with lead, for example, has been shown to endanger the health of a fetus in the earliest stages of pregnancy. Others, however, clearly seem to indicate the operation of old prejudices surrounding women's "frailty." General categories of prohibited occupations include work under water and work at heights of more than five stories.[36]

There have been a few attempts to explain the newly issued restrictions. Marifeli Perez Stable, in her article, "Toward the Emancipation of Cuban Women," puts forward what she calls an "educated guess" that the issuance of the restrictions at this point has to do with the revolution's effort to reorganize the economic and governmental structure. She suggests that "it may well be that the economic rationale behind the 1976 resolution is to free jobs occupied or which could be occupied by women so that men who have been rationalized out of their jobs can be once again employed. Women without jobs, after all, do not present the same type of social problems as men without jobs."[37]

It is our impression, derived from visits to some fifteen work centers in June and July of 1974, that by and large women were not working in the sorts of areas cited in the new resolution. The reason given, at workplace after workplace, when we asked why women did not work on this or that machine or in this or that area of the factory, was "considerations of health." It can be assumed that, as with Resolutions 47 and 48, there will be exceptions to the new rule. But the fact remains that Resolution 40 gives the force of law to a systematized sexual division of labor.

That such contradictions exist should not be surprising. The roots of patriarchy are deep, the problems of underdevelopment severe, and the process of transition to socialism has been going on only twenty years. At the same time, the degree to which the Cubans resolve these contradictions will be the measure of the success of their effort to achieve a truly liberated, truly equal society.

Notes

1. Isabel Larguia and John Dumoulin, "Toward a Science of Women's Liberation," *NACLA's Latin American and Empire Report* 4, no. 10 (December 1972): 4.
2. Cubans use the term "labor force" to mean all those engaged in salaried work. Throughout this article, the term is employed in the same manner.
3. Che Guevara, "Man and Socialism in Cuba," in *Venceremos: The Speeches and Writings of Ernesto Che Guevara*, ed. John Gerassi (New York: Macmillan, 1968).
4. James O'Connor, *Origins of Socialism in Cuba* (Ithaca: Cornell University Press, 1970), p. 333. For further information on conditions in Cuba prior to the revolution, see also Fidel Castro, "History Will Absolve Me," in *Revolutionary Struggle*, ed. Rolando Bonachea and Nelson Valdes (Cambridge: M.I.T. Press, 1972).
5. Fernando Ortiz, *Cuban Counterpoint: Tobacco and Sugar* (New York: Vintage, 1970), p. 84.
6. Figures taken from Population Census of 1953.
7. C. Wright Mills, *Listen Yankee: The Revolution in Cuba* (New York: Ballantine, 1960), p. 15.

8. For further information on these efforts undertaken on behalf of women in the early years of the revolution, see Margaret Randall, *Cuban Women Now* (Toronto: Canadian Women's Educational Press, 1974) and Elizabeth Sutherland, *The Youngest Revolution: A Personal Report on Cuba* (New York: Dial Press, 1969).
9. Alberto Pozo, "Female Labor Force of Cuba," in Prensa Latina Feature Service, *Direct from Cuba*, 1 June 1974.
10. Fidel Castro, "Speech at the Closing Session of the Second Congress of the FMC," 29 November 1974 (Havana: Book Institute), p. 11.
11. *Memories: Second Congress of Cuban Women's Federation* (Havana: Editorial Orbe, 1975), p. 33.
12. Ana Ranos, "Women and the Cuban Revolution," *Cuba Resource Center Newsletter* 2, no. 2 (March 1972): 8.
13. "Sobre el Pleno Ejercicio de la Igualdad de la Mujer" in *Tesis y Resoluciones: Primer Congreso del Partido Comunista de Cuba* (Havana: DOR), p. 574.
14. Anne Sterling and Martha Vicinus, "Women in Revolutionary Cuba" (Providence, 1973).
15. From Clara Zetkin, "Lenin on the Woman Question," in *The Woman Question: Selections from the Writings of Karl Marx, Frederick Engels, V.I. Lenin, Joseph Stalin* (New York: International Publishers, 1951), p. 93.
16. Stasia Madrigal, "The Feminists of Cuba," *Off Our Backs* (May 1974).
17. *Memories: Second Congress*, p. 19.
18. "Sobre el Pleno Ejercicio," p. 585.
19. *Granma Weekly Review* (4 January 1976), p. 12.
20. "Sobre el Pleno Ejercicio," p. 585.
21. Ibid., p. 586.
22. Ibid., p. 589.
23. Ibid., p. 584.
24. "Women: Decisive Force in Economic Development," an interview with Rosario Fernandez, Secretary of Production of the FMC, *Mujeres* (August 1971).
25. Castro, "Speech at the Closing Session," p. 17.
26. Madrigal, "Feminists of Cuba," p. 10.
27. *Memories: Second Congress*, p. 37.
28. Ibid., pp. 39, 175.
29. Ibid., p. 39.
30. Ibid., p. 54.

31. "Sobre el Pleno Ejercicio," pp. 563, 571.
32. Ibid., p. 596.
33. Heidi Steffens, "A Woman's Place," Cuba Review 4, no. 2, p. 29.
34. "Sobre el Pleno Ejercicio," p. 573.
35. Castro, "Speech at the Closing Session," p. 45.
36. Granma, 1 June 1976.
37. Marifeli Perez Stable, "Toward the Emancipation of Cuban Women" forthcoming, Latin American Perspectives.

INTRODUCING THE FAMILY CODE

Margaret Randall

One of the most exciting aspects of the Cuban Revolution is the way the country's economic and social progress involves a constant physical dialogue between leadership and masses, between economic possibilities and ideological mass consciousness, a real interrelationship between collective gains and future possibilities. This general feeling among working women, and the population in general, that old ideas about women's roles simply have no place in the new society, had reached an unofficial peak when the draft of the new Family Code was first discussed in the newspaper and became subject matter for interminable street-level discussions. I say street level as opposed to the official discussions of each new law which take place in workplaces, military units, mass organizations, and schools. A lot of unofficial discussion goes on first— in grocery stores, on buses, in waiting rooms.

As I write this, the official discussions of the Family Code draft are just beginning. What are some of the new proposals included in this vastly revised Family Code? (Legislation in this area is not new.) All the new proposals point to great advances in a real workable equality between the sexes. Among other things, if the draft becomes law without modification, men will be required by law to shoulder 50% of the housework and child care when women work. Other features include totally equal duties and responsibilities for men and women in

This article is excerpted from the Afterword to *Cuban Women Now* (Toronto: Canadian Women's Educational Press), written in Havana in July 1974.

marriage, divorce, child support, etc. It goes without saying that there will be no such thing, even on paper, as an illegitimate child, and the old bourgeois concepts of adultery, mental cruelty, etc. will no longer be on the books as necessary "requirements" for divorce. Adopted children will have the same rights as all others. The new code rests entirely on mutual respect between women and men and respect on the part of parents for their children. The family nucleus as we know it is in fact strengthened, but its private property or bourgeois capitalist-sexist aspects are largely removed.

Cuba may be the only country in the world to introduce this kind of a law governing social relations within the home in just this way. It's also clear that in a country like Cuba, with its history of Spanish-Christian male dominance and its still prevailing sexist residue, this clause will, at least in the beginning, mainly serve an educational role. It will, after all, require an exceptionally strong woman to charge her husband with nonfulfillment of the law, and we all know the variety of emotional weapons a man can wield over a woman to make sure she grants him certain privileges.

But, as more often than not in the past, Cuban leadership has again chosen just the right moment to introduce these duties and rights. The ideological campaign has been on the upswing for more than two years. Discussions concerning women's rights have been encouraged at all levels. Women are being promised support in this through their mass organizations and workplaces. And the FMC's Second Congress has promoted a series of preliminary activities which have given women new strength and a new sense of broader collective possibilities.

The street-level discussions of this new code have been lively. Cuban women and men, always outspoken and opinionated, go at it anywhere and all the time. Often men try to put forth "historical" or "biological" reasons for objecting— especially—to the clause concerning their 50% participation in household and childcare duties. In markets and on buses there are always plenty of women on hand, with well-founded arguments borne out by their own experience to defend their imminent legal gains.

My comrade was standing in line at the supermarket the other day and a man behind him said to no one in particular or anyone in general: "This business of shopping is really women's work—women are really specialists at this kind of thing, much more than men!" A woman in the same line turned on him in violent glee and—her face two inches from his—came back at him with "oh, yes, women are such specialists at this and some men sure are specialists at talking crap!"

Our block-level CDR held its discussion of the draft on two consecutive nights this week. With a lawyer explaining each clause as it was read, the people took the discussion of the law seriously. Men seemed to understand the essential justice involved and, at least in this collective context, didn't contest their new role. Women were told they would receive support from the party at their workplace and from the CDR in their neighborhood in enforcing their new rights.

Some of the women commented that they felt their husbands would feel less uneasy about doing housework "now that everyone's in the same boat." Some said they didn't really expect older men to change but that the new law would help enforce the tendency—already evident among the youth—toward more real equality in marriage. One woman said: "Young women around here drew up this law before the government ever thought about it, and young men just have to go along with it these days!"

WHEN PATRIARCHY KOWTOWS: THE SIGNIFICANCE OF THE CHINESE FAMILY REVOLUTION FOR FEMINIST THEORY

Judith Stacey

> The commencement is in the family and state;
> the consummation in the Empire.
> E-Yun, B.C. 1539

Woman's oppression starts right at home. The family is the central institutional context for the transhistorical, transcultural oppression of women. Feminists and socialists have focused on the modern nuclear family as a particularly pernicious incubator of male supremacy. Classical socialist theory ties the nuclear family directly to private property and dates woman's oppression from its inception.[1] But the USSR example has led feminists and others to recognize that the abolition of private property is at best a necessary, but insufficient, condition for women's emancipation. It is now generally recognized that male supremacy predates both class society and the nuclear family. Likewise it is apparent that the nuclear family has survived socialism as well as capitalism and that sexism in varying guises and degrees exists in all societies known to woman. Increasingly feminists have come to speculate that

This article was originally published in Feminist Studies 2, no. 43 (1975). Feminist Studies Inc., 417 Riverside Drive, N.Y., N.Y. 10025. It was also presented as part of the lecture series in socialist feminism at Ithaca College in the spring of 1976. For the most painstaking criticism and generous support, I wish to thank George Ross and Diane Ostroffsky. Critical readings of an earlier version of this paper by the editors of Feminist Studies have also contributed significantly to whatever improvements appear in the present essay.

patriarchy is itself woven into the base, into the material conditions of female oppression which transcend historical modes of production.[2]

The biological family is the universal human institution. It is here, therefore, that feminists have begun to seek the theoretical roots of the universal aspects of our oppression. And while the modern nuclear family has no historical monopoly on patriarchal values, it increasingly appears to be developing one in industrial societies. Thus the nuclear family has been identified as the critical institution in the contemporary oppression of women, and it is within its specific set of social and psychological relations that we have begun to seek the roots of the conditions of our oppression. From this dual-level exploration of the universal and the historically specific nature of the family is emerging a dialogue that will etch the theoretical basis for a feminist revolution. It is within this context that I wish to discuss the "family revolution" in the People's Republic of China.

China provides us with an especially rich and fascinating case study for building feminist family theory. In traditional China, even more than in most preindustrial societies, family life was the indisputable nexus of the social system. Further, the Chinese family was a virtual citadel to patriarchy. Few family systems can compete with the Confucian for degradation and brutality toward women. From female infanticide to crippled feet to childbride sale, wife-beating, polygyny, and more. Chinese women tasted no end of bitterness in their short, mostly poverty-ridden lives. Today the situation is unrecognizably transformed. In the context of a socialist revolution, mainland Chinese women have perhaps moved closer to equality with men than have women in any other contemporary society. At the same time, the Chinese family system has undergone a dramatic transformation in the direction of the modern conjugal family—both in practice and ideology. And while the economic, political, and social hegemony of the family has been categorically eclipsed by party, state, and commune, the modern Chinese family remains a remarkably strong, reputedly harmonious, and peculiarly unquestioned element in Communist Chinese society.

What I intend to present here is an admittedly thrice-removed analysis of the significance of the Chinese family revolution for Western feminists. Relying heavily on secondary source material, I shall attempt to reconstruct the significant structural and historical events.[3] I will then discuss the implications of the Chinese experience for feminist theory.

The Decline of the Traditional Family

The contradictions within the structure of the traditional Chinese family contribute their share to a revolutionary dialectic. At the same time, however, it must be acknowledged that this argument can cut two ways. The same divisive kinship loyalties that weakened imperial authority also inhibited the development of collective consciousness of nationality or social class. Further, the particularistic norms and inherent nepotism of the classical Chinese family probably served to retard the growth of industrialization.[4] But ultimately history came down on the other side. It had a powerful accomplice in the imperialism of the West.

A trickle of Western missionaries had penetrated China since the seventh century, but their numbers and ideological impact did not attain significance until after the British victories in the mid-nineteenth-century Opium Wars. As the dynastic curtain was forcibly parted in the late nineteenth and early twentieth centuries, Western traders and industrialists began to mine the markets and resources of the immense Manchu empire.[5] Particularly in the urban areas, the combined effects of Western commerce, industry, and ideology were disastrous for the already badly strained family and social structure.[6]

The effects of commerce were felt first. An influx of new, cheap commodities—particularly textiles—had a disruptive effect on both consumption and production patterns. As it became less costly to remove domestic production from the home, the economic self-sufficiency of the traditional household began to erode. The introduction of exchange transactions outside the home, which were dependent on cash, further exacerbated this trend. The spread of domestic industry and the gradual introduction of machine technology were ultimately shattering. Together they challenged the central norms and relationships which supported the Confucian order.

Universalistic job criteria, specialization, and competition were disabling enough, but the opportunity for even a small proportion of women and youth of both sexes to be employed outside the home was probably the decisive factor in the undermining of traditional authority. Industrial capitalists found a ready pool of cheap labor in women of the poorer classes. Because their families were unable to forego the added income which their labor could contribute to family sustenance, young girls by the thousands poured into the silk and textile factories of Canton, Shanghai, and other developing urban industrial centers.[7] Although factory conditions were abysmal, the status and independence of the women they employed was immeasurably enhanced. For the first time in Chinese history, some Chinese women had a legitimate escape route from their family prisons. With the increasing economic and physical autonomy of even small numbers of women and youth, all the restrictive familial regulations and customs came to be questioned. As the family began to lose its role as a productive unit, the material basis for arranged marriage, polygyny, footbinding, ancestor worship, veneration of elders, and the double standard began to vanish.

An exceptional minority of women even found the collective strength to refuse marriage entirely. Early in the twentieth century, the women silk spinners of Canton formed a "collective spinsterhood, leading a pseudo-family life in highly organized societies."[8] Agnes Smedley reported that these young women were notorious and thought to be lesbians because they refused to marry, supported themselves and their families, formed secret sister societies, and even organized for higher wages and shorter hours.[9]

The Cantonese women were exceptional, but indices of family decay were prevalent. Divorce, delinquency, and suicide increased ominously. The degree of social and economic security provided by the extended family, which in its best moments belied the gracious myth, continued to decline. As Olga Lang has pointed out, the only assistance on which an individual could generally rely was that provided by the conjugal group.[10] Although family ties did count for something, affluent clan members were as likely as not to charge their impoverished relations usurious interest rates—that is, if they were willing to acknowledge the relationship at all. And even in most extended households, income was generally pooled along conjugal-unit lines. Because woman's contribution to this pool was apt to be negligible, her portion of security was correspondingly dim. If her husband was one of the many who became addicted to opium, gambling, or negotiable sexual amusements, there was not much a Chinese woman could do to prevent the sale of bed, board, offspring, or self to his debtors.[11]

The trend toward the modern nuclear family appeared first among the urban working classes. At the same time, upper classes were subjected to Western ideological influence. For the first time, educational privileges were extended to upper-class girls, and bourgeois women entered the university and the professions.[12] While economic conditions were creating the material basis for the physical emancipation of working-class women, women of the upper classes felt the stirrings of cultural emancipation. Indeed, as Lang observed, there was a contradiction between the theory and practice of the different social classes: "The workers and peasants often behave in new ways toward their parents, husbands, or children without realizing that they are repudiating the old Confucian rules; the young intellectuals often have new ideas about paternal authority, marriage, etc., without being able to put them into practice."[13] The Chinese Communist Party early perceived that to resolve this contradiction was one of its important revolutionary tasks.

There is little purpose in joining the debate over whether it was the internal contradictions of the Confucian social structure or the intrusion of the West that was ultimately decisive in bringing down the patriarchal order. More likely, as Joseph Levenson has pointed out, the two were mutually reinforcing. Weaknesses in the traditional order inspired massive rebellions for whose suppression the Manchus relied on increasing Western support, which in turn exacerbated the disintegrating trends, thereby inciting ever more serious rebellions.[14]

Suffice it to underscore that, as with the whole of the classical order, by the dawn of the twentieth century both the practice and ideology of the Confucian family were subject to relentless attack. The Chinese family had begun to lose its privileged position as the institutional center of the Chinese social order. While the Nationalist movement of Sun Yat-sen was by no means the first to incorporate family reform and feminist demands (the two were practically synonymous) within its political program, from that time forth it became foolhardy for any viable social or political Chinese movement to overlook the crumbling familial order.[15]

In 1916 intellectuals of the Chinese renaissance movement spent much of their venom in a frontal attack on the Chinese family. During the May Fourth Movement in 1919, the term "family revolution" was first publicized, and from that time forward, to students, nationalists, and progressives, the family came to symbolize China's weakness in the modern world.

The "family revolution" in pre-liberation China consisted of a series of spontaneous, uncoordinated, sporadic attacks on the Confucian patriarchal order. Although they directly affected the lives of a small minority, student protests, individual experimentation, and legal reforms patterned on Western models chipped away at tradition. Even Chiang Kai-shek's Kuomintang, which was loathe to condone youthful insubordination of any sort, and indeed launched the New Life Movement in 1934 artificially to resurrect the ancient Confucian virtues, could not afford to ignore the insistent demand for family reform. Largely in response to bourgeois pressure, in 1930 the KMT adopted a compromise measure, the Law of Kinship Relations. Although the Chinese family remained patronymic, patrilocal, patrilineal, and patriarchal, the law incorporated principles of freedom of marriage and monogamy. Most important, women received the legal right to inherit property.

The KMT code was not enforced and remained a paper protection for the privileged few, but by giving official sanction to spontaneous social practice, it bore witness to the historical inevitability of family transformation. I do not wish to retrace the details of that lengthy historical process. Yet it is important for our purposes to pay some attention to the pre-liberation history of Communist Party policy on the family.

Communist Policy before Liberation

When in 1919 Miss Chao Wu-chieh of Changsha chose the time-honored route for female martyrdom in China by slitting her throat in her bridal chair in order to escape the intolerable fate of her arranged marriage, she gave young Mao Tse-tung the inspiration for some of his earliest and most impassioned writings on the subject of women's oppression.[16] Mao condemned the brutal social structure that rendered suicide a prosocial act of individual protest, and he called for the collective struggle of a family revolution to eliminate the provocation for such acts of individual futility.

Mao's political consciousness was formed in the context of the liberalism and nascent feminism of the May Fourth period, but he had come by his feminist sympathies in a much earlier, more direct manner—at home.[17] Like many outstanding revolutionaries, Mao's earliest political sensibilities were nurtured in the family, where a warm, intimate relationship with his mother taught him to identify his cold, tyrannical father as one source of his and his mother's common persecution.[18] Neither Mao nor his future revolutionary comrades forgot their early commitment to women's liberation and family reform. When their politics matured from liberalism to Marxism they incorporated into their revolutionary program an awareness that family reform was one key to social change in China.

The women's movement in China was nurtured by war and affected by its vicissitudes. In the course of the Communist movement's twenty-eight-year struggle to liberate the homeland, its policy toward women and the family underwent many fits and starts. In 1922 the young CCP issued a proclamation for women's rights which established a special women's bureau.[19] Little attention was paid to this at first, probably because there was scant female participation in the early Chinese party. Moreover, both women and men among the early radicals considered women's issues secondary to the proletarian struggle.[20] Leftist women, like Hsiang Ching-yu, opposed crusaders for women's rights as too individualistic and bourgeois.

Hsiang, who headed the new CCP women's bureau, was influential in shaping early party policy on women. She opposed the tendency of Chinese feminists to perceive of their struggle in sexual terms. Hsiang attributed woman's low social status to the Chinese social structure and argued that woman's emancipation could only come through a structural change.

Throughout the 1920s, during the period of the CCP's urban proletariat strategy, Hsiang devoted most of her political energies to organizing women silk and cotton workers. Particularly in Shanghai, where women comprised a majority of the laboring class, the policy was initially successful. Female workers overcame their centuries of docility with a vengeance. They participated heavily in the wave of militant strikes which punctuated the decade. Another revolutionary heroine, Tsai Chang, organized provincial women during the Northern Expedition; Madame Sun Yat-sen established a training school in Hankow to train women organizers. The women's unions served a dual purpose, at times operating in a quasi-judicial fashion as marriage and divorce bureaus—a practice which encountered significant male resistance. The KMT response to the social and economic threat was brutal. The successes of the prolabor, anti-imperialist activities of the mid-1920s helped to provoke the White Terror of 1927 which decimated the urban proletarian struggle and set the desperate framework for the acceptance of the ultimately victorious peasant strategy of Mao Tse-tung.

The violent bloodbath of the counterrevolution which Chiang Kai-shek's forces unleashed against the Communists reserved some of its most sadistic brutality for the women organizers. More than a thousand female leaders (not all of them Communists) were hunted down, tortured, and executed. Hsiang Ching-yu was among the infamous fatalities of the terror.[21]

Thus the Communists were brutally persuaded to abandon their orthodox urban strategy. For the next two decades they redirected their energies to the construction of a peasant-based revolution. The Kiangsi Soviet became an early testing ground for policies on women and the family. There the central executive committee passed its first two marriage laws in 1931 and 1934. The marriage laws, patterned after those of the Soviet Union, were essentially liberal. They established the principle of free association in marriage. Women received the right to retain custody over children. By requiring the registration of marriage and divorce with local government, the state entered the marriage sector for the first time. The 1934 law, which protected Red Army soldiers from divorce by their wives, reflected aspects of the experience of the party in implementing the earlier code. Even though the earlier law had not been vigorously enforced, the right to divorce aroused considerable enthusiasm among young peasant women and widespread resistance from men and older women.

Throughout the revolutionary period party policy and practice veered a shaky course between the exigencies of the class and sex wars. Needing to attack the traditional family, if only to liberate women to mobilize their political and economic support, afraid to antagonize the men upon whom the "liberated" women were justifiably wont to vent their long pent-up fury, the CCP leadership was racked with conflict and dissension on this issue.[22]

Although the struggle for women's emancipation was never as central nor as militant as that for land reform, women in the liberated areas derived significant benefits from both these programs during the War for Liberation. Land reform granted women equal rights to land—the first condition for peasant women's economic independence. Women, quick to grasp the implications of land reform for their status within the family, participated actively in reform struggles.[23] Further, as the war expanded, and male labor power in the villages dwindled, women were forced to take up the slack. Women's associations developed mutual aid teams, undertook sabotage and intelligence operations, devised makeshift hospitals, and strained to maintain the subsistence economy for the duration. Their growth in consciousness and morale must have been stupendous.

Accordingly, in 1948 the party issued a new resolution encouraging women to struggle against their subordinate family status. The resolution declared that oppression of women was "an ideological struggle amongst the peasants and should be radically different from the class struggle against the feudal landlords."[24] In Maoist terms the class struggle is antagonistic, whereas contradictions among the people can be resolved through persuasion and propaganda.[25] The implication of the resolution was that women should refrain from violence against men. For the most part they did, but more than a few women's associations found their collective fury roused them to physical retribution against particularly oppressive, unrepentant men.[26] Once more the cadres found themselves on the tightrope. Sex antagonism posed a threat to class solidarity. Moreover, women's associations split along generational lines as older women fought younger women over the right to free choice in marriage. Until the civil war was ended and a stable social and economic order could be established, radical family policy was a tricky, sometime business. Yet when that time came in 1949, peasants and cadre in the liberated zones had established the economic, political, social, and even psychological basis for a permanent transformation of the family.

Feminist Controversies

A number of controversies continue to rage over certain facts and the meaning of the revolutionary period. As they have significance for contemporary feminist politics, it is worth trying to sort them out. First, there is rather passionate disagreement concerning the motivation and integrity of CCP feminist policy. Essentially the controversy is between those who affirm and those who distrust the feminist commitment of the Communist leadership. The former assert that from beginning to end women's liberation was at best a secondary concern—a means to an end. In its most hostile version, the argument claims that women's rights policy was sacrificed to the personal, political interests of a Stalinist leadership.[27] The less sectarian version charges that economic and political considerations consistently, and often misguidedly, shaped CCP policy on women and the family.[28] Such arguments point to the silencing of Ting Ling in 1942 as evidence of the party's repressive response to feminism. Those who differ place emphasis on the precarious balance of the revolutionary alliance which the Communists had to forge.[29] This position is essentially one of realpolitik. It excuses the Communists their antifeminist policies on the grounds that there was no other road to socialist victory—a destination they assert was in women's own best interests.

There is no denying the enormous strides Chinese women made under Communist leadership. To pit feminism against the goals of a socialist revolution is to make a prematurely divisive distinction. Socialism is not now, and was not then, exclusively a male project. Yet it is not inappropriate to raise questions about the process of feminist policy-making. The matter of Ting Ling is a case in point. I think it is incorrect to view the imposition of party discipline, which silenced her feminist protest in 1942, as a simple case of male chauvinism. The incident occurred during the height of the anti-Japanese mobilization, when deviationism of any form was considered highly dangerous.[30] Whatever one thinks of the political merits of ironclad party discipline, either under those specific historical circumstances or more generally (and I myself have visceral misgivings), it is sectarian to overlook the context of the Ting Ling affair.

It is equally wrong, it seems to me, for feminists to let it go at that. For the fact remains that what Ting Ling was presenting (and her life before and after the incident bore witness to the integrity of her motivation) was a feminist appeal. The leadership may well have been correct in judging the military situation as being too precarious to withstand the strain of feminist, or any other deviationist, militancy. But a significant detail for feminists to note is that the decision to subordinate the struggle for women's emancipation was made by a body overwhelmingly dominated by men. Given the historical context, particularly that of the patriarchal family system, it is unlikely that it could have been otherwise. But it makes me uneasy to see women so hasty to justify antifeminist policies made by agencies from which their sisters were systematically or otherwise excluded.

Why it is that women played so small a part in revolutionary leadership is also a matter of concern to contemporary Western feminists. Only four women's names appear on a list of one hundred top party leaders in 1928.[31] A mere thirty women were among the fifty thousand who set out from Kiangsi on the Long March.[32] Women were generally miserably underrepresented in the ranks of the vanguard. While it is likely that a garden-variety chauvinism in the CCP contributed its share to this unfortunate situation, structural aspects of sexism were probably more important. Suzette Leith has argued that the peasant base of the revolution goes a long way toward explaining women's low profile. Working women, who shared economic concerns with working men, were easily integrated into the class struggle, but when the party was forced to abandon its urban strategy, it ran smack up against the contradiction between class and sex antagonisms.[33] In the rural areas, the easiest method for organizing peasant women was around their repressive family conditions. These specialized concerns lent a separatist tendency to the women's associations. Moreover, the conservatism and sexism that was deeply entrenched in the countryside made it difficult for women to participate in military or other public, counterstereotyped roles.

Lest we take this to mean that a proletariat base assures sex equality, Leith concedes that even in the early period with its urban labor focus, few women leaders emerged at the top. This, she believes, can be explained by two major factors. First, the leadership was for the most part initially drawn from the ranks of the educated. Long-term sex discrimination in education kept the available pool of female leadership recruits low. The few women who received formal education were from the bourgeoisie and likely to be more attracted to the cause of liberal feminism. Secondly, it was the tendency of the CCP leadership to confine party women to the women's movement. Even Hsiang Ching-yu, who was an early labor sympathizer, was relegated to the leadership of the women's bureau.

Chinese women were caught on the horns of a strategic dilemma familiar to feminists. When they tried to participate as equal members of an integrated movement, they were required to overlook their specific oppression as women. Yet when they organized autonomously around women's issues, they were considered divisive to the cause of class solidarity.

There is disagreement over which horn Chinese women favored. Did they perceive their oppression primarily in sexual or in economic terms? Underlying this question are shades of the contemporary political dispute over whether sex or class is "the basic contradiction." It is difficult to make generalizations, particularly ex post facto, of subjective perceptions. From the available evidence it seems that Chinese women were variously aware of the dual nature of their oppression. There, as elsewhere, bourgeois women tended to focus on their status as women. Radical women, it would seem, accepted, and even helped formulate, the party analysis that sexual equality would follow from economic liberation. Yet given the practice of democratic centralism, it is not possible to speculate how many party women silently shared Ting Ling's misgivings about this approach. Peasant women probably ran the political gamut from sex to class hatred or indifference. Yet there is reasonable cause to assume they were at least as concerned with liquidating the patriarchy as they were with establishing socialism.

The most heated controversy over this period surrounds assessments of the success of feminism and the family revolution in the War for Liberation. I will reserve till later fuller consideration of the complexities of this issue, which, after all, is the crux of the political matter for feminist socialists.[34] Certainly even the CCP recognized that the family revolution was far from complete when the war ended in 1949. The nature of the obstacles that CCP revolutionary strategy placed in its way is the subject of the controversy.

Janet Salaff, who feels "the Communist Revolution stopped far short of transforming the social status of women," rests her case for this on her contention that "women were not organized *as women* during the revolutionary period." We have just seen that it was exactly because women were organized as women that their revolutionary commitment was called into question, but I do not think that is quite what Salaff has in mind. It is the fact that women, "despite their heavy contribution to the revolution, never gained control of the means of coercion—armed force—which would have guaranteed their power" that disturbs Salaff most.[35] Whatever the merits of this position for a contemporary feminist movement, it seems a rather academic judgment to make of the Chinese liberation struggle—one, perhaps, that mistakes an effect for a cause. Far more crucial, it seems to me, is to understand just why it was that women did not play an autonomous role in the military struggle.

There is little evidence, of which I am aware, that women were systematically thwarted in a sustained attempt to seize, or even to share, military power. We are left with the more likely, if unfortunate, conclusion that they did not try. It would be foolish to judge them too harshly. To have tried would have required the existence of a mass-based revolutionary feminist consciousness. Even here and now it is far from clear that the material and ideological conditions for such a development are yet ripe. In semifeudal, patriarchal China, it was probably out of the question.

Feminism and the Family in the People's Republic

Political History

When the victorious CCP adopted its first national marriage law on 1 May 1950, it was making official policy out of the social processes of family reform that had long been underway. What had been sporadic and uncoordinated experimentations now became a matter of explicit legal doctrine and intense propaganda. The May 1 law officially put an end to all the patriarchal, authoritarian abuses of the Confucian family order. It explicitly repudiated "the arbitrary and compulsory feudal marriage system, which is based on the superiority of man over woman."[36] The bill was a victory for the monogamous, conjugal family based on principles of free association and sexual equality. Polygamy, concubinage, child betrothal, marriage by purchase, infanticide, and illegitimacy were abolished. Divorce, remarriage, inheritance, and property rights were guaranteed to women as well as men.

In the twenty-four years since the passage of that revolutionary bill, CCP policy on women and the family has been through a variety of stages and formulations. Every three to four years policy on the family seems to vacillate along the lines of the broader political struggle. As party strategy shifts from the political to the economic front of the socialist transformation, woman and family policy steers a choppy course between emphasis on the special aspects of women's oppression and the submergence of women's liberation within the broader class struggle. The vicissitudes of family reform recall the preliberation tension between sex and class antagonisms. Accordingly, Chinese family life in the People's Republic has been through alternating periods of upheaval and restabilization.

While it is possible to chart the approximate course of official party policy, a social history of actual family life must be sketchy and impressionistic. We have little more to go on than the accounts of Westerners whose visits have been widely scattered in time, geography, and perspective, and whose access to primary material has been limited. Bearing this limitation in mind, it seems reasonable to divide the post-liberation era into six periods.[37]

(1) From liberation until approximately 1953, the family revolution was a political priority. This early period was marked by concentrated political mobilization around the issues of land reform and the marriage law. So intensive was the agitation that the marriage law soon came to be known to the masses as the "divorce law." Women and men of all ages participated enthusiastically in land reform struggles, but, as in the earlier period, many men and older women put up serious resistance to the marriage bill. Women inundated the courts with their divorce suits. They were the plaintiffs in 76.6 percent of the 21,433 divorce cases of the 32 cities and 34 rural county-seats reported in the *Jen-min Jeh-pao (People's Daily)* of 29 September 1951.[38] They were answered by the same brutality and obstruction that their sisters in the liberated areas had experi-

enced earlier. Beatings, confinement, and murder were the fate of many young women who sought to exercise their new freedoms. Nor, as official party statements recognized, were local party cadre aloof from this violent, obstreperous behavior. The peasant women came to say: "To get a divorce, there are three obstacles to overcome: the obstacle of the husband, the obstacle of the mother-in-law, and the obstacle of the cadres. The obstacle of the cadres is the hardest to overcome."[39]

Once more a wave of female suicides led party leadership to reconsider pursuit of the militant policy. Marjory Wolf attributes to this the ensuing slowdown on family policy: "The fact that women, supposedly the primary beneficiaries of the campaign, resisted it cannot help having had some influence on the social planner's decision to turn aside for awhile."[40] Yet to interpret suicide as female resistance to family reform is to curiously misread the evidence.

It was in resistance to the old, not the new, family system that most of these young women gave their lives. Much more in the way of political and economic reconstruction had to be done before it was safe for women to exercise their rights. Far-reaching as it seemed at the time, the 1950 law was only a partial measure. It was based on a system of private land ownership, which was a significant advance, but still provided women with inadequate economic security to take full advantage of their legal opportunities.

(2) The inadequacy of the economic base was, most likely, as much responsible for the retrenchment of the second period (1953–1957) as were the alarming female suicide and murder rates. During this period of the first five-year plan, political agitation was discouraged, as Communist policy concentrated on economic development. The party attempted to justify a time of reaction, or restabilization, if one prefers, on issues of family reform by pronouncements that women had already achieved liberation. Divorce policy underwent the most dramatic reversal—one from which it has never since recovered. Divorce became, and remains, exceedingly difficult to obtain, on the principle that if one makes one's own bed, one must lie in it. Or in the words of a village secretary: "Even if the mar-

riage is childless, people still consider divorce immoral, because now that people can choose whom they will marry, they will have chosen each other, and should put up with the consequences."[41]

Divorce on the basis of "incompatibility" was denounced as bourgeois and divisive, and marriage came to be promoted as a positive socialist political act. Women were urged to further the revolution both by participating in agricultural work and by resuming "their" domestic responsibilities uncomplainingly. This latter directive was intended primarily for urban women, for whom there were not yet sufficient employment opportunities to provide feasible alternatives to familialism.

(3) The Great Leap Forward (1958–1961) was particularly well-named from the point of view of feminist progress. The establishment of the people's communes represented an important structural innovation for women, replacing the family as the source of an individual's economic and social security. There is some evidence that the communes were a popular response to local need rather than simply an edict from Peking.[42] Women had everything to gain from the innovation.[43] Before agricultural production was socialized, women in Ten Mile Inn "eked out their grain with chaff for part of the year" to conserve energy-giving nourishment for the harder-working men.[44] Not only were labor opportunities for women limited, but, before the institution of the commune, wages were paid to the family rather than to the individual. With collectivization, the countryside experienced its first labor shortage. Women were called upon to fill the gap. It was an instance when the needs both of the society and of women's emancipation were in close harmony. To free women for productive activity such social services as canteens (collective dining halls) and nurseries were introduced. A new era for women and socialism appeared close at hand.

Rapidly, however, the communes experienced serious setbacks. Soviet aid was abruptly withdrawn in 1960. China was devastated by three years of natural diasters. Production quotas went by the boards. It is also thought that collectivization was pushed too fast. Whether or not Katie Curtin is correct in her claim that peasants reacted with a massive sitdown to unreasonably high production and labor quotas, there is evidence from village studies that peasant consciousness was not yet prepared to accept socialized housework. The canteens in Yangyi commune, for example, were shut down in response both to natural disasters and to complaints from diners (mainly men), who preferred their meals cooked at home. Sheila Rowbotham maintains that throughout contemporary China "the peasant women particularly seem to prefer their individual families to communal facilities."[45]

(4) Predictably, in the fourth period (1962–1965) China entered a second phase of retrenchment. The Liu Shao-chi faction assumed party leadership, economic development was once more the national priority, and restabilization of the family was again the order of the day. The party issued a handbook on *Love, Marriage, and the Family,* which put forth the official ideology on the family. Marriage, it was asserted, is the single appropriate response to love, an emotion which it would seem was expected to be guided primarily by the dictates of political priorities. As senior editor of *Women of China,* Tung Pien promoted the back-to-the-home revival by printing such articles as: "Women Live for the Purpose of Raising Children," "Women Should Do More Family Duties," and "For Women to Engage in Enterprises is Like Flying Kites under the Bed."[46] Communist stories of this period, in contrast to those published during the Great Leap Forward, also resurrect some of the Confucian family virtues. Respect for elders, the closeness of the father-son relationship, and semiarranged marriages are common themes in these stories. On the basis of a comparative survey of stories of this period from the People's Republic and Taiwan, Chin concluded that the shift was no casual matter. It appeared to her to represent a partial return to a celebration of paternal authority, father-son solidarity, and the subordination of youth to their elders.[47]

In the villages, many women seemed to accept their familiar subordinate status. Women pioneer Li Kuei-ying of Liu Ling village explained to Jan Myrdal: "You see, not all women by any means are aware that they are their husbands' equals. Some still look up to their husbands as in the old days, before women became free. They suffer because of that, and they must be freed from it."[48]

(5) The Cultural Revolution (1966–1968) was, in part, an attempt to shake the masses out of their lethargy. Maoists denounced the "right-wing revisionist" politics of Liu Shao-chi, who was also blamed for the reactionary policies on women and the family. Tung Pien, too, was purged and denounced as a "black gang element" who had "plotted to use the bourgeois thesis of human nature to corrode readers so that they would pursue and be content with the warmth of small families, thereby destroying their revolutionary will." Instead, *Women of China* began publishing articles attacking arranged marriages, betrothal gifts, and extravagant wedding celebrations. Women were encouraged to participate in the widespread political criticism and fervor that marked the period, but the official woman's movement was disbanded. International Women's Day disappeared from Chinese calendars. Women were asked once more to throw in their revolutionary lot with men. One Chinese author proclaimed: "Revolution differs according as it is true revolution or false revolution. It does not differ according to sex."[50]

The Cultural Revolution was a complex event from a feminist point of view. The massive politicization, and particularly the renewed emphasis on women as equal revolutionary agents, was crucial to women's progress, but during the two-year suspension of all normal social activity, education and the birth control campaign were among the casualties. Despite official propaganda to the contrary, youthful marriages also increased—perhaps in response to the suspension of schooling and the general relaxation of social control. Since a history of sex discrimination in education and inferior literacy rates are key factors in women's continued subordinate status, the two-year holiday was a very mixed blessing. Yet the Cultural Revolution broke the stranglehold on the family. Women, and men, seemed to gain a renewed respect for women's productive, political, and cultural capabilities—an ideological triumph it would be foolish to minimize.

(6) It is difficult to so neatly categorize the period since the Cultural Revolution. The earlier pattern would suggest that once more political and feminist issues would recede, economic concerns become paramount, and family life enjoy renewed emphasis. There is evidence that at least part of the pattern holds firm. Mark Selden reports that the family, "including the extended family of several generations," has taken on renewed vitality. Courtyard living arrangements which accommodate extended families who share a common kitchen are popular in the countryside. Comprehensive daycare is still a rarity in rural areas, and women continue to participate less and earn less in socialist production.[51]

Yet it would be incorrect to characterize the post-Cultural Revolution period as thoroughly reactionary on feminism. Women continue to be exhorted to assume full membership in the revolution. Recent issues of *Peking Review* are instructive for ascertaining the official line on women's emancipation. Most of the articles on women take the form of inspirational autobiographical addresses, intended to reaffirm faith in women's steady progress under Chairman Mao, the CCP, and the socialist road. Hsu Kwang, for example, recounts her long history (since 1937) in the Chinese women's movement. At first, Hsu claims, she thought that women had to wage their fight for freedom against men and in the home. Now she knows this was a mistake. "This was trying to settle the woman's problem in isolation and proved to be quite impractical."[52] Instead Hsu has learned that the oppression of women has its social roots in private ownership and class exploitation. The only path for women's emancipation is through the revolutionary historic mission of the proletariat. The bourgeois women's rights movement is a digression. "Since the women's rights movements of the bourgeoisie pursue equality of the sexes in form, and do not take into account classes and class struggle and are divorced from the social revolutionary movement, they can only sidetrack the women's liberation movement."[53] Overlooking her own admission that women are significantly underrepresented in positions of greatest responsibility, Hsu claims that women enjoy equal status with men in all spheres.

She enthusiastically reports that public dining halls, creches, and communal facilities are increasing, that family planning progresses, and that housework is shared between women and men.

Fu Wen, in another issue of *Peking Review*, adopts the familiar Chinese propagandistic technique of scapegoating.[54] She blames Confucius and Mencius for the doctrine of women's oppression and links Liu Shao-chi and Lin Piao to the reactionary antifemale line. Women are exhorted to participate in the mass movement to criticize Lin Piao and Confucius in order to rid the nation of the feudal ideology so oppressive to women.

Hsing Yen-tzu offers another rousing success story of women's progress under Mao and the party. She claims that domestic problems are quickly being solved and that women are taking an increasing role in all levels of leadership. In a revealing anecdote of hero worship, Hsing recounts the most exciting moment of her life when she sat next to Mao at a National People's Congress dinner in 1964: "Every time I recall that occasion my heart beats with excitement and I feel incomparable warmth in my heart. . . . Only in socialist New China, under the leadership of Chairman Mao and the Communist Party, is it possible for us working women to live as happily as we do today."[55]

I think there are a number of important lessons to be drawn from such material. First, the articles appear to serve a dual political function. Obviously, they attempt to consolidate support for the Maoist faction of the CCP. More importantly, the self-congratulatory technique of reciting women's accomplishments is probably intended to serve a self-fulfilling purpose. It puts forth the prevailing political line on women and the goals of feminist policy. The current emphasis on shared housework, communal facilities, family planning, equal status, and increased political leadership roles for women bodes well for feminism. It demonstrates that there is official ideological backing for all of those reforms. Second, the scapegoating device indicates the awareness of the party that women's emancipation depends on ideological struggle as well as structural reforms.[56] By exhorting women to participate in criticism campaigns, the party is indirectly encouraging a revival of women's consciousness-raising activity, reminiscent of the earlier "speak bitterness" campaigns.

The feminist analysis revealed in the propaganda literature will be recognized as orthodox Marxism-Leninism. It ties women's oppression to the private ownership of property and links their liberation to the proletarian revolution. Although specialized aspects of women's oppression are recognized, they tend to be downplayed, while sex antagonism is projected onto scapegoats. There is one rather disturbing facet of this literature (two, if one includes the doctrinaire quality of the language itself) in the incestuous father-worship aspect of the Chairman Mao cult. As Rowbotham has pointed out, it is not clear whether "self-activity at the base can be reconciled with the magnified figure of Chairman Mao directing from the top,"[57] particularly, I might add, when he has assumed such paternalistic proportions.

The Current State of the Family Revolution

By now it should be clear that the family revolution in modern China has been an integral aspect of a long, complex process of broad social change. It has taken close to a century for the Chinese Revolution to transform a decaying semifeudal social order governed by a system of bureaucratic despotism—with the patriarchal lineage as its social cement—into a powerful modernizing society that guarantees security, dignity, and opportunity to almost all its members, through the most egalitarian example of a socialist system the world has yet seen.

In the course of that process the Confucian patriarchal family is perhaps the most dramatic, unmourned casualty. It has been replaced by a particularly Chinese variant of the increasingly universal pattern of modern conjugal family life. It might be useful at this point to review the prominent features of the Chinese family revolution and to take stock of exactly how far the People's Republic has and has not gone in transforming family life in general, and woman's status in particular.

On the level of structural change, the first striking fact is that kinship is no longer the central organizational fact of life in China. Through the socialization of the forces of production, the family has been transformed from a self-sufficient unit of production to a unit of consumption whose members are highly integrated into the larger social order. Hence, the family has lost its former significance as the sole source of its members' economic security. Even more than in other industrializing nations, the family has also forfeited many of its educational, religious, medical, and recreational responsibilities. In China, the work team, production brigade, commune, neighborhood association, state, and party now provide more assurance of an individual's right to eat, work, study, survive, and prosper than the family ever did or could. Small wonder that these agencies have begun to compete successfully for an individual's allegiance.

While the large conjoint family of classical legend is but a faint archival memory, it would be a mistake to exaggerate the disappearance of the extended family. As we have already seen, the conjoint family was never more than a prerogative of the very rich. The "famille souche," or stem family, was more typical. Although the two-generational conjugal household has become more widespread, there is evidence that the stem family retains popularity. Particularly in rural areas, where grandparents assume major responsibility for child care (and even in the cities this is by no means an unusual arrangement),[58] widowed parents are apt to live with their married children. Even when households are separate, grandparents are likely to be nearby and daily contact between parent and male child is unlikely to be severed by marriage.[59]

Most of the other important structural changes in the Chinese family read like a catalog of modern, conjugal family features. The husband-wife relationship has replaced the father-son as the pivotal relationship in the family structure. Polygamy, betrothal by purchase, arranged marriages, ancestor worship, infanticide, and prostitution are disappearing with varying rates of haste.[60] Youth has begun to eclipse its elders in social status and authority. However, children are still required by law to support their aged parents—probably as much a reflection of the limitations of the Chinese economy as of the traditional veneration of the aged.[61]

The acceptable age for marriage in China has been raised, both by statute and, increasingly, by custom. The marriage law prohibited marriage by females under eighteen and by males under twenty, and intensive propaganda has been directed toward delaying the event considerably longer. Although reports of actual practice vary, there is evidence that rural women typically marry between the ages of twenty-one and twenty-three to men who are twenty-three to twenty-five, while in the cities marriage is typically delayed a couple of years longer.[62] At the same time the trend has been toward having fewer children. The two facts are intimately and intentionally related. The CCP campaign for later marriage is the central element in its population limitation policy. Because premarital chastity is nearly universal practice in China, later marriage is the most effective method of birth control the Chinese have at their disposal. However strange it falls on Western ears, abortion and "illegitimate" births are reported to be rare.[63]

This is probably gratifying to party officials, a factor of some significance, because initially the rest of its birth control program met with only uneven success. As Salaff has pointed out, it is essential for the Chinese to limit population growth as long as their economic development is dependent upon a strong labor force rather than on high consumption patterns.[64] It is important for China to avoid a disproportionately greater infant-child population during this developmental period. However, in the rural areas especially, childbearing, which has long been highly valued but economically disastrous, enjoyed a new popularity under conditions of economic security. As a 1971 peasants' ballad in Szechwan ran: "Better produce a little flesh dumpling [a baby], than produce work points."[65] Han Suyin reports that initially the birth control drives were incompetently managed. Respect for traditional sentiment, she claims, was responsible for Mao's apparent reversal on population control policy in 1958 when he proclaimed that China's greatest strength lay in her enormous population. Although the party remains anti-Malthusian, it never really abandoned its attempt to limit population growth. By all reports its more recent campaign has been enormously successful.[66]

Advocacy of delayed marriage probably serves political as well as economic purposes. By postponing the potential conflict in loyalty an intimate marital relationship might pose, the zestful energies of China's youth are left free for service to their country. One young Chinese woman described her exemplary marriage arrangements in a 1966 issue of *Women of China*: "We also agreed with each other to have a later marriage so as to completely use our youthful vitality in the service of constructing socialism."[67]

The structural changes in Chinese family life both initiate and reflect important changes in familial values. The priority on service to the revolution is unquestionably the most striking characteristic of Chinese social life today. Loyalty to one's family is properly subordinate to loyalty to the party and the state. To the extent that this has been internalized, it is a radical reversal of classical Confucian sensibilities.

No longer are children pardoned for shielding parental crime in the practice of filial piety. C. K. Yang records several examples of Communist youth and women who were encouraged to report, capture, and surrender their subversive parents and husbands.[68] One Communist youth describes his agonizing internal struggle before he helped capture and deliver his reactionary father to the authorities. Yet after his father was imprisoned, the son was relieved: "My duty was at last done. I felt light-hearted; I was happy, for I had rid the people of a dangerous character."[69]

Private life has been officially assigned a very feeble second place in the People's Republic. In countless interviews, cadres make this point explicit: "One's private life is a small matter; it's the state, the society, that's important."[70] Political and work assignments that require long-term separations of married couples, while atypical, seem to be accepted easily by the parties involved. The director of the Woman's Association of Chin-An district, Shanghai, sees her husband only two weeks a year. They send each other study material on the thought of Mao Tse-tung and accept their situation philosophically: "We do not regard separation too seriously, as a bad thing. We accept it as it is necessary for the good of the country. We must think about our whole family, the Motherland, rather than our own small interests. Without the party and Chairman Mao, our lives would not be so happy."[71]

In view of this apparently widespread sentiment, it is not surprising that political criteria are expected to dominate selection of one's marriage partners and decisions concerning divorce.[72] The emphasis in marital relationships is on comradeship. Reason dictates passion, and it is considered the height of good sense to seek out a hard-working, frugal, even-tempered, service-oriented mate.[73] The young woman who cheerfully delayed her marriage to sublimate her "youthful vitality" in political work describes her engagement to a party cadre: "After a period of time we got to know each other well, our ideas were similar, and we fell in love."[74] Putting politics in command is a basic Maoist principle. When marriages run into difficulty, the political thought of Mao Tse-tung is employed to serve as therapy:

> We sat down with Chang Yu-chen and her husband and read what Chairman Mao had written about the correct handling of contradictions amongst the people. When Chang Yu-chen and her husband had their quarrels these weren't a contradiction between ourselves and the enemy, but a contradiction amongst the people. So we tried to apply what we'd studied and had a deep, thorough-going discussion and a frank exchange of views with Chang Yu-chen and her husband. After that they stopped quarreling. They seem happy together. At least for the time being.[75]

One consequence of this political approach is that divorce has become exceedingly rare in China.[76] Generally every effort is made to discourage unhappy couples from dissolving their bonds. Plaintiffs must first win the approval of their production brigades or local associations. This is by no means a simple matter, particularly as production and political considerations guide the verdicts. When the husband of a certain Mrs. Li requested a divorce on the grounds that his wife, who had been given special responsibilities as a rural production brigade official, was neglecting her home and children, his peers decided against him: "Members of the production brigade testified that while it was true that Mrs. Li was doing less housework, she was carrying out important duties for the brigade. Accordingly, the husband was in the wrong and after 'education and criticism' he withdrew his divorce suit."[77]

Closely related to this highly rationalistic and political approach to love is the much-remarked-upon asceticism that seems to pervade contemporary China. We have already referred to the apparent near-universality of premarital chastity in China. Monogamy, fidelity, and exclusive heterosexuality are equally esteemed sexual values, so much so that adultery is punishable by law. Despite the fact that birth control devices are readily available, so that sex and reproduction can reasonably be separated, sexual freedom is considered a product of bourgeois decadence. Yet the Chinese are not pleased with their reputation for puritanism. K. S. Karol found in his discussion with Chinese filmmakers that "in their view present-day China is, on the contrary, antipuritanical because it wants to break with the superpuritanical Confucian morality which prevailed throughout the countryside."[78] In addition, the Chinese are quick, and correct, to point out the liberating aspects of a society devoid of consumerism in which female sexuality is not objectified. Furthermore, Chinese women are justifiably proud of their progress in eliminating the double standard, even if what they have replaced it with is a single standard which Carol Tavris has dubbed, "all for none and none for all, at least until marriage."[79]

Nevertheless, it is the apparent near-absence of sexual experimentation in China that sits most mysteriously on Western consciousness. Add to this the homogeneity of life patterns—the total absence of viable alternative life styles to that of monogamous marriage—and you have a morality which few foreign individualists are prepared to covet.

On the positive side, indeed the paradoxical side, Chinese family life appears to be exceptionally harmonious, morale remarkably high, and a spirit of civic optimism characterizes the national consciousness. As Ezra Vogel has pointed out, the lack of tension in the family is probably a function of the absence of power relationships created by the loss of economic functions. Family roles are stripped of power when they do not determine the individual's access to economic security. Further, family equanimity is probably helped along by the segregation of social networks of individual family members. Individuals in China are tightly integrated into small extrafamilial groups—typically the work group, school, or neighborhood association—which meet weekly under the direction of an activist to discuss all manner of public and personal issues. As other voluntary groups (aside from party, Youth League, and affiliated mass organizations) are discouraged, and there is little overlap between family members' groups, families rarely participate in group activities together.[80] These factors, with the structured opportunity to air conflict in a group setting, probably go a long way toward minimizing the customary tensions and frustrations of family life. Nor is the widespread optimism difficult to comprehend. Chinese women and men are tightly integrated into a society that has brought dignity and purpose to a people with powerful memories of degradation and despair. The contrast between their national mood and ours is not difficult to fathom.

There is no denying that Chinese women and the Chinese family have come a very long way. But we would be remiss to overlook the limitations which remain to China's progress toward sex equality and family reform. The most obvious inequity is the serious underrepresentation of women in positions of high-level leadership, in the party, and in the military.[81] Handicaps in literacy, education, and leadership experience contribute to women's secondary status.[82] The fact that a good many of the most prominent female leaders (like Ching Soong-ling, Teng Ying-chao, Chiang Ching, and until recently, Yeh Chun) are the wives or widows of the male leadership has unfortunate implications for female mobility.[83]

Second, despite impressive gains, sex-typing is far from dormant in Chinese economic and social life. Women uniformly perform the traditionally female tasks. All nursery and kindergarten teachers are women. Domestic production inside and outside the home is typically defined as women's work. For example, when women, who composed one third of a special tract work force in Yangyi commune, worried that they would not find time to make shoes for their families, the branch committee decided to release them from production work an extra half-day each week.[84] When Lio Shao-chi's "black line" that women should only do housework was condemned during the Cultural Revolution, political discussion groups in Lio Ling village decided that men should *help* with the housework. However, the village men opposed the plan. Finally they agreed to watch their children when their wives went to meetings. A cooperative sewing-house was established to help reduce *women's* household burdens.[85]

It has been difficult to overcome the culturally embedded conviction that family work is woman's work. Economic and theoretical factors reinforce the difficulty. Even today women are not yet fully integrated into the productive work force. Salaff estimates that while women comprise 40 percent of the agricultural labor brigades, their workforce participation is sporadic compared to men's, revolving around the demands of their household and childrearing responsibilities. Since the mid-1960s, political organizational work has been directed toward urging women to redefine themselves as workers rather than as family members, but thus far, for rural women at least, a good many of their links to the community continue to relate to their childbearing and childrearing activities.[86]

In urban areas the situation is different, but not dramatically superior. Urban men appear to participate more often in household chores,[87] communal childcare facilities in factories and neighborhoods are more widely available than in the countryside; women factory workers receive paid maternity leaves; and women play central leadership roles in the urban residents' committees. However, women are the first to be laid off when employment drops, and they are concentrated in the low-wage neighborhood "housewife" industries.[88] Although their familial burdens are lighter than those of their rural sisters, urban women retain more responsibility than do their husbands for childcare and domestic chores.

Even when women are fully integrated into the work force, they are likely to encounter residual sex-typing right on the job.

In the textile factories of model production brigade Ta Chai, women operate the looms while men have primary responsibility for machine repair and supervisory positions.[89] Women in the People's Liberation Army have separate battalions that generally perform service tasks.[90]

Although sex-typing is far from eliminated, it appears that a conscientious attempt is being made to open traditionally male-defined roles to women. The Yangyi commune branch committee, for example, decreed that every brigade and work team was to have a woman as vice-head.[91] The Iron Girls of Ta Chai, the military women of the Red Detachment of Women, and the Yang Family Circle are held up as models of revolutionary womanhood. However, men do not seem to be entering traditionally female occupations. Moreover, sex differences are accepted as natural and desirable by most Chinese. They believe women are better with children and seem to let it go at that.[92]

Perhaps the critical area of discrimination against women concerns their unequal access to economic rewards. Women in China do receive equal pay for equal work; but they do not have the opportunity to perform what is considered equal work. As long as they retain primary responsibility for household and childcare tasks, this is likely to remain the case. The commune work-point system is a critical structural factor in perpetuating this inequity in rural China. Current CCP policy is "to each according to his work." Work points are awarded on the basis of annual self and peer evaluations of an individual's average daily work rate. Physical strength and experience are among the criteria employed, and hence fully employed women typically earn approximately two fewer points than men per day.[93] The work-point system and the conjugal family reinforce each other to women's disadvantage. Because the family remains the critical income unit, women are apt to shoulder the household responsibilities in order to free their husbands for the more lucratively awarded work-point jobs. In turn, the emphasis on physical criteria and experience reinforces the tendency to sex-type workforce and domestic tasks.[94]

The halt of the communalization movement in the early

1960s probably accounts for much of this double-bind. The unsuccessful attempt fully to socialize domestic work sent traditional woman's work, and thus woman's identity, back to its original family base. As we have already seen, economic factors had much to do with this setback. The commune could not yet afford to assume full responsibility for domestic services. The canteens of Yangyi commune were closed down because it was cheaper to have everyone (that is, women) cook at home, where the fuel that heated their kangs could serve its traditional dual purpose (cooking and heating), rather than expend work-team funds on additional precious fuel. The natural disasters of the early commune years overtook the drive to release women from housework.[95]

The other side of this dilemma is that work performed in the home continues to be regarded as individual rather than socially productive labor. Hence it receives no wage from the collective. I do not wish to embark upon an application of the contemporary Western feminist wages-for-housework dispute. Certainly there would be enormous potential for sex-typing in introducing public compensation for domestic chores. I simply wish to point out that the current arrangement obscures the social utility of work involved in the reproduction of labor power. This is also reflected in the loss of pay that rural women suffer when they avail themselves of maternity leaves. And while grandparents often mind their grandchildren, the continuing shortage of comprehensive childcare facilities in rural areas remains a barrier to women's autonomy.

Similarly in the urban areas, economic pressures have kept wages down in the small, labor-intensive neighborhood "housewife" factories. Cadres justify the wage inequity on the grounds that the women do not require further remuneration because their husbands earn sufficient wages in the larger state-owned factories.[96]

A final factor cries out for examination. Of the traditional oppressive "4 Ps" in China (patriarchy, patriliny, patrinomy, and patrilocality), one remains as index and buttress of male supremacy. The majority of Chinese marriages continue to be patrilocal. At least in the rural areas, which contain 80 percent of the Chinese population, it is customary for the bride to move to her new husband's village. This immediately places many Chinese women at a social, political, economic, and psychological disadvantage. They lack the local reputations and experience to win them positions of responsibility and power. They lose seniority at work. They must build from scratch the loyalties and friendships which they will need to support them in their domestic and public trials.

But it is not only the practical consequences of patrilocality which are significant for women. There is evidence that Chinese women and men alike accept the asymmetrical arrangement unquestioningly. It is thought to be "natural," like sex differences, and that is simply that.[97] Patrilocality must appear equally unremarkable to Western commentators, because aside from its recent mention in Juliet Mitchell's *Psychoanalysis and Feminism* I do not recall ever having seen it mentioned in print.[98] Whatever the merits of Mitchell's analysis of patrilocality as the symbolic exchange of women by men, it is certain that patrilocality reflects a deeply embedded cultural subordination of women. That it operates in such apparent anonymity reveals the psychological depth of women's secondary status.

Conclusion

After surveying the history of family revolution in China one cannot help but feel that the transformation in the status of Chinese women is little short of miraculous. It is true that New China has participated in the universal trend of social evolution from a form of the self-sufficient extended family to the highly interdependent conjugal family system. In China, as elsewhere, the family has lost its exclusive responsibility and control over the socialization, employment, inspiration, and nurturance of its members. Yet the People's Republic variant of the modern conjugal family is unique. The Chinese family today appears to be stronger, more harmonious, more agreeable to its participants than does the family life of any modern society we know about.

The family revolution in China is far from complete. In fact, the Chinese repeatedly remind themselves and others that their revolution is a never-ending process in which the revolutionary masses must continually rededicate themselves to progress from socialism to communism. But there are a variety of barriers which retard the feminist aspect of this advance.

The historic material poverty of China imposes one primary structural impediment to feminist revolutionary advance in China. It was primarily economic scarcity that halted the movement to communalize housework and child care. While the party urges men to do their share of the household work "which social institutions have not yet been able to take over,"[99] it is economic scarcity that restricts the Chinese to the less-than-communist remuneration principle of "to each according to his (and not quite to her!) work." Scarcity maintains the premium on physical strength which underlies the discriminatory work-point system. The family still must shoulder certain economic burdens as a consequence, and it is women, as always, who draw the short straw.

There are those who argue that scarcity is a red herring. The real culprit is the authoritarian CCP:

> The repressive defense by the Stalinists of the nuclear family, and with it of female oppression, flows not primarily from the lack of funds for social services to replace it. If that were the case, economic necessity alone would hold the family together until it could be replaced. The coercive attitudes of the CCP toward sexuality and divorce stem rather from the need to defend hierarchical privilege against democratic and egalitarian demands by the masses.[100]

This claim is difficult to legitimate on several grounds. There is little evidence, and Curtin offers none, that the masses in China have presented any such demands. Nor is there a great deal to complain about on the matter of equality. The People's Republic is more advanced in this respect than any other modern society. Nevertheless there is likely some purpose beyond economics that leads the CCP systematically to encourage stable family life. The family in China still contributes its portion to social and political stability. Whether or not this is just cause for political suspicion is difficult to assess. We simply do not know enough about the inner workings of family-policy decision-making in China. Yet it is a cause for concern that men, who have real privileges to maintain, appear to be primarily in control of this process.

Not all of the barriers to sexual equality and family revolution in China are structural. There is an aspect of social life in the People's Republic that is extremely paradoxical from the vantage point of advanced, industrial Western culture. Limitations on sexual equality in China are apparent. Sexual morality is rigid. Alternate life styles to marriage and childbearing are virtually nonexistent. Freedom of expression is sharply curtailed. Each of these restrictions is considered cause for outrage in the West. Yet so far as we are able to discern (and there are genuine limitations to this capacity), there is little corresponding outcry in New China. Chinese women with high levels of political consciousness do not seem concerned about the unequal distribution of power between women and men: "But what does it matter if we do not have statistical representation? Our interests and our needs are more than adequately met."[101] Puritanical sexual codes incite no youthful rebellion we can learn about. Doctrinal orthodoxy seems to cause few qualms. All in all, popular and feminist morale appear exceptionally high.

The seeming equanimity of the Chinese in regard to the rigidity of Chinese sexual codes excites the greatest degree of curiosity in Western political circles. Many explanations have been put forth to account for it. Certainly the history of sexual exploitation is an important consideration. As it was for middle-class women in Victorian America, the first stage of sexual liberation in China may well be the right to say no. Monogamous, faithful marriage may have been a basic feminist demand. Helen Snow claims that "to one who has lived in China in the old society, there is no mystery about this strange new Puritanism. It was promoted by women as part of their attempt to demand respect for themselves and for the home and marriage in a new style."[102]

This argument is certainly plausible. Yet by itself it is an inadequate explanation of such widespread asceticism on the part of men as well as women. Sublimation seems to be governmental policy as well. We have already seen how youth is encouraged to expend its vital juices in the service of the people.[103] Sexual relationships of passionate intensity might pose a serious threat to the collective ethos and contribute to unwelcome population growth. The homogeneity of life styles may serve economic and political functions. Karol has pointed out that the celebration of the "moral and psychological simplicity of the poor" is useful to a regime interested in guiding its youth toward a "family functionalism."[104] Indeed, as Sidel has observed, the Communist Chinese have quite a different view of personal life from our own:

> While the Chinese are clearly concerned about their personal lives, they see themselves at the same time as part of a larger scene . . . and consequently, one's obligation is not merely to achieve a "happy" or "fulfilled" life for oneself but also to participate actively in the larger world. . . . Thus personal life is not the ultimate goal or even expectation but rather a subtle interplay between personal well-being and the role or contribution one can make to one's environment.[105]

Moreover, China remains a peasant-based society, only recently embarked upon a course of modern development, whereas ideologies of liberal individualism emerged in societies undergoing capitalist industrialization. For skeptical Westerners, it must be left a possibility that our own presumptions of what is "human nature" are ethnocentrically bound.[106]

Still, if one is to avoid a hopelessly relativist position, it is legitimate to raise questions about the degree of coercive indoctrination that underlies the apparent intellectual, social, and sexual conformity of the contemporary Chinese. A cause for concern in any instance, doctrinaire socialization is of particular concern with regard to women whose historic experience has subjected them to a disproportionate share of obedience-training and social control.

There are barriers to women's emancipation in China that

transcend both the structural and the cultural. On the subject of women and the family, Marxism and Maoism suffer from many theoretical limitations. Central to Marxism is the conviction that "the history of all hitherto existing society is the history of class struggles." Social class analysis is Marxism's pivotal theoretical tool. The dialectic of history is propelled largely by the contradictions in class society. Class struggle is the stuff of revolution, and Marxism is the "science" that attempts to understand its process to help move it along progressively.

It has never been easy to fit women and the family into this historical scheme. To begin with, it is difficult to define women as a group in terms of social class. Women are members of all the traditionally defined social classes, but there is oppression specific to women which cuts across socioeconomic class lines. While Marxism has never denied the specific aspects of women's oppression (indeed, it was among the earliest social theories to take this seriously), it has never been able to accommodate us within its categories. The repercussions of this failing are not mundane. As Rowbotham has pointed out: "There is still no concept of an historical agency of women. Woman is still the other, part of the world outside as perceived, grasped, controlled by man. It is not clear how woman is going to act from her specific form of prostitution. She appears as an indication of the state of society, not as a social group in movement, developing consciousness in history."[107]

The strategic consequence of this inadequacy is the emphasis on point-of-production organizing; hence, of getting women into the labor force. Under Maoism this latent tendency has been heightened. In People's China equal participation in production is seen as the central platform of women's liberation. While it is true that the CCP has been sensitive to many of women's special needs, the guiding principle of most feminist reforms is to liberate women for production. Chen Hsi-lien, a Politburo member, intoned the conventional Maoist position on women at a recent women's congress in Shenyang:

> Women's organizations at all levels should regard the mobilizing of women to take part actively in socialist construction as their

important task. . . . Women can completely emancipate themselves and acquire a position equal to that of men only by extensively participating in social productive labor.[108]

It has become increasingly clear to Western feminists that women's task is not nearly so simple as that. We are not merely victims of social-class oppression. Our oppression inheres in the most intimate, private areas of life which transcend culture and history. It is in relationship to the mode of reproduction, not production, that woman's specialized oppression originates. It is here, therefore, that Western feminists have begun to seek theoretical understanding of the universal aspect of woman's oppression.[109] The major theoretical stranglehold remains the one Rowbotham underscored—envisioning a role for women as historical agents. It is not yet clear how women's biocultural form of oppression can contribute to a revolutionary dialectic.

There is a second theoretical factor, particular to Maoism, that is problematic for feminism. Mao divides social contradictions into two classes—those between the people and their enemies, and those among the people themselves. Contradictions of the first order are serious and antagonistic. Contradictions among the people, on the other hand, are not considered antagonistic, because there is thought to be an identity of underlying interest among the contending groups. Here, persuasion, education, and patience are prescribed in application of the principle, "Unity, criticism, unity."[110] This position is politically expedient (perhaps essential) as a safety net beneath the sex and class tightrope we have spoken of before. And as Linda Gordon suggests: "If indeed the contradiction between women and their masters has been reduced to a nonantagonistic contradiction, that is powerful evidence for the efficacy of socialism as a way of attacking women's oppression."[111] However, I do not believe it is possible for such a reduction to be genuine. There is a level at which men are indeed "the enemy" vis-à-vis women. Only in the most abstract, idealistic sense can it be said that there is complete identity of interest between the sexes. To deny the real privileges, spiritually deranging as they may be, that men obtain at women's cost, is to set feminism back several important years. This is a mistake the Chinese make.

My third objection to Maoist feminism follows from the preceding. The anti-individualist ideology of the Chinese Communists is particularly limiting in the area of women's emancipation. The rejection of private life as a sphere of bourgeois decadence means that many strategic Western feminist concerns are theoretically off-limits. The right to exercise control over one's body and autonomy over one's life choices is antithetical to the hegemony of the collective that Maoism embodies. Birth control is not an instrument that provides reproductive options to individuals; it is a means of service to the state—both through limitation of population and by liberating female labor power for productive activity. Free choice in marriage and divorce is not just a path to sexual and emotional liberation; it is also intended to destroy the patriarchal bases of power and to secure the stability of the new familial order. Chinese feminism is repeatedly couched in quasi-instrumental terms. Its demands are rarely good in and of themselves but because they contribute to the collective goals.

The point of this criticism is not to fault the Chinese movement for its collective bias. Nancy Milton is correct in saying Chinese women should not be criticized for not finding that they need what Western feminists think they ought to need or for not getting what they haven't asked for.[112] It is of interest, however, if Chinese women neither ask for nor crave the liberties which we feel in their places we would.

Finally Maoism, and Marxism only slightly less so, is an extraordinarily rational, secular world view. It views the individual as inherently good but corruptible; it perceives the state in similar tabula rasa terms. Faith in the perfectability of the individual is, perhaps, the radical linchpin of a revolutionary system. It is grounded in the assumption that proper socialization guarantees proper social life. The search for a psychology compatible with Marxism has always been a complicated undertaking. While Marxism leaves theoretical room for the development of "false consciousness," it gives the unconscious short shrift. Maoism exaggerates the inherent Marxist faith in conscious socialization. This is a faith that Western feminists are finding more and more difficult to share. Sexism seems to prevail in the deepest recesses of human culture. The processes of its transmission and perpetuation are far from apparent, and correspondingly distant from our powers of conscious control. Feminist theorists are just beginning to explore the complexities of the unconscious transmission of sexism. Maoists have no theoretical space for a comparable effort.

Having surveyed the scope and limitations of the Chinese family revolution and Maoist feminism, it is time to draw what specific political and theoretical implications we can from the Chinese experience with family reform. First, it is important to know what the Chinese situation teaches Western feminists about the relative merits of the extended and nuclear families. The lesson is simple. Chinese Confucian history should permanently debunk any illusions concerning the harmonious beauty of extended family life. Contemporary Chinese reports should perform a similar service on tales of the horrors of the nuclear family. What the Chinese experience makes clear is that social context is all-important. The extended family can be a nightmare, the nuclear one a bed of roses, depending on the social functions it is required to perform and the powers it is allowed to exercize over its dependents.

The second major lesson to be learned is not news to feminists. The Chinese example lends support to the view that no family system yet devised assures full equality to women. If the social context is all-important, it is not yet exactly clear what it must contain to counteract the discriminatory processes that inhere in all family structures known to women. Nor is it clear if there is a portion of the burden that social structural solutions can never address.

In sum, the positive political lessons of the Chinese family revolution teachings are essentially these:

(1) Socialism has proven itself to be an important aspect of women's liberation. The relationship between women's eco-

nomic contribution, security, and recognition are closely related to their social status and to family reform.[113]
(2) Structural reforms in familial relationships can contribute
impressively toward eliminating women's oppression. The
most effective reforms are those which remove power relationships from the family.
(3) Women seem to progress most during periods of militant
political activity.[114]
There are negative lessons to be drawn as well:
(1) Sexual equality must cut both ways. It is not sufficient
that formerly "for men only" doors be opened to women. As
long as traditionally female roles go unchallenged, sexism
keeps its heavy foot safely in the corridor. It seems particularly important for women to be delivered of their primary
identification with children and their responsibility for
domestic work.[115]
(2) The social evaluation of work requires considerable re-
consideration. So long as physical strength, intergenerational experience, and a public arena are significant criteria,
women's access to status is likely to be disadvantaged.
(3) Sexism is deeply ingrained in the human psyche. Although psychological differences by sex are social products,
they have been part of human society long enough to develop
a semiautonomous existence of their own. The barely noticed
persistence of patrilocality in China is evidence of the depth
of sex conditioning.
(4) Women must make their own revolution in their own
name. It cannot be handed us by "another" revolution. We
must find some way as women to form our own base of
power.

Perhaps, if one is absolutely truthful, there is at least as much
we cannot learn from the Chinese. China made its revolution
starting from a very different place from where we must start.
Our revolution must be one that takes account of our long
tradition of bourgeois individualism and that gives equal measure to personal liberation. The material conditions appear
nearly at hand for such a revolution. Sex and reproduction are

substantially separate. Physical labor has lost most of its early significance. Women participate in the labor force in increasing proportions. Consumption, a particularly female domain, is as strategic as production to çapitalist exploitation. The family is in a state of severe dislocation. It has lost its economic raison d'etre at the same time emotional demands on its limited resources have become most acute.

But feminist ideology seems to lag far behind. We have individual visions of personal liberation a-plenty, but confusion is widespread. Even those genuinely committed to feminist socialism are not sure where or how to focus their energies. We lack a theoretical basis for defining women as revolutionary agents. Wearily we reconsider old questions—is socialism a precondition for feminism? How can feminism be built into the revolutionary project? Nevertheless, China should serve as an inspirational example to us in moments of little faith. In spirit and fact its people have lived a miracle. Inside our own house of patriarchy, there are also grounds for encouragement. Feminist theoretical efforts are in progress. We have begun to reclaim and understand our past. This is the laborious, but necessary, preamble to the construction of a liberated future.

Notes

1. Friedrich Engels, *The Origin of the Family, Private Property, and the State* (1884; New York: International Publishers, 1972).

2. I first encountered this specific notion when it was suggested by Sherry Ortner during a panel discussion on patriarchy held at Sarah Lawrence College in April 1973. Recent works, such as those by Juliet Mitchell, *Psychoanalysis and Feminism* (New York: Pantheon, 1974) and Nancy Chodorow, "The Reproduction of Mothering" (Ph.D. diss., Brandeis University, 1974) proceed from the question of the universal conditions of woman's oppression.

3. I draw largely from the following major sociological works on the Chinese family: Olga Lang, *Chinese Family and Society* (New Haven: Yale University Press, 1946), Marion Levy, *The*

Family Revolution in Modern China (1949; New York: Octagon, 1971), and C. K. Yang, Chinese Communist Society: The Family and the Village (Cambridge, Mass.: M.I.T. Press, 1959). Hung-Lou Meng, The Dream of the Red Chamber (1792; New York: Pantheon, 1958), and Ida Pruitt, A Daughter of Han (New Haven: Yale University Press, 1945), are among the important literary and biographical works which flesh out the academic portrait.

4. This is a central thesis in Levy, Family Revolution. Lang, Chinese Family, and William Goode, World Revolution and Family Patterns (New York: Glencoe Free Press, 1963) concur.

5. Han Suyin, in The Crippled Tree (New York: Bantam, 1972), includes a rich description of the imperialistic activities of missionaries and railroad financiers, particularly of the Belgians.

6. For discussions of the internal strains on the traditional political and economic order before the Opium Wars, see Ping-ti Ho, "The Population of China," in The China Reader: Imperial China, ed. Franz Schurmann and Orville Schell (New York: Vintage, 1967), pp. 76–78, and Wolfram Eberhard, A History of China (Berkeley: University of California Press, 1971), pp. 272–77. One of the most serious of the economic strains appears to have been a precipitous rise in the rate of population growth which began in the middle of the eighteenth century and increased drastically throughout the nineteenth century (Eberhard, p. 273).

7. Agnes Smedley claimed that because of this, only in silk market towns did female births become welcome. Daughters here were apt to become the main support of their families, and their dignity and self-pride was correspondingly high (Battle Hymn of China [New York: Knopf, 1943], p. 87).

8. Yang, Chinese Communist Society, p. 198.

9. Smedley, Battle Hymn. According to Lang, Chinese Family, they had good precedent. In the early nineteenth century, girls of Canton employed as silk workers formed a movement, "Girls Who Do Not Go to the Family." They refused to live with their husbands, remained virgins, and lived in "Girls Homes."

10. Lang, Chinese Family, pp. 158–60.

11. Pruitt, Daughter of Han, Yang, Chinese Communist Society, Jack Belden, China Shakes the World (New York: Monthly Review Press, 1970), William Hinton, Fanshen (New York: Vintage, 1966), K. S. Karol, China, The Other Communism (New York: Hill and Wang, 1967), and Meng, Dream of the Red Chamber, all provide graphic examples of such events.

12. Han Suyin, in *A Mortal Flower* (New York: Bantam, 1972), describes the author's own experience as a member of the second generation of female pioneers in the professions. Helen Snow, *Women in Modern China* (The Hague: Houton and Co., 1967) includes similar biographical material on outstanding Chinese women leaders. Ester Boserup reports that in 1932, girls made up 12 percent of the Chinese university population (*Woman's Role in Economic Development* [London: George Allen and Unwin Ltd., 1970], p. 122).

13. Lang, *Chinese Family*, p. 337.

14. Joseph Levenson, *Confucian China and Its Modern Fate* (Berkeley: University of California Press, 1958), pp. 147–52. Western academics consistently emphasize the role of the West, often it seems, to belittle the role of the Communist Party in organizing opposition. See, for example, Goode, *World Revolution*, Levy, *Family Revolution*, and Yang, *Chinese Communist Society*.

15. The Taiping Rebellion (1851–1864) included equality of the sexes and prohibitions against concubinage, footbinding, arranged marriage, and so on in its social program.

16. Roxanne Witke, "Mao-Tse Tung, Women, and Suicide," in *Women in China*, ed. M. Young (Ann Arbor: Center for Chinese Studies, 1973), pp. 7–31, is my major source for the material on Mao's early feminism.

17. Lang, *Chinese Family*, Levy, *Family Revolution*, and Yang, *Chinese Communist Society*, provide structural-functional analyses of sources of stability and strain in the Confucian family.

18. See H. Snow, *Women in Modern China*, for biographical examples of such revolutionary mother/child alliances.

19. The following historical survey relies heavily on material from Young, *Women in China*. Suzette Leith, "Chinese Women in the Early Communist Movement" is my major source for the early Communist period, and Davin, "Women in the Liberated Areas," for the later period. H. Snow, *Women in Modern China*, and Smedley, *Battle Hymn* are useful for more journalistic documentation on the period.

20. Indeed, this is true not only of the early Chinese radicals, but is a constant in CCP history, and in fact, a basic tenet of all Marxist theory. I am grateful to Diane Ostroffsky for pointing out to me that my focus on women and the family revolution tends to overemphasize the centrality of these issues in CCP strategy and deliberation.

21. According to Helen Snow, over 120,000 revolutionaries were killed. Yang Kai-hui, the first freely chosen wife of Mao Tse-tung, was executed in 1930.

22. George Ross has reminded me that an equally delicate political balancing act was required for all the central issues of revolutionary strategy—land reform, class analysis, military tactics, etc.

23. See Hinton, *Fanshen*, for the best account of the nature of this participation and for the interrelationship between land reform and female status. For example: "One woman said: 'Always before when we quarrelled my husband said, "Get out of my house." Now I can give it right back to him. I can say, 'Get out of my house yourself' " (p. 397).

24. Davin, "Women in the Liberated Areas," p. 84.

25. Mao Tse-tung, "On the Correct Handling of Contradictions Among the People," *Four Essays on Philosophy* (Peking: Foreign Languages Press, 1968).

26. See Davin, "Women in the Liberated Areas," Belden, *China Shakes the World*, and Hinton, *Fanshen* for examples.

27. Katie Curtin, "Women and the Chinese Revolution," *International Socialist Review* 35, no. 3 (March 1974): 8–11, 25–40.

28. Janet Salaff and Judith Merkle, "Women and Revolution: The Lessons of the Soviet Union and China," *Socialist Revolution* 1, no. 4 (1970): 39–72.

29. Nancy Milton, "Women and Revolution," *Socialist Revolution* 1, no. 6 (1970): 139–44. Charlotte Cohen, "Experiment in Freedom: Women of China," in *Sisterhood Is Powerful*, ed. Robin Morgan (New York: Vintage, 1970), pp. 385–417; Leith, "Chinese Women in the Early Communist Movement," differ with this view. Davin, "Women in the Liberated Areas," takes an intermediate position.

30. The question of the purge of Ting Ling after the Hundred Flowers episode is quite another, although not unrelated, matter. See Karol, *China*, for an illuminating discussion of that period.

31. Leith, "Chinese Women in Early Communist Movement," p. 66.

32. Davin, "Women in Liberated Areas," p. 75.

33. Davin reports Mao's estimates that in Ts'ai-hsi (Kiangsi), 30 percent of the representatives in the lower district congresses in 1931 were women, and 62 percent and 64 percent(!) in 1932 and 1933 when more men had joined the army.

34. See below, pp. 322–30 and conclusion.

35. Salaff, "Women and Revolution," p. 59, 71.

36. Quoted in Cohen, "Experiment in Freedom," p. 399.
37. The following historical and sociological summary is drawn largely from the following sources: Yang, *Chinese Communist Society*; Cohen, "Experiment in Freedom"; Sheila Rowbotham, *Woman, Resistance and Revolution* (New York: Vintage, 1974). Isabel Crook and David Crook, *The First Years of Yangyi Commune* (London: Routledge and Kegan Paul, 1966); Curtin, "Women and the Chinese Revolution"; Jan Myrdal, *Report from a Chinese Village* (New York: New American Library, 1965); Jan Myrdal and Gun Kessle, *China: The Revolution Continued* (New York: Pantheon, 1970); Janet Salaff, "Institutionalized Motivation for Fertility Limitation," in Young, *Women in China*, pp. 93–144; Ruth Sidel, *Women and Child Care in China* (Baltimore: Penguin, 1973); Ruth Sidel, *Families of Fengsheng: Urban Life in China* (Harmondsworth, England: Penguin, 1974); Karol, *China*; and Simone de Beauvoir, *The Long March* (Cleveland, Ohio: World Publishing Co., 1958) provide useful analyses of some of the salient issues.
38. Yang, *Chinese Communist Society*, p. 71.
39. Ibid., p. 81.
40. Marjory Wolf, "Chinese Women: Old Skills in a New Context," in *Woman, Culture, and Society*, ed. Michelle Rosaldo and Louise Lamphere (Stanford: Stanford University Press, 1974), p. 171.
41. Myrdal, *Report from Chinese Village*, p. 58.
42. Crook and Crook, *The First Years*, for example, make this claim. Myrdal and Kessel, *China: The Revolution Continued*, and de Beauvoir, *The Long March*, lend some support. Curtin, "Women and Chinese Revolution," however, disputes this heatedly: she presents the Trotskyist view that collectivization was a Stalinist process.
43. H. Snow actually maintains women were the driving force behind socialization: "It was women who chiefly hastened the development of socialist ownership in China, as they were not adequately protected under a system of private ownership" (*Women in Modern China*, p. 50). Attractive as this may sound to feminists, there is little hard data available to substantiate Snow's claim.
44. Crook and Crook, *The First Years*, p. 37.
45. Rowbotham, *Woman, Resistance and Revolution*, p. 196.
46. Quoted in Salaff, "Women and Revolution," p. 65.

47. Ai-li Chin, "Family Relations in Modern Chinese Fiction," in *Family and Kinship in Chinese Society*, ed. M. Freedman, p. 108.
48. Myrdal, *Report from Chinese Village*, p. 259.
49. Wu Yuan-chi et al., "The Great Conspiracy of Spurious Discussion and Bona Fide Poisoning," *Chinese Sociology and Anthropology* 1, no. 2 (1968): 59.
50. Quoted in Cohen, "Experiment in Freedom," p. 413.
51. Mark Selden, "Report from a People's Commune," *Eastern Horizon* 12, no. 2 (1973): 37–50. See Salaff, "Institutionalized Motivation," for precise data on women's participation in the labor force. Sidel, *Families of Fengsheng*, pp. 99, 111 gives examples of urban wage differentials between the sexes.
52. Hsu Kwang, "Women's Liberation Is a Component Part of the Proletarian Revolution," *Peking Review* 17, no. 10 (1974): 12.
53. Ibid., p. 13.
54. Fu Wen, "Doctrine of Confucius and Mencius—The Shackle that Keeps Women in Bondage," *Peking Review* 17, no. 10 (1974): 16–18.
55. Hsing Yen-tzu, "Training Women Cadres," *Peking Review* 17, no. 14 (1974): 18–21.
56. See Karol, *China*, for a provocative discussion of the practice of exorcizing "demons" in China today.
57. Rowbotham, *Woman, Resistance and Revolution*, p. 198.
58. Sidel reports that "at least 50 percent of urban children under the age of three are cared for at home, usually by grandparents" (*Families of Fengshen*, p. 132).
59. Liu Yung-huo, "Retirees and Retirement Programs in the People's Republic of China," *Industrial Gerontology* 1, no. 2 (Spring 1974): 72–81.
60. The story of the CCP campaign to eliminate prostitution and restore self-pride, dignity, and social purpose to its former victims is one of the most inspirational of the Chinese success stories. See, for example, Joshua Horn, *Away With All Pests* (New York: Monthly Review Press, 1969).
61. See Liu Yung-huo, "Retirees and Retirement Programs," for a description of the sources of economic and social security for the elderly.
62. Myrdal and Kessel, *China: Revolution Continued*, Sidel, *Women and Child Care*, Sidel, *Families of Fengsheng*, and Han Suyin, "Population Growth and Birth Control in China," *Eastern Horizon* 12, no. 5 (1973): 8–16.

63. Sidel, *Women and Child Care*, Han Suyin, "Population Growth," Salaff, "Institutionalized Motivation," and Myrdal and Kessel, *China: Revolution Continued*.

64. Salaff, "Institutionalized Motivation."

65. Han Suyin, "Population Growth," p. 9.

66. Horn, *Away With All Pests*, Han Suyin, "Population Growth."

67. Ning Ming-yeh, "The Party Supports Me in My Struggle for Self-Determination in Marriage," *Chinese Sociology and Anthropology* 1, no. 1 (1966): 52–56.

68. See Ezra Vogel, *Canton Under Communism* (Cambridge, Mass: Harvard University Press, 1969), for a discussion of pressure for familial surveillance and betrayal during the 5-Anti Campaign of 1952 in Canton. One must be conscious, however, of Vogel's strong anti-Communist bias.

69. Yang, *Chinese Communist Society*, p. 178.

70. Quoted in Sidel, *Women and Child Care*, p. 37.

71. Quoted in Carol Tavris, "Women in China: The Speak-Bitterness Revolution," *Psychology Today* 7, no. 12 (1974): 93.

72. See also Myrdal, *Report from Chinese Village*, p. 346, and Sidel, *Families of Fengsheng*, p. 41.

73. See, for example, Myrdal, *Report from Chinese Village*, p. 54.

74. Ning Ming-yeh, "The Party Supports Me," p. 56.

75. Myrdal and Kessel, *China: Revolution Continued*, p. 135.

76. Sidel reports that out of 9,100 families in Ching Nian commune (Sian), from January to September 1972, only seventeen couples requested divorces; of these six were "united" and eleven "whose characters and feelings were different," had their requests granted (*Families of Fengsheng*, pp. 73–74).

77. Ian Steward, "Divorces in China Decided by Peers," *New York Times*, 31 October 1973. This is an instance of a progressive application of political and economic considerations to a personal matter. At times, however, the motivations seem more questionable. Women have been asked to be patient with their sexist and abusive husbands. See Felix Green, "A Divorce Trial in China" (Boston: New England Free Press, n.d.) for a full description of one such instance. Sidel also presents a detailed example of the laborious process of divorce litigation and concommitant marital counseling (*Families of Fengsheng*, pp. 112–19).

78. Karol, *China*, p. 178.

79. Tavris, "Women in China."

80. Ezra Vogel, "A Preliminary View of Family and Mental Health in

Urban Communist China," in *Mental Health Research in Asia and the Pacific*, ed. William Caudill and Tsung-yi Lin (Honolulu: East-West Center Press, 1969).

81. See Salaff, "Institutionalized Motivation," for data on this.
82. In 1958 females accounted for 23 percent of Chinese university students. At the same time only 31 percent of secondary and 39 percent of primary students were female (Boserup, *Woman's Role*, p. 122n.). After the Cultural Revolution, which originated in and had a profound effect on Chinese higher education, the proportion of women in the universities remained unequal. Despite a conscious effort to allot more university places to females, "especially at medical, normal, political and art colleges, only 20 percent of the first students admitted to Tsinghua and 30 percent to Peking University were women" (John Gardner and Wilt Idema, "China's Educational Revolution," in *Authority, Participation and Cultural Change in China*, ed. Stuart Schram (Cambridge: Cambridge University Press, 1973), p. 280.
83. It is certainly true that this is far preferable to the Western counterpart of the First Lady. However the defense of this policy by Maria Macciocchi, *Daily Life in Revolutionary China* (New York: Monthly Review Press, 1972), p. 352, that this is a means of insuring top (male) leadership support for "highlighting the role of women at the very core of political life," is neither persuasive nor appealing.
84. Crook and Crook, *The First Years*, p. 82.
85. Myrdal and Kessel, *China: Revolution Continued*, p. 134.
86. Salaff, "Institutionalized Motivation."
87. Ibid., p. 129.
88. Sidel, *Women and Child Care*, p. 23.
89. Jane Uptegrove, "Women in China" (slide-talk, Cambridge, Mass., 24 March 1974).
90. Tavris, "Women in China."
91. Crook and Crook, *The First Years*.
92. Tavris, "Women in China," and Sidel, *Women and Child Care*.
93. Myrdal, *Report from Chinese Village*; Sidel, *Women and Child Care*; Crook and Crook, *The First Years*.
94. Selden, "Report from a People's Commune."
95. Crook and Crook, *The First Years*.
96. Sidel, *Families of Fengsheng*, p. 122.
97. Information received from Kathy and Susanna Yeh, citizens of the People's Republic, in personal discussion, June 1974.

98. Juliet Mitchell, *Psychoanalysis and Feminism* (New York: Pantheon, 1974). It is gratifying to report that this statement is no longer accurate. During the past few years, feminists and other social analysts have begun to direct serious analytical attention to the persistence and significance of patrilocality and male lineage links. See, for example, Norma Diamond, "Collectivization, Kinship, and the Status of Women in Rural China," in *Toward an Anthropology of Women,* ed. Rayna Reiter (New York: Monthly Review Press, 1975) and William L. Parish, "Socialism and the Chinese Peasant Family," *Journal of Asian Studies* 34, no. 3 (May 1975).

99. Liu Chao, "Safeguarding Women's Interests," *Peking Review* 17, no. 13 (1974): 17.

100. Curtin, "Women and the Chinese Revolution," p. 38.

101. Joyce Marvin, "Sisterhood Is Indeed Powerful," *China Notes* 12, no. 1 (1973), p. 4.

102. H. Snow, *Women in Modern China,* p. 62. See also de Beauvoir, *The Long March,* p. 154.

103. The Red Army consciously attempted to absorb the sexual energies of its soldiers in training and recreational activities to facilitate its policy which made violation of women a criminal offense (Smedley, *Battle Hymn,* p. 180). In Chinese universities today, sexual affairs are so frowned upon they can lead to expulsion. Westerners in Peking claim that students are therefore encouraged to expend their energies in sports (Karol, *China* p. 305).

104. Karol, *China,* p. 179.

105. Sidel, *Families of Fengsheng,* p. 62.

106. Susan Sontag, "Trip to Hanoi," *Styles of Radical Will* (New York: Dell, 1969), reached a similar conclusion after her trip to Hanoi. Although at first she found herself skeptical and alienated by the simplicity, homogeneity, and moralism of Vietnamese communication, her condescension was short-lived. In brief time she came to appreciate how different were the historical and geographical antecedents of the sensibilities and emotional responses of the Vietnamese. Sontag concluded that the Vietnamese had much to teach us about how culturally specific is the Western psyche, and that this is an important lesson for radicals to learn.

107. Rowbotham, *Woman, Resistance and Revolution,* p. 63.

108. "Old Role for Women in China Resisting Change," *New York Times,* 16 September 1973, p. 43.

109. See for example, Mitchell, *Psychoanalysis and Feminism*, "The Reproduction of Mothering," and Chodorow, this volume, as well as the Rosaldo and Lamphere collection, *Woman, Culture and Society*, particularly the articles by Rosaldo, Ortner, and Chodorow.
110. Mao Tse-tung, "On the Correct Handling of Contradictions."
111. Linda Gordon, "The Fourth Mountain," *Working Papers* 1, no. 3 (1973): 39.
112. Nancy Milton, "Women and Revolution," *Socialist Revolution* 1, no. 6 (1970): 137.
113. An analysis of crosscultural anthropological data on women's status by Sanday, "Female Status in the Public Domain," p. 198, indicates a curvilinear relationship between women's contribution to productive activity and their public status. Women's public status is highest when they contribute approximately equally with men. It is lowest when they are excluded from or overburdened with productive tasks.
114. Rowbotham, *Woman, Resistance and Revolution.*
115. Nancy Chodorow has worked extensively on this issue. See her article in Rosaldo and Lamphere, *Woman, Culture and Society*, "Being and Doing," in *Woman in Sexist Society*, eds. V. Gornick and B. Moran (New York: Basic Books, 1971), and "The Reproduction of Mothering." Also see this volume.

SOCIALIST FEMINISM
IN AMERICA

The socialist feminist part of the women's movement has been developing in new and important ways since a conference held in Yellow Springs, Ohio, 4–6 July 1975. This conference of 1600 women marked the first organized attempt at gathering together a group of women as socialist feminists. It was initiated by several women's groups (from New American Movement and from East and West coast socialist feminist groups). The lack of a clearly defined feminist analysis that became apparent during the course of the conference, emphasized the need for greater clarity among feminists. Before the conference began, the organizing committee had distributed a statement of principles of unity:

I. We recognize the need for and support the existence of the autonomous women's movement throughout the revolutionary process;
II. We agree that all oppression, whether based on race, class, sex, or lesbianism, is interrelated and the fights for liberation from oppression must be simultaneous and cooperative; and
III. We agree that socialist feminism is a strategy for revolution.
IV. We take our movement seriously; discussions at the conference should be in the spirit of struggle and unity, to move socialist feminism forward.
Members of groups which have taken stands contrary to our principles of unity and groups whose practice does not promote open discussions are not welcome and should not come.

This attempt at creating unity was unsuccessful in that many women attended as members of established sectarian groups rather than as members of a newly developing autonomous socialist feminist community. As a result, many of the theoretical developments that small socialist feminist collectives had made were not shared publicly at this time.

Since this conference was a first attempt at clarifying socialist feminism, it probably should be no surprise that the commitment to socialism was stated more clearly and easily than the statement of a socialist feminist position. This doesn't speak to the greater validity of the socialist analysis but to the fact that it has had more time to develop. Because there were many women who—despite the principles of unity—attended as socialist women, rather than as socialist feminists, the latter were most often unable to spell out their concerns when attacked by women from some of the established Marxist and socialist groups. As a result, the conference was clearly more Marxist than feminist.

In 1977, after two years of changing and growing and learning, socialist feminism has reached a different place. An integrated analysis of capitalism, racism, and patriarchy has been better elaborated. Political commitments are clearer as a result. The conference can be considered the beginning of socialist feminism as a political force because it was there that the commitment to the feminist part of socialist feminism surfaced as a self-conscious political statement. It was no longer sufficient to discuss issues theoretically in our collectives; it was now necessary to develop the ability to articulate these ideas publicly so that there would be a more focused and fruitful dialogue between male Marxists, socialist women, and socialist feminists.

Socialist feminist collectives over the past two years reflect the lack of resolution of the sometimes conflicting relationship between Marxism and feminism, although the conflict often surfaces in other forms. The questions of the relationship between the personal and the political, of the importance placed on group process and means, and of the importance of theory being tied to practice all reflect the basic issue of *how* feminism and Marxism can be synthesized in practice. Once a theoretical framework for the relationship between patriarchy and capitalism has been defined, the difficult stage of learning how to use it begins to take precedence. The conflicts in the socialist feminist community now are very much over the question of *how* to use the ideas we say we are committed to. How do we move forward politically, for instance, in trying to build a socialist feminist movement, without denying the importance of the way we organize and the way in which we work together? How do we move forward to the question of taking power when we are also committed to maintaining an autonomous structure as women of socialist feminism? We are really only first articulating what that socialist feminist strategy may be. And the conflict that plagues us is part of that process.

Most often, it seems to happen that in some collectives the Marxist Leninists win out as they plaster theory onto reality rather than creating a blend, or as they refuse to really understand how patriarchy defines our personal lives and that this is as crucial to understanding society as capitalist class relations. The other side of socialist feminist conflict is the collective that begins to define itself so much in terms of abstracted personal relations that the concern for process overrides the concern for the goal of the process; dealing with politics or power becomes a dynamic internal only to the group, or to the society only through the dynamics of the group. To say that process is part of politics is not to say that group process is politics. It is the relationship between the spheres of our existence that we must try to construct, not the replacement of one with the other.

Revolutionary politics is hard, and the commitment to building a viable socialist feminist movement, especially with the rest of the left as disorganized as it is today, makes it even more difficult. Hopefully, the selections in this section will revitalize those of you who are tired, redirect those of you who have found it difficult to define your politics or concerns, and renew the energy of those who are in the struggle. Hopefully, also as socialist feminism becomes recognized publicly and politically, a level of analysis and struggle that has been difficult because of a lack of public communication will become possible.

The three pieces included here are meant only to represent the spectrum of activity taking place within the socialist feminist movement in the United States. The Berkeley-

Oakland principles of unity were drawn up in 1973, before the Yellow Springs Conference. Although the Berkeley-Oakland Women's Union disbanded in January 1977, they agreed that their principles represent an important political document that should be shared with other socialist feminists. As a group they were committed to developing programs "that dealt with the family as a part of the capitalist system and with housework and children as socially necessary labor." They organized as an autonomous union because they saw socialist feminism growing out of the attempt of women to "integrate what we had learned in the women's movement with a Marxist analysis of the society and the economy." The Combahee River Collective, a black feminist group in Boston, presents its history and commitments as black lesbians committed to socialism. They do not identify as socialist feminists to the degree that they see it as a part of the white women's movement and they are primarily committed to understanding and changing racism. Their statement makes clear they see the struggle against racism as connected to the struggle against sexism, heterosexism, and capitalism, but they believe that their struggle must be rooted in an autonomous base which focuses upon racism.

The paper presented by Ros Petchesky to the first joint conference of Marxist Feminist Groups 1–5 at Barnard College, 19 March 1977, outlines the theoretical work being done by the group to which she belongs, Marxist Feminist Group 1. The Marxist Feminist groups are mainly made up of women from the Boston and New York area and meet about eight times yearly. Her paper is a discussion of the recent developments in socialist feminist theory and the current directions in research that have laid the basis for a fuller integration of Marxism and feminism. (It should be noted that the terms Marxist and socialist are used interchangeably in this section.)

Related Reading

"Principles of Unity," adopted by The Lexington Socialist/Feminist Union.

Redstockings, *Feminist Revolution* (New York: Random House, 1976).

"Socialist Feminism—A Strategy for the Women's Movement," Hyde Park Chapter, Chicago Women's Liberation Union.

"Statements from the National Conference on Socialist Feminism," *Socialist Revolution* 5, no. 26 (October–December 1975).

"Theories of Revolution," *Quest* 2, no. 2 (Fall 1975), especially Nancy Hartsock, "Fundamental Feminism: Process and Perspective," pp. 67–79.

"Working Papers on Socialist Feminism," New American Movement.

THE BERKELEY-OAKLAND
WOMEN'S UNION STATEMENT

Principles of Unity

Part 1: Why We Form a Women's Union

We come together now to form a women's union to develop a position of increasing strength and to transform our society into one that will meet our needs and the needs of all people as full human beings. We form a *women's* union in recognition that sexism shapes our lives. By sexism we mean a system which takes a physical characteristic, sex, and builds on it divisions of labor, ability, responsibility, and power which are then called "natural." Historically, these divisions have benefited men and oppressed women, preventing women from developing themselves to their full potential. Sexism directly upholds the capitalist system and benefits individual men within it.

With the awareness of our oppression we have developed over the last several years, particularly in our small groups, we have reached a deeper understanding of the society we want to create. We have also realized, however, the limitations of small groups for moving to create that society. We are now forming an organization, a women's union, in order to overcome the fragmentation of the women's movement and to build a structure within which we can most effectively carry on the struggle of the women's movement. Through this organization we will be able to share what we have learned, further develop a com-

This statement originally appeared in *Socialist Revolution* 4, no. 1 (January–March 1974).

mon analysis, and organize direct political action as we work toward the revolutionary transformation of society.

Over a century ago, women came together to fight their oppression. We can learn from them both what they were able to accomplish and what they failed to do. Third World, immigrant, and working women had needs and priorities different from those of the predominantly upper-class and white feminists of the nineteenth century. Though their movement started with progressive social and political goals, these feminists, fighting for the one goal of suffrage, ended up pursuing their own interests in opposition to the interests of working and Third World women. Thus, ultimately, they did not challenge the basis of capitalist society. We in the women's union have learned that those who run the capitalist system will try to divide us, by absorbing our energy and by granting specific reforms which benefit some women at the expense of other women but which in the end benefit none of us.

Many women worked in the civil rights, antiwar, and student movements of the middle sixties. As they became increasingly aware of their oppression as women, within society and within the male-dominated radical movements, they joined with other women, many of whom had never related to radical politics, to form the growing women's liberation movement. Although we feel connected to the struggles of the left, our experience and our history teach us that a male-dominated revolutionary movement can ignore our oppression in the name of its own priorities and expediency. Not defining ourselves in reaction to the left, we assume the legitimacy of our movement. We are an autonomous women's union which will embody and struggle for the new forms of organization and relations between people which we define as socialism.

Part 2: How We See Our Struggle

Our priorities for struggle are determined not only by our own immediate needs but by our evolving analysis of society as a whole. As women, we seek liberation in conjunction, not in competition, with others who are oppressed.

We recognize that our liberation and that of other oppressed groups cannot be achieved within the existing system. Therefore, our struggle against sexism necessarily involves us in the struggle against capitalism, racism, imperialism, and all other forms of oppression, and must be waged simultaneously with these struggles if we are to achieve our vision of socialism.

We stand united against the capitalist system, which is based on a division of labor that separates and alienates people, exploits their labor for the profit of a few, and creates false needs without meeting the real needs of the people. We will struggle to achieve redistribution of wealth and of control of the resources that produce wealth in this society. We will struggle for people to gain control of the conditions and the product of their work—all unpaid labor, including work in the home, as well as work in the traditional sense. We will struggle to combat in ourselves and around us the values—such as individualism, possessiveness, and competiveness—that sustain capitalism.

We stand united against racism, in society and within our movement. We will resist all attempts by those in control of this country's resources to pit us, as women, against other oppressed groups for an inadequate share of those resources. In formulating and implementing our programs and policies, we will work toward a greater awareness of the needs of women oppressed by racism. We recognize that racism, like sexism, has oppressive cultural and psychological manifestations which we must combat.

We stand united against imperialism, which we understand to be integral to advanced capitalism and not a separate system of oppression. Imperialism is the system by which the ruling class in the dominant capitalist nations extracts the resources and wealth of Third World and other peoples, and imposes on them an oppressive economic, social, and political system. We too are oppressed by this international system of advanced capitalism that wages war against revolutionary struggles for liberation and destroys the culture and resources of Third World countries. We cannot achieve our goals without a just division of wealth worldwide and self-determination for all peoples.

Recognizing that our own liberation is contingent on the

liberation of all, and that such liberation requires the elimination of the causes of oppression, we seek to work with other organizations also committed to achieving these goals. We realize that this can be done only on a basis of mutual respect.

Part 3: How We See What We Want

Our vision of the future rests upon the recognition that the separation of the public and the private spheres of our lives is used by the capitalist class to further alienate people not only from the means of production but from themselves, from what they need and want, and from each other. The public aspects of people's lives—for example, jobs or participation in government—have become separated from the private or personal aspects of people's lives, such as one's self-image or relationships. Those whose lives are now restricted to the private sphere—children, older people, and women in the home—are disrespected and considered marginal to the public life of the society. The split between the public and the private also leads to a distorted view of human energy which has to be either work or leisure. Our recognition that the split between the public and the private is functional to capitalist domination makes our vision of a transformation of the whole of women's lives a historical possibility.

Most movements that have worked for the revolutionary transformation of society have confined their vision and analysis to the aspects of people's lives which are public or "political." Socialists of the nineteenth century challenged the concept of "natural" greed or competitiveness which was put forth to rationalize workers' responses to the brutally exploitative working conditions of early industrial capitalism. These socialists did not extend their critique of the concept of human nature to the "natural" division of labor between men and women. The private or personal aspects of people's lives were considered less important to analyze. They were to be considered after the transformation of the institutions of public life. Now we consider both people's subjective experience and their public lives as the focus of a socialist movement.

The people who ranked the public over the private were usually men because their identity was supposed to come from their public selves. Women's emotional reality was always supposed to have been our only reality. The division of labor between men and women was accepted and justified as "human nature." Women's capacity to bear children was misconstrued to be a biological necessity like that of each woman to eat or drink. As women we have come to know that the personal is "political" because we were isolated in the personal sphere.

Ideologies have always been created to convince people that what they see around them is inevitable, in order that they not challenge any of it. We challenge the notion of "human nature" which enforces the split between public and private spheres. We see the integration of these spheres, beginning now, as the way to struggle against our alienation and exploitation.

Our task then is to integrate the public and private spheres of our lives within the context of a revolutionary movement. We reject the idea that the personal sphere is women's sphere, in practice, by working to transform the whole of people's lives. In capitalist society productive work is defined as labor that receives pay. Labor that does not receive a wage, especially work in the home—raising children, doing daily maintenance, and caring for people's emotional needs—is not regarded as work. We need to acknowledge this and other unpaid work as socially necessary. We now begin to build a concept of human activity which in a socialist society includes all forms of work, human interaction and creative effort necessary to maintain the whole society. All productive human activity becomes the collective responsibility of the whole society. More than this, old people and children will not have their lives segregated from those of the adults who are now seen as the work force. We will work to integrate all human beings into the common life of the society.

The people of the society can decide what needs to be produced and the people who work in a particular workplace can determine their own working conditions and can initiate and develop changes in the process of production. As workers take control of the processes of production, the process of reintegrating mental and manual work will begin. We will cease to comprehend people's time only as either work, or its opposite, leisure. As working people control their own workplaces they will make the decision about the time-rhythm of their lives and about how to reclaim the technology they have developed. The decisions about resources and technology will ultimately have to be made by the people of the earth as a whole as this country must no longer take the natural resources of other countries.

We understand that the conditions of our work determine the potential of interpersonal relations. When everyone is involved in activity that is meaningful, we will be able to meet our needs for personal relations in many different forms with many different people.

As we overcome our alienation, it will become possible for people to fully love themselves and each other. What's called homosexuality/heterosexuality will no longer be labeled and judged. We can reclaim all of our sexuality and freely express it.

In building a revolutionary movement which embodies these ideas, we begin to build a culture in which we will use our energy to achieve both collective goals and the fulfillment of our individual needs. Such experience now takes place only in isolated parts of our lives while the alienated capitalist context still distorts most human energies. We are striving toward the full integration of the private and public aspects of our lives.

It is the realization of this vision that we define as socialism.

Part 4: How We See Our Work

We are a socialist feminist organization. Our task is to confront the immediate realities of women's oppression under advanced capitalism, and this is integral to our struggle to achieve a socialist society. A socialist feminist movement will grow out of the rage and indignation we feel at the exploitation of our lives. We think that women will move toward making a revolution through an analysis of the oppression we experience—not through a moral or abstract intellectual commitment to socialism. Because we seek to integrate the public and private aspects of people's lives, we understand ourselves to be working toward the only kind of socialist revolution that could ever involve most of the people in this country. Socialism is more than a description of a future society, as it also describes the process by which we struggle to create that society.

Our strategy is to struggle for changes that improve our lives while exposing the limitations of the capitalist system. It has been common in the past to look for the perfect revolutionary demand that capitalism or "the system" cannot coopt by adopting. The idea has been that a demand or a struggle is either reformist or revolutionary. In the absence of a coherent socialist movement, all reforms will be coopted. A reform is only revolutionary when the movement is capable of showing that more than that particular reform is needed to solve problems people face in their lives.

In our programs, we will fight for the fulfillment of women's immediate needs. We will seek those reforms that materially improve women's lives and give women a sense of their own power. In doing so, we will struggle to include and connect the various aspects of the present women's movement: workplace organizing—in the home and on the job, consciousness-raising, struggles within the family, and alternative institutions. Through our struggle to formulate long-range strategy, we will all be involved in an educational process. This education is a crucial part of our work.

For a society to be socialist means that the process of reexamining people's control of their lives will be continual. Socialism involves a radical transformation of all human relations, and we believe that this process of change must begin now. In our organization, we will work to change those attitudes in ourselves which reflect the capitalist ideology we have all internalized. We will struggle against manipulative and competitive attitudes and actions. Increasingly, our lives under capitalism are unlivable and we know this will become clear to large numbers of people. We know that people have continuing energy and ability to change, and that out of our experience we can create a revolution in this country.

THE COMBAHEE RIVER COLLECTIVE

A Black Feminist Statement

We are a collective of black feminists who have been meeting together since 1974.[1] During that time we have been involved in the process of defining and clarifying our politics, while at the same time doing political work within our own group and in coalition with other progressive organizations and movements. The most general statement of our politics at the present time would be that we are actively committed to struggling against racial, sexual, heterosexual, and class oppression and see as our particular task the development of integrated analysis and practice based upon the fact that the major systems of oppression are interlocking. The synthesis of these oppressions creates the conditions of our lives. As black women we see black feminism as the logical political movement to combat the manifold and simultaneous oppressions that all women of color face.

We will discuss four major topics in the paper that follows: (1) The genesis of contemporary black feminism; (2) what we believe, i.e., the specific province of our politics; (3) the problems in organizing black feminists, including a brief herstory of our collective; and (4) black feminist issues and practice.

1. The Genesis of Contemporary Black Feminism

Before looking at the recent development of black feminism, we would like to affirm that we find our origins in the historical reality of Afro-American women's continuous life-and-death struggle for survival and liberation. Black women's extremely negative relationship to the American political system (a system of white male rule) has always been determined by our membership in two oppressed racial and sexual castes. As Angela Davis points out in "Reflections on the Black Woman's Role in the Community of Slaves," black women have always embodied, if only in their physical manifestation, an adversary stance to white male rule and have actively resisted its inroads upon them and their communities in both dramatic and subtle ways. There have always been black women activists—some known, like Sojourner Truth, Harriet Tubman, Frances E. W. Harper, Ida B. Wells Barnett, and Mary Church Terrell, and thousands upon thousands unknown—who had a shared awareness of how their sexual identity combined with their racial identity to make their whole life situation and the focus of their political struggles unique. Contemporary black feminism is the outgrowth of countless generations of personal sacrifice, militancy, and work by our mothers and sisters.

A black feminist presence has evolved most obviously in connection with the second wave of the American women's movement beginning in the late 1960s. Black, other Third World, and working women have been involved in the feminist movement from its start, but both outside reactionary forces and racism and elitism within the movement itself have served to obscure our participation. In 1973 black feminists, primarily located in New York, felt the necessity of forming a separate black feminist group. This became the National Black Feminist Organization (NBFO).

Black feminist politics also have an obvious connection to movements for black liberation, particularly those of the 1960s and 1970s. Many of us were active in those movements (civil rights, black nationalism, the Black Panthers), and all of our lives were greatly affected and changed by their ideology, their goals, and the tactics used to achieve their goals. It was our experience and disillusionment within these liberation movements, as well as experience on the periphery of the white male left, that led to the need to develop a politics that was antiracist, unlike those of white women, and antisexist, unlike those of black and white men.

There is also undeniably a personal genesis for black feminism, that is, the political realization that comes from the seemingly personal experiences of individual black women's lives. Black feminists and many more black women who do not define themselves as feminists have all experienced sexual oppression as a constant factor in our day-to-day existence.

Black feminists often talk about their feelings of craziness before becoming conscious of the concepts of sexual politics, patriarchal rule, and, most importantly, feminism, the political analysis and practice that we women use to struggle against our oppression. The fact that racial politics and indeed racism are pervasive factors in our lives did not allow us, and still does not allow most black women, to look more deeply into our own experiences and define those things that make our lives what they are and our oppression specific to us. In the process of consciousness-raising, actually life-sharing, we began to recognize the commonality of our experiences and, from that sharing and growing consciousness, to build a politics that will change our lives and inevitably end our oppression.

Our development also must be tied to the contemporary economic and political position of black people. The post-World War II generation of black youth was the first to be able to minimally partake of certain educational and employment options, previously closed completely to black people. Although our economic position is still at the very bottom of the American capitalist economy, a handful of us have been able to gain certain tools as a result of tokenism in education and employment which potentially enable us to more effectively fight our oppression.

A combined antiracist and antisexist position drew us together initially, and as we developed politically we addressed ourselves to heterosexism and economic oppression under capitalism.

2. What We Believe

Above all else, our politics initially sprang from the shared belief that black women are inherently valuable, that our liberation is a necessity not as an adjunct to somebody else's but because of our need as human persons for autonomy. This may seem so obvious as to sound simplistic, but it is apparent that no other ostensibly progressive movement has ever considered our specific oppression a priority or worked seriously for the ending of that oppresssion. Merely naming the pejorative stereotypes attributed to black women (e.g., mammy, matriarch, Sapphire, whore, bulldagger), let alone cataloguing the cruel, often murderous, treatment we receive, indicates how little value has been placed upon our lives during four centuries of bondage in the Western hemisphere. We realize that the only people who care enough about us to work consistently for our liberation is us. Our politics evolve from a healthy love for ourselves, our sisters, and our community which allows us to continue our struggle and work.

This focusing upon our own oppression is embodied in the concept of identity politics. We believe that the most profound and potentially the most radical politics come directly out of our own identity, as opposed to working to end somebody else's oppression. In the case of black women this is a particularly repugnant, dangerous, threatening, and therefore revolutionary concept because it is obvious from looking at all the political movements that have preceded us that anyone is more worthy of liberation than ourselves. We reject pedestals, queenhood, and walking ten paces behind. To be recognized as human, levelly human, is enough.

We believe that sexual politics under patriarchy is as pervasive in black women's lives as are the politics of class and race. We also often find it difficult to separate race from class from sex oppression because in our lives they are most often experienced simultaneously. We know that there is such a thing as racial-sexual oppression which is neither solely racial nor solely sexual, e.g., the history of rape of black women by white men as a weapon of political repression.

Although we are feminists and lesbians, we feel solidarity with progressive black men and do not advocate the fractionalization that white women who are separatists demand. Our situation as black people necessitates that we have solidarity around the fact of race, which white women of course do not need to have with white men, unless it is their negative solidarity as racial oppressors. We struggle together with black men against racism, while we also struggle with black men about sexism.

We realize that the liberation of all oppressed peoples necessitates the destruction of the political-economic systems of capitalism and imperialism as well as patriarchy. We are socialists because we believe the work must be organized for the collective benefit of those who do the work and create the products and not for the profit of the bosses. Material resources must be equally distributed among those who create these resources. We are not convinced, however, that a socialist revolution that is not also a feminist and antiracist revolution will guarantee our liberation. We have arrived at the necessity for developing an understanding of class relationships that takes into account the specific class position of black women who are generally marginal in the labor force, while at this particular time some of us are temporarily viewed as doubly desirable tokens at white-collar and professional levels. We need to articulate the real class situation of persons who are not merely raceless, sexless workers, but for whom racial and sexual oppression are significant determinants in their working/ economic lives. Although we are in essential agreement with Marx's theory as it applied to the very specific economic relationships he analyzed, we know that this analysis must be extended further in order for us to understand our specific economic situation as black women.

A political contribution which we feel we have already made is the expansion of the feminist principle that the personal is political. In our consciousness-raising sessions, for example, we have in many ways gone beyond white women's revelations because we are dealing with the implications of race and class as well as sex. Even our black women's style of talking/ testifying in black language about what we have experienced has a resonance that is both cultural and political. We have spent a great deal of energy delving into the cultural and experiential nature of our oppression out of necessity because none of these matters have ever been looked at before. No one before has ever examined the multilayered texture of black women's lives.

As we have already stated, we reject the stance of lesbian separatism because it is not a viable political analysis or strategy for us. It leaves out far too much and far too many people, particularly black men, women, and children. We have a great deal of criticism and loathing for what men have been socialized to be in this society: what they support, how they act, and how they oppress. But we do not have the misguided notion that it is their maleness, per se—i.e., their biological maleness—that makes them what they are. As black women we find any type of biological determinism a particularly danger-ous and reactionary basis upon which to build a politic. We must also question whether lesbian separatism is an adequate and progressive political analysis and strategy, even for those who practice it, since it so completely denies any but the sexual sources of women's oppression, negating the facts of class and race.

3. Problems in Organizing Black Feminists

During our years together as a black feminist collective we have experienced success and defeat, joy and pain, victory and failure. We have found that it is very difficult to organize around black feminist issues, difficult even to announce in certain contexts that we *are* black feminists. We have tried to think about the reasons for our difficulties, particularly since the white women's movement continues to be strong and to grow in many directions. In this section we will discuss some of the general reasons for the organizing problems we face and also talk specifically about the stages in organizing our own collective.

The major source of difficulty in our political work is that we are not just trying to fight oppression on one front or even two, but instead to address a whole range of oppressions. We do not have racial, sexual, heterosexual, or class privilege to rely upon, nor do we have even the minimal access to resources and power that groups who possess any one of these types of privilege have.

The psychological toll of being a black woman and the dif-ficulties this presents in reaching political consciousness and doing political work can never be underestimated. There is a very low value placed upon black women's psyches in this society, which is both racist and sexist. As an early group member once said, "We are all damaged people merely by virtue of being black women." We are dispossessed psychologically and on every other level, and yet we feel the necessity to struggle to change our condition and the condition of all black women. In "A Black Feminist's Search for Sisterhood," Michele Wallace arrives at this conclusion:

> We exist as women who are black who are feminists, each stranded for the moment, working independently because there is not yet an environment in this society remotely congenial to our struggle—because, being on the bottom, we would have to do what no one else has done: we would have to fight the world.[2]

Wallace is not pessimistic but realistic in her assessment of black feminists' position, particularly in her allusion to the nearly classic isolation most of us face. We might use our position at the bottom, however, to make a clear leap into revolutionary action. If black women were free, it would mean that everyone else would have to be free since our freedom would necessitate the destruction of all the systems of oppression.

Feminism is, nevertheless, very threatening to the majority of black people because it calls into question some of the most basic assumptions about our existence, i.e., that gender should be a determinant of power relationships. Here is the way male and female roles were defined in a black nationalist pamphlet from the early 1970s.

> We understand that it is and has been traditional that the man is the head of the house. He is the leader of the house/nation because his knowledge of the world is broader, his awareness is greater, his understanding is fuller and his application of this information is wiser. . . . After all, it is only reasonable that the man be the head of the house because he is able to defend and protect the development of his home. . . . Women cannot do the same things as men—they are made by nature to function differently. Equality of men and women is something that cannot happen even in the

abstract world. Men are not equal to other men, i.e., ability, experience, or even understanding. The value of men and women can be seen as in the value of gold and silver—they are not equal but both have great value. We must realize that men and women are a complement to each other because there is no house/family without a man and his wife. Both are essential to the development of any life.[3]

The material conditions of most black women would hardly lead them to upset both economic and sexual arrangements that seem to represent some stability in their lives. Many black women have a good understanding of both sexism and racism, but because of the everyday constrictions of their lives cannot risk struggling against them both.

The reaction of black men to feminism has been notoriously negative. They are, of course, even more threatened than black women by the possibility that black feminists might organize around our own needs. They realize that they might not only lose valuable and hard-working allies in their struggles but that they might also be forced to change their habitually sexist ways of interacting with and oppressing black women. Accusations that black feminism divides the black struggle are powerful deterrents to the growth of an autonomous black women's movement.

Still, hundreds of women have been active at different times during the three-year existence of our group. And every black women who came, came out of a strongly felt need for some level of possibility that did not previously exist in her life.

When we first started meeting early in 1974 after the NBFO first eastern regional conference, we did not have a strategy for organizing, or even a focus. We just wanted to see what we had. After a period of months of not meeting, we began to meet again late in the year and started doing an intense variety of consciousness-raising. The overwhelming feeling that we had is that after years and years we had finally found each other. Although we were not doing political work as a group, individuals continued their involvement in lesbian politics, sterilization abuse and abortion rights work, Third World Women's International Women's Day activities, and support activity for the trials of Dr. Kenneth Edelin, Joan Little, and Inez Garcia. During our first summer, when membership had dropped off considerably, those of us remaining devoted serious discussion to the possibility of opening a refuge for battered women in a black community. (There was no refuge in Boston at that time.) We also decided around that time to become an independent collective since we had serious disagreements with NBFOs bourgeois-feminist stance and their lack of a clear political focus.

We also were contacted at that time by socialist feminists, with whom we had worked on abortion rights activities, who wanted to encourage us to attend the National Socialist Feminist Conference in Yellow Springs. One of our members did attend and despite the narrowness of the ideology that was promoted at that particular conference, we became more aware of the need for us to understand our own economic situation and to make our own economic analysis.

In the fall, when some members returned, we experienced several months of comparative inactivity and internal disagreements which were first conceptualized as a lesbian-straight split but which were also the result of class and political differences. During the summer those of us who were still meeting had determined the need to do political work and to move beyond consciousness-raising and serving exclusively as an emotional support group. At the beginning of 1976, when some of the women who had not wanted to do political work and who also had voiced disagreements stopped attending of their own accord, we again looked for a focus. We decided at that time, with the addition of new members, to become a study group. We had always shared our reading with each other, and some of us had written papers on black feminism for group discussion a few months before this decision was made. We began functioning as a study group and also began discussing the possibility of starting a black feminist publication. We had a retreat in the late spring which provided a time for both political discussion and working out interpersonal issues. Currently we are planning to gather together a collection of black feminist writing. We feel that it is absolutely essential to demonstrate the reality of our politics to other black women and believe that we can do this through writing and distributing our work. The fact that individual black feminists are living in isolation all over the country, that our own numbers are small, and that we have some skills in writing, printing, and publishing makes us want to carry out these kinds of projects as a means of organizing black feminists as we continue to do political work in coalition with other groups.

4. Black Feminist Issues and Practice

During our time together we have identified and worked on many issues of particular relevance to black women. The inclusiveness of our politics makes us concerned with any situation that impinges upon the lives of women, Third World, and working people. We are of course particularly committed to working on those struggles in which race, sex, and class are simultaneous factors in oppression. We might, for example, become involved in workplace organizing at a factory that employs Third World women or picket a hospital that is cutting back on already inadequate health care to a Third World community, or set up a rape crisis center in a black neighborhood. Organizing around welfare or daycare concerns might also be a focus. The work to be done and the countless issues that this work represents merely reflect the pervasiveness of our oppression.

Issues and projects that collective members have actually worked on are sterilization abuse, abortion rights, battered women, rape, and health care. We have also done many workshops and educationals on black feminism on college campuses, at women's conferences, and most recently for high school women.

One issue that is of major concern to us and that we have begun to publicly address is racism in the white women's movement. As black feminists we are made constantly and painfully aware of how little effort white women have made to understand and combat their racism, which requires among other things that they have a more than superficial comprehension of race, color, and black history and culture. Eliminating racism in the white women's movement is by definition work for white women to do, but we will continue to speak to and demand accountability on this issue.

In the practice of our politics we do not believe that the end always justifies the means. Many reactionary and destructive acts have been done in the name of achieving "correct" political goals. As feminists we do not want to mess over people in the name of politics. We believe in collective process and a nonhierarchical distribution of power within our own group and in our vision of a revolutionary society. We are committed to a continual examination of our politics as they develop through criticism and self-criticism as an essential aspect of our practice. As black feminists and lesbians we know that we have a very definite revolutionary task to perform and we are ready for the lifetime of work and struggle before us.

Notes

1. This statement is dated April 1977.
2. Michele Wallace, "A Black Feminist's Search for Sisterhood," *The Village Voice*, 28 July 1975, pp. 6–7.
3. Mumininas of Committee for Unified Newark, *Mwanamke Mwananchi (The Nationalist Woman)*, Newark, N.J., c. 1971, pp. 4–5.

DISSOLVING THE HYPHEN: A REPORT ON MARXIST-FEMINIST GROUPS 1–5

Rosalind Petchesky

The paper attached to this "report" is a product of the collective thought and four-year interaction of something called "Marxist-Feminist Group 1." "M-F 1" was formed in 1973 out of an informal network of women, many of them radical academics but others involved principally in community organizing, health care, clerical organizing, or other kinds of work. It was never an "organization"; much less does it, at the present time, represent a "movement." At best it can be called the structural expression of a political and personal tendency: the urge of a considerable number of women, long active in both the women's movement and the independent left, to integrate the two major aspects of their own political thought and practice. Working alone or in small isolated groups in our individual families, communities, colleges, offices, and institutions, the tensions between our Marxism and our feminism often seemed overwhelming. Coming together, as we have several times a year for four years, to reflect upon, compare, and analyze our diverse and common situations, the possibility of a synthesis, in our ideas and our practice, has begun to seem more real.

Because the members of M-F 1 come from widely dispersed

In addition to the general, pervasive influence of my sisters in M-F1 on the thinking in this paper, I owe a particular debt to Ellen Ross, who read the original draft and lent it her unique insight, and to Sarah Eisenstein for her encouragement.

places—New York, New Haven, Hartford, Buffalo, western Massachusetts, Boston, Washington, D. C.—and work in a variety of political frameworks, it was never imagined that we could undertake common organizational activity or formulate a strategy as a group. Thus our activity has mainly been of a theoretical nature, consisting of weekend-long intensive discussions around a large array of subjects: women and unions, motherhood, patriarchal ideology in the Victorian period, the fiscal crisis and its impact on women, sexuality and psychoanalytic theory, racism in health care and population control policies, feminism and culture, building a feminist movement—these are but a small sample of the more formal topics of study that have engaged our attention. In addition, we have spent time discussing subjects of a more "personal" nature—men, sexuality, living arrangements, work, money, and our feelings about all these things—as a regular part of every weekend conference. Clearly, this division between "heavy" and personal ("soft") topics reflects a continued dichotomy in our consciousness, a continued inability to concretize the "connection between the personal and the political" that we all believe in steadfastly. Yet the desire to combine theory, personal experience and consciousness, and organizing strategies in our discussions remains an evident and pressing concern.

M-F 1 has been slow and reticent about committing itself to paper, in the form of a collective writing project. But we have kept a diligent record of our theoretical work in the form of notes and in the subtle but innumerable ways that our collective thinking has entered the individual writing, teaching, and political practice of all our members. Perhaps the most concrete product of our work together has been the formation of Marxist-Feminist Groups 2, 3, 4, and now 5, in the past three years. The ease and enthusiasm, indeed yearning, with which our sister groups came together suggests that the development of a genuine Marxist-feminist politics is a deeply felt need, shared by many women in the cities (primarily New York and Boston) where these groups have emerged. We now have an aggregate membership of some 175 women. On 19 March 1977, about seventy of us met together for a first joint, all-day conference at Barnard College, to share our ways of working and our tentative ideas about Marxism-feminism as a perspective and as a potential movement. At this conference, the single political issue that commanded the most interest as an appropriate area for future work was the politics of reproduction, and specifically the ongoing campaign against sterilization abuse. It was felt that this issue presented a broad potential for integrating questions of sex, race, and class, as well as for building the bridges which we see as critical between the feminist movement and Third World, anti-imperialist, and socialist revolutionary movements.

More generally, there was a spirit of cautious hopefulness that infused the day's proceedings, of awareness that the ambiguities in our politics, like the contradictions in our personal lives, are far from having been resolved. This spirit was best captured for everyone present in the words of Mary Bailey, spokeswoman for M-F 2:

> As Marxist-feminists we straddle an uneasy horse. We have not worked out what this means, this hyphen. We think that a revolution which proceeds from the insights of Marxism and feminism is what we want; our own practice as a group leaves everything but the formalistic aspects of such a revolution to be delineated. All too often all this has meant is that we are Marxists to our feminist sisters and feminists to our Marxist brothers. The gravest danger . . . facing us right now is that we will settle for this hyphen, we will settle in with it comfortably as a self-explanation. It will become a counter, a cipher, instead of a project. It will be used as a way to get and insure our place in a declining economy, as a way of finding a comfortable berth that we try to curl into among the available niches in capitalist society, as a way of defining ourselves for the rest of our lives. What prevents this: contradictions of our own lives which will not withstand this static definition; contradictions of capitalism which will make this attempt an immensely difficult, we hope impossible, process. What intervenes in this relationship of two terms is desire, on every level. Hyphen as wish. We have heard its whisperings.

The following paper is an expanded version of the talk I gave at the conference.*

Marxism-Feminism: Transcending the "Separate Spheres"

A couple of years ago a very exciting manuscript began circulating among the Marxist-feminist "underground." It was "The Traffic in Women," by Gayle Rubin, and it pointed the way to a mode of analysis which we could call our own, a genuine Marxist-feminist methodology.[1] I single out Rubin's article not to eulogize it, but because I think it was a kind of watermark for Marxist-feminists' theoretical growth. It signaled the beginning of a much richer, more integrated analytical approach than we had been able to achieve before, in our anxiety either to locate women solidly and respectably in the volumes of *Capital,* or to politicize the "personal" by simply describing it in exhaustive (and depressing) detail.

Rubin, in her proposal for a "political economy of sex-gender," thoughtfully suggested to us that sexuality and gender, and the kinship-family structures in which they are reproduced, "are themselves social products," that they consist of historically determined relationships in which material production, wealth, exchange, power, and domination—as well as feelings and sensibilities—are all directly involved. This, in turn, led to a further analytical insight: that "production" and "reproduction," work and the family, far from being separate territories like the moon and the sun or the kitchen and the shop, are really intimately related modes that reverberate upon one another and frequently occur in the same social, physical, and even psychic spaces. This point bears emphasizing, since many of us are still stuck in the model of "separate spheres" (dividing off "woman's place," "reproduction," "private life," the home, etc. from the world of men, production, "public life," the office, etc.). We are now learning that this

---

* Because the author is a member of Group 1, and not because that group is more important or has exercised any particular "vanguard" role, these remarks will disproportionately reflect Group 1's experience. The five groups have not as yet established any machinery for mutual consultation on a regular basis.

model of separate spheres distorts reality, that it is every bit as much an ideological construct as are the notions of "male" and "female" themselves. Not only do reproduction and kinship, or the family, have their own, historically determined, products, material techniques, modes of organization, and power relationships, but reproduction and kinship are themselves integrally related to the social relations of production and the state; they reshape those relations all the time. One implication of this theoretical breakthrough (and I don't think that's too grandiose a term) is that the two tasks of analyzing patriarchy and analyzing the political economy—whether capitalist, precapitalist, or socialist—cannot be separated. The very process of developing a Marxist-feminist mode of analysis will necessarily deepen the Marxist dialectic and enrich its ways of seeing and reflecting the world.

My self-appointed role on this panel is to share with you my ideas about how and in what areas this process has already begun. I have great confidence that a Marxist-feminist theory and methodology are no longer just a wish (or an "unhappy marriage"). We ourselves, in our own discussion groups as well as in our writings, have helped to make such a theory a serious political and intellectual project. As I look over where we are at this point, it seems to me that we've begun to analyze four critical relationships; and that, within these relationships, the dynamic interconnections between the public and the private, production and reproduction, are surfacing in a concrete and historically precise way. They are:

(1) The relationship between kinship, or the family, and class structure. I have in mind the various ways that family and kinship systems both reflect and help to reshape social relations outside the family.

(2) The relationship between control over the means of reproduction (specifically, sexuality and childbirth) and male power. This refers to our growing understanding of the fact that control over the material conditions and techniques of childbirth and sexuality is an important instrument of patriarchal and capitalist/imperialist domination, and thus is an important object of socialist feminist struggle.

(3) The relationship between patriarchal, or male suprema-cist, ideology and the state, its form and its legitimacy. Simply showing a coincidence between patriarchy and a state form of organization, as Engels did, isn't enough; we are beginning to learn how patriarchy underwrites state power. This involves the function of dominant antiwoman ideologies, such as the "double standard," misogynistic pollution taboos, cults of motherhood, etc. as major legitimations for the ancient and modern bourgeois states.

(4) The relationship between all this and women's con-sciousness and between women's consciousness and the nature of revolutionary transformation. The more we understand about women's actual conditions, of course, the more we understand the specific ways that women have acted to trans-form those conditions, and to transform revolutionary movements from within.

There is no time here to analyze all of these relationships or even to illustrate them in any detail. What I will do is to give some examples of recent intellectual work that has moved us forward in the first two areas and then offer some brief specula-tions about the third and fourth.

1. Kinship and Class Structure

As Marxist-feminists, probably our most shared and well-communicated understanding is the extent to which (a) the particular material and social conditions of women as a group are determined largely by kinship structures; and (b) the family itself—both its form and its functions—is determined by wider economic and social forces. We now have plenty of an-thropological evidence that male supremacy in certain forms predates not only capitalism but class and state society gener-ally.[2] Because studies of preclass societies focus directly on kinship, they may be helpful in developing a sort of typology of patriarchal systems, the sexual division of labor, and forms of women's resistance. Such studies, done from a Marxist-feminist perspective, indicate, for instance, that women's mate-rial condition and power differ substantially according to whether there is matrilocal or patrilocal kinship; according to whether social environments exist in which stability and peacefulness or militarism and danger prevail; according to whether there are possibilities for female community and kin networks to operate, and the like. It seems to me (a nonanthropologist) that we have a long way to go before we know when, and under what conditions, the sexual division of labor in preclass societies is a relation of domination—i.e., a patriarchal or male-supremacist relation—and when it is simply a division.[3] But we do know a lot about the particular ways in which kinship and the family define women's situation in class/state societies—partly because, as Marxists, we understand power in those societies better. And we can look more precisely at how the so-called "spheres" of production and reproduction interpenetrate there.

For example, Laura Oren's article on laboring families in industrializing England shows us in specific, material terms how the husband's control over the wage both mediates the wife's relation to the capitalist economy and determines the social relations between husband and wife.[4] Through the analysis of the distribution of the wage within the household economy, we learn about one material basis of male domination within working-class families and about the housewife's particular form of alienation. But we also learn about how the wage relationship is itself reproduced through the family economy. Oren's article suggests that the particular family form created by capitalism—woman confined to monogamy, housework, and economic dependency, man defined as breadwinner—itself helps to legitimate and stabilize the wage labor–capital relationship. The hierarchical/patriarchal family relation, in other words, is a necessary condition of male wage labor. Oren's analysis of how the wage gets transformed into unequal shares of food, health, and other amenities provides empirical evidence for what we suspected all along: that working-class men, too, get something material, and not just illusory, out of patriarchy; and that this material system of power, privilege, and extra resources creates an objective tie between them and capitalist men, as well as an objective division between them and "their" women—an obvious double contradiction from the standpoint of the working class as a whole.

One more set of examples will do to illustrate the two-way relationship between kinship and class structure. The many excellent analyses of women's work growing out of Marxism-feminism have made us aware that kinship patterns and family functions embedded deep within the capitalist system shape women's position within that system.[5] Women in advanced capitalist societies still find not only our domestic lives but also our social and workforce status, our job definitions and working conditions, determined largely by kin-oriented rituals; by patrilocal residential patterns; by, above all, motherhood and mothering functions. Moreover, as people like Judith Stacey and Norma Diamond have shown with regard to contemporary China, patriarchy may remain the norm within socialist societies, too, to the extent that basic aspects of patriarchal kinship systems—such as patrilocal residence and exclusive female childrearing—still govern women's lives and determine their place within the economy and the state.[6]

But while our healthy focus on women makes all this clear, we less often pay attention to how the class structure itself is affected by kinship and family relations. Let me cite just two examples of inquiries that reveal this dimension of the family-society relationship. One that is quite familiar has to do with the effect of marriage patterns on the identity and solidification of the upper class in eighteenth-century Europe. Studies by French and English historians (such as Bloch and Habbakuk) show the exogamous patterns between high commercial and finance capital and the more enterprising elements of the aristocracy.[7] Between male members of these classes, the "traffic in women" (specifically, daughters of the nobility and gentry) was a primary agent during the period of preindustrial capital accumulation in Western Europe in cementing a new ruling class. Looking closely at patterns of endogamy and exogamy can reveal a lot, not only about systems of inheritance but about the process of class formation and the nature of class consciousness. Seen from a Marxist-feminist perspective, such analyses show that the so-called "sphere of reproduction," or kinship, actually produces wealth as well as reproducing the class as a whole (and not only its individual members).

Another example that belies the image of a split between the domain of the family and the domain of political economy can be taken from a contemporary context. Writings by Amy Bridges, Batya Weinbaum, and Ruth Milkman transcend the abstract notion of the family as a private sphere by analyzing how the family and women's "consumption work" take up the slack during periods of economic crisis, providing a necessary precondition for inflation, layoffs, and cutbacks in social services.[8] As women tighten up the household budget and take care of elder family members released early from hospitals, children turned out of daycare centers, and teenagers who can't afford college tuition, the family (i.e., women) takes over the state's job, smoothing the rough edges of the crisis and making it humanly endurable.

It may sound as though I'm mixing many sorts of apples and oranges with these diverse examples, but the point is a very general one: that the relationship between family systems and class systems is a complex and dialectical process and that this process is the stuff that Marxist-feminists are fruitfully engaged in explaining.

2. *Patriarchal Power and Control over the Means of Reproduction*

Feminist movements have always been characterized by a deep-rooted conviction, often carried to the level of individual resistance or broad social demand, that matters such as birth control and abortion, or definitions of "illegitimacy," are political in the highest degree. In large part, the slogan "the personal is political" was meant to convey this reality: how and how often people have sex, practice birth control, or give birth are issues of great political consequence; that there is no isolated "private sphere" where such issues are concerned. Recent feminist scholarship such as that of Linda Gordon and Sarah Pomeroy gives this slogan historical content.[9] Their work begins to provide us with a concrete historical base from which to develop a Marxist-feminist theory of the relationship between reproduction control and patriarchal, class, and state power. Both Pomeroy and Gordon—one speaking of fifth-century

(B.C.) Athens, the other of nineteenth-century America—show, for example, that the meanings of concepts such as "legitimacy" and "illegitimacy," as reflected in laws and judicial pronouncements, shift markedly in relation to changes in the state's population control policies and the social and economic conditions governing those policies. Pomeroy in particular, arguing that the status of women in classical Athens was a function of their primary duty as producers of citizens, indicates that Athenian laws regarding legitimacy, intercourse, abortion, infanticide, marriage between citizens and noncitizens, and adultery were all aspects of a deliberate reproduction control policy that directly satisfied military manpower needs and indirectly solidified state power.[10] Control over the means of reproduction gives substantial human resources to the patriarchal (capitalist or precapitalist) state. Policies, for example, that directly control the numbers and types of children born give the state, and the class in power, control over numbers, over the distribution of the population among various classes or castes, over the size of potential labor or slave pools in relation to potential market fluctuations, etc. Similarly, dominant norms defining legitimate and illegitimate expressions of sexuality (e.g., legal sanctions for husbands' sexual coercion of wives, state laws either regulating or sponsoring prostitution, sodomy laws, restrictions against homosexuality, etc.) not only reinforce a certain type of patriarchal family structure and sexual repression (especially of women and homosexuals). They also further remove from families, particularly mothers, control over their own children and their children's destinies, placing that control effectively within the hands of the state.

The analysis of reproduction control emerging from the Gordon and Pomeroy studies differs from what one may identify as a "radical feminist" perspective on such questions, as well as from a "Marxist-Leninist" approach.[11] On the one hand, Marxist-feminist inquiry confirms the class basis of much of reproduction control policy in practice, showing that, on one level, control over the means of reproduction is indeed a class issue. Clearly, it is not all men who control the population resources mentioned above, but those men who compose a capitalist-imperialist ruling class. Moreover, as Gordon's book demonstrates, the libertarian movements for individual birth control (as opposed to a state policy of systematic population control) have themselves at times reflected particular class biases—the support of eugenics theory and policy, for example, by the later "voluntary motherhood" proponents and the twentieth-century birth control reformers like Margaret Sanger.[12] Finally, reproduction control is a class issue in the sense that its form and impact are different for different classes and national groups of women. The most blatant example of this class—national division is, of course, the systematic involuntary sterilization imposed by AID and other state population control agencies on Puerto Rican, Native American, and other Third World women throughout the imperialist periphery.

But to argue that reproduction control, including involuntary sterilization, is entirely or even primarily a class question ignores the fact that such practices grow out of and are legitimated by some 4,000 years of patriarchal tradition. As Gordon convincingly points out, insofar as simple, effective means of birth control have been well known to women throughout most of recorded history, the suppression of such means in particular times (or their replacement with irreversible surgical techniques) is not a question of technological change but of politics—specifically, the antifeminist response to women's attempt to achieve their own liberation. It is true that involuntary sterilization programs pose very different kinds of problems for Third World women from those faced by women of other classes and national groups in trying to secure cheap, safe abortions and birth control. But both problems grow out of the control by dominant groups of men over reproduction itself. Marxism-feminism relocates the analysis of specific historical forms of population control within the broader framework of male supremacy over the means of reproduction, over women's bodies, and over the terms and material conditions of motherhood. While this control takes specific forms with regard to particular class and national groups of women, it cuts across such divisions and affects the position of all women. It is therefore preeminently a feminist issue.

3. *Patriarchal Ideology and the State*

We have only just begun to understand the wider political implications of misogynistic ideologies, how they not only reinforce the patriarchal family itself but provide one of the most fundamental and most persistent legitimations of the modern capitalist state.[13] It seems to me, although I have little concrete data as yet to prove it, that ideologies which mythologize women either as sources of pollution and taint or as purity and motherlove incarnate, or which raise the sexual double standard to a maxim of the public good, become unusually prevalent in periods of state consolidation. These are periods in which there is severe class division and social instability, or heightened militarism and warfare, and in which a centralized state apparatus develops (as Engels explains) as a general antidote to social disorder and a solidifier of ruling class hegemony. In the course of development of the Western state, it would appear that misogynistic ideologies attempt to resolve such disorder by unifying groups of men across class lines around the abstract notion of "citizenship." In this way, the state develops on a very definite patriarchal as well as class basis. Pomeroy illustrates this pattern abundantly in her analysis of sexual politics in fifth-century Athens. Citing the legal "reforms" of Solon, which established state-owned brothels (thus "institutionalizing" the distinction between good women and whores), degraded the status of lower-class women, and subjected upper-class (citizen-breeder) women to a rigid physical and legal confinement, she remarks:

> These regulations, which seem at first glance antifeminist, are actually aimed at eliminating strife among men and strengthening the newly created democracy. Women are a perennial source of friction among men. Solon's solution to this problem was to keep them out of sight and to limit their influence.[14]

Much evidence points to a similar pattern occurring—a pattern which has deep cultural roots in the classical world—in the rise of the modern bourgeois state. As people like Christopher Hill and Eli Zaretsky suggest, the commonwealth based on "equality," contract, and "voluntary consent" that emerged from the English civil wars represented a victory for male heads of households, its dominant rhetoric obscuring both the exclusion of the majority of men from "liberty" as well as the economic and social contradictions within the citizen body itself.[15] By the eighteenth century, and culminating in the Jacobin ideal of "virtue," the definition of citizen has a solidly male overtone, whose silent partner is the definition of woman as dependent, docile, and domesticated. And again as in classical Greece, this ideological tendency is reinforced by the increasing physical, legal, and economic confinement of women within the patriarchal family. I am suggesting that misogynistic ideology and institutions help to legitimate the bourgeois political ideology of "liberty and equality" for all males, serving thus to secure national (male) unity, loyalty, and military service, among other things. The ideology of legitimate and illegitimate birth itself not only functions as one prop or patriarchal control over the means of reproduction, discussed above; it also helps to elevate and mystify the very notion of citizen. (It is not trivial that Jean-Jacques Rousseau, ideologue par excellence of both republican virtue and female subordination, declared that for woman to violate the sexual double standard constituted, on her part, an act of "treason."[16])

4. Women's Consciousness and Revolutionary Change

Before ending, I want to say a word about what I listed as the fourth critical relationship—that between women's consciousness and the nature of revolutionary transformation. As Marxist-feminists I think we have a natural revulsion to mechanistic modes of thought. Out of our political understanding we have initiated a rigorous investigation of how women themselves, in different cultures and periods, have perceived their situations and attempted to survive in and struggle against them. Clearly, forms of organization and protest that arise out of women's "reproductive" work and collective consciousness as reproductive workers—like food riots and rent strikes and school sit-ins—are not inherently more or less radical than other forms of struggle, like trade-union organizing. In both cases, the extent to which such forms are revolutionary in content and effect will depend upon their historical context, the quality of their leadership, their connection to a mass base, their adoption of a long-range strategy for transforming all of society, and so forth. But it seems important to me that we've begun to study concrete revolutionary situations in order to determine whether women, because of their particular material conditions, develop particular ways of fighting and organizing. If we understand that patriarchal kinship relations are not static but, like class relations, are characterized by antagonism and struggle, then we begin to speculate that women's consciousness and their periodic attempts to resist or change the dominant kinship structures will themselves affect class relations. Take, for example, the systematic attempt by the church, poor law officials, moral reformers, and others to impose legal marriages and bourgeois norms of legitimacy on the customary sexual practices of the preindustrial working class in eighteenth- and nineteenth-century Europe and America. These attempts were clearly resisted massively by individual women, but during periods of heightened revolutionary struggle, such as those in 1848 and 1871 in France, the demand for legal recognition of "free unions" and the payment of equal benefits to the children of such unions became a primary rallying call of working-class women.[17] Will Marxist-feminist analysis show that, like the moral campaigns around disease, religion, and the work ethic, sexuality and kin ties have themselves been a vital terrain of class struggle—with the important distinction that this terrain is one women have fought on in their own behalf?

And what of our own struggle? How do we begin to articulate our felt experience that fights around child care, birth control, cutbacks in the schools and hospitals, housework, and sexual oppression are part of a socialist revolutionary process, and to make the link in practice?[18] Getting out of the false dichotomy of separate spheres is just as critical for our revolutionary strategy as it is for our theoretical analysis. Given all the interconnections between the public and the private alluded to above, these must have important implications for women's consciousness and women's revolutionary activity. We do our reproductive work in the market, in the wider reach of state institutions, in the paid workplace, and in the home; we mediate the public and the private. Without us, and without a frontal attack on the sex-gender systems that "produce" us as women in capitalism, socialist movements to revolutionize the capitalist economy and state really are bound to fail.

Notes

1. Rubin's article is available in *Toward an Anthropology of Women*, ed. Rayna Reiter (New York: Monthly Review Press, 1975).
2. See the important essays by Marxist-feminist anthropologists in *Toward an Anthropology of Women* and *Woman, Culture, and Society*, ed. Michele Rosaldo and Louise Lamphere (Stanford: Stanford University Press, 1974), particularly those by Kathleen Gough, Patricia Draper, Paula Webster, Rubin, Ruby Rohrlich-Leavitt, in the former and Michele Rosaldo, Louise Lamphere, and Nancy Tanner in the latter.
3. A similar view is expressed by Rayna Reiter, Introduction to *Toward an Anthropology of Women* and Eleanor Leacock, Introduction to Friedrich Engels, *The Origin of the Family, Private Property, and the State* (New York: International Publishers, 1972). Both of them suggest, though in different ways, that in order to better understand the position of women in preclass societies, we need a much sharper definition of what we mean by "power."
4. "The Welfare of Women in Laboring Families: England, 1860–1950," in *Clio's Consciousness Raised: New Perspectives on the History of Women*, ed. Mary S. Hartman and Lois Banner (New York: Harper and Row, 1974).
5. The most influential among those Marxist-feminist works that attempt not only to analyze the political economy of housework but to connect women's family work to their work outside the home have been Juliet Mitchell, *Woman's Estate* (New York: Pantheon, 1971); Sheila Rowbotham, *Woman's Consciousness,*

Man's World (Baltimore: Penguin, 1973); and Ann Oakley, *Woman's Work: The Housewife, Past and Present* (New York: Pantheon, 1974). See also Rosalyn Baxandall, Elizabeth Ewen, and Linda Gordon, "The Working Class Has Two Sexes," in *Technology, the Labor Process, and the Working Class: Essays in Honor of Harry Braverman* (New York: Monthly Review Press, 1977), and Batya Weinbaum and Amy Bridges, "The Other Side of the Paycheck: Monopoly Capital and the Structure of Consumption" in this volume.

6. Judith Stacey, "When Patriarchy Kowtows: The Significance of the Chinese Family Revolution for Feminist Theory," *Feminist Studies* 3, no. 2 (1975), and in this volume, and Norma Diamond, "Collectivization, Kinship, and the Status of Women in Rural China," in *Toward an Anthropology of Women*.

7. Marc Bloch, *French Rural History: An Essay on Its Basic Characteristics* (Berkeley: University of California Press, 1966) and H. J. Habbakuk, "English Landownership, 1680–1740," *Economic History Review* 10, no. 1 (1940).

8. Weinbaum and Bridges, in this volume, and Ruth Milkman, "Women's Work and the Economic Crisis: Some Lessons from the Great Depression," *Review of Radical Political Economics* 8, no. 1 (Spring 1976).

9. Sarah Pomeroy, *Goddesses, Whores, Wives, and Slaves: Women in Classical Antiquity* (New York: Schocken Books, 1975), and Linda Gordon, *Woman's Body, Woman's Right: A Social History of Birth Control in America* (New York: Viking, 1976).

10. Pomeroy, *Goddesses, Whores,* ch. 4.

11. For a recent example of the latter, see Bonnie Mass, *Political Economy of Population Control in Latin America* (Toronto: Canadian Women's Educational Press, 1976). I am indebted to Joan Kelly-Gadol, M-F 3, whose thoughtful remarks on this subject, presented at the March 19 conference, have been incorporated into this paragraph.

12. Gordon, *Woman's Body,* chs. 5–7.

13. Much work remains to be done in this area, particularly for the critical period during the seventeenth and eighteenth centuries in Western Europe, when the early capitalist state and classical liberal doctrines of the state and citizenship made their appearance. For some insights into the relationship between the rise of the ancient state and the decline in women's position, see Pomeroy, *Goddesses, Whores;* Ruby Rohrlich-Leavitt, "Women in Transi-

tion: Crete and Sumer," in *Becoming Visible: Women in European History*, ed. Renate Bridenthal and Claudia Koonz (Boston: Houghton Mifflin, 1977); and, of course, Friedrich Engels, *The Origin of the Family*.

14. Pomeroy, *Goddesses, Whores*, p. 57.

15. Christopher Hill, *Society and Puritanism in Pre-Revolutionary England* (New York: Schocken Books, 1967), ch. 13; and Eli Zaretsky, *Capitalism, the Family, and Personal Life* (New York: Harper and Row, 1976).

16. Jean-Jacques Rousseau, *Emile* (New York: Dutton, 1974), p. 325. David Hume, in his *Treatise of Human Nature* (1751), had remarked that female chastity within marriage was in fact a "law of nature"; that for men to remain willing to work and support their families, they must be assured that their children are their own. The logical conclusion is, of course, that female chastity and the double sexual standard become a prerequisite of labor productivity and thus of capitalism itself!

17. See Sheila Rowbotham, *Women, Resistance, and Revolution* (New York: Pantheon, 1972), ch. 5; and Edith Thomas, *The Women Incendiaries* (New York: George Braziller, 1966), ch. 4. Ivy Pinchbeck, *Women Workers in the Industrial Revolution* (Clifton, N.J.: Augustus Kelly, 1969), p. 81; and Mary Lynn McDougall, "Working-Class Women During the Industrial Revolution, 1780–1914," in *Becoming Visible*, pp. 271–72, show that the so-called "high illegitimacy rates" among eighteenth-century rural women in England represent a similar struggle. Premarital sex and out-of-wedlock childbearing for these women were both an assertion of rural working-class culture and a means of material survival.

18. See Weinbaum and Bridges, who note the activities of the miners' wives in the Brookside miners' strike and of Chilean women during the *Unidad Popular* government, in the *Juntas de Abastecimientos* (Prices and Supplies Committees), as recent examples of how women's work in their families and local communities may become an integral part of the class struggle as a whole.

NOTES ON THE CONTRIBUTORS

Carollee Bengelsdorf teaches political science at Hampshire College and is the author or coauthor of various articles on Cuba, focusing particularly on women and the post-1970 institutionalization process. She has been a member both of the Africa Research Group (ARG) and of the North American Congress on Latin America (NACLA).

Berkeley-Oakland Women's Union was an autonomous, socialist feminist organization committed to struggle for the new forms of organization and relations between people which they defined as socialism.

Amy Bridges is a member of the editorial board of *Politics & Society*. Her work has appeared in the *American Journal of Sociology, Science & Society*, the *Review of Radical Political Economics*, and *Administration Science Quarterly*. She is writing a dissertation in the political science department of the University of Chicago.

Nancy Chodorow teaches sociology at the University of California, Santa Cruz. She received a Ph.D. from Brandeis University. Drawing extensively on psychoanalytic theory, she has published articles and has a forthcoming book on the social and psychological implications of women's mothering. She works on the editorial collective of *Socialist Revolution* and is also working on questions of psychoanalysis and Marxism.

The Combahee River Collective is a black feminist group in Boston whose name comes from the guerrilla action conceptualized and led by Harriet Tubman on 2 June 1863, in the Port Royal region of South Carolina. This action freed more than 750 slaves and is the only military campaign in American history planned and led by a woman.

Margery Davies is an editor of *Radical America* and is finishing her doctoral dissertation on the proletarianization of clerical work and the feminization of clerical workers in the United States.

Ellen DuBois is an assistant professor of history and American studies at the State University of New York, Buffalo. She is the author of *No More Silence: Woman Suffrage and the Emergence of Independent Feminism, 1848–1869*, to be published by Cornell University Press, Ithaca, N.Y. She teaches women's history and has been active in the women's liberation movement since 1969.

Zillah Eisenstein teaches feminist theory and political philosophy in the politics department of Ithaca College, Ithaca, N.Y. She received her Ph.D. in 1972 from the University of Massachusetts, Amherst, having written her dissertation on "The Concept of Species Being in Marx and Durkheim: Its Import for Feminist Idology." She is currently active in the socialist feminist women's movement.

Jean Gardiner is a lecturer at Leeds University Extramural Department and is also active in the women's liberation movement in England.

Linda Gordon is associate professor of history at the University of Massachusetts, Boston. She is the author of *Woman's Body, Woman's Right: A Social History of Birth Control* (New York: Viking, 1976) and coeditor (with Rosalyn Baxandall and Susan Reverby) of *America's Working Women: A Documentary History* (New York: Random House, 1976). She is an editor of

Radical America and active in socialist and feminist movements.

Alice Hageman, who visited Cuba in 1969 and 1971, partici- pates in the Boston Friends of Cuba group and collaborates with the New York-based Cuba Resource Center, publisher of the quarterly *Cuba Review*. She has written several articles on politics, religion, and sexism; she also edited *Religion in Cuba Today: New Church in a New Society* (New York: Association Press, 1971) and *Sexist Religion and Women in the Church: No More Silence!* (New York: Association Press, 1974). She is cur- rently liturgist at the Church of the Covenant in Boston and is completing a law degree at Northeastern University.

Heidi Hartmann is an economist who has taught and written about the economic status of women. She has been active in the women's liberation movement, in Marxist-feminist groups, and in URPE (Union for Radical Political Economics) for several years. She received a Ph.D. degree from Yale University in 1974; her dissertation was entitled "Capitalism and Women's Work in the Home, 1900–1930." She is currently at the U.S. Commission on Civil Rights, where she is studying employ- ment discrimination against women and minority members.

Nancy Hartsock is an editor of *Quest: a feminist quarterly* and an assistant professor of political science at Johns Hopkins University.

Ros Petchesky has been teaching in the social relations and women's studies programs at Ramapo College of New Jersey for the past five years. She received her Ph.D. in political science from Columbia University in 1974. She has long been active in the women's movement in New York City, where she lives with her child, Jonah.

Margaret Randall lives and works in Cuba. She has four chil- dren. Her recent books concern the situation of women in Vietnam, Nicaragua, and Chile. She is currently involved in bringing her concept of oral history into the poem.

Mary P. Ryan teaches at the State University of New York, Binghamton and is the author of *Womanhood in America from Colonial Times to the Present* (Washington: Viewpoints, 1975). She is completing a social history of women, the family, and early industrial capitalism based on a study of Utica, New York between 1800 and 1870.

Judith Stacey, a doctoral candidate in sociology at Brandeis University, is writing a dissertation about the family and social revolution entitled "Thermidorian Reaction to Family Revolution." She is also the sociology editor of *Feminist Studies*.

Batya Weinbaum has worked with the women's project of the Union for Radical Political Economics and published in the special women's issues put out by the organization's *Review of Radical Political Economics*. She works with the women's project of the Theology of the Americas and with Project Chance, a return-to-college program for community women at Brooklyn College. She is working on a book, *The Curious Courtship of Women's Liberation and Socialism*, and also does research, writing, and speaking about agribusiness.